# Speaking My Mind

# Speaking My Mind

*Expression and Self-Knowledge*

DORIT BAR-ON

CLARENDON PRESS · OXFORD
2004

# OXFORD

### UNIVERSITY PRESS

Great Clarendon Street, Oxford OX2 6DP

Oxford University Press is a department of the University of Oxford.
It furthers the University's objective of excellence in research, scholarship,
and education by publishing worldwide in

Oxford New York

Auckland Cape Town Dar es Salaam Hong Kong Karachi
Kuala Lumpur Madrid Melbourne Mexico City Nairobi
New Delhi Shanghai Taipei Toronto

With offices in

Argentina Austria Brazil Chile Czech Republic France Greece
Guatemala Hungary Italy Japan South Korea Poland Portugal
Singapore Switzerland Thailand Turkey Ukraine Vietnam

Oxford is a registered trade mark of Oxford University Press
in the UK and in certain other countries

Published in the United States
by Oxford University Press Inc., New York

British Library Cataloguing in Publication Data
Data available

Library of Congress Cataloging in Publication Data
Data available

ISBN 0-19-926320-5
ISBN 0-19-927628-5 (pbk)

1 3 5 7 9 10 8 6 4 2

Typeset by Newgen Imaging Systems (P) Ltd, Chennai, India
Printed in Great Britain
on acid-free paper by
Biddles Ltd, King's Lynn, Norfolk

*To my father, Elimelech Bar-On, to Manya,*
*and*
*To the memory of my mother Margalit, my aunt Malka,*
*my brother Palti,*
*and my friends Yael Barash and Ezra Moria*

# Acknowledgments

I was led to the ideas developed in this work by seeking a systematic motivation and defense of the account of avowals presented in Bar-On and Long (2001). I am greatly indebted to Doug Long for numerous stimulating discussions on the status of avowals and self-knowledge, and for several years of philosophical conversation and collaboration.

The roots of the ideas go back further, to my time as a graduate student at UCLA, where I was fortunate to study closely with Tyler Burge (my dissertation advisor), Philippa Foot, Tony Martin, and David Pears. I owe them and my other teachers at UCLA a great intellectual debt. The particular combination of philosophical interests in language, mind, and knowledge that has led me to the present work goes back even further, to my undergraduate years in Tel Aviv, where I was turned on to analytic philosophy by Asa Kasher.

Of all my teachers, the one who has most influenced my thinking about the issues that occupy me in this work is Rogers Albritton. Seminars I took from Albritton while at UCLA and several marathon conversations with him have set me on a philosophical path to which I shall always find myself returning. I deeply regret not having been able to present this work to him before he died, especially given his generous encouragement at a crucial stage of its inception. But I find some comfort in the thought that he, of all people, would not have urged me to let go of it any earlier.

Three people provided close readings of the manuscript, intellectual support, and editorial help at various stages of this work. Bijan Parsia was my research assistant during the earlier stages of my work on the manuscript; I am grateful to him for his philosophical and editorial suggestions. Dylan Sabo has been my research assistant for the last two years. His help in preparing the manuscript for publication has been invaluable. Ram Neta, now my colleague provided extensive comments on a complete earlier draft of the manuscript, and later continued to read draft after draft of various chapters, never failing to offer insightful and challenging comments and constructive suggestions. I thank him for pushing me to go deeper and make myself clearer.

I also wish to thank colleagues and graduate students at UNC-Chapel Hill for intellectual stimulation and support, both direct and indirect, during the writing of this book. Several people have read earlier drafts of chapters and have given me feedback and helpful comments: Peter Alward, Simon Blackburn, Tony Brueckner, Tyler Burge, Brad Cohen, Nancy Daukas, Fred Dretske, Don Garrett, Brie Gertler, Bill Lycan, David Reeve, Keith Simmons, and Carol Voeller. My thanks to the participants in seminars on self-knowledge taught at UNC-Chapel Hill in 1996 and 2001, to Rogers Albritton and Richard Moran who commented on the paper presented by Doug Long and myself at the Pacific APA symposium on self-knowledge in March 1998, to the participants in a workshop on self-knowledge at UCLA in May 1998, especially David Kaplan, and to audiences at the University of South Carolina, the meetings of the North Carolina Philosophical Society, the College of William and Mary, Virginia Commonwealth, the meetings of the Canadian Philosophical Association, a conference on Language, Mind, and the World in Tlaxcala, Mexico, the University of Maryland, Davidson College (especially David Robb), UC Santa Cruz (especially Julia Tannenbaum), UC Santa Barbara (especially Tony Brueckner, Kevin Falvey, and Aaron Zimmermann), and to participants in a recent seminar at Duke University led by Fred Dretske and Guven Guzeldere. Special thanks to Mitch Green for many conversations, as well as comments he provided on some of the chapters, which have greatly helped shape my view on expression. Finally thanks to the editors at OUP, and especially to Peter Momtchiloff.

My work on this manuscript was supported by a semester's fellowship from the Institute for the Arts and Humanities at UNC-Chapel Hill and a semester's University Research and Study Leave. A small Research Grant from the UNC University Research Council helped support the preparation of the index. The publishers of the following journals have kindly given me permission to use materials from published papers: *Philsophical Topics* ("Speaking My Mind"), *Philosophy and Phenomenological Research* ("Avowals and First-Person Privilege", co-authored with Douglas Long). *Ashgate Publishing Limited* has given permission to use materials from "Knowing Selves: Expression, Truth, and Knowledge" (also co-authored with Douglas Long). My chairman, Geoff Sayre-McCord, stepped in at various crucial stages with much-appreciated support for research and editorial assistance. Ben Theis helped with last minute work on the footnotes and the bibliography and Ted Parent helped prepare the Index. My friend Michal Goldman has graciously allowed me to use one of her beautiful works of art for the book cover.

I would have found it impossible to engage in a project of this length without the love and support of those closest to me. I am ever so grateful to my friends, both in the profession and outside it, and to my family: my father Elimelech and his wife Manya, my sisters Sigi, Ranit, and Noa, and most of all, to my husband (and colleague) Keith Simmons, always a source of philosophical insight and sound advice, and to Leah, my bright and shining light.

*Chapel Hill, North Carolina*
*Spring 2004*

# Contents

# I

# Introduction: The Special Security of Some "I" Talk

"I have a terrible headache," I mutter, rubbing my temples.
"I am so tired," you say, as you stretch out on the couch.
A gloomy child says to her caregiver, "I hope Mommy is coming soon."
Looking at the sky, your friend says, "I'm wondering whether it's going to rain."
At the sight of a mean-looking pit bull, you say, "I am scared of that dog."
Staring at the newest painting by one of my favorite artists, I say, "I'm finding this painting utterly puzzling."

We have here a handful of examples of everyday utterances in which speakers tell us certain things about themselves. Each of these utterances mentions a particular sensation, or feeling, or thought that the speaker ascribes to herself at the moment of utterance. Such utterances—"avowals", as they are sometimes called—ascribe states of mind that the speaker happens to be in at a given time. On their face, avowals resemble other everyday utterances in which we report various occurrences, such as:

"There is a red cardinal at the bird-feeder."
"We've just run out of dog food."
"I have a mosquito bite on my leg."

Like these reports, avowals appear to inform us of certain contingent states of affairs; they tell us of states of mind that the speaker happens to be in at a given moment. Yet avowals have a unique status. For, when compared to ordinary empirical reports, avowals appear to enjoy distinctive security.

## The Distinctive Security of Avowals

Imagine three-year old Jenny walking into the room and saying, "Mom, I want to go play outside." Jenny's mom can surely question the wisdom of Jenny's going to play outside at this time. But she is highly unlikely to question the fact that Jenny *wants* to go and play outside. We, too, as we consider Jenny's utterance, would take it at face value. As long as we do not suspect some kind of dissimulation or insincerity on Jenny's part, we would take her pronouncement as straightforwardly and unquestionably true. We may think it inappropriate to credit Jenny, being a child, with very sophisticated self-knowledge. We may think Jenny does not know much about what she 'really wants in life'. But surely she knows this much about herself: that she wants to go and play outside right now!

Or imagine your spouse putting down the phone after a conversation with his dad, saying, "I'm so mad at my dad for always trying to put me down!" You may think it unfair to your father-in-law to portray him this way; you may disagree that he always tries to put your spouse down. But you would hardly venture to question that, right now, your spouse is indeed mad at his dad for always trying to put him down. Nor would you dream of asking your spouse why he thought he was mad at his dad, or how he knew that he was, and so on. As far as your own belief that your spouse is mad at his dad, his telling you: "I'm so mad at my dad . . ." is not just the beginning of the story, it is also its end.

Now consider the situation from the point of view of the person issuing an avowal. I say, "I'm hoping it's not too late to buy tickets for the show." In the normal case, I do not consult my own behavior or memory; I do not reason, or draw some inference; I do not even use ordinary sense perception. For all appearances, my avowal is 'baseless'. Yet, in the typical case, I would have no doubt whatsoever regarding its truth. The avowal seems to articulate a piece of information that is immediately available to me and that I can state with great confidence—something I unquestionably know.

Here, then, are already some notable features of avowals. Avowals are apparently *non-evidential*. Yet, like ordinary empirical reports (e.g., that there's a red cardinal on the bird-feeder, or that the street traffic is heavy, or that there's a bump on my head), they are typically taken to provide us with particular *truths* about contingent states of affairs, and to represent things that the subject straightforwardly *knows*. In this, avowals differ from mere grunts, grins, and gurgles. On the other hand, unlike ordinary empirical reports, avowals are *not* normally *subjected to ordinary epistemic assessment*. As suggested above, it would be highly irregular to request of someone issuing an avowal to offer reasons for her pronouncement, or to criticize her for lacking an adequate basis or justification. And, except under very special circumstances, we do not expect the sincere author of an avowal to stand corrected. A subject who avows being tired, or scared of something, or thinking that *p*, is normally presumed to have the last word on the relevant matters; we would not presume to criticize her self-ascription or to reject it on the basis of our contrary judgment. Furthermore, unlike ordinary empirical reports, and somewhat like apriori statements, avowals are issued with a very high degree of confidence and are not easily subjected to doubt. I take these to be salient features that mark the distinctive security of avowals.

We can think of avowals as having the 'normal form' "I am (in) M", where "I" refers to the subject of the ascribed state, and "M" refers to a (type of) mental state the subject is said (or thought) by herself to be in. One aspect of the security of avowals, which will occupy us in the earlier chapters, has to do with the fact that they are ascriptions to *oneself* in which the subject picks herself out in a special way. However, I will be arguing that the distinctive security of avowals goes beyond that. Avowals also enjoy what I shall call *ascriptive security*: security in the component that ascribes a certain state to the self-ascriber. This security in turn has several aspects that are worth separating out. Doing so is important both for seeing why explanations of avowals' security currently on offer fall short and for appreciating some of the advantages I will be claiming for the view I shall myself be offering.

While we may take it that all avowals involve an ascription of a present mental state to oneself, avowals differ in terms of the degree of articulation of the ascription. Some avowals simply ascribe the presence of a mental state, others ascribe a mental state specifying some object toward which it is directed, still others ascribe a mental state assigning to it a particular propositional content. Corresponding to the differences we can identify distinct aspects with respect to which avowals can be said to enjoy security. We have:

**(a) So-called phenomenal avowals: avowals ascribing the presence of a state with no specification of intentional content[1]**

e.g.: **"I am feeling thirsty."**

    Are you really *feeling thirsty*?

      Are you feeling any particular sensation at all?

      Is it *thirst* (not hunger, e.g.) that you are feeling?[2]

**(b) So-called intentional (or attitudinal avowals): avowals ascribing a state with intentional content**

**(b₁) Avowals ascribing a state with intentional object**

e.g.: **"I am mad at John."**

    Are you really *mad at John*?

      Do you have any emotions at all (toward John)?

      Is it *being mad* (not loving, e.g.) that you feel?

      Is it being mad *at John* (not at Mary, e.g.) that you feel?

**(b₂) Avowals of propositional attitudes** (i.e., of a state with propositional content)

e.g.: **"I believe it is going to rain."**

    Do you really *believe* that it is going to rain?

      Do you have any attitude at all (toward *p*)?

      Is it a *belief* (not a wish) that you have?

      Is it a belief *that it is going to rain* (rather than *that it is going to snow*) that you have?

      Is it *true* that it's going to rain?

Part of my task will be to offer an explanation for why, in the normal case, these kinds of different questions do not arise (with the exception of the very last question).

We can see that the gradual increase in grammatical complexity reflected in (a)–(b₂) corresponds to an increase in the number of aspects

---

[1] "Intentional content" is a shorthand for intentional object or propositional content (see below). I want to remain neutral on the question whether there are mental *states* that have no such content. Whether or not there are, it remains a fact that some avowals do, and others do not, involve the *specification* of the relevant content. (See Ch. 4, n. 10.)

[2] Some phenomenal avowals may not have the overt grammatical structure of an "I"-ascription. "It hurts" is perhaps the most familiar example. I think that the two questions below could still have analogues in that case (viz.: Does it feel like anything at all? Is it hurtfulness (as opposed to pressure)?) It may be feasible to treat such avowals as containing covert self-reference. This may be supported by cross-linguistic evidence.

of the self-ascription that could, in principle, be questioned, by either the avowing subject or her audience (actual or potential). So one might expect that the grammatical differences among avowals—viz., the absence versus presence of intentional content—will correlate in some way with differences in the degree of security to be assigned to avowals in the different categories. To put it crudely, it may seem that, since there is less to be wrong about in the case of, e.g., avowals of emotions than in the case of avowals of propositional attitudes, and still less in the case of avowals of sensations, avowals of sensations should enjoy more security than avowals of emotions, and avowals of emotions should, in turn, enjoy more security than avowals of propositional attitudes.

It is not unusual to find claims that there are indeed systematic differences in the security of avowals. For example, in his summary of the traditional view of avowals' security, Wright (1998) presents so-called phenomenal avowals—of sensations such as pain, fatigue, thirst, malaise, non-specific anxiety—as "strongly authoritative": "If somebody understands such a claim, and is disposed sincerely to make it about themselves, that is *a guarantee of the truth* of what they say. A doubt about such a claim has to be a doubt about the sincerity or the understanding of the one making it" (1998: 13, my emphasis). Wright contrasts phenomenal avowals with what he calls "attitudinal avowals", which are only supposed to be "weakly authoritative": "You may not suppose me sincere and comprehending, yet chronically unreliable about what I hope, believe, fear, and intend" (1998: 17). However, "to the extent that there is space for relevant forms of self-deception or confusion, sincerity-cum-understanding is no longer a guarantee of the truth of even basic self-ascriptions of intentional states" (1998: 17).[3]

In what follows, I will be trying to bring out an element of special security that separates *all* avowals—whether intentional or phenomenal—from other ascriptions. While I do not want to deny that there are interesting differences between phenomenal and intentional *states*, I think that attending to the ordinary treatment of *avowals* warrants grouping phenomenal and intentional avowals together, for purposes of understanding their distinctive security. Intuitively, one who avows having a thought that *p* would no more be inclined to

---

[3] We shall see later that other authors also think we should treat avowals of sensations separately from avowals of intentional attitudes.

doubt that the thought has the propositional content she has assigned to it than she would be inclined to doubt that it's fatigue that she's feeling, when she avows feeling tired. Nor would her audience be more readily inclined to correct or request reasons for an avowal just because it involves an assignment of propositional content to a state. By the same token, it is not as though phenomenal avowals are absolutely immune to correction or failure. There are circumstances in which even a phenomenal avowal may be thought to be false. My goal will be, then, to identify and explain a kind of security—special, even if not absolute—that we seem to enjoy whenever we issue an avowal, with respect to the state we self-ascribe, *as well as* with respect to the intentional object we specify for it, or the propositional content we assign to it, if any.

## Avowals: Semantic Continuity and Epistemic Asymmetry

The strikingly high degree of security that avowals enjoy relative to other pronouncements has led some philosophers to regard them as infallible, indubitable, and incorrigible. Thus regarded, avowals should hold great interest for those who harbor hopes of grounding our knowledge of the world around us on an absolutely secure foundation. If avowals were indeed guaranteed to be true, could never be doubted, and could never be corrected by others, then they would articulate things we know of ourselves in an absolutely secure, unassailable way. They could serve as a kind of epistemological starting point for any investigation into our knowledge of the world.

But even apart from their potential to constitute an epistemic foundation, avowals should be of special interest to anyone who is inclined toward some kind of mind–body separation. If avowals can indeed be taken to represent absolutely unassailable self-judgments, they would seem to stand in sharp contrast with all bodily self-ascriptions. When it comes to bodily features and conditions such as height and weight, disease, heart rate, digestive processes, etc., our self-ascriptions are made on the same kinds of bases as our ascriptions to others (or theirs to us). Now, it is true that some bodily self-ascriptions are not made on such bases. For example, we do not normally tell that we ourselves are standing, or that our own legs are crossed, by looking at ourselves. Even so, such bodily self-ascriptions are still open to straightforward rejection and correction by others. If I say, "My legs are crossed," it would be entirely open to you to deny what I say. In the normal case, you and I use different means for telling the state of my legs. But as regards the truth of what I say, you seem to have as much authority as I have. By contrast, when it comes to present mental states, it is normally assumed that 'the subject knows best'. It is far from straightforward to conceive of circumstances in which you would be prepared simply to contradict my avowal, "I *think* my legs are crossed", or "I *feel* as though I am standing", or "I feel nauseous". And this is not just a feature of our social practices. As we consider someone else's *thought* in which she ascribes to herself a present sensation, feeling, or thought, as opposed to some non-mental bodily state, we would be equally inclined to assign the mental self-ascription a much higher degree of security. To the extent that the contrast is thought to be genuine, we may chalk it up to the special *nature* of that of which avowals speak. Avowals and non-mental bodily self-ascriptions differ in their subject matter: in avowing, we speak of our *minds*, which are genuinely distinct from, and are only contingently coexistent with, our bodies. (And, conversely, if we are reluctant to accept that there are differences of substance between mind and body, we may try to play down the apparent contrast between mental and bodily self-ascriptions.)

We may be encouraged to assign absolute security to avowals by considering Descartes-inspired ascriptions such as "I am thinking that I may be deceived right now". At least on one way of understanding this self-ascription, it is *self-verifying*: one cannot make the self-ascription without it being true. Though it ascribes to the thinker a contingent, present mental occurrence, it seems to enjoy apriori certainty. Using the model of self-verifying thought, one may seek to identify a special subclass of mental self-ascriptions that are equally certain, characterized in terms of how things *seem* to us at a given moment.[4] However, among the self-ascriptions of occurrent mental states that I refer to as "avowals" there are many that do not share this absolutely secure status.

It seems that we can sensibly question an avowal at least under certain circumstances. The most obvious examples involve self-ascriptions

---

[4] See Wilson (1978) for discussion of Descartes's attempt to identify such a class of avowals.

of states such as beliefs, intentions, and desires. Here are a few such examples.

(i) You tell your therapist, sincerely, that you want to help your friend. It may emerge, in the course of therapy, that you actually despise your friend, and secretly wish him ill.

(ii) Distraught at the thought of having lost his son forever, a father may sincerely say, or think, "I do believe he's still alive", even in the face of compelling evidence to the contrary, which he has carefully reviewed.

(iii) I show you my latest painting, and in response to my implicit invitation to react, you say, "I like the painting". I may doubt that you really like it. My doubt may initially seem only to address your sincerity: "Do you really like it, or are you just saying that?" But it is conceivable that I should continue to have my doubts, even after being convinced that you meant what you said. I know you intensely dislike paintings in this style. I also know how much you *want* to like my work. Maybe *that* is why you said—sincerely—that you like my painting.

Self-deception and wishful thinking can clearly issue in avowals of propositional attitudes that may be questioned and become subject to doubt. But even in the case of avowals of so-called phenomenal states, the possibility of a sincere but false self-ascription is not out of the question. For example, sitting in the dentist's chair, and having had a long history of painful dental work, I may exclaim, "This hurts!" just before the drill reaches the infected tooth. It may be doubted that I really feel pain, even in the face of my sincere avowal. Given the circumstances, there is a perfectly good explanation of how I could issue a sincere self-ascription of pain, even though I am not really in any pain. Insistence on the absolute infallibility or certainty or incorrigibility of all avowals would fly in the face of such examples. But such insistence is not required in order to acknowledge that all avowals—self-verifying or not—are treated significantly differently from other empirical pronouncements. As I shall now explain, despite being semantically (and logically) continuous with other empirical pronouncements, there are significant epistemic asymmetries between them.

Semantically speaking, an avowal will typically identify an individual—the speaker—and ascribe to her a certain condition—being thirsty, feeling scared, hoping that . . . , etc. It will be true under the same circumstances as any ascription that identified that same individual and ascribed to her the same condition at the same time (e.g., "*She* is scared of the dog", or "*DB* was scared of the dog yesterday").[5] It can also serve as a premise in humdrum logical inferences, such as "I am scared of the dog, and so are you; so that makes two of us". Avowals thus exhibit continuity of logico-semantic structure and are interchangeable *salva veritate* (in context) with ordinary, unproblematic statements. I shall call this claim Semantic Continuity.[6] (To accept Semantic Continuity, note, is not to prejudge the issue whether terms in avowals refer in the same way as they do in other ascriptions; nor is it to presuppose anything about the *kinds* of things referred to by avowals.)

However, epistemically speaking, avowals seem radically different from their semantic close cousins. As already noted, avowals at least do not appear to be made on any ordinary evidential basis, nor are they normally subjected to ordinary kinds of epistemic assessment. Not only do we normally take avowals to be true, but it is also very unusual to reject, deny, or criticize avowals as mentioned earlier, this is not just a matter of social decorum or politeness. As we consider, hypothetically, a 'thought avowal'—i.e., a present-tense self-ascription of a mental state that someone is spontaneously producing in thought rather than speech—we would also not presume to question or criticize it. Now, some philosophers think of simple perceptual reports as not made on any evidential basis, and such reports do enjoy some security. If someone we know to have normal eyesight, who is standing in front of the window, tells us, "There is a red cardinal at the feeder", we would not be inclined to question her report. A perceptual report, though, is clearly open to what we may call *brute error*. A brute error is one that is simply due to the world failing to cooperate, rather than being due to some kind of failure of the subject's concepts or faculties. The judgment that there is a red cardinal at the bird-feeder can be mistaken simply because, as a matter of fact, there is no red cardinal at the bird-feeder, even though in making the judgment the person has exercised conceptual and perceptual capacities that are in perfect working order. (Perhaps someone has placed a very con-

---

[5] I set aside the question whether there is *full* semantic equivalence—"sameness of meaning"—among statements of the forms "I am F", "She is F", and "DB is F", where the subject term in each case is used to refer to the same individual.

[6] Following Bar-On and Long (2001). See also Bar-On (2000) and Bar-On and Long (2003).

vincing decorative papier-mâché cardinal on the feeder.[7]) By contrast, although I think we must allow that avowals can be false, when this is so, it seems that it is always due to some kind of failure or irregularity on the part of the avowing subject.

Thus, even if avowals are not absolutely infallible, incorrigible, or indubitable, important questions remain regarding their status, the fact remains that they exhibit notable epistemic asymmetries with respect to ordinary empirical ascriptions, including all bodily self-ascriptions, as well as some ascriptions that are truth-conditionally equivalent to them. When compared to other non-apriori ascriptions, even non-self-verifying avowals are much more certain, much less subject to ordinary mistakes, significantly less open to a range of common doubts, and highly resistant to straightforward correction. I shall call this claim Epistemic Asymmetry.

My main task in this book is to provide an account of the unique status assigned to avowals that respects both Semantic Continuity—the claim that avowals are interchangeable *salva veritate* in context with certain unproblematic statements and can figure in certain logical inferences—and Epistemic Asymmetry—the claim that there are genuine and important epistemic contrasts between avowals and their semantic cousins. I take this task to be of considerable philosophical interest. For, even if avowals do not enjoy absolute security, their relatively high degree of security as compared with all other empirical statements should make us wonder. Why should my own pronouncements regarding my present states of mind, in speech or in thought, carry so much more weight than anyone else's pronouncements on the same matters? Why should they carry more weight than my knowledgeable pronouncements about other matters? Why should they be so much less vulnerable to doubt, so much more resistant to criticism, and so on? Answering these questions may help us uncover something significant about the relation between mind and body. At the very least, understanding the special status of avowals may reveal something about the knowledge we are said to have of our own minds.

I try to accomplish my main task by offering an account of avowals' distinctive security that does not invoke any special epistemic method or access we have to our own present states of mind. However, I aim to

---

[7] For some discussion of the notion of brute error, see Burge (1996).

show that the account I develop, unlike other 'non-epistemic' accounts, respects the fact that, though avowals are epistemically different from other ascriptions, they are nonetheless *epistemically continuous* with other pronouncements in one important respect. Like other pronouncements, avowals can represent articles of genuine *knowledge* we have about ourselves. Thus, part of my task will be to pave the way toward a positive, *non-deflationary* account of ordinary, or 'basic', self-knowledge, which we can take avowals to represent.

## The Distinctive Security of Avowals and Privileged Self-Knowledge

The first question I will be trying to answer regarding avowals' distinctive security is the following one:

(i) What accounts for the *unparalleled security of avowals*? Why is it that avowals, understood as true or false ascriptions of contingent states to an individual, are so rarely questioned or corrected, are generally so resistant to ordinary epistemic assessments, and are so strongly presumed to be true?

Another way of putting this question is: How can avowals be understood in a way that preserves Semantic Continuity while fully respecting Epistemic Asymmetry? It is important to recognize that one can acknowledge avowals' special security without subscribing to a particular explanation of this special status. For example, one need not take the special security of avowals to be due to the fact that they involve self-judgments made on an especially secure epistemic basis, thereby subscribing to what I shall call the Epistemic Approach. My own answer to question (i) will be *non-epistemic*, in that it will not derive avowals' special security from the security of a special epistemic method, or privileged epistemic access.

However, there is a second question, intimately connected with question (i), which is often of most interest to philosophers studying avowals, namely:

(ii) Do avowals serve to articulate *privileged self-knowledge*? If so, what qualifies avowals as articles of knowledge at all, and what is the source of the privileged status of this knowledge?

Question (ii) asks whether there is a special kind of knowledge that subjects have with respect to their present states of mind, and which avowals articulate. Note that question (ii) concerns avowals only indirectly, as attesting to the existence of a special kind of knowledge. Its more direct concern is with the existence and nature of a special kind of self-knowledge. Do we have a special kind of self-knowledge that avowals represent? If so, what is the source of the privileged status of this kind of self-knowledge? One can deny that we possess privileged self-knowledge that avowals articulate without thereby denying that avowals *qua* performances, in speech or in thought, do enjoy special security, in that they are not subjected to ordinary epistemic scrutiny and challenge.[8] That is, one can answer (ii) in the negative, and yet offer a substantive answer to (i).

However, philosophical discussions of self-knowledge sometimes appear directly concerned with a third question:

(iii) Avowals aside, what allows us to possess privileged self-knowledge? That is, how is it that subjects like us are able to have privileged, non-evidential knowledge of their present states of mind, regardless of whether they avow being in the relevant states or not?

Question (iii) presupposes that we do have privileged self-knowledge, whether it is articulated by avowals or not, and seeks to find out what puts us in a position to have such knowledge. Whereas questions (i) and (ii) begin with the fact that we often pronounce on our mental states through avowals (in speech or in thought), and that when we do, our pronouncements enjoy a special security (as characterized by Epistemic Asymmetry), (iii) takes these facts to be incidental. It invites us to explain privileged self-knowledge in complete abstraction from the special security of avowals.

In what follows, I shall begin with question (i). Because question (iii) assumes that we do possess privileged knowledge of our present states of mind, it does not leave open the possibility of offering a negative answer to (ii). What is worse, at least on one way of reading (iii), it assumes that a subject will have a privileged way of knowing what mental state she is in simply in virtue of being in that state. But suppose this assumption is mistaken. In that case, it would be

[8] There is an affinity between my two questions and the two sub-tasks Fricker (1998) identifies for a philosophical account of self-knowledge (see esp. sect. II). I address (ii) in Ch. 9.

misguided to begin an investigation into self-knowledge by attempting to answer (iii). Yet rejecting the assumption still allows us to acknowledge a certain relatively less controversial claim: when we do avow being in a mental state, our avowals enjoy special security (characterized by Epistemic Asymmetry) and appear to represent things we know about ourselves. We may still want to explain the special status of avowals, and determine whether avowals indeed qualify as articles of privileged knowledge. That is, we can still seek answers to (i) and (ii).

As between these two questions, I believe there is good reason to begin with (i). First, answering (i) is arguably a necessary prerequisite for addressing (ii). The phenomena that give rise to epistemological questions regarding self-knowledge involve asymmetries in the ways avowals (made in speech or in thought) are issued by subjects and regarded by others. Before we can determine whether avowals reflect a special kind of knowledge we possess, we need an understanding of what it is that subjects do when avowing, and why it is that avowals are treated so differently from other pronouncements. Secondly, if we begin instead with the question whether avowals reflect a special kind of knowledge, we may be tempted to suppose that the only way to answer the question positively is by invoking, as did Descartes, a specially secure method or way we have of finding out or making judgments about our present states of minds. This may in turn tempt us to suppose that question (i) can be answered only by appealing to this special way of knowing. That is, we may think that, in answering (i), we are forced to adopt the Epistemic Approach. On the other hand, if we begin with a relatively neutral set of observations about the status of avowals, and try to understand that status, we leave the door open for non-epistemic accounts. We can then take up questions of self-knowledge with a more open mind.

Thirdly, answering (ii) requires a properly epistemological investigation, which would explain what (if anything) qualifies avowals to represent items of knowledge in the first place. If it is determined that avowals do represent a form of genuine self-knowledge, we would need to locate it in the context of other kinds of knowledge, and bring out what makes it privileged by comparison. It seems to me that such an investigation is best undertaken once we have gained a proper understanding of the character and status of avowals. As I mentioned before, I think a good answer to (i) should involve respecting Epistemic Asymmetry in its full scope. That is, it should avoid putting avowals on epistemic par with other pronouncements, non-mental self-ascriptions included. This places constraints on what we should accept as an adequate answer to (ii). In particular, it should caution us against answers that require us to regard avowals simply as representing true judgments produced by highly secure epistemic mechanisms, since such answers risk assimilating avowals too closely to certain non-mental self-judgments. And conversely, answering (ii) first may lead us to ignore or deny answers to (i) that *would* allow us to respect Epistemic Asymmetry in its full scope.

Thus, I propose to begin by attempting to offer an answer to question (i). But note that certain answers to (i) may leave no room for substantive answers to (ii). Suppose one were to claim that what is distinctive about avowals is that they simply belong to a different *grammatical* category from other ascriptions. Thus, on one familiar version of this view, mentalistic terms such as "in pain", or "believes that *p*", are ambiguous between their first-person and third-person uses. When I say that *I* am in pain, or that *I* believe that *p*, I am no more ascribing a state to myself than when I wince, or simply utter *p*.[9] In that case, though, avowals belong to the wrong category to be proper candidates for any kind of knowledge, let alone privileged self-knowledge. Or, suppose one held, less radically, that avowals are true or false self-ascriptions, but that it is simply a bedrock constitutive feature of our practice of mentalistic attributions that they should be accorded special status.[10] Then it would still seem misguided to search for an account that establishes avowals as representing a special kind of knowledge that we have of our own present states of minds. In general, purely 'grammatical' answers to question (i) seem inconsistent with substantive answers to question (ii). As we shall see, grammatical accounts are not well placed to respect various continuities between avowals and other ascriptions. This provides sufficient motivation for seeking an alternative to such accounts of avowals. In addition, however, anyone who believes that avowals do represent a special kind of knowledge that subjects have of their own present states of mind has good reason to seek an account of avowals that is at least consistent

---

[9] This ambiguity account is sometimes attributed to Wittgenstein. As I shall explain in Ch. 7, this account would be in violation of what I have called Semantic Continuity.

[10] An account along these lines is offered on Wittgenstein's behalf in Wright (1998) under the title 'the Default View'. The view is discussed in Ch. 9 below.

with a substantive answer to (ii). Thus I believe that we should keep
question (ii) in mind as we develop an answer to question (i).

My first goal will be to motivate and develop a non-epistemic
answer to question (i). I will be offering an account of avowals' special
security that does not take it to be a matter of some specially secure
epistemic basis or method. Nor will it resort to the Cartesian idea that
avowals concern a special subject matter: viz., states of immaterial
minds. Having offered a non-epistemic, non-Cartesian answer to (i), I
will then try to show that this answer is consistent with a range of
non-deflationary answers to question (ii). Even if one does not regard
avowals' distinctive security to be a matter of their epistemic pedigree,
one can still maintain that we *do* have privileged self-knowledge that
is articulated by avowals. Furthermore, one can attempt to explain
the privileged status of self-knowledge partly in terms of the special
security of avowals understood non-epistemically. As for question (iii),
after I give my answer to (i) and examine answers to (ii) that are consistent with it, we will be in a position to see that there is something
misleading about question (iii).

In a sense, my approach reverses the order we are used to in philosophical discussion of these matters. Following Descartes's lead in his
*Meditations*, many philosophers begin with the thought that we *must*
have an especially secure way of knowing our own (present) mental
states, far more secure (e.g., more immune to doubt, error, and correction) than the ways we have of knowing both the minds of others
and our own bodies. We are then primed to expect that the only way
one could explain the special security of present-tense mental self-
ascriptions without giving up the idea that we possess privileged self-
knowledge is to adopt an overtly epistemic explanation for avowals'
security. I hope to show that departing from tradition in this matter
will bear philosophical fruit.

## Avowals' Security and Self-Knowledge: Some Conditions of Adequacy

Earlier I pointed out that avowals do *not* in general share the absolute
certainty of self-verifying self-ascriptions. Nonetheless, their status
contrasts with that of a wide array of non-apriori ascriptions. Thus,

contrast an avowal such as "I'm so tired!" made by me at a particular time with the following:

(a) "She is very tired," said (or thought) by someone else about me at that same time;

(b) "I was very tired then," said by me at a later time;

(c) "John is very tired," said by me about someone else;

(d) "DB is very tired," said by me about myself when I fail to recognize that *I* am DB;

(e) "I am very tired," said by me on the basis of, say, looking in the mirror, or inference from some test results;

(f) "I am 5'5" tall," or "There's a scar on my forehead";

(g) "I am a very patient person," or "I have a sense of humor," or "I am attentive to my friends";

(h) "There's a red car right there!" said upon seeing a car outside;

(i) "My legs are crossed," or "I'm standing in front of the house."

(j) "I am seeing a red cardinal," or "I am hearing a loud noise."

A careful look at the epistemic asymmetries between avowals and the ascriptions in (a)–(j) reveals that there is no obvious single feature shared by avowals alone. For instance, avowals are not alone in being ascriptions *to one's self* (consider (b), (d), (e), (f), (g), (i), and (j)). Nor are they alone in being *present-tense* ascriptions to one's self (see (d), (e), (f), and (i)), or in being *mental*, or *psychological* present-tense ascriptions to one's self (see d, e, and g). Also, there are other types of ascriptions that are not based on evidence or explicit inference. Ordinary perceptual reports (such as (j)) share this feature. Furthermore, arguably, ascriptions of mental states to *others* (a and c) are often also non-evidential and non-inferential. Typical attributions of propositional attitudes regarding present states of affairs to others often seem to be spontaneous projections of one's own propositional attitudes. Seeing the terrified face of a friend as we are walking on a trail, I look ahead, and noticing a bear, I attribute to my friend fear of the bear—a fear I myself would be prepared to avow.[11] And attributions of present feelings and states of minds to people very close to us often strongly resemble reports of direct perceptions. Consider a mother's pronouncement, upon seeing her child: "He's not feeling well," or a husband's declaration, looking at

---

[11] The example is due to Robert Gordon (1986).

his wife: "She's mad at me." 'Projective' and 'perceptual' psychological attributions do not seem like hypotheses advanced on the basis of evidence in an effort to provide a (proto-) theoretical explanation of others' behavior.

It might be thought that, unlike perceptual reports, avowals do not require *any* ordinary observation. But it is not clear that observation is necessarily implicated in all perceptual reports. As I understand it, observation is a deliberate cognitive act, which involves the deployment of some faculty or sense for the purpose of reaching a verdict on some matter. Now consider a standard case of perception. I stand facing the window, and a bright red cardinal flies by, landing on a tree outside. I exclaim: "Look! There's a beautiful red cardinal on that pine tree!" Must my report be backed up by an active procedure of *observing*, or *looking at*, or *checking to see* what is outside? Could I not have, more passively, *seen* or *perceived* or *noticed* the bird, simply in consequence of the fact that my eyes were open and I was appropriately placed? But then it seems that at least some perceptual reports can share in the non-observational immediacy of avowals. Yet they do not share in their security.

Finally, we must recognize that many non-mental present-tense *self-ascriptions* are not based on ordinary evidence or inference. Some of them (most notably, those like i) are different from perceptual reports precisely in not being based on ordinary sense perception. These are proprioceptive reports and reports on one's bodily position, location, or orientation. Yet, as suggested earlier (and as will be discussed at length in later chapters), avowals seem much more secure than these bodily self-ascriptions. It might be suggested that such self-ascriptions are nonetheless based on some kind of *internal* perception. But then we should consider self-ascriptive reports of perception of the kind exemplified in (j). It does not seem plausible to suppose that reports that one is seeing or hearing something are based on any kind of perception of *one's seeing or hearing* (in addition to perceptions of *what* one claims to be seeing or hearing). Yet, to the extent that such reports are factual, they are straightforwardly corrigible by others, and, at any rate, seem to be much less secure than avowals.

I take it as a non-negotiable condition of adequacy on an account of avowals' special security that it should respect both Semantic Continuity and Epistemic Asymmetry. Yet it may be more difficult than might first appear to come by an account that does not compromise one or the other claim.[12] Of particular interest is what I have referred to as the Epistemic Approach to explaining the security of avowals. On this popular approach, avowals are taken to represent judgments that we make about ourselves, and their distinctive security is to be explained by identifying a different way of knowing, a special epistemic access, route, or basis associated with avowals. In keeping with Semantic Continuity, epistemic views portray avowals as representing subjects' judgments about the states of a certain individual (oneself), which judgments could be made by others as well. The epistemic contrasts between avowals and other ascriptions are attributed to the fact that avowals are arrived at through a different epistemic method, or rely on a different epistemic basis, from other ascriptions. Thus described, the Epistemic Approach includes traditional Cartesian introspectionism as well as contemporary materialist introspectionism. But it also includes non-introspectionist views, as we shall see.

The Epistemic Approach may seem very tempting, if not inevitable, when we combine the following:

- the non-evidential character of avowals, i.e. their immediacy and lack of reliance on ordinary inference, evidence, or observation;
- the supposition that avowals represent judgments that we make about contingent matters of fact that are not based on pure reason;
- the fact that avowals appear to be *epistemically* more secure than judgments about the same matters of facts that *are* evidentially based, for avowals are not only less readily questioned or challenged; they are presumed to be more apt to be correct and knowledgeable.

Putting these together encourages the thought that there must be some special epistemic way or basis each of us has for determining certain things about what is currently going on with us. Using this basis, each of us can issue claims about our present states of mind that would be more epistemically secure than truth-conditionally equivalent claims

---

[12] For discussion of how leading accounts currently on offer fail to respect one or the other claim, see Bar-On and Long (2001). Smith (1998) has independently argued that the main difficulty in reaching a satisfactory philosophical account of so-called first-person authority is to reconcile (what I here call) Epistemic Asymmetry and Semantic Continuity. Focusing on the difficulties in accounting for Epistemic Asymmetry, Wright (1998) also points out the importance of preserving features grouped here under Semantic Continuity.

made by others, or by oneself at other times, or ones that would be made by oneself on a different basis.

The Epistemic Approach encompasses several views. On the familiar Cartesian introspectionist view, avowals enjoy absolute security that is epistemic in nature. It is the result of the operation of an *infallible* mode of obtaining knowledge, an "inner sense", which operates only when one is making judgments about one's own *immaterial* mind. Preserving the idea of "inner sense", but abandoning Cartesian infallibility as well as Cartesian dualism, contemporary materialist versions of introspectionism have offered a variety of modes of internal 'tracking' of some of our own brain states to explain the high reliability of our own mental self-pronouncements. One difficulty with materialist introspectionism is that it fails to capture adequately the striking contrast noted above between avowals and present-tense proprioceptive reports such as "My legs are crossed", as well as self-ascriptions of position (e.g., "I am sitting down") and orientation (e.g., "I am in the middle of the room"). Such present-tense non-mental self-ascriptions are as non-evidential as avowals: they are not normally based on inference, evidence, or ordinary observation. In this case it seems very plausible to suppose that there is a distinctive way of knowing associated with such self-ascriptions. After all, no one can tell that my legs are crossed, or that I am standing up, and so on, the way I can, and normally do. Yet avowals seem strikingly more secure than these non-evidential non-mental self-ascriptions, in ways that will be explored below. I think that full appreciation of this contrast in security will diminish the appeal of contemporary introspectionist views.

I shall also consider non-introspectionist views that still fall under the umbrella of the Epistemic Approach. I will be arguing that these views, too, fail to do full justice to Epistemic Asymmetry. My critique of the Epistemic Approach will set the stage for the alternative, non-epistemic explanation of the distinctive status of avowals that I shall defend later on. Dissatisfaction with the Epistemic Approach will provide critical motivation for my search for an alternative account. At the same time, I will be developing a more 'analytical' motivation; that is, I will try to make a compelling case for a non-epistemic account through a more direct analysis of the character, role, and status of avowals.

In the course of my discussion, I will attempt to motivate the following desiderata for an adequate account of the distinctive security of avowals:

**D1.** The account should explain what renders avowals protected from ordinary epistemic assessments (including requests for reasons, challenges to their truth, simple correction, etc.).

**D2.** It should explain why avowals' security is unparalleled: why there are asymmetries in security between avowals and all other empirical ascriptions, including (truth-conditionally equivalent) third-person ascriptions and non-mental first-person ascriptions. In particular, it should explain why avowals are so strongly presumed to be *true*.

**D3.** It should explain the non-negotiable character of the security—the fact that it is 'non-transferable' and 'inalienable'.

**D4.** It should apply to *both* intentional and non-intentional avowals alike, and allow us to separate avowals from other ascriptions in terms of their security.
(Meeting D1–D4 would amount to accounting for Epistemic Asymmetry in its full scope.)

**D5.** It should accommodate the continuities in semantic and logical structure between avowals and other ascriptions. In particular, it should present avowals as truth-assessable.
(Meeting D5 would amount to accommodating Semantic Continuity.)

**D6.** It should avoid portraying avowals as absolutely infallible or incorrigible.
(I take meeting D6 to be part of remaining faithful to the ordinary treatment of avowals.)

**D7.** It should avoid appealing to Cartesian dualist ontology.
(Meeting D7 should make my account acceptable to those who accept some of Descartes's key observations about our relation to our own mind, but who find Cartesian dualism unacceptable.)

**D8.** It should allow for the possibility that avowals represent privileged self-knowledge.
(Meeting D8 would make room for a non-deflationary view of self-knowledge.)

Grammatical accounts of the security of avowals seem potentially better placed than non-Cartesian epistemic accounts to meet desiderata

D1–D4. Non-Cartesian epistemic accounts, on the other hand, seem better placed to meet D5–D8. None of the accounts I shall be criticizing meets all the above desiderata in a satisfactory way. I hope to convince my reader that the account I shall be developing in this work does.

## The Plan of this Book

The uniquely secure status of avowals clearly has something to do with the special way an avowing subject picks herself out. Ascribing an occurrent thought or feeling or sensation to myself under the description "DB", or "so and so's philosophy teacher" will not, in the normal case, afford me the security characteristic of an avowal. It has thus seemed to many that focusing on the way the pronoun "I" (or its equivalents) is typically used to pick out the subject of an avowal holds the key to understanding their special status. While I agree that our understanding of the status of avowals is aided by understanding the special character of "I"-ascriptions, I believe that excessive focus on the way "I" refers has led many astray. In Chapter 2, I show how such a focus generates a false dilemma. Attending to the distinctive security of avowals as *"I"-ascriptions*, we may feel compelled to find a peculiar object, such as a Cartesian Ego, which can serve as the special subject that each avowal characterizes. Alternatively, we may feel driven to maintain that avowals are 'subjectless'—i.e., that they involve no ascription to an individual at all. Both these alternatives are problematic as accounts of the semantic functioning of "I", and each in its way involves compromising Semantic Continuity. What is worse, neither alternative results in an acceptable explanation of the secure status of avowals.

A more promising account of the way "I" refers, which derives from the works of Sidney Shoemaker and Gareth Evans, is discussed in Chapter 3. This account, which I shall dub the Reference Without Identification account, preserves Semantic Continuity, while explaining various epistemic asymmetries between "I"-ascriptions and other ascriptions. On Shoemaker and Evans's account, we can understand these asymmetries better if we properly understand a phenomenon Shoemaker has dubbed "immunity to error through misidentification". I shall argue that Shoemaker and Evans's account still focuses too narrowly on the subject part of "I"-ascriptions, and, it turns out, still fails to account for Epistemic Asymmetry in its full scope. Examining the merits and limitations of the Shoemaker and Evans account will set the stage for the alternative account developed in later chapters.

I begin Chapter 4 by briefly outlining and criticizing the contemporary materialist incarnation of the traditional epistemic account. On this version, the security of avowals is due to the operation of a special mechanism for detecting or 'tracking' our own mental states, where these states are to be understood as forming a certain subset of our internal physical states. I then discuss a certain alternative to introspectionist views that has received much attention in recent years. The alternative view is centered on the idea that avowals of propositional attitudes are marked by a special feature, which I dub 'transparency-to-the-world'. When I avow, "I believe it's raining outside," though I say something about a state of my mind, my attention is focused directly on a state of the world outside me, rather than on what goes on inside me. Avowals of beliefs, desires, emotions, and so on reflect our ability to tell how things are with us, mentally speaking, by using an epistemic 'transparency procedure' by which we directly consider how things are in the world around us. I argue that although this account respects Semantic Continuity, it fails to capture Epistemic Asymmetry in its full scope. I also examine a non-epistemic version of the transparency view (due to Richard Moran). I argue that it fails to provide a viable alternative to the Epistemic Approach.

In Chapter 5, I examine a recently much-discussed puzzle regarding the security of, specifically, avowals that involve the specification of intentional content. The puzzle is how such security can be reconciled with *externalism about content*. It has been argued that if externalism is true, then we must face a form of *skepticism* about content, analogous to the more familiar skepticism about the external world. I argue that the argument relies on a *recognitional conception* of ordinary knowledge of content (and self-knowledge more generally), which we ought to reject. I propose that ordinary self-ascriptions of contentful mental states, even if not absolutely infallible or incorrigible, are protected from external-content skepticism precisely because they do *not* represent recognitional self-judgments.

I develop this proposal in Chapter 6 by appeal to the notion of 'ascriptive immunity to error', a notion I explain by analogy to the notion of immunity to error through misidentification discussed in earlier chapters. I try to show that the epistemic immediacy that attends ascriptive immunity to error is no bar to achieving both genuine and correct self-ascription. I do this by considering first a special case of avowals: self-verifying avowals of presently entertained thoughts. I then argue that this case exhibits some key features that are shared by all avowals. Using an insight that I derive from my earlier discussion of content skepticism and content externalism, I locate the source of avowals' distinctive security—what accounts for their *ascriptive* security—in the *expressive character* of avowals. This allows me to portray security in content assignment as a special case of avowals' ascriptive security.

In Chapters 7 and 8, I turn to a fuller development of my non-epistemic, *Neo-Expressivist* account of avowals' special security. The account builds upon the familiar idea that avowals, whether made in speech or in thought, are expressive performances that serve *directly to express the self-ascriber's mental condition*, rather than report it. However, it avoids the difficulties that are thought to beset expressivist views of avowals. On the Neo-Expressivist view, avowals, like natural expressions, serve to express the subjects' first-order mental conditions rather than report them. But unlike natural expressions, and unlike non-self-ascriptive verbal expressions, avowals self-ascribe the very conditions that they express. Avowals are expressive acts whose products are genuine ascriptions of occurrent mental states to oneself that pick out a particular individual and ascribe to her a certain occurrent condition. After investigating key similarities and differences between avowals and natural expressions, I argue that, properly understood, the expressive character of avowals can explain why avowals are regarded as immune to epistemic errors of ascription and why they are strongly presumed to be true. It can account for Epistemic Asymmetry in its full scope. At the same time, avowals are seen as pronouncements that can be true or false, and can be interchanged *salva veritate* in context with other ascriptions. Thus, in contrast with more familiar expressivist accounts, the account I offer adheres to Semantic Continuity.

By itself, the Neo-Expressivist account of avowals I develop does not explain the special claim to knowledge that subjects have with respect to their present states of mind, and it does not provide an explanation of the special status of self-knowledge (see questions (ii) and (iii) above). The Neo-Expressivist account of avowals' security is consistent with a variety of views of self-knowledge. In particular, it is compatible with a *deflationary* view, which maintains that the seemingly privileged status of self-knowledge is fully exhausted by the special security of avowals understood non-epistemically. However, while such a deflationary view is consistent with my account of avowals, it is not entailed by it. Since I believe subjects *do* have a special claim to knowledge of their own present mind, I seek an account of avowals that is at least consistent with a substantive answer to (ii). In Chapter 9, I argue that the account of avowals I offer meets this desideratum. I sketch several proposals concerning the privileged status of self-knowledge that should be compatible with my account of avowals. I also offer a more direct explanation of the privileged status of self-knowledge in terms of the notion of first-person *privilege* (as contrasted with so-called first-person *authority*).

My final chapter, Chapter 10, offers reflections on possible implications of the account of avowals defended in this work for certain metaphysical issues in the philosophy of mind. In particular, I address two metaphysical issues that are kept in the background in earlier chapters: the reality of mental states, and the extent to which they are ontologically independent of expressive behavior.

## Some Terminological Preliminaries

So far, I have presented everyday *utterances* as my paradigmatic examples of avowals. However, I intend my discussion to apply *mutatis mutandis* to self-ascriptions made in either speech or thought. The puzzles surrounding the status of avowals remain (and in some cases become sharper) when we consider, e.g., my *thought* "I'm so tired", "I wish this headache would go away", "I hate this painting", "This dog really scares me". For, it is equally natural to take such thoughts to represent truths about their subject which the subject is in a special position to deliver. And, upon considering such thoughts, we would normally credit the subject who harbors them with privileged knowledge of their truths. If you consider that I am now *thinking* to myself, "I feel so tired," you would hardly take yourself to be in a position to question my feeling tired. (Note that here questions of sincerity do not even arise: the case is one where we are supposing that I am thinking that thought to myself.)

My use of the relatively neutral notion of *ascription* is intended to cover both utterances and thoughts or judgments. In keeping with common practice, I shall allow myself to speak of the "semantics", as well as "truth-conditions" of ascriptions, as well as of the "I"-component of an ascription and its "reference". I shall also use quotation marks to cite the relevant ascription, without presupposing that self-ascriptions in thought must consist in one's *talking* to oneself (at least in some sense). Presumably, one can think, as well as say, something properly expressed in English by the words "I am $\phi$", where $\phi$ refers to an occurrent mental state. That is what I have in mind when I speak of mental self-ascriptions made in thought, as opposed to speech. And I am allowing that, among such self-ascriptions, there are those that can properly count as avowals. (Exactly what qualifies them as such is something that I will take up later.) However, I do not want to suggest that there are no important differences between ascribing in language and ascribing in thought.[13] Where these differences matter, I shall indicate it.

I have initially characterized avowals in a very rough-and-ready way, as present-tense self-ascriptions of occurrent mental states. Part of my task will be to refine this characterization. A first, obvious refinement pertains to "self-ascriptions". Ascribing an occurrent (as opposed to dispositional) mental state at the time of ascription to an individual who is *in fact* oneself is not sufficient for avowing the mental state. It seems as though one must also be thinking of the individual *as* oneself. Where the context makes it clear, I will allow myself simply to speak of self-ascriptions; otherwise, I shall speak of an "I"-ascription. Furthermore, avowing seems to require ascribing to oneself the relevant state in a certain way. Saying, or thinking, "I am mad at my mother" purely in consequence of being convinced by a therapist's analysis would not constitute *avowing* anger, since such an "I"-ascription is made on a kind of basis available to others as well. So it is not even the case that all present-tense "*I*"-ascriptions of occurrent mental states will count as avowals. Thus, when I use "avowal", I intend to signal that

---

[13] One difference has already been noted in passing: where we consider a self-ascription that is made in thought, rather than in speech, questions of insincerity or dissimulation do not arise.

the relevant self-ascription is not to be understood as a theory-driven self-ascription.

It should be noted, however, that some ascriptions of occurrent mental states that fail to use "I" may also qualify as avowals. For instance, I consider ascriptions such as "My tooth hurts", or "This hurts", or "This feels cold" to be avowals, even though such ascriptions do not contain the pronoun "I" (the last two contain no overt element referring to the ascriber). I think it is plausible to treat such ascriptions as elliptical, and as containing a covert indexical reference to the utterer/thinker. This receives some support from considering languages such as Hebrew and French, which do require an overt indexical pronoun, at least in some of these cases (cf. Hebrew: "Ko'ev *li*" ("It hurts *to me*"), or French: "Il *me* fait froid" ("It makes *me* cold")). Furthermore, it would not be unreasonable to suggest that, at least in speech, avowals can use terms other than an indexical pronoun to refer to the self-ascriber. Thus consider, "Stop it, Jenny! *Daddy* doesn't like this," said by a parent to a child, or "*Jenny* wants to eat now," said by the child of herself.

The foregoing examples illustrate what will become increasingly clear as I develop my account of avowals. The class of avowals cannot be circumscribed purely in terms of the surface grammar of certain self-ascriptions. It also cannot be delineated by attending to obvious aspects of the meaning of the relevant self-ascriptions. Indeed, this is part of our difficulty: avowals contrast in their security with ascriptions that are grammatically and even semantically indistinguishable from them. "I am very happy" can sometimes be an avowal and sometimes not. (The account of avowals I shall be developing is partly motivated by this difficulty.) Thus I will not begin my investigation with a clear definition of my explanandum. Nor will I be aiming to produce at the end of my investigation a stable definition of avowals in terms of necessary and sufficient conditions. My starting point is a familiar phenomenon, which can be characterized ostensively as it were, and which is philosophically puzzling for reasons I began to explain in this chapter. If I can offer an illuminating account of this phenomenon that will make the puzzles go away, I will be satisfied. So, I hope, will my reader.

# 2

# Using "I" 'as Subject': Cartesian Reference or No Reference?

Self-ascriptions such as "I am thirsty", "I have a terrible headache", "I feel like taking a nap right now", "I'm thinking about my poor aunt in the hospital", "I hope this noise stops soon", "I'm so annoyed that I can't get this computer to work", and so on, as normally made, have a seemingly unique status. Whether volunteered spontaneously or offered in response to questions, whether made in speech or in thought, such *avowals*, as I shall refer to them, appear to enjoy a special security. Unlike typical apriori judgments, avowals concern contingent matters of fact. Yet their production does not seem to involve consulting any evidence, inference, or ordinary observation. Like perceptual reports, they are seemingly 'effortless' and are strongly presumed to be true, but, unlike such reports, they are not based on ordinary perception. In fact, they appear to be made on no basis at all. And in contrast to all other pronouncements, avowals are strongly resistant to epistemic criticism, not subject to ordinary doubts and corrections, and invulnerable to brute error.

## The Use of "I" 'as Object' versus 'as Subject'

It is no doubt crucial to the special status of avowals that they are *self*-ascriptions. However, recall the ascriptions in the contrast class of avowals:

(a) "She is very tired," said (or thought) by someone else about me at that same time;

(b) "I was very tired then," said by me at a later time;

(c) "John is very tired," said by me about someone else;
(d) "DB is very tired," said by me about myself when I fail to recogn-
    ize that *I* am DB;
(e) "I am very tired," said by me on the basis of, say, looking in the
    mirror, or inference from some test results;
(f) "I am 5′ 5″ tall," or "There's a scar on my forehead";
(g) "I am a very patient person," or "I have a sense of humor," or
    "I am attentive to my friends";
(h) "There's a red car right there!" said upon seeing a car outside;
 (i) "My legs are crossed," or "I'm standing in front of the house."
 (j) "I am seeing a red cardinal," or "I am hearing a loud noise."

Many of these are self-ascriptions. Many of them do not merely ascribe a property to someone who is in fact the self-ascriber (as in (d)). Rather, they are self-ascriptions that use the first-person pronoun "I" to pick out the self-ascriber. (Consider (b), (e), (f), (g), (i), and (j).) Even so, they do not share in the secure status of avowals. Part of the task of accounting for this status, then, is to explain how avowals are different from these other, less secure "I"-ascriptions.

In *The Blue and Brown Books*, Wittgenstein offers the following distinction:

There are two different cases in the use of the word 'I' (or 'my') which I might call 'the use as object' and 'the use as subject'. Examples of the first kind of use are these: "My arm is broken," "I have grown six inches," "I have a bump on my forehead," "The wind blows my hair about." Examples of the second kind are: "*I* see so and so," "*I* hear so and so," "*I* try to lift my arm," "*I* think it will rain," "*I* have a toothache." (1958: 66 f.)

At first glance, it is not clear what the distinction amounts to. For, in both "I think it will rain" and "I have grown six inches", "I" serves as the grammatical subject. As will become clearer below, however, the distinction does not pertain to a difference in surface grammar, but to the way the subject of predication is picked out. Wittgenstein is pointing out that certain uses of "I"—its uses 'as subject'—in some sense do not involve picking oneself out as just another item in the world, a particular object or individual, of which something is to be predicated. As Wittgenstein explains:

One can point to the difference between these two categories by saying: The cases of the first category involve the recognition of a particular person, and there is in these cases the possibility of an error. . . . It is possible that, say in an accident, I should feel a pain in my arm, see a broken arm at my side, and think it is mine, when really it is my neighbour's. . . . On the other hand, there is no question of recognizing a person when I say I have tooth-ache. To ask 'are you sure it is *you* who have pains?' would be nonsensical. (1958: 67)

Using Wittgenstein's distinction, it may be suggested that avowals are self-ascriptions that use "I" 'as subject', not 'as object'. This may provide an important insight for understanding the distinctive secur-ity of avowals. It may be suggested that, in trying to understand this security, we should focus attention on the *"I"-component* of avowals. Though avowals are not alone in being self-ascriptions, and though other self-ascriptions also use the grammatical pronoun "I", avowals should be marked by the fact that they involve a special use of "I": its use as subject. Thus, consider the ascriptions in the contrast classes for avowals (i.e., (a)–(j) above). Ascriptions of present mental states to others (c), or by others to oneself (a), or by oneself to oneself in the past (b) and so on, are all subject to various kinds of potential errors, corresponding to possible aberrations in the 'epistemic routes' that lead one to the judgments they express. (Perception, observation, inference, memory, etc. are all notoriously subject to various failures.) This explains why such ascriptions do not enjoy the maximal degree of epistemic security. By parity of reasoning, we might take the secur-ity of avowals to be due to the fact that they are somehow protected from these kinds of epistemic failure. Following Wittgenstein, we may also notice that avowals involve uses of "I" as subject, whereas the ascriptions in the contrast class involve uses of "I" as object. A proper understanding of what is characteristic of such uses will show why ascriptions involving them are not vulnerable to certain errors. And this may go a long way toward explaining why avowals seem to enjoy such a high degree of security.

## Cartesian Egos as the Targets of Reference for "I"

What kind of protection from error or failure is afforded by using "I" as subject? Wittgenstein suggests that the protection has to do with the special way we identify the individual of whom we predicate something. When using "I" as subject, "there is no question of recognizing a person . . . . To ask 'are you sure it is *you* who have pains?' would be nonsensical." The errors that we seem to avoid when using "I" as subject are, then, errors of recognition. But we must ask why, and in what sense, one is protected from such errors when using "I" as subject.

As Descartes famously recognized, just thinking an "I"-thought seems to guarantee both the existence and the presence of the referent of "I". It makes no sense to suppose that one has used "I" to refer to no object at all. Moreover, at least with certain uses of "I", it seems impossible to doubt that one has got 'the right object'—namely, oneself. So the invulnerability to error seemingly involved in the relevant uses of "I" is rather remarkable. It begs for explanation.

Now, according to Wittgenstein, the historically familiar Cartesian account is an attempt to explain the seemingly guaranteed success of "I" in a particular way:

We feel then that in the cases in which "I" is used as subject we don't use it because we recognize a particular person by his bodily characteristics; and this creates the illusion that we use this word to refer to something bodiless, which, however, has its seat in our body. In fact *this* seems to be the real ego, the one of which it was said, "Cogito, ergo sum." (1958: 69)

On Wittgenstein's diagnosis, since uses of "I" as subject do not seem to require recognition of bodily features in picking out, or identifying the referent of "I", the Cartesian is moved to supply a special object— 'something bodiless'— that each of us could refer to without relying on the use of such features, namely, her Self. Uses of "I" as subject then turn out to involve *reference to this special object*.

On this reading of the Cartesian view, when I say, or think, "I feel overcome by joy," for instance, I am guaranteed success in identifying the subject of my ascription, since I cannot be in error regarding *which* object I am trying to pick out. But we may wonder how it is that I can be guaranteed success in picking out the Ego, understood *as one object* (or individual substance) *among others*. Do I perhaps have a special access to my own Ego—a special way of recognizing it, or some kind of direct acquaintance with it? But what could that amount to? Talk of recognition *of*, acquaintance *with*, or access *to* implies an epistemic relationship between an epistemic subject (someone who is a potential believer or knower) and some object (an individual or thing, or perhaps a fact). In paradigmatic cases, there is a kind of 'epistemic gap' between the two relata, which the relationship allows the subject to bridge. But it is very unclear what could be made of these ideas within the Cartesian framework, in which I simply *am* my Ego and every belief, thought, impression, etc. that I have is necessarily a feature of it. (Talk of *my* Ego seems equally misleading.)

Suppose, on the other hand, it is suggested that when "I" is used as subject, we pick out the subject of the ascription (viz., the Ego) neither through features of the body associated with it nor through direct acquaintance with the Ego itself. Instead, we pick it out as the bearer of certain features, which present themselves to us directly. The suggestion is that we have direct access to (or awareness of) our present mental states, and we use "I" to refer to the subject of these states, namely, our Ego. But it is not clear why identifying a subject of ascription in this way should afford more security, more protection from epistemic error, than identifying a subject of ascription through its bodily features. We would still be left with the question why "I", understood as referring to the subject of certain present mental states, should be a more secure referential device than other referring expressions, or than "I" understood as referring to one particular object among others. The detour via Cartesian Egos will seem to have got us no further.[1]

Be that as it may, notice that the Cartesian explanation (on the above diagnosis) takes it for granted that uses of "I" as subject, perhaps like uses of other referential expressions, must rely on some form of access to, or recognition of, the referent of "I". (This idea will be criticized in the next chapter.) This, in turn, presupposes that "I", in its use as subject, is a referential expression. It presupposes that, like uses of other subject-terms in grammatically similar ascriptions, uses of "I" as subject *purport* to refer to an object of which something is to be predicated.[2] On the present diagnosis, the Cartesian begins with the correct observation that certain self-ascriptions are not subject to the same *epistemic* failures as other ascriptions. Seduced by surface grammar,

---

[1] Doug Long and Bijan Parsia have both independently raised questions that prompted the points made in the last two paragraphs. (I return to some of these points below.)

[2] I allow myself to speak of reference here, since, presumably, on the Cartesian picture, even a self-ascription made in thought would contain a distinct element whose function is to refer to the self-ascriber.

he tacitly makes the tempting *semantic* assumption that "I" (and its equivalents) in such self-ascriptions is an ordinary referring expression whose function is to identify some object of which something is then to be predicated. (As noted above, he further assumes that performing this semantic function requires some form of epistemic access to the referent.) But then, to reconcile this semantic function with the role of "I" in epistemically secure self-ascriptions, he is moved to make an *ontological* postulation, assigning as the referent of "I" something quite extraordinary—a Cartesian Self or Ego.

Putting the above reasoning more explicitly, we get:

(1) "I" is a referring expression whose semantic function in all its uses is to pick out, or refer to, a particular object.
(This is the semantic presupposition identified above. It can be seen as an application of the Semantic Continuity claim to "I". For it may seem that, unless "I" were taken to refer to a particular individual, we could not accommodate the logico-semantic continuities between "I"-ascriptions and other ascriptions.)

(2) Certain "I"-ascriptions—where "I" is used as subject—enjoy a distinctive security: the user of "I" in such ascriptions cannot make an epistemic error in picking out the referent of "I". Uses of "I" as subject are guaranteed correct reference.
(This is the epistemic observation attributed above to Descartes. It can be seen as an application of Epistemic Asymmetry to the "I"-component. For it manifests a contrast between certain "I"-ascriptions and various other ascriptions.)

(3) If we took "I" to refer to an 'ordinary' object, say one's body (or, more fashionably, one's brain), there could be no apriori guarantee for the user of "I" that she is referring to what she thinks she is referring to.

So,

(4) Uses of "I" as subject cannot be taken to refer to any ordinary object, such as one's body, or a distinct part of it (e.g., one's brain).

(5) Given (2), the intended referent of "I" must be an object whose presence can only be ascertained in the act of making the relevant "I"-ascription.

(6) For (5) to hold, the essential characteristics of the referent of "I" must be accessible to the user of "I" in the act of using it.

(7) The only object that meets this condition is a Cartesian Ego.

So,

(8)  The referent of certain uses of "I" must be a Cartesian Ego.

The foregoing is an attempt to spell out in an explicit argument form the reasoning imputed to the Cartesian by Elizabeth Anscombe, in her celebrated article "The First Person" (1975).[3] The basic idea behind the argument can be presented more simply, in terms of the following dilemma. Adhering to Semantic Continuity and accepting that "I" is a referring expression, the referent of "I" must be either an ordinary object (such as a human body) or some extraordinary object. Given the special epistemic security of avowals as captured by Epistemic Asymmetry, "I" cannot be taken to refer to an ordinary object. So, the referent of "I" must be an extraordinary object: an object securely knowable in a way no ordinary object can be. The Cartesian Self or Ego can be seen as an ontological invention tailored to fit the bill.[4]

The Cartesian strategy may seem a promising one for explaining the contrasts between avowals and other ascriptions. Avowals, unlike ascriptions that are superficially similar to them, involve reference to a special kind of object, Egos. That is what sets apart uses of "I" as subject. The nature of Egos and our own special epistemic relation to them guarantee that the ascriptions we make to them when using "I" as subject are not vulnerable to any of the ordinary epistemic failings. Adhering to this picture, we can explain how your ascription, "DB is feeling very sad", can be exchanged for my self-ascription, "I am feeling very sad". We both ascribe a certain state to a particular subject of mental states, namely, me (= my Ego). However, you make the

---

[3] Anscombe qualifies the Cartesian argument's conclusion, remarking that the referent of "I" is perhaps not to be taken as a Cartesian Ego, but "rather, a stretch of one" (1975: 58). This is presumably by way of conceding the point famously made by Russell (1912) (and others), that reference to a substantial persisting Ego would require more than what can be provided by momentary mental ascriptions. (See also Strawson (1994).) We shall return to Anscombe's view shortly.

[4] Given the problematic character of the reasoning in the above reconstruction, it may be historically inadvisable to attribute it to Descartes. Indeed, Descartes says things that go against some of the above steps. As is well known, Descartes's Sixth Meditation contains an argument for dualism that does not depend on the greater epistemic security of "I"-ascriptions, but rather depends on the difference in metaphysical nature between the mental and the physical. Still, it does not seem unfair to take Descartes's Second Meditation as an attempt to form an explanatory link between Epistemic Asymmetry and onto-logical separation. (And many contemporary philosophers who do not accept Descartes's metaphysical argument for substance dualism are nonetheless seduced by the idea that there is some such link.) I should say that my purpose in this discussion, however, is not Descartes exegesis. (My thanks here to Don Garrett. Also thanks to Bijan Parsia for trying to keep me honest about the historical Descartes.)

ascription on the indirect basis of observations and inferences regarding my bodily behavior, and your ascription is subject to all sorts of epistemic failures. I, on the other hand, make the ascription in a way that is protected from all such failures.

Accepting Cartesian dualism, with its commitment to mind–body interaction, requires embracing an ontology that includes immaterial particulars that exert causal influence on, and are causally affected by, goings-on in the physical world. The difficulties with this idea are widely appreciated. It also requires making good sense of the idea of contingently existing, objective particulars whose modifications can be known infallibly. We have seen some difficulties with this idea earlier. However, even setting aside qualms about Cartesian ontology and epistemology, one may question the adequacy of the above Cartesian account as an acceptable *semantic* account of the reference of "I".

First, we may observe that the account requires compromising Semantic Continuity to a certain extent. For, although the account preserves the idea that "I" refers, it requires postulating a systematic semantic ambiguity in uses of "I". To explain the security of uses of "I" as subject, the Cartesian proposes that we see them as referring to a different (kind of) object from uses of "I" as object. But then it is not clear how we can preserve the palpable grammatical and logical continuities across the two types of uses. If I say to someone (or just think to myself), "I'm just getting out of bed, but I feel so tired," I seem to be ascribing two things to a single individual (myself): getting out of bed and feeling tired. Yet, on the Cartesian picture, the first ascription has as its subject a particular body, or perhaps a particular human being, whereas the subject of the second ascription is a particular immaterial Ego. This means that my conjunctive attribution will involve a certain—unmarked and unnoticeable—shift in reference. A corresponding shift will presumably occur in the third person: in "DB just got out of bed, but she feels tired". "DB" will presumably refer to the human being DB, whereas "she" will have to refer to DB's Self (where "She feels tired" will be taken to express a fallible conjecture about a state of that Self). But if we can no longer take for granted the notion of pronominal preservation of reference, it is not clear how we are to preserve the validity of everyday inferences that seem to trade on such preservation. (e.g.: "If someone has had a lot of sleep, then she is not likely to be tired. DB got a lot of sleep. So she is not likely to be tired.")[5]

We may assume that this problem can be circumvented; still, there is a difficulty with the Cartesian way of explaining Epistemic Asymmetry. The Cartesian explains the security of avowals as a matter of the guaranteed *semantic success* of "I" in referring to the 'right object'. This guaranteed success he explains by invoking the guaranteed *epistemic success* each of us enjoys when we identify ourselves as the targets of reference. And this success in turn is explained by the existence of certain objects that are, by their nature, susceptible to such unfailing identification. We can summarize this by saying that, for the Cartesian, the target of reference of "I" is (semantically) unmissable because (epistemically) unmistakable. But perhaps we ought to be wary of the very idea of unmissable targets of reference.

Naively, the notion of a target of reference suggests the idea of someone *aiming* at and/or *hitting* some object. Conceptually speaking, the possibility of hitting a target requires at least the possibility of missing it. Correlatively, it ought to be at least conceptually possible for one who aims at a target to *think* she has hit the target without her *actually* having succeeded. With ordinary targets of reference—by which I mean people, and everyday physical objects, but also things such as hurricanes, countries, wars, and numbers—these conceptual possibilities seem preserved. For such entities have identity conditions that are independent of any particular individual's success in identifying them. Not so with Cartesian Egos. To play the role of securing apriori guaranteed success of reference, Egos are required to be targets that each of us *cannot*—logically or conceptually—fail to recognize, and is thus able to name unerringly using "I". This means that their identities are essentially tied to individuals' successful acts of identification. As Anscombe remarks, "I" is supposed to have 'sure-fire' reference. But this could only be so "if the referent of 'I' were both freshly defined with each use of 'I', and also remained in view so long as something was being taken to be *I*" (Anscombe 1975: 57).

---

[5] Ram Neta has suggested to me that the validity of such inferences can be preserved on the Cartesian view by claiming that they tacitly employ auxiliary premises that connect the human being with the immaterial Ego. I would be suspicious of any claim to the effect that in going through ordinary reasoning we must be 'tacitly employing' a highly controversial metaphysical view. However, I do not wish to rest too much weight on this point.

With ordinary referring expressions, there has to be what I shall call *"semantic distance"* between applications of a referring expression and its putative target of reference. A referring expression has an extension: a range of things to which it is supposed to apply. Some things will be in the extension of the expression, others will not. But the expression is of course distinct from its extension. And it must always be in principle possible for the expression to be *misapplied* to a given item. That is to say, it must be possible to use the expression to refer to something outside its extension. The expression (or its user) aims to pick out an item, but may—at least as a matter of logical or conceptual possibility—fail to 'latch onto' the right item (or to any item at all). This implies that whenever a speaker uses a referring expression, there ought to be a conceptual distinction between her *thinking* she applied the term correctly and her *actually* having applied the term correctly. For example, we take it that the word "chair" is a referring expression; it is a term that purports to refer to some items—viz., the chairs of this world. To say this is to say that the word is *supposed to apply* to chairs only. But all this could mean is that it would be incorrect to apply it to something that is not a chair (as when someone says, pointing to a hammock, "Don't sit on this chair"). And this, in turn, implies that it is in principle *possible* to apply it to a non-chair, even if no one ever actually mistakenly calls a non-chair "chair".

Now, the Cartesian picture painted so far portrays "I" as an ordinary referring expression—indeed, very much like a name. However, "I" on this picture has an extraordinary item as its putative target of reference: an unmistakable Ego. Though each Ego is to be a genuine target, to be hit by particular uses of "I", it is logically guaranteed to be unmissable. Failure to hit this kind of target is logically ruled out, and so we may wonder whether we can speak of attempting to hit a target in the first place.[6] If success in picking out the referent of "I" is logically guaranteed, the semantic distance required for ordinary reference seems to be eliminated. Thus Descartes's "I" is a very peculiar referential device: in using it, we supposedly try to single out an item in the world (an Ego) the way we do with proper names or general

---

[6] To use another metaphor, the Cartesian Ego is like an invisible hand whose contours are defined to have a shape that fits a found glove. In such a case, it seems at best misleading to speak of a genuine fit between the hand and the glove.

terms. But, unlike in these cases, our uses of "I" are guaranteed success. I think we may legitimately wonder whether the Cartesian picture manages to preserve the idea of "I" as a referring expression on the model of ordinary referring expressions.[7]

The foregoing can serve to fill out Anscombe's own rejection of Egos.[8] A natural reaction to this reasoning is to suggest that "I" does not qualify as an ordinary referring expression. Later on, I will consider various possibilities of altering the requirements on reference so as to accommodate the special behavior of "I". Some of these possibilities may well be available to the Cartesian, in which case the above argument against reference to Egos will be blocked. However, it may also turn out that such possibilities are consistent with taking all uses of "I" to refer to a more ordinary object, such as a human being. In that case, the Cartesian would no longer be able to cite the special security of "I" as a motivation for postulating Egos.

## The Wittgensteinian Rejection of Private Sensations

Anscombe's argument against Cartesian Egos can be seen as running parallel to Wittgenstein's rejection of private sensations (encapsulated in his so-called Private Language Argument). On one plausible, if limited, reading of the passages surrounding Wittgenstein's *Philosophical Investigations* §258, the so-called Private Language Argument is an attempt to reduce to absurdity a very specific conception of sensation talk, one which can be described as Cartesian.[9] The conception under attack is a combination of four substantive assumptions regarding the character of sensations and sensation terms.

(a) that sensations—the putative referents of the diarist's private signs—are *objective particulars* of sorts, which can be recognized,

---

[7] See Bar-On and Long (2001: sect. 1), where the present objection to Cartesianism is also discussed. We point out that, on the Cartesian picture, each Ego is fixed to the muzzle of the relevant self-ascriber's "I"-gun, so to speak. As we shall see later, this metaphor is actually a useful one for bringing out the distinctive way "I" is supposed to function, which is importantly different from the way ordinary referring expressions work. But once this is understood, the temptation to invoke a special *target* of reference for "I" should disappear.          [8] See Anscombe (1975: esp. 56 ff.).

[9] Though I believe the argument I reconstruct below brings out an important strand in the passages that have come under the title "The Private Language Argument", I cannot claim to be providing a proper exegesis of those passages. My interest here is only in those aspects that bear on the present investigation into the special status of "I"-talk and avowals.

grouped together into kinds, and named, just like ordinary physical objects. However, their recognition is subserved by 'inner sense', rather than by ordinary perception;

(b) that sensations are logically *private* objects: only the 'host' of a sensation can possibly recognize it or verify its presence (from which it follows that she is *incorrigible*);

(c) that the 'host' of a sensation can recognize it *transparently* as well as *infallibly*: a sensation is the sort of thing which, if it is present, its presence will be immediately recognizable by its host. And if it seems to the host that she has it, then she does have it. (See Wittgenstein 1953: §§244, 246, 256.);

(d) that sensation terms, like all "individual words in language name objects", and that the meaning of a word "is the object for which it stands". (This is the core assumption of the Augustinian model of language described at the start of the *Philosophical Investigations*.)

The alleged trouble with setting up a language for which these four assumptions hold is that it will turn out that, in such a language, it would be in principle impossible to *mis*apply words. To borrow a metaphor from David Pears, applying words in such a language would be like throwing stones and declaring the target to be where the stones land. Where putatively objective targets are thus locked on to individual acts of shooting, the whole idea of *aiming* at a target collapses. The private speaker, whose words are supposed to name (and thus have as their meanings) logically private objects, is like the idle stone-thrower: his objects of reference are necessarily tied to his individual acts of references. In this way, whatever is going to seem right to him is right. "And that only means that here we can't talk about 'right' " (1953: §258).[10]

How did we get into this trouble? Let us imagine, with Wittgenstein, a diarist whose task is to set up a language with terms which name his private sensations. He begins by trying to set up some symbol, say "S", as a meaningful sign in his own language, which purports to name one of his sensations. According to the Augustinian assumption (d), the act of endowing "S" with meaning is the act of singling out some object which would *be* its meaning. Since "S" is supposed to be

---

[10] Kenny (1966: 368) makes a related point: that in the case of an utterance in a private language there can be no distinction between the criterion for its content and the criterion for its truth. See also Pears (1987).

a term in a sensation language, the relevant object to be singled out would be some sensation, S. By assumption (a), S is an objective particular, a recognizable individual item in the world. However, by assumption (b), the putative referent of "S"—some particular sensation—will be a logically *private* item. So, if the diarist *could* succeed in setting up "S" as a name for some sensation, he would have introduced a term with a private meaning, since (by assumption (d)) "S"'s meaning is the object for which it stands. How could the diarist achieve this feat? Let us suppose the diarist has some sensation. By assumption (c), the diarist will recognize that he has the sensation, perhaps by introspection. Having introspected its presence, our diarist is in a position to make it the referent (and thus, by (d), the meaning) of "S", perhaps by some kind of inward ostensive definition (he focuses his attention on S and dubs or tags it "S"). Furthermore, by assumption (b), on any future occasion of using "S", our speaker is, logically, the only one in a position to determine whether "S" was correctly applied. Now, suppose the diarist's 'inner sense' tells him that he has S (i.e., that S is present now), and he writes down in his diary "S" (or 'tokens "S" in his language of thought'). In that case, he is using the term "S" because it *seems* to him that he has S. However, by the infallibility part of assumption (c), if it seems to him he has S, then he *does* have S. Which means that the private diarist cannot, logically, go wrong in his linguistic applications of "S".

What is the alleged problem with this? In my discussion of Cartesian reference to Egos in the previous section, I suggested that, in the case of ordinary linguistic expressions, there is a conceptual distinction between correct and incorrect applications of the term. There is what I called a "semantic distance" between applications of a referring expression and the items to which it is used to refer. To recapitulate, referring expressions have an extension: a range of things to which they correctly apply. Some things will be in the extension of the terms, others will not, and it ought to be possible in principle for the expression to *misapply* to a given item. Thus, whenever a speaker uses a referring expression, there ought to be a conceptual distinction between him thinking he applied the term correctly and his actually having applied the term correctly. Now, on a Cartesian way of construing sensations, the subject of a sensation is *infallible* about the presence and character of his sensations: if it seems to the subject that he has a particular sensation, then he has it. Furthermore, sensations are *self-intimating*: if the subject has a particular sensation, then he is bound to recognize that he does. Sensations, as putative targets of reference, would thus be objects that are essentially tied to the subject's recognition of them. There would be, even in principle, no *epistemic distance* between a subject's sensations and his affirmations of their presence—no possibility of a mismatch between the subject's judgment about the presence and character of a sensation and the relevant facts. However, if all there is to the meaning of "S" is (as per (d)) "the object for which it stands", then affirmations of the presence of S would be all there is to meaningful uses of the term "S". But then it seems that there will be no semantic distance between S's and applications of "S" by a speaker, either.

Even supposing there could *be* infallibly recognizable objects, they could not serve as appropriate targets of private linguistic reference. To reiterate, suppose that our private diarist experiences some sensation. How can he undertake to use, say, the sound "S" as a name for that sensation? That is, how can he make it so that, from that point on, "S" should be correctly applicable only to that same sensation (or, perhaps, to all and only future sensations that are 'relevantly similar to' the sensation he dubbed "S")? The problem is that our diarist would only be inclined to use "S" to refer to something if he thought he was experiencing a sensation that is the same as the one he originally dubbed "S". But, by the infallibility assumption, if he thinks he is experiencing a sensation of a certain character, he would be right. Which means that our private diarist *cannot* go wrong in his linguistic applications of "S". Whenever he is inclined to apply "S", his application will be correct. But this means, as Wittgenstein says, that here we cannot speak of correctness *or* incorrectness. And the diarist's original "S" would turn out to be no more than an empty mark made on the occasion of something going on in him.

The parallel to the argument against Cartesian Egos can be brought out as follows. The epistemic security of present-tense "I"-ascriptions of sensations may encourage the idea that avowing speakers have an unfailing way of successfully picking out their sensations, ostensively perhaps. The Cartesian recognizes that, with ordinary objects, there can be no apriori guarantee of successful recognition. So, to secure such guarantee, the putative referents of sensation terms would have to be quite extraordinary items. But, on the above reading of the Private Language Argument, Wittgenstein argues that no language could be set up to talk about sensations understood as such items, if we think of the words of such a language as having these items as their meanings (as per the Augustinian assumption (d)). For the conditions necessary for genuine reference will not be met by the terms of such a language. The analogous argument in the case of the Ego was that no word intended to name an object whose successful identification was logically or conceptually guaranteed could be a genuine name referring to that object.

For all that this version of the Private Language Argument shows, it may be possible for someone to use an existing public language to speak of things about whose occurrence he is epistemically infallible. It may even also be possible to invent one's own private language—a language governed by completely idiosyncratic rules—to speak of publicly accessible entities. What is unique to the case of the private language Wittgenstein envisages is that it is set up to talk about logically private items that are also taken to provide the *meanings* for its terms. It would follow that the meanings of terms in such a language would be logically inaccessible to anyone but their inventor. In a truly logically private language, the extensions of terms like "S" would be fixed by items whose presence and character the speaker in principle cannot fail to recognize, neither at the time of defining "S" nor subsequently. To summarize, the problem with setting up (and using) such a language is that *the lack of epistemic distance needed to secure genuine logical privacy undermines the semantic distance required for linguistic reference.* As targets of reference, private sensations would be completely locked onto the individual applications of the terms putatively referring to them. Whatever practice the private-sensation diarist will manage to set up using terms like "S" is bound to be an idle practice, and emphatically not one involving Augustinian linguistic reference.

It is important to recognize how different the private linguist's use of "S" would be from our use of an ordinary referring expression, such as "tiger". Someone who uses "tiger" to refer to something is potentially subject to at least the following three kinds of errors. Setting aside slips of the tongue, a speaker may call a leopard "tiger" due to a *semantic* error, because he thinks that the word "tiger" covers (or is a word for) both leopards and tigers. Or, the speaker may make a *conceptual* error. She may call a leopard "tiger" because she has in her conceptual repertoire no classification that separates tigers from leopards; she simply lumps them together. (This of course means that she also has the meaning of the word "tiger" wrong, but not because she matches it with a conjunction of two distinct concepts she possesses.) Finally, the speaker may make an *epistemic* error: she may use the term "tiger" to refer to a non-tiger because she thinks mistakenly that there's a tiger in front of her, due to some perceptual defect or poor observation conditions. Alternatively, her error may be *brute*: though her recognitional faculties are intact, and conditions are favorable, she may be confronted with a perfect counterfeit. The differences between these kinds of errors can be appreciated, *inter alia*, by considering the kinds of corrections that would be appropriate, and the revisions that the subject in error would be susceptible to.

Note that, in the ordinary case, the possibilities of making these types of errors are intertwined. Thinking that someone has made an epistemic error when calling a non-tiger "tiger" depends on crediting her with the relevant concepts and on the meaning of the word "tiger" being in place. Ascribing to someone a purely semantic error presupposes that they possess the relevant concepts. And taking some-one to be making a conceptual error involving "tiger" would strongly tend to undermine the attribution to her of thoughts or judgments about tigers (though of course she may still use the relevant *words*, even successfully).

Now, in the private case we are trying to imagine, there are no meanings in place. The private linguist's task is to *set meanings up*. Presumably, however, we cannot suppose that the relevant *concepts* are in place either. At least we should not suppose that the private diarist shares *our* sensation concepts. For if he did, then the invention of "S" would be like the invention of some new word to express the familiar concept TABLE. Such an effort would hardly qualify as the invention of a private term in Wittgenstein's sense. On the above reading of Wittgenstein's Private Language Argument, the conceptual difficulty arises when trying to make sense of someone setting up "S" as a gen-uinely private term designed to refer to items concerning which the possibility of epistemic errors is ruled out (by the Cartesian hypothesis), but where all there is to the semantic application of "S" is the marking of the presence of such items. For, by the Augustinian assumption (d),

"S" is to be a term whose only meaning is the object for which it stands; and that object is to be an item whose presence is infallibly recognizable by the putative user of "S".

It might be thought that the Cartesian need not be accused of trying to establish private meanings for sensation terms. Why couldn't the Cartesian preserve the semantic distance, allow for the possibility in principle of semantic and conceptual mistakes in uses of sensation terms, but insist only on closing the epistemic distance, by denying the possibility of epistemic errors? After all, even the most staunch Cartesian, it seems, would agree that a person can utter a false self-ascriptive sentence about her present state of mind through a slip of the tongue or a misunderstanding. Linguistic competence is always presupposed as a background condition of claims about infallibility and self-intimation. In addition, it is typically presupposed that the subject is sincere and is not engaged in deliberate lying, deceit, or dissimulation. (This is where direct consideration of thought rather than speech comes in handy, as it seems to eliminate these kinds of distortion.) And, clearly, possession of the relevant concepts must also enter into the background conditions. The Cartesian, it seems, need only insist on one's infallible recognition of the presence (and character) of one's own present sensations. Thus she need only rule out the possibility of epistemic errors about them.

However, the Cartesian conception requires more than the merely contingent reliability of subjects in recognizing their sensations (and other occurrent states of mind). It requires some *conceptual guarantee* of correctness or impossibility of epistemic error. And it is this idea that, according to the above reading of the Private Language Argument, undermines the conditions necessary for genuine reference to sensations understood as private objects—objects infallibly recognized by their host. For it seems as though the only way to secure the conceptual impossibility of epistemic error in the case of sensations is by essentially tying their presence and character to acts of recognition by their hosts. If we suppose in addition that the meanings of the relevant terms are to be logically private, then it would turn out that the host of a sensation not only has the final word on whether a particular sensation of hers falls within the extension of a sensation term on a particular occasion of use; she also has the final (and only) word on what sensations are *supposed to* fall within the term's extension. Add to that the Augustinian assumption (d), that the meaning of a sensation term is exhausted by its extension, and the requisite semantic distance between uses of the relevant terms and what they are supposed to apply to would seem to vanish.

The Cartesian may try to secure the semantic distance between sensation terms (as used in avowals) and sensations that is required for reference by insisting on the independent existence of sensations as states of subjects' minds. This seems to be the point of invoking minds as immaterial substances. However, it is not clear how this can be reconciled with the conceptual impossibility of a recognitional failure. For, on this option, a subject who ascribes a present mental state to herself is making a higher-order judgment about an independently existing first-order mental state. And it is not clear why the judgment could not in principle fail, however superior the mode of access deployed in achieving it is, and even supposing the subject to be sincere and conceptually and linguistically competent.[11]

Finally, it is worth highlighting the fact that the problem raised by the Private Language Argument on the above construal is not restricted to *talk* about sensations understood in the Cartesian way. It extends to *thought* about them as well. If the argument succeeds, it shows that we cannot as much as think about private sensations, at least insofar as thinking about an item requires referring to it in thought (i.e., singling it out, or bringing it under the relevant concept). For the argument readily generalizes to the possibility of establishing and achieving genuine reference, period. The problem facing the private diarist is not merely that of managing to communicate linguistically about private sensations; it is the problem of setting up any referential link to putatively private object. It may be, however, that the argument does not yet show that private sensations could not *exist*, even if we could not talk or think about them.[12]

To sum up, having construed sensation avowals on the model of ordinary descriptive reports about certain goings-on (albeit 'inside' the self-ascriber), the Cartesian still wants to maintain that they enjoy

---

[11] This points to a certain tension between Cartesian ontological dualism and Cartesian infallibility. For some discussion, see Bar-On and Long (2001: sects 1 and 2).

[12] To be able to deny their existence, we may have to take a further step, so as "to shew the fly the way out of the fly-bottle" (see Wittgenstein (1953: §309) ). Still, if the argument is successful, it would show that the *idea* of sensations as private objects can play no role in communication or understanding. (This may provide one way of understanding Wittgenstein's famous 'beetle-in-the-box' passage (see Wittgenstein (1953: §293) ).

absolute infallibility. This must amount to the claim of the impossibility of epistemic errors of recognition. There is no possibility of a sincere, conceptually and linguistically competent subject who makes a false present-tense self-ascription of a sensation because he merely thinks he has that sensation, even though in fact he has not. In addition, the Cartesian view endorses self-intimation: the impossibility of having a sensation without recognizing it and judging that one has that sensation. But the Cartesian seems to be facing a certain dilemma. To do justice to the uniquely secure status of sensation avowals, he insists that the impossibility of recognitional error in the case of certain mental states is a conceptual one. Yet it seems as though the only way to secure such a conceptual impossibility is by essentially tying the presence and nature of sensations to acts of recognition by their hosts. The first horn of the dilemma is that doing so closes the semantic distance required for reference. On the other hand, the Cartesian may try to secure the semantic distance between the self-ascription and the state of affairs that is required for reference by insisting on the independent existence of sensations as states of subjects' substantial minds. The second horn of the dilemma is that doing so inevitably reintroduces an epistemic distance between subjects and their present sensations and opens the door for brute errors of recognition.

On the above reading, the impossibility of 'a language in which I speak of my private sensations' is either that a private linguist's efforts would fail to culminate in a sensation *language* or that the language he might manage to set up would fail to be *private*, in the sense that its terms would have logically private meanings, accessible only to the private linguist.[13] Recall, however, that the argument to that effect depended on four assumptions concerning the character of sensations and sensation terms. These were: (a) that sensations are genuine objects; (b) that sensations are private (only the host of a sensation can conclusively attest to its presence); (c) that sensations are transparently and infallibly recognizable by their hosts; and (d) that sensation terms are names for the relevant private objects. These are strong and, on their face, not very plausible assumptions. In the chapters to come, I will be considering, explicitly and implicitly, various ways of relaxing one or the other assumption, so that we can see our way clear to

---

[13] For this way of portraying the impossibility of a private language, see Stroud (1983).

preserving key Cartesian intuitions about 'first-person' talk and thought about mental states without falling afoul of Wittgensteinian concerns about private language.

## Getting Rid of Cartesian Egos: The 'No Reference' Thesis

Let us now return to "I". The very same feature of "I"—the apparent apriori guarantee of success in reference—may disqualify both Cartesian Egos and material human beings as potential targets of reference for "I". Material entities are apparently disqualified, because when it comes to such entities, it is hard to see how one could be guaranteed to hit the right target. Cartesian Egos, on the other hand, are apparently disqualified, because it is hard to see how they can retain their status as targets of ordinary reference, given that their identity is tied to guaranteed success in hitting them. Notice that what leads to trouble here is the attempt to preserve the combination of Semantic Continuity—treating "I" as a referring expression—and Epistemic Asymmetry—treating "I"-ascriptions as enjoying peculiar security, or protection from epistemic failure. If Epistemic Asymmetry is what we seek to explain, then perhaps we should reject Semantic Continuity.

This is precisely the strategy adopted by Anscombe in "The First Person". Anscombe suggests that the source of our problems is the idea that the security of "I" is a matter of guaranteed referential *success*. Perhaps "I"-users are protected from various failures of reference *not* because they are guaranteed to succeed in picking out the right object, but because they make no attempt to get hold of an object in the first place:

Getting hold of the wrong object *is* excluded, and that makes us think that getting hold of the right object is guaranteed. But the reason is that there is no getting hold of an object at all. With names, or denoting expressions (in Russell's sense), there are two things to grasp: the kind of use, and what to apply them to from time to time. With 'I' there is only the use. (1975: 59)

Anscombe is thus led to what I shall refer to as the No Reference View: if "I" cannot fail to hit its target of reference, it is because "I" is not even in the business of referring to an object. Grammatical appearances notwithstanding, " 'I' is neither a name nor another kind of expression whose logical role is to make a reference, *at all*" (1975: 60).[14]

If the surface subject-term in "I"-ascriptions is not a referring expression, then there should no longer be any need, or room, to seek a special kind of item that could serve as the unmissable target of reference for "I" (namely, a Self). So, once the philosophical grammar of such ascriptions is properly understood, we may be freed of the Cartesian illusion.

Instead of appealing to ontological dualism, the No Reference View attempts to save Epistemic Asymmetry by abandoning Semantic Continuity. But this is too heavy a price to pay. As Anscombe herself points out, *all* "I"-ascriptions must be seen as governed by what she calls "a logician's rule" which gives their truth-condition:

If X makes assertions with "I" as subject, then those assertions will be true iff the predicates used thus assertively are true of X. (1975: 60)[15]

Thus, my "I"-ascription, "I feel really tired", will be true if, and only if, it is true *of this person*, DB, that she feels really tired. But how can that be if no component of my self-ascription has the semantic function of referring to me (DB)? Anscombe remarks that "[t]he truth-condition of the whole sentence does not determine the meaning of the items within the sentence" (1975: 60). Presumably, she means that the fact that the self-ascription as a whole is made true by the actions, movements, or states of some particular individual does not entail that any component of the ascription has the semantic function of referring to some distinct entity. But while this is true, it is not clear what model we are to follow here.

In his discussion of Descartes's *cogito*, Lichtenberg (1971: 412) proposes that "Cogito", which is typically translated as "I am thinking" (or "I think"), should be translated by a less committal locution that avoids a personal pronoun. He proposed *Es denkt*, on the model of *Es blitzt* ("There's lightning").[16] "There's lightning", "It's raining",

---

[14] Anscombe's proposal seems clearly inspired by Wittgenstein's discussion of "I" in *The Blue and Brown Books*, in particular, by remarks such as: "To say, 'I have a pain' is no more a statement about a particular person than moaning" (Wittgenstein 1958: 67). I believe that the discussion surrounding this remark is open to less radical interpretations than Anscombe's, although Wittgenstein is reported to have held something like the No Reference thesis at some point. See Moore 1959a: 306–10. Wittgenstein exegesis, however, is not my concern here.

[15] For our purposes here, "assertions" can be replaced *mutatis mutandis* by "ascriptions".

[16] For some discussion, see Burge (1998a: 244). See also McDowell (1997: sect. 4). McDowell suggests that Lichtenberg is better read as pointing to a certain absurdity we are led to if we follow Descartes's reasoning, rather than as endorsing the proposed translation of the *cogito* into a subjectless ascription.

"It's thundering", are examples of statements whose truth-condition does not require the grammatical subject-term to refer to any entity. Such statements, to be sure, are made true by events and happenings in a certain region of space and time. But they do not involve picking out any individual of whom something is predicated. Similarly, Anscombe may be taken to suggest that "I"-ascriptions do not contain a distinctive component whose function is to pick out a particular individual. This, despite the fact that "I"-ascriptions are made true by the actions, states, etc. of a particular individual.

However, the difficulty is that "I" in, e.g., "I am really tired" functions logically, as well as syntactically, just like a singular referring expression. For example, it can replace (in context) singular terms *salva veritate*. On the basis of my contextually interpreted avowal, you could infer "*She* (or *DB*) is really tired", where your ascriptions presumably *do* involve reference to me. If I say, "You are really tired, and so am I," you would be entitled to conclude that DB is (also) really tired, and thus that at least two people are tired. If you say to someone, "DB will be giving a talk here tomorrow," I can truly report: "She thinks that I will be giving a talk here tomorrow." And so on. Denying that "I" refers flies in the face of such continuities between "I"-ascriptions and other ascriptions. Unlike "It" in "It's raining", or "There" in "There's a storm", "I" does not behave like an idle surface element. It appears to have a robust logical function. It is hard to see how it could serve this function without being semantically on a par with referential devices.

It may be more appropriate to invoke in this connection Russell's famous analysis of definite descriptions (in his (1905)). Consider the familiar example: "The present King of France is bald." On the Russellian analysis, the surface singular term—the definite description "the present King of France"—dissolves. The proposition expressed by the sentence turns out to have no proper subject. Rather, the proposition as a whole is construed as a quantified claim, asserting the unique existence of an individual satisfying a certain description ("is a present King of France") and ascribing to him a property (being bald). Thus, on Russell's 'translation', the statement becomes, roughly: "There is one and only one individual who is a present King of France, and whoever is a King of France is bald." This translation contains no constituent that works like a singular term whose function is to pick out a particular individual. Surface-grammatical appearances to the contrary, Russell maintained, definite descriptions are not expressions whose function is to refer to particular individuals.

The case of "I" seems different, however. The Russellian analysis of definite descriptions still leaves some room for interchanging the surface singular term with other (genuine) singular terms that would pick out the individual uniquely satisfying the relevant description. For, provided the relevant individual exists, the unique existential claim into which the surface singular term dissolves in effect provides a recipe for getting to a particular individual. And that individual can then be referred to using genuine singular terms. (Russell himself mentions the possibility of a "verbal substitution" of "Scott" for "the author of Waverly" in his analysis of "George the IV believed that Scott was the author of Waverly" (1905: 489).) By contrast, simply denying that "I" refers does not tell us how we could preserve the idea of the interchangeability (in context) of "I" with genuinely referring expressions, which successfully single out the user of "I".

The problem runs deeper. Accepting the No Reference thesis would have the undesirable consequence that an "I"-ascription does not really have the form "$a$ is F", where "$a$" is taken to refer to the individual who must satisfy the predicate "F" in order for the ascription to be true. But, as emphasized by Evans (1982: ch. 7), "I"-ascriptions are logically linked with other ascriptions which clearly do have this form. To make the self-ascription "I am happy", I must be able to conceive what it is for anyone, myself included, to be happy (I must grasp: $x$ is happy for arbitrary $x$'s). Also, at least for some form of identification, $|\delta|$, I must grasp what it is for [$\delta = I$] to be true.[17] In other words, my self-conscious thought requires that I be able to understand what it would take to latch onto some person in the world as myself; it is *about* some particular individual. My "I"-ascriptions, like all ascriptions of the form "$a$ is F", conform to the Generality Constraint, which "requires us to see the thought that $a$ is F as lying at the intersection of two series of thoughts: the thoughts that $a$ is F, that $a$ is G, that $a$ is H ... on the one hand, and the thoughts that $a$ is F, that $b$ is F, that $c$ is F... on the other hand" (for any F, G, H, and $a$, $b$, $c$, of

---

[17] $\delta$, for Evans, stands for what he calls a "fundamental description" of an object (see Evans (1982: 107–9) ).

which the subject has a conception) (Evans 1982: 209). Yet the No Reference thesis seems to imply that "I"-ascriptions are not subject to this constraint, since they are not on a logical par with ascriptions of the form "*a* is F".

In order to retain Epistemic Asymmetry while avoiding appeal to Cartesian Egos, one might be prepared to pay a rather high price. One might be willing to deny that "I"-ascriptions have the logical form "*a* is F", and to reject Semantic Continuity. But the point of doing so will be lost if the promised pay-off is not forthcoming. The Cartesian offers us reference to infallibly known immaterial Egos as the distinctive mark of avowals, which can serve to separate them from other self-ascriptions (the idea being that only when making first-person mental self-ascriptions do we refer to our Ego). By contrast, the No Reference thesis, understood as a flat-out denial that "I" refers, would fail to distinguish avowals from many "I"-ascriptions. Even if the thesis were restricted to present-tense "I"-ascriptions, it would still apply to a variety of non-mental present-tense "I"-ascriptions. Anscombe's own prime examples are all of that kind (see below). This means that accepting No Reference would not achieve for us what the Cartesian appeal to Egos is designed to do: namely, to explain why avowals should seem epistemically more secure than all other "I"-ascriptions.

Suppose (*contra* Anscombe) that we were to restrict the No Reference View to certain uses of "I"-ascriptions only—specifically, to their uses as subject. The idea would be to maintain that the distinction between the use of "I" as object and its use as subject coincides with the distinction between referential and non-referential uses of "I". Only uses of "I" as subject would then be claimed to be non-referential. After all, as noted earlier, the Cartesian cannot offer a uniform treatment of the reference of "I" either. He must allow that at least sometimes—e.g., in "I have a scar on my arm"—"I" is used to refer to something other than one's immaterial Self. Similarly, it may be suggested that the No Reference claim should be regarded as a claim only about certain uses of "I", rather than a claim about "I" as an expression type.

In support of this move, one might invoke Peter Strawson's claim (1950) that referring is not something that components of ascriptions do, in the abstract, but rather something speakers or thinkers do in context. We can see an application of this claim that is relevant to our present discussion in Keith Donnellan's familiar distinction between "attributive" and "referential" uses of definite descriptions.[18] A speaker can use a definite description such as "Smith's murderer" on an occasion attributively: to pick out *whoever* satisfies the description "the man who murdered Smith". Or the speaker can use the same description referentially: to pick out a particular, contextually salient individual, who may or may not in fact be the man who murdered Smith. Donnellan suggests that Russell's aforementioned 'no reference' analysis of definite descriptions is appropriate only for the "attributive" use of definite descriptions. If so, then, in agreement with Strawson, we could maintain that whether or not a definite description has a referential function depends on its use. Definite descriptions purport to refer when used referentially; they do not purport to refer when used attributively.

Somewhat similarly, it might be suggested that there are two uses of "I", one referential, the other not. When using "I" as object, speakers do intend to single out a particular object or individual in the world, of whom they want to predicate something (being 6′ tall, or having a scar on the arm, and so on). This would constitute a use of "I" as a more or less ordinary referring expression. However, when using "I" as subject, the expression does not serve a referential function. It is not intended to pick out a particular individual; it is rather more like an idle surface element that contributes no distinct logico-semantic component to the proposition expressed.

Notice, first, that this modified No Reference View would still not allow us to preserve semantic and logical continuities between ascriptions that involve uses of "I" as subject and other ascriptions. The view would still face the question: what licenses the inference from "I have a headache" (in which "I" is presumably used as subject) and "He has a headache" to "Two people here have a headache". And so on. The modified No Reference View would still have to buy Epistemic Asymmetry at the cost of Semantic Continuity, and would require denying that uses of "I" as subject involve ascriptions of

---

[18] See Donnellan (1966) for the distinction. Kripke (1977) argues that the distinction only has pragmatic significance. Donnellan (1979) responds to Kripke's argument. By presenting the distinction as a distinction between two uses of definite description I do not intend to preclude the possibility that the distinction has semantic significance, though I am inclined to agree with Kripke's view. For relevant discussion, see, e.g., Devitt (1981: 36–56) and Neale (1990).

the general form "a is F". But, more importantly, portraying avowals as "I"-ascriptions that do not involve reference to an object still seems insufficient for explaining their distinctively secure status. The reason is as follows. Presumably, the security that would result from using "I" non-referentially would be a kind of negative security: where there is no attempt to target oneself as an object of reference, there is no room for failure in picking out the right referent. However, the security of avowals goes beyond this (a point I shall take up further in Chapters 3 and 4). It is manifested also in a relatively high degree of security in applying the relevant predicates. To understand this further security, it looks as though we must attend, in addition, to the kinds of states avowals ascribe (viz., occurrent mental states). But then the worry is that, even after we rid ourselves of the need for 'sure-fire' reference for "I", the temptation to postulate Cartesian Egos may remain. This is because Cartesian immaterial substances may be required as appropriate 'substrata' for the securely ascribed states. If that is so, then we will not have escaped the Cartesian illusion. And we might as well use Egos as referents for certain uses of "I".

We should pause to reflect on what an Anscombe-style explanation of the seeming predicative success of avowals would look like. Assuming that predicates such as "tired", "hungry", "thinking about Descartes", or "hoping for rain", etc. purport to refer to instances of the relevant mental states or events, and given Epistemic Asymmetry as applied to the predicative component of avowals, the Cartesian view would urge us to suppose that mental predicates refer to extraordinary types of property (at least as applied to oneself). Otherwise, how could the striking predicative success of avowals be explained? Rejecting this Cartesian view, the Anscombian strategy would dictate denying that this security is a matter of guaranteed success. Instead, it would portray it as a matter of impossibility of failure due to the fact that the relevant predicates *do not purport to refer to the relevant states*, at least not in their first-person use. This would be the No Reference View applied to the predicative component of avowals. Note that here too we have an analogue for the assumption that uses of "I" require some way of identifying the referent of "I". The analogue would be the assumption that the application of mental predicates to relevant instances always requires using some epistemic method for determining the presence of the relevant state, be it in the case of others or oneself. This is an assumption I shall later dispute.[19]

It should be evident that putting together the two No Reference views would yield absurd results.[20] It would turn out that no part of an avowal has the function of referring to anything—either to an individual or to a state of that individual. Avowals, then, would not be *about* anything, they would not *say* anything. As thoroughly inarticulate noises, avowals could not obey the "logician's rule" of which Anscombe speaks, for they could not possess truth-conditions. Accepting this would amount to no mere compromise of Semantic Continuity—it would constitute a complete abandonment of it.

Toward the end of her paper, Anscombe notes that the "I"-thoughts she has been considering "have been only those relating to actions, postures, movements, and intentions"—e.g., "I jumped", or "I am standing"—"[n]ot, for example, such thoughts as 'I have a headache,' 'I am thinking about thinking,' 'I see a variety of colours,' 'I hope, fear, love, envy, desire,' and so on" (1975: 63). Her reason for focusing on the former kind of thoughts and avoiding the latter, 'Cartesianly preferred thoughts' (as she calls them) is that "only thoughts of actions, postures, movements, and intended actions . . . both are unmediated, non-observational, and also are descriptions (e.g., 'standing') which are directly verifiable or falsifiable about the person of E. A. Anyone, including myself, can look and see whether that person is standing" (1975: 63). If we regard these ascriptions as grammatically 'subjectless', there will be no need to invoke anything extraordinary to understand how they can be made true or false. For such ascriptions are made true or false by the readily observable "actions, postures, movements" of a particular individual—the individual who happens to make the ascriptions using the semantically idle "I".

Contrasting the "I"-ascriptions that concern Descartes with the ones that can be handled simply by treating them as 'subjectless',

---

[19] Foot (1982) argues that Wittgenstein rejected this assumption; that he accepts that mental terms—"pain", for example—can be understood as referring to mental states while rejecting the idea that the meaning of those terms in any way involves a relation of designation which sets up a connection between the term and the state through a prior act of identifying the state via a private ostensive definition, and then introducing the term as a name for what is designated by the ostension.

[20] My thanks to Bijan Parsia for impressing on me this difficulty for Anscombe's view. The combined view is very close to what I later call the Simple Expressivist View (see Ch. 7).

Anscombe says: "The Cartesianly preferred thoughts all have this same character, of being far removed in their descriptions from the descriptions of the proceedings, etc., of a person in which they might be verified. And also, there might not be any. And also, even when there are any, the thoughts are not thoughts of such proceedings, as the thought of standing is the thought of a posture" (1975: 63). Anscombe acknowledges that this raises a difficulty for her anti-Cartesian position, and proposes to address it on another occasion. But she does not seem to recognize that the difficulty undermines the only attraction that the No Reference proposal has in the first place. The point of denying that "I" refers (at least in some of its uses) was to allow us to avoid the temptation to postulate peculiar objects—immaterial Egos—to which uses of "I" can securely refer. But if this temptation remains even after we accept the No Reference View of "I" (on however limited a basis), we seem to have made no progress. And if, to avoid the temptation, we would also have to resort to a No Reference View of mental predicates, we ought to question the cogency of the No Reference approach and re-evaluate some of the assumptions that gave it its initial appeal.

# 3
# "I"-Ascriptions: The Semantic and the Epistemic

On the Cartesian view presented in Chapter 2, "I", like other surface singular terms, has the function of referring to a particular individual. "I"-ascriptions involve picking out a particular individual in the world and ascribing to that individual some property. Thus, like other ascriptions similar to them in surface grammar, "I"-ascriptions have the logical form "*a* is F". Since the individual referred to by "I" may be referred to using other singular terms, "I"-ascriptions should be interchangeable in context with other ascriptions *salva veritate*. This much of Semantic Continuity seems preserved. At the same time, there would be notable epistemic asymmetries between (certain) "I"-ascriptions and other ascriptions. This is so because the entity referred to by "I" (at least in some of its uses)—namely, one's Ego—is understood to be infallibly knowable only by the user of "I". Others' epistemic access to that same Ego is inevitably indirect, and the ascriptions based on such access are open to various failures.

By contrast, the No Reference View found in Anscombe attempts to capture the epistemic asymmetries between "I"-ascriptions and other ascriptions through an alleged semantic *dis*continuity between them. For, on the No Reference View, "I", unlike expressions that are similar to it in surface grammar and that are substituted for it in non-"I"-ascriptions, is not a referential device, at least not when it is used as subject. The No Reference View thus shifts attention from the epistemology of "I"-ascriptions to their philosophical grammar, in the hope that this will obviate the need to resort to infallibly knowable, immaterial Cartesian entities.

We should note, however, that, as presented here so far, both the Cartesian and the No Reference views are equally informed by a presupposition concerning reference, namely: *that "I" could only refer if its use were backed up by an epistemic ability of the "I"-user to recognize or identify the referent of "I"*, an ability which she must exercise in order to succeed in referring. The idea is that the user of "I" could not succeed in genuinely referring to herself unless she had available to her *and was deploying* epistemic means for singling herself out as the referent. Given this presupposition, and assuming that "I" must refer to some thing, the Cartesian feels compelled to postulate Egos. For, only reference to such infallibly recognizable objects could explain the special security of certain "I"-ascriptions. The champion of No Reference, on the other hand, thinks that no cogent appeal to such unmistakable targets of reference can be made. But she agrees that the special security of "I"-ascriptions is inconsistent with uses of "I" referring to ordinary objects, such as embodied human beings. So she is moved to deny altogether that "I" refers (at least when used as subject).[1]

The above presupposition—that successful reference with "I" requires some form of recognition or identification of "I" 's referent—is rejected by an account of the semantic functioning of "I" that is derivable from Shoemaker (1968) and Evans (1982). Like Anscombe, both Shoemaker and Evans seek to take the mystery out of uses of "I" as subject. Unlike her, however, they try to avoid the temptation to invoke a mysterious referent for "I" *without* denying that "I" refers. On their view, the key to finding a non-Cartesian referential account of "I"-ascriptions lies in seeing "I" as belonging in a special subset of genuinely referential devices: namely, ones that do *not* require their users to employ specific epistemic means for identifying their referents.

## Immunity to Error through Misidentification

Both Shoemaker and Evans use as a starting point Wittgenstein's way of drawing the distinction between uses of "I" as subject and uses of "I" as object, to wit:

One can point to the difference between these two categories by saying: The cases of the first category involve the recognition of a particular person, and

---

[1] I think it is not unreasonable to regard the historical Descartes, as well as Anscombe of "The First Person", as tacitly presupposing that uses of "I" (or its equivalents in other languages, and also in thought) require some 'epistemic backing', if "I" is to be a genuinely referring expression. However, I am not here concerned to settle the exegetical question whether Descartes, or Anscombe, could be read as avoiding this presupposition.

there is in these cases the possibility of an error, or as I should rather put it: the possibility of an error has been provided for. . . . It is possible that, say in an accident, I should feel a pain in my arm, see a broken arm at my side, and think it is mine, when really it is my neighbour's. And I could, looking into a mirror, mistake a bump on his forehead for one on mine. On the other hand, there is no question of recognizing a person when I say I have tooth-ache. To ask 'are you sure it is *you* who have pains?' would be nonsensical. (1958: 67)

Wittgenstein here notes that with certain uses of "I", it makes little sense to question the self-ascriber's success in identifying the right individual as the subject of the ascription. In the normal case in which I make the self-ascription, "I have a toothache", there is no room for me to ponder: "*Someone* has a toothache, but is it *me*?" By contrast, if I see someone walking toward a house, and, taking him to be Joe, I say, or think, "Joe will get to the house in a minute", it would make perfect sense for me to wonder, "*Someone* will get to the house in a minute, but is it Joe?"

Shoemaker takes Wittgenstein to be drawing attention to a certain phenomenon that he dubs "immunity to error through misidentification" (1968: 556–7).

The statement "I feel pain" is not subject to error through misidentification: it cannot happen that I am mistaken in saying "I feel pain" because, although I do know of someone that he feels pain, I am mistaken in thinking that person to be myself. . . . [T]his is also true of first-person statements that are clearly not incorrigible; I can be mistaken in saying "I see a canary," since I can be mistaken in thinking that what I see is a canary or (in the case of hallucination) that there is anything at all that I see, but it cannot happen that I am mistaken in saying this because I have misidentified as myself the person I know to see a canary. (1968: 557)

The suggestion is that Wittgenstein's uses of "I" as subject are ones where the user of "I" cannot err in identifying the subject of her ascription. Uses of "I" as object, on the other hand, can be assimilated to ordinary uses of names, for example, since the user *can* fail to identify the subject of her ascription.[2]

Suppose I make an ordinary perceptual ascription that Sheila is sitting on a chair. Presumably, my ascription is based on my recognizing

---

[2] In my discussion of Shoemaker and Evans I often substitute "ascription" for their "judgment". My exposition of Shoemaker and Evans on immunity to error through misidentification partially follows Wright (1998). See also Pryor (1999) for helpful discussion of this notion.

in some way the presence of an individual whom I take to be Sheila, and on my perception that she's sitting on a chair. I may be victim to at least two kinds of error in this case. First, I may think Sheila is sitting on the chair, when she is really only leaning against it in a peculiar way, or I may think it is a chair she is sitting on, when in fact it is a small table. But, second, I may also think that it is *Sheila* who is sitting on the chair, when in fact it is Dinah (or maybe no one at all!). Now consider my self-ascription, "I am sitting on a chair". *In the normal way* of making this "I"-ascription (see below), I have no reason, grounds, or basis for judging that *someone* is sitting on a chair over and above, or separately, from whatever grounds my judgment that *I* am sitting on a chair. This means that although my "I"-ascription may well be mistaken—I may not be sitting on a chair but on a table, or I may not be sitting but squatting—it will not be vulnerable to the error of misidentifying *who* it is that is sitting on a chair. This is what it means, on Evans's and Shoemaker's analysis, to say that my ascription enjoys immunity to error through misidentification. What protects it from such error is the fact that, in an important sense (to be explained below), my ascription does not rely on an identification of its subject—namely, myself. To put the point more abstractly, in the case of ascriptions that are immune to error of misidentification (IETM, for short), reasons for retracting the ascription *a* is F (e.g., that I am sitting on a chair, or that I have a toothache) are grounds for abandoning the existential judgment, that *someone* is F. For, in such cases, one has no other reason for thinking that *someone* is F over and above the thought that *she herself* is F. Not so in case of ascriptions that are not IETM. If I discover that it is not true that Sheila is sitting on a chair, my belief that *someone* is sitting on a chair may still survive. (The same will be true of some "I"-ascriptions, as we shall see shortly.)

Shoemaker points out that the phenomenon of immunity to error through misidentification "is one of the main sources of the mistaken opinion that one cannot be an object to oneself, which in turn is a source of the view that 'I' does not refer" (1968: 558 f.). As Wright summarizes it, the line of thought here "runs from the impossibility of misidentifying myself to the conclusion that, in reflection about myself, there is no identification of any object, that such reflection is not object-directed at all, and that 'I' accordingly has no referential function" (1998: 19). Indeed, Wittgenstein continues the above-quoted passage by making a pronouncement that may have fueled Anscombe's No Reference View: "To say, 'I have pain' is no more a statement about a particular person than moaning is" (1958: 67). Shoemaker and Evans, on the other hand, think that the move to No Reference is unwarranted. They agree that uses of "I" as subject do *not* rely on a certain kind of self-identification. But, unlike Anscombe, they do not take this to be reason for supposing that in such ascriptions the subject-term "I" is not being used to refer to, or talk about, a particular object. The key to avoiding the mistaken move is to deny the presupposition that genuine reference requires identification, in the demanding sense of employing a distinct procedure for identifying or descriptive means for recognizing the relevant target of reference. Abandoning this presupposition should lead us to consider a thesis I shall dub Reference Without Identification.

Before assessing this thesis, some clarificatory remarks are in order. As I shall present it, Reference Without Identification is an account of the semantic functioning of "I". It is designed to explain how "I" can refer successfully even when its user does not use robust identificatory means for picking out the referent of "I". Both Shoemaker and Evans see this possibility as allowing us to avoid the need for Cartesian Egos as referents for uses of "I" as subject, as well as Anscombe's No Reference claim. Now both Shoemaker and Evans link this account of "I" to their explanation of the phenomenon of immunity to error through misidentification. As we saw earlier, Shoemaker thinks it is misunderstanding of this phenomenon that encourages the No Reference view (1968: 558 f.). And Evans thinks that a proper understanding of the phenomenon should diminish considerably the plausibility of the Cartesian view, since it takes the mystery out of uses of "I" as subject (1982: 218 f.).

As will become increasingly clear, however, immunity to error through misidentification of certain "I"-ascriptions is a phenomenon distinct from the success of "I" as a referring expression. So, in what follows, I shall try to keep the two separate as much as possible. In the next two sections, I will present Reference Without Identification as a *semantic account*—an account of the semantic functioning of certain referential devices, "I" included. I will argue that this view does not adequately explain the guaranteed success of "I" in picking out its referent. I will then offer an alternative view of the semantic functioning of "I". Next, I will return to the phenomenon of immunity to error through misidentification and explain how it goes beyond the phenomenon of the guaranteed referential success of "I". I will conclude the chapter by arguing that *neither* phenomenon holds the ultimate key to the special security of avowals. Nonetheless, understanding how these two phenomena can each contribute to the security of "I"-ascriptions will set the stage for the positive account of the security of avowals that I shall be developing in subsequent chapters.

## Reference Without Identification: Demonstratives

Before turning to the semantic functioning of "I", let us consider linguistic reference by means of demonstratives. Demonstratives such as "this" and "that" provide useful examples of genuinely referential devices that do not require descriptive identification of an object. The competent user of "this" in English, for example, does not succeed in referring to some particular object in virtue of associating with the linguistic expression some condition that the object has to satisfy in order to be the referent and ascertaining that the object referred to indeed satisfies the condition. Still, an utterance of "This is blue" can undeniably be *about* a particular object; it can express a singular proposition with the logical form "*a* is F", where "this" picks out an object to which the predicate "is blue" is applied (truly or falsely). Demonstrative pronouns do purport genuinely to refer to particular objects. "I'd like to buy *that* one" seems as much an instance of trying to single out some particular item as "I'd like to buy the red shirt on the top shelf" or "I'd like to buy item No. 36". However, demonstratives seem to work in an epistemically more direct, or unmediated, way than other referential devices. A demonstrative picks out an object more by giving it a verbal pat on the back, as it were, than by describing it. Arguably, the same applies to demonstrative thought. A person who is thinking "*That thing* is moving very fast" can be thinking about a specific object—can have *it* in mind—without having to think of the object as a such-and-such, and certainly without possessing uniquely identifying information about it. (We shall later see what might nevertheless allow such a thought to latch onto the relevant object.)

Russell famously claimed that in order for a thinker to be capable of thinking of a particular object—in order to make 'singular reference' in a thought of the form "*a* is F"—the thinker must have some kind of *knowledge* that allows her to be thinking of that object in particular. As Evans puts this requirement:

[I]n order to be thinking about an object or to make a judgement about an object, one must *know which* object is in question—one must *know which* object it is that one is thinking about. (1982: 65)

[A] subject cannot make a judgement about something unless he knows which object his judgement is about. (1982: 89)[3]

At first blush, it may seem that admitting demonstratives as genuinely referring expressions, even though their use is not backed up by the possession of identifying information, conflicts with Russell's 'knowing which' requirement. It may also seem to conflict with the Fregean requirement that an object that is thought or talked about must be *given* or presented to the speaker or thinker in a certain way, which is what is represented by the 'sense', or 'mode of presentation' associated with the relevant referential item.[4] Indeed, Anscombe cites this Fregean demand for an *Art des Gegebenseins* as part of her reasons for concluding that "I" cannot be a genuinely referential device.[5]

However, it is important to recognize that what was said above regarding demonstrative reference (in speech or in thought) is consistent with Russell's 'knowing which' requirement, as well as with the Fregean demand for sense. As Evans points out, in order for Russell's requirement to have substance, it should be understood to require what he calls "discriminating knowledge",: viz., "the subject must have a capacity to distinguish the object of his judgement from all other things" (1982: 89). But there may be different ways of satisfying the requirement so understood. Possessing identifying information or uniquely descriptive beliefs is only one such way. One can also distinguish an object from all other objects by being able to single it out in

---

[3] This 'knowing which' requirement, which Evans dubs "Russell's Principle", is the subject of ch. 4 of Evans (1982). The requirement is also discussed by Strawson (1974), and more recently by McDowell (1990) and Cassam (1997).

[4] For Frege's canonical discussions of "sense" and "mode of presentation", see Frege (1960) and (1967).

[5] See Anscombe (1975: 48). Hints of this requirement on "I" can be found in the remark which concludes Wittgenstein's discussion of "I" in the *Blue Book*: "The kernel of our proposition that that which has pains or sees or thinks is of a mental nature is only, that *the word 'I' in 'I have pains' does not denote a particular body, for we can't substitute for 'I' a description of a body*" (1958: 74, my emphasis). (I do not think it's clear whether Wittgenstein himself accepts the 'kernel.')

one's field of perception, or by being able to recognize it when presented with it. For instance, my thought "That thing is moving fast" can succeed in latching onto a particular object in virtue of my being appropriately related to it—my being able to locate it in space, or track it as it moves, and so on. Indeed, it may be argued that such non-descriptive discriminatory capacities are more basic and are pre-supposed by the more cognitively-laden modes of discrimination that are encapsulated in identifying information or descriptive beliefs.[6]

We can perhaps think of the distinction between two types of 'knowledge which' with the help of two familiar distinctions. Having descriptive beliefs or identifying information about an object amounts to *knowing that* so-and-so is the object one is referring to. It is having some kind of *propositional knowledge* about the referent. It is a matter of knowing the object *by description*. On the other hand, hav-ing non-descriptive discriminatory capacities with respect to the object is a kind of *knowing how*—having certain *practical abilities* with respect to it. Such knowing how may be grounded in knowledge *by acquaintance* of the object.[7]

If knowing how to single out the relevant referent is a legitimate form of 'discriminating knowledge'—i.e., of distinguishing the object "from all other things"—then it is not necessary to suppose that knowing which object one is thinking about requires possessing identifying information about it. Similarly, it may not be necessary to suppose that the Fregean sense of every referring item must consist in some descriptive (and uniquely identifying) belief, which must be true in order for the user to succeed in referring to the relevant object. In its most general form, Frege's idea of the sense of a referring expression is the idea of a way the referent is given to one, which affords a *route to the reference*—a means of getting to the referent.[8] In the case of demonstratives, the idea can perhaps be preserved by

---

[6] I am here following Evans and Shoemaker in allowing that demonstratives pick out in an epistem-ically unmediated way *public* objects, which could be recognized by individuals other than the user of the demonstrative, and could also be recognized by the user herself in a mediated way. This requires liberat-ing Russell's own treatment of demonstratives (his "logically proper names") from the restriction to privately ostended sense-data. (For discussion, see Evans (1982: 42–63).)

[7] Neither the distinction between knowing that and knowing how nor the distinction between knowledge by description and knowledge by acquaintance is unproblematic. I trust, however, that they have gained enough philosophical currency to be of some suggestive help in this context.

[8] See Frege (1960). The relation between sense and reference has been much discussed. For some dis-cussion of Frege's idea of sense in connection with demonstratives, see Perry (1977); Evans (1981), and Kaplan (1989).

considering *how* the user gets to the referent, rather than *what* she thinks of it—i.e., what descriptive beliefs or information she has about it. Corresponding to the two general ways of satisfying Russell's 'knowing which' requirement, we may distinguish two categories of referential devices, according to what it takes for a user of the device to know which object is the referent. In one category, we will have devices whose use must be backed up by propositional or descriptive knowledge regarding the referent. In the other category, we will have devices whose use need only be backed up by certain practical abilities, which can be acquired through appropriate causal contact or acquaintance with the referent, and whose exercise can ground successful reference to it.

It is useful to recognize that Russell's 'knowing which' requirement is not, strictly speaking, a requirement that pertains to the semantics of expressions. Rather, it pertains to what we may call "semantic epistemology": the study of what one must know in order to be a competent user, or to have a proper understanding of some expression. In the case of thought (which is what Russell was focusing on), the study concerns what a thinker must know in order to qualify as having a thought with a particular semantic content. The division I just proposed between two categories of referential devices was likewise intended to belong in semantic epistemology. It is a distinction in terms of the kinds of *knowledge* required for competent use or understanding of the relevant devices in speech or in thought. It is not implausible to suggest that a competent user of a general term such as "whale" need not know which items in the world are whales. She can succeed in saying or thinking things about whales (e.g., that whales are the largest mammals) without having discriminating knowledge that allows her to separate whales from other animals. By contrast, it may be claimed, with Russell, that competent use of (at least certain) singular terms *does* require knowing which particular item in the world one is talking or thinking about. And what I have suggested above is that this epistemic requirement on singular reference may be satisfied in different general ways.

It would be interesting and important to investigate the various alternative ways there may be for satisfying Russell's 'knowing which' requirements, as well as the various candidates for playing the role of a Fregean 'route to the reference', besides identifying descriptions. Such an investigation goes beyond my scope here.[9] For present purposes, it suffices to recognize demonstrative pronouns as plausible examples of genuinely referential devices whose use can satisfy the 'knowing which' requirement in some way other than through the user's mobilizing identifying information or descriptive beliefs she possesses concerning the object.[10]

Both Shoemaker and Evans point out that the use of demonstratives will often issue in ascriptions that are IETM. Thus, suppose I say (or think), "This is blue", or "That is moving fast" (pointing, or attending, to some perceived object). While my ascriptions in these cases may be false, because I may be wrong about the color or movement, respectively, it seems to make no sense to suggest that the ascriptions could fail *because of an erroneous identification* of the object of my ascription. Though I am attending to a particular perceived object, I am not mobilizing any information or beliefs that allow me to identify it as a (the) such-and-such and which could be mistaken. Yet there seems no other basis for the suggestion that I may have mistaken the object referred to by "this" or "that" for some other object (*what* other object?). My demonstrative thought is not 'identification-dependent', but, in a sense, 'object-dependent': whatever thought I managed to have (if any) cannot fail to be about *this object*.[11]

---

[9]  Though see next note and pp. 80 f. below. For helpful discussion, see McDowell (1977) and (1984). Also relevant is Boër and Lycan's (1975) discussion which points to another dimension of flexibility in satisfying Russell's requirement. They argue that the knowing which/who requirement is always relative to a purpose, and that different tests for whether it is satisfied are made appropriate by different purposes.

[10]  It seems reasonable to suggest that the competent user of a definite description, such as "the present US president", need *not* know which individual in the world satisfies the description. At least as long as the description is used attributively, one can use the description competently (in speech or in thought) without having discriminating knowledge allowing her to distinguish the individual who is the present US president, viz. George W. Bush, from all other things. (For the relevant distinction, due to Donnellan, see above, p. 51.) She need not even know *that* George W. Bush is the present US president. By the same token, however, it may be denied that (attributive) uses of definite descriptions issue in saying or thinking things about *particular* individuals. But if this is so, then it seems puzzling how possession of descriptive beliefs or identifying information could allow one to satisfy Russell's knowing which requirement. It may begin to look as though, to satisfy the requirement, the descriptive beliefs that back up one's use of the singular term would ultimately have to be grounded in *non-descriptive* discriminatory knowledge. (For relevant discussion, see Strawson (1959: 15–30).)

The foregoing observation seems in keeping with Russell's own ranking of knowledge by acquaintance as epistemologically prior to knowledge by description. (For Russell's discussion of the distinction, see Russell 1912: 31–40. (Note that one can accept this ranking without following Russell in insisting that the only items one can be acquainted with in the requisite way are private sense-data.)

[11]  See Shoemaker (1968: 558), and Evans (1982: 179–91, 215–20, esp. 218, including n. 25.) See also Pryor (1999). Evans himself points out the possibility of a case in which "there is no one object with which the subject is in fact in informational 'contact' [so he] is hallucinating, *or if several different objects succeed each other without his noticing*", but he claims that in such a case, the subject "has no Idea-of-a-particular-object, *and hence no thought*" (1982: 173, my emphases). In other words, a case like this would

Note that the case of demonstratives contrasts nicely with that of proper names. Consider my ascription, "John is wearing a coat." This ascription can clearly fail due to my failing to identify *John*. This could be either because I have mistaken Jack for John, or because the person I am thinking of is not wearing a coat. Notice that even if I fail in either of these ways, my success in making some ascription is not undermined. For I can still have succeeded in ascribing something, though not something *about John*, viz.: "*Someone* (though perhaps not John) is wearing a coat." (Of course, if the person I take to be John is not wearing a coat, then my judgment will be false.) The demonstrative case seems different. Suppose, as I direct my attention to something that appears to be moving fast, I think, "*That* is moving fast." If my thought is purely demonstrative, there seems to be no analogue here for the case of mistaking Jack for John. I cannot be said to have judged, "*Something else* (though perhaps not that) is moving fast."

Evans argues that the case of demonstratives is also distinctive with respect to the possibility of complete failure of reference, where there is no object at all to which one could be referring. Suppose there is in fact no one around me at all, but due to some perceptual mistake, or illusion, I come to think, "John is wearing a coat." In this case, my use of "John" will fail to latch onto anyone. Still, I may have managed to think something: that there *is* someone here, someone whom I take to be John, who is wearing a coat. But, Evans argues, in the demonstrative case, if there is *nothing* in my vicinity for my use of the demonstrative to single out, there will be no candidate for constituting the thought I had. If there is no object for my demonstrative thought to have latched onto, the thought itself seems to evaporate.[12] This claim of Evans's may be disputed. For it could be argued that I may still be said to have had some thought: namely, that *something* is moving fast.[13] Be that as it may, it does seem right to point out that

not illustrate the possibility of a demonstrative thought that is not immune to error through misidentification; rather, it's a case in which one fails to have any thought at all.

This is not to say, however, that uses of demonstratives are immune to all failure. As we shall see next, a use of "this" or "that" will fail to refer altogether if there is *no* object at all to which the demonstrative pronoun can latch on.

[12] See Evans (1982: 173). (See previous note and p. 72 below.)

[13] Bill Lycan has mentioned to me in this connection the possibility of *de re* thoughts about non-existents. And Bijan Parsia suggested the case of attending to a rainbow, saying, or thinking, "Look how bright that is!" as an intermediary case. Another case in the same spirit: traveling in the desert, I say, pointing to what I take to be an oasis, "That is so beautiful!" And there are, of course, Hamlet's ostensible

demonstratives work differently from proper names with respect to failure of reference. An ascription such as "John is wearing a coat" can survive a wider array of failures than an ascription such as "That is moving fast!"; there is more for it to fall back on, cognitively speaking. And this suggests that the former kind of ascription is more underwritten by descriptive information, as we might put it.

It is worth pausing to consider the case of proper names for a moment. It has been persuasively argued by several philosophers that, in their semantic functioning, proper names resemble demonstratives more than they resemble definite descriptions. Proper names, it is claimed, do not pick out their referents in virtue of the applicability of some associated identifying description(s). Like demonstratives, they seem to single out their referents 'directly'.[14] As a point about the *semantics* of proper names, this seems to me correct. However, it may be tempting to carry this point over to what I earlier called the semantic epistemology of proper names. The temptation is to suppose that competent uses of names are epistemically on a par with uses of demonstratives. But, at least in the case of thought (and perhaps also in the case of linguistic communication), there are important differences between the use of demonstrative devices and the use of proper names. The use of a proper name is arguably more 'epistemically involved' than the use of a demonstrative. For the user to succeed in thinking about *John* rather than Jack, for her to know *which* individual is John, she needs to have identificatory means that are in some ways richer than those required in the case of a purely demonstrative thought.[15]

Even as regards their semantics, however, there is an important difference between proper names and demonstrative pronouns, which difference cuts across the use of these referential devices in speech and in thought.[16] Suppose we think of proper names as devoid of descriptive content, and maintain that they function like labels or tags that attach to their referents in some non-descriptive way. Even if it is

dagger-thoughts. Must Evans insist, quite radically, that in these cases there are, appearances to the contrary, no thoughts to be had or conveyed by the subjects? Or could he perhaps insist only that the thoughts are not *singular* thoughts, appearances to the contrary? This is not something that needs to be settled for present purposes.

[14] See, e.g., Marcus (1960, 1961); Kripke (1972); Kaplan (1975); and Salmon (1986).

[15] For instructive discussion of prevalent misunderstandings regarding the implications of "direct reference" views for thought and the connection to Russell's 'knowing which' requirement, see Evans (1982: 73–85, 89–120).      [16] My thanks here to Bijan Parsia.

further maintained that proper names have an indexical element built into them, it is still the case that proper names work differently from demonstratives.[17] For proper names attach to specific individuals in a discriminating way. If proper names are tags, they are relatively 'dedicated' tags. By contrast, demonstrative pronouns are 'generic' tags; they can potentially apply to any object. (It would make no sense to suggest that someone might dub some particular object "this" or "that" unless, of course, she offered to use these words as, well, proper names!) If so, the difference between proper names and demonstratives can be put as follows: whereas successful reference using a proper name requires applying the *right* tag to the object, in the case of demonstratives, though reference can fail, there is no question of applying the right tag to an intended object of reference. All in all, then, demonstratives have a distinctive role and semantic function among referential devices.

## Reference Without Identification: "I"

We are now in a position to consider indexical pronouns such as "here", "now", and "I". Applying the above considerations regarding demonstratives, we might accept that a subject who says or thinks "The cat is *here*" can succeed in picking out a particular location without having any specifically identifying information about the place, and without possessing descriptively correct beliefs about it. It may still be correct to say of such a subject that she *knows which* place she is talking (thinking) about—in virtue of her being able to orient herself in relation to other objects, for example. And similarly for "now"-ascriptions. Along the same lines, a subject may be credited with thoughts about herself even in the absence of any kind of identifying information about herself, and while failing to think of herself *as* a such-and-such; she may not even harbor any minimal description such as "the user of this sentence" or "the thinker of this thought". When a subject picks out herself using "I", or her location using "here", or the time of her ascription using "now", her ascription concerns a particular person, place, and time, respectively. "Here", "now",

---

[17]  For an indexical treatment of proper names, see Burge (1988).

and "I", like "this/that [F]", have the semantic function of singling out particular items in the 'objective order' of things. In that sense, ascriptions involving them are *about* the relevant items. But in the indexical case, as in the case of demonstratives, a subject may have a thought about, or pick out, or refer to, an object even without deploying any identifying information or descriptive beliefs concerning her target of reference. As Shoemaker puts it:

If I say "I feel pain" or "I see a canary," I may be identifying for someone else the person of whom I am saying that he feels pain or sees a canary. But there is also a sense in which my reference does not involve an identification. My use of the word "I" as the subject of my statement is not due to my having identified myself as something of which I know, or believe, or wish to say, that the predicate of my statement applies to it. (1968: 558–9)

Still, as Evans points out, the fact that my ascription does not involve, or require deploying, an identification procedure does not impugn my thinking *about* myself. Referring to an object (in speech or thought) may require being able to identify it, but only in a minimal sense. In this minimal, or 'thin' sense, the ability to identify an object consists in possessing—and perhaps also standing ready to mobilize—some means of latching onto the object. It implies some knowledge of *how* to single it out from among other objects.[18] However, referring to an object does not always require being able to identify it in any 'thick' sense— i.e., possessing a set of descriptive beliefs or identifying information that the object fits or satisfies uniquely.[19]

So far, the suggestion has been that "I" functions semantically more like demonstratives, in that its use does not require thick identification of its referent. This is not to say that a complete assimilation of the workings of "I" and other indexicals to the workings of demonstratives is in order. As linguistic expressions, personal pronouns such as "I", "you", etc., as well as other pronouns, such as "here", "today", and the like have associated with them *some* descriptive content; they possess so-called linguistic, or dictionary, meaning, more so than

[18]   Rovane (1987) offers what she considers a Fregean treatment of "I". It is a disadvantage of her discussion that she does not consider the possibility of satisfying the Fregean requirement with respect to "I" without insisting that users of "I" must associate with it what is traditionally thought of as a Fregean sense: viz., a set of descriptive beliefs.

[19]   For the distinction between the 'thin' and 'thick' senses of identification that I am using here, see Evans (1982: 218).

proper names. This allows sentences containing pronouns to be interpreted by speakers even when they have no clue as to what the relevant indexical expressions refer to. (Take the sentence "I am unable to keep my office hours today", for example. Readers of the sentence would understand what it says even if it were written on an office door with no indication of the time it was produced.)[20] I believe similar remarks can be made regarding the use of indexical pronouns as opposed to demonstratives in thought.

Nonetheless, from the point of view of their semantic functioning, there is an important affinity between demonstratives and indexical pronouns, which separates them from other singular terms. This affinity can be further brought out by considering again immunity to error through misidentification. Understood as a referential device that does not require thick identification of its referent, the use of "I" is suitable for making ascriptions that are identification-free and are thus immune to error through misidentification. By contrast, however directly referential proper names are thought to be, their successful use to refer to the right individual must be backed up by the availability of richer means of identification. Given that, ascriptions containing them become identification-dependent (in Evans's sense). As a result, ascriptions involving proper names are not in general candidates for being IETM. An ascription that makes an essential use of a proper name such as "John" will always presuppose a judgment to the effect that *John = such-and-such*, where "such-and-such" stands for some way used by the ascriber to represent John to herself.[21]

Now it may seem that the Reference Without Identification View already allows us to explain the security of uses of "I" as subject without invoking Cartesian Egos as referents for "I", on the one hand, and without denying that "I" refers, on the other. The Reference Without Identification view seems to do away with the idea of guaranteed *epistemic* success that drives the Cartesian to invoke infallible recognition of a special object. The difficulty with Cartesian reference to unmistakable Egos, recall, was that it required the notion of a referential device that is *supposed* to work via a mediating conception, but

---

[20]   For some discussion of the differences between proper names and pronouns and the connection to direct reference views, see Lycan (2000: ch. 4).

[21]   I speak of making an "essential" use of proper names to rule out cases where one uses one's own proper name simply in place of the pronoun "I" in order to refer to oneself (as when a child says of herself, "Jenny wants teddy," or her dad says, "Daddy would like you to stop crying").

where the possibility of recognitional failure is ruled out conceptually. But on the Reference Without Identification view, "I" is understood as a referential device that is capable of successful reference independently of the user's correct beliefs or judgments regarding the identity of the referent. Furthermore, in contrast with proper names, "I" does not require reliance on the user's ability to identify the referent through any other recognitional means.

We saw that, in the case of demonstratives, there was no need to credit the successful user of a demonstrative pronoun such as "this" or "that" with some mysterious epistemic ability of recognizing infallibly her target of reference or having unmistaken beliefs about it. The same is true for "I". A speaker or thinker's success in picking out herself as the referent of "I" may depend only on her exercising normal abilities—abilities that do not require postulating extraordinary targets of reference. For example, Evans cites the capacity we have for perceiving our own bodies (1982: 220). This ability may enable you to track yourself reliably even when your beliefs about yourself might lead you astray, by being false of you, or true of someone else, for example. Thus, if you have been struck by amnesia, and have no true beliefs about who you are, you may still successfully pick yourself out using "I" as you say or think, "I am really tired", since you are still able to perceive your own body and track yourself reliably.

On the present proposal, the user of "I" can pick out the referent of her "I"-ascriptions (namely, herself) in a relatively unmediated way, epistemically speaking. This may be thought to account, at least in part, for the security of uses of "I" as subject. Inasmuch as my success in referring to myself does not depend at all on the correctness of any identifying information I have about myself, mistaken information, or total lack of information, does not impugn it. Not so when I refer to myself as, say, "So-and-so's philosophy teacher", or "The person now teaching in room 213", or even, more directly, as "DB". Success in referring to an individual using a definite description (at least when the use is attributive) may depend on whether or not the individual uniquely fits the relevant description or is assigned the right "tag". And we saw that even success in referring to an individual using a proper name requires using the *right* name for the individual. I will only succeed in referring to *myself* using one of these devices if it is true that I *am* so-and-so's philosophy teacher, or the person teaching at . . . , or DB. The use of such devices involves some kind of thick identification of the referent. Thus, it may be thought to introduce an *identification component* on which the relevant ascriptions rely, thereby rendering the ascriptions vulnerable to errors through misidentification. Since the identification component can straightforwardly fail— the judgment identifying me as such-and-such can simply be false—the ascriptions which rely on it are relatively less secure than "I"-ascriptions.

There are two problems with the above explanation. The first problem is that it runs together the two phenomena distinguished earlier (pp. 59 f.). The first phenomenon, which so impressed Descartes and Anscombe, is that of the guaranteed success of referring, and of referring to the 'right' object, which users of "I" enjoy, even when they lack all identifying information concerning "I" 's referent. The second phenomenon is that of the immunity to error through misidentification of "I"-ascriptions. It is easy to conflate these two phenomena, but it is important to avoid the conflation, as I shall explain later. The second problem is that, although the Reference Without Identification View improves considerably on other accounts of "I" we have seen, it still does not adequately explain the guaranteed referential success of "I". I begin the next section by explaining this second problem, thereby identifying the limits of the Reference Without Identification account of "I". Then, after suggesting an alternative semantic account of "I", I explain why the guaranteed *semantic* success of "I" is a different phenomenon from the *epistemic* immunity to error through misidentification of certain "I"-ascription. I conclude the chapter by arguing that even a proper understanding of the phenomenon of immunity to error through misidentification affords us only partial understanding of the phenomenon with which we began: namely, the special security of avowals.

## The Guaranteed Referential Success of "I"

The Reference Without Identification View as presented so far is intended as an account of the semantic functioning of "I". Its promise seems to lie in the fact that it relaxes the epistemic demands on successful reference, thereby allowing us to see how "I" can succeed in referring even without the backing of extraordinary epistemic acumen. However, what is puzzling about "I" is not simply how "I"-ascriptions *can* succeed in being about the right object, but why their success seems *guaranteed*—or why they seemingly cannot fail— in referring to the relevant object. It is this feature that appeared to force a choice between reference to extraordinary objects (Descartes) and no reference (Anscombe). My task in this section is to argue that the guaranteed success of "I" in referring is not adequately accommod- ated by the Reference Without Identification account of "I". Though this account moves in the right direction, it does not go far enough in relaxing the epistemic requirements on reference with "I". This will motivate an even more epistemically 'bare' account of the way "I" refers, which I present in the next section.

As noted in Chapter 2, uses of "I" have two special (and related) features. They are:

(a)  The referent of "I" is guaranteed to exist and be present.
(b)  The user of "I" seems guaranteed success in referring to the *right* object—namely, herself.

Feature (a) separates "I" from ordinary demonstratives such as "this" or "that". If I say, while pointing to something that is rolling fast toward us, "That thing is moving fast," there is no room for error in *mis*identifying the thing that's rolling. But I *may* say "That thing . . . ," while pointing to empty space—if I am hallucinating, for example. Of course, I may also be referring to something that is not moving at all. As already mentioned, with an ordinary demonstrative, unlike with "I", there is always room for complete failure of reference. This possibility of failure also exists for uses of indexical pronouns such as "she", "he", "it", or "you". By contrast, if an "I"-ascription takes place, the user of "I" seems guaranteed to succeed in referring to *someone* present. Uses of "I" are thus not subject to complete failures of reference. This shows that, by itself, the possibility of reference without thick identification is insufficient for capturing feature (a) of the use of "I" (which feature clearly fuels Descartes's *cogito*, and par- tially motivates Anscombe's No Reference View).

What explains the possibility of complete failure of reference in the case of demonstratives and indexical pronouns? On the Reference Without Identification View, the use of such devices, in general, does not require deploying epistemically rich means for identifying the referent. However, to explain how a user can nonetheless succeed in referring to the relevant object, the view invokes the user's exercise of various abilities that allow her to single out the object. For example, even in the absence of a (correct) set of informative descriptions of the relevant object, the user may have (and may be deploying) perceptual abilities to track the object as it moves. The claim is that the exercise of such abilities is sufficient to put the user in epistemic contact with the referent, which is in turn sufficient for the user's use of the referential device to refer to the relevant item (since it provides for the user's knowledge of *which* object she is thinking about). Now, since hallucination, perceptual illusions, etc. are always possible, there can be no apriori guarantee that the exercise of non-identificatory abilities (as we might call them) will in fact issue in contact with *any* object. In such cases, then, the use of a demonstrative or indexical pronoun will be empty; it will fail to refer.

It might be suggested that uses of "I" are *not* subject to such failures, because in the normal case, when an "I"-ascription is made, the user does—or at least is disposed to—exercise certain non-identificatory abilities that allow her to track herself in a special way. As Evans observes, when tracking our own bodies, we are not restricted to the use of normal perception. We have proprioception, kinesthetic sense, and so on (1982: 220 ff.). These non-identificatory abilities may remain intact even when one is subject to hallucination or perceptual illusions, allowing one still to be referring to herself when using "I". However, uses of "I" seem to be guaranteed reference even in the face of damage to or total loss of, *both* identificatory and non-identificatory abilities. So suppose that I am floating through empty space in a sensory deprivation tank, having been struck by amnesia as well as paralysis.[22] This combination of mishaps would presumably result in a radical damage to my abilities to track myself through either own-body perception or normal perception, as well as to my ability to pick myself out through descriptions stored in memory. I would be receiving no sensory stimulation or information and would be unable to locate myself in relation to other objects. And I would not be disposed to have my thoughts and actions controlled by sensory information or

---

[22] This imaginary case is inspired by Anscombe (1975).

through kinesthetic sense. For all that, it does not seem that I should be unable to think to myself, "I don't like this one bit!" and be guaranteed the existence and presence of a referent for my use of "I".[23]

Indeed, not only would I be guaranteed reference to someone in such a case, but I would be guaranteed successful reference to *myself*. In other words, as I use "I" in the imagined situation, I am guaranteed the existence and presence of the referent of "I" (feature (a) above) *and* am guaranteed that my use of "I" refers to the right object (feature (b) above).[24] There are no similar guarantees in the case of demonstrative and indexical pronouns. Because the Reference Without Identification View requires the exercise of some abilities to assure successful reference, it fails to capture this difference between "I", on the one hand, and other indexical pronouns and demonstratives, on the other. It thus fails to explain the semantic functioning of "I".

In view of the special guarantees of reference enjoyed by uses of "I", if we continue to insist that such uses are referring uses, are we again open to the threat of Cartesianism? I do not think so. It is instructive to note that crucial aspects of these guarantees are also shared by uses of the indexical pronouns "here" and "now". If I say (or think), "It feels very hot now," my success in referring to the time of utterance (or thought) with my use of "now" does not seem to depend on my ability to know (descriptively or otherwise) the time at which the utterance (thought) takes place. If I say, "It's cold in here," it seems I can similarly succeed in referring to the place where I am with my use of "here" even if I do not know where I am. For a vivid limit case combining the use of these indexical pronouns with the use of "I", consider the familiar "I am here now". Though the ascription may represent a useless piece of information (to the self-ascriber or to her audience), at least it has the merit that its pronouns are guaranteed referential success. When making the ascription, I seem guaranteed to pick out myself, the place where I am, and the time of the ascription, respectively, even if my tracking abilities are as damaged as in the case described earlier. Even if I have no idea—or

---

[23] Evans requires that an individual have the aforementioned dispositions in order to have an adequate Idea of herself, which, according to him, is required for successful self-reference in thought; see Evans (1982: ch. 6 and 7). What I am imagining, though, is a case where having acquired the dispositions necessary for acquiring an adequate Idea of myself in the normal way, I get afflicted in the ways described. It would seem odd to suggest that I thereby lose my capacity to have thoughts about myself, such as "I'm so unfortunate!" or "I wish I could *feel* something" (though Evans may be committed to this).

[24] The two guarantees are, of course, linked. See again Anscombe (1975).

have a completely *wrong* idea about—who I am, where I am located, or what time it is, my uses of "I", "here", and "now" will refer to me, the place where I am, and the time of utterance or thought, respectively.

Note that, insofar as in thinking "I am here now" I rely on no identification judgment regarding the subject, the place or the time of the ascription, my ascription will *also* be completely immune to errors of misidentification.[25] Since in the case described I am not identifying the subject, place, and time by judging that I am such-and-such, that the place where I am is so-and-so, or that the time of my thought is such-and-such, there is no room for my making a mistake of identification about whether it is *I* who am here now, whether it is *here* I am now, or *now* that I am here.[26]

It might be argued that "I" is more resistant than "here" to failure of reference in cases of misinformation. Suppose, unknown to me, my ears have been wired to receive auditory information from a distant place, and I say, "It's loud here".[27] In that case, my use of "here" may be thought ill-grounded. This is because I cannot be said, in such a case, to know *what* place I am thinking about. On the present view of reference, I can only refer to a place if I know which place it is, since I have no suspicion that anything is unusual. So it would seem odd to suggest that I'm thinking about that other place—the place where the noise is coming from. On the other hand, given that my thoughts and actions are not controlled by any information received from my immediate environment in this case, it would seem wrong to suggest that, nonetheless, I manage to pick out my own location by my use of "here". By contrast, if, unknown to me, I were so wired as to receive non-descriptive information about someone *else*'s limb position or posture and were to think, "I am sitting down," my use of "I" would

---

[25] I say "also", since, as mentioned before, the guaranteed success in reference is a phenomenon separable from that of immunity to error through misidentification. (See below, p. 84.) And, recall that not everyone would agree that the absence of identification judgment suffices for rendering the ascription immune to error through misidentification. (See, again, Pryor (1999).)

[26] See Evans (1982: 179–91, 215–20). For some suggestive remarks about the status of "I am here," see Wittgenstein (1958: 61–9, 108–9). Don Garrett and Brad Cohen have both suggested that this absolute immunity to errors of misidentification of "I am here now" may be an artifact of certain contingent features of "I"-ascriptions—in particular, e.g., the fact that it takes a very short time to make them, or the fact that the brain crucially involved in producing an "I"-ascription is typically lodged within one's body. Relevant here is Dennett (1981) and Evans (1982: 253 ff.). I leave discussion of the extent to which changes in such contingent facts would affect the immunity of "I am here now" for another occasion, since I do not think the issue bears directly on my claims below.

[27] See Evans (1982: 184–7) for a discussion of this kind of case.

still be plausibly taken to refer to *me*, issuing in a false ascription (assuming *I* am *not* sitting).[28]

I am not entirely convinced that "I" is different from "here" in the respects highlighted above. This is because I am not certain that on Evans's view we should count my use of "here" in the auditory cross-wiring case as ill-grounded.[29] But I do not wish to dwell on this point, since my present purpose is only to establish the insufficiency of the Reference Without Identification View specifically as an account of "I". If there is a difference between "I" and "here" along the lines suggested above, then the Reference Without Identification View fails to capture the semantic profile of "I", even if we think it captures the way "here" works. If, on the other hand, "here" is as indifferent to loss of (even) non-identificatory abilities as "I", then we need to go beyond the Reference Without Identification View as presented so far, in order to be able to explain the semantic functioning of *both* "I" and "here" (and perhaps "now", too).

To sum up, though the Reference Without Identification account relaxes the epistemic demands on successful reference, it still requires the exercise of some abilities apt to put the user in epistemic contact with the relevant referent. The point of the above examples was to show that, however minimal the epistemic backing required for success in reference is, we can still conceive it missing, or leading to the wrong object. In that case, by the lights of the Reference Without Identification View, we should be faced either with complete failure of reference, or failure to refer to the right object, respectively. Yet such failures seem ruled out for "I". "I", in Ayer's apt phrase, has an 'adhesive quality'; it appears to stick no matter what.[30]

If we agree that "I" is set apart from other referential devices, demonstratives and other indexical pronouns included, we may legitimately

---

[28]  For an argument to this effect see O'Brien (1995).

[29]  Davies (1998: 338) cites another example from Evans which seems to indicate that changes in location unbeknownst to the subject may simply issue in different determinate thoughts, rather than the lack of any thought at all.

[30]  The phrase is attributed to Ayer by Lucy O'Brien, who suggests that the special feature of guaranteed reference of "I" amounts to its unique "propensity to refer and to stick with its object of reference, even though the waves of information might seem to want to buffet it this way then that." (1995: 241). It may be denied that "I" is unique in this regard, since, as remarked earlier, it may be thought that "here" and "now" share in the adhesive quality of "I" (and if so, this may be due to the intimate interrelations among these indexicals). On the other hand, it may be denied that "I" enjoys absolute guarantee of reference. Rovane (1987) tries to describe a case (which is unconvincing, in my opinion) where "I" could be said to fail to refer.

demand of an adequate account of how "I" refers that it capture its unique features. The Reference Without Identification View, with its reliance on non-identificatory abilities of perceptual recognition, tracking, etc., does not seem to do so. Thus, although this view may represent the semantic functioning of "I" more faithfully than either a semantic theory inspired by the Cartesian View or the No Reference View offered by Anscombe, it still falls short.

## How "I" Refers—An Indexical Account

On the Reference Without Identification View, reference to oneself is still thought of on the model of *targeting an object*. And the minimal epistemic abilities thought sufficient for reference all pertain to one's reliability in hitting the relevant target. Though this is not thought to be achieved through the ascriber's possession of identifying information about the target of reference, it still involves the capacity to track it, or locate it, or receive information about it. But there may be room for relaxing the epistemic conditions on successful reference for "I" even further than is allowed by the Reference Without Identification View. Perhaps "I" should not be thought as used by an ascriber to hit a target at all. Instead, perhaps we could think of "I" as a referential device intended to mark the *source*, or origin, of the ascription. In this section, I would like to sketch a view that tries to improve on the Reference Without Identification account of how "I" refers along these lines. I shall refer to it as the Indexical Reference View.

According to the Indexical Reference View, in the special case of "I", referring to the right object does not require the exercise of any ability to hit the relevant target, or make epistemic contact with it. Consider what we may call "indexical propositions", such as "It's raining", or "The door is open". If someone asserts such a proposition, the value of certain parameters—notably, the time and place of utterance—has to be fixed in order for the ascription's truth-value to be determined. (John Perry proposes that these are "unarticulated constituents" of the proposition expressed; see his (1979).) However, there is no need for the person making the assertion to direct her attention to, or recognize in any way, the time and place of her utterance. I want to suggest that we compare the epistemic position of the

"I"-user with respect to the referent of "I" to the position of the user of an indexical proposition with respect to the parameters of time and place. The suggestion is that, from the point of view of the *epistemic* requirements on reference, the user of "I" need be able to do no more than mark or tag one such parameter.

It should be emphasized that the comparison to indexical propositions is not made with an eye to the *semantic* analysis of the relevant expressions, but only with an eye to their *semantic epistemology*. The claim is only that the epistemic requirements on the user of "I" vis-à-vis the identification of the referent of "I" may be as minimal as those on the user of an indexical proposition vis-à-vis the parameter of time and place. If the Indexical Reference View is to adhere to Semantic Continuity (and respect Evans's Generality Constraint (see p. 49 above) ), it must recognize a logico-semantic difference between "I"-ascriptions and indexical propositions. In the case of the latter, although the truth-condition of the proposition essentially involves some particular place and time (and, on some views, a speaker, too), no distinct component of the ascription actually makes reference to a time or place. Intuitively, "The door is open" is not *about* the time or place of utterance, even though its truth-condition is required to specify the time and place of its utterance. Whereas in the case of "I"-ascriptions, we want to preserve the idea that a self-ascription such as "I am very tired" *is* about a particular person, that it has a distinct component that *refers* to someone.

But perhaps it could be suggested that an "I"-ascription can still be about a particular person (and "I" can still be thought to refer to that person) in the following sense.[31] *Making manifest, or marking, what would otherwise be a mere index can still serve to introduce an object into discourse* (or thought). With genuine indices (time, place, person), no such marking takes place by the person issuing the proposition. All reference to such parameters recedes in to the background and becomes a matter of presupposition. But with "I"-ascriptions, the person index is dragged to the foreground, as it were, so as to make an appearance in the ascription itself. If so, then the user of "I" can still be credited with having a thought about an object (herself), even though she is not herself locating a target of reference (any more than

---

[31]   I owe the following suggestion to Bijan Parsia.

she does when issuing an indexical statement). She may also be regarded as offering up a potential target of reference for others, or for herself at other times, as opposed to representing that target to herself at the time of making the "I"-ascription, or prior to it.

The Indexical Reference View may be able to explain why "I" always singles out the speaker or thinker of the relevant "I"-ascription. And it may also explain why very little, if anything, can go wrong with the way "I" picks out its referent. Having mastered the logical rule governing the use of "I"—namely, that it refers to the origin of "I"-ascriptions—the user of "I" does not need to bring to bear any (further) epistemic acumen to achieve reference. So various possibilities of reference failure that can afflict other referring devices, such as demonstratives (and perhaps even indexical pronouns like "he"), have no purchase in the case of "I". The Indexical Reference View may thus have a better chance than the Reference Without Identification View of explaining why uses of "I" are more secure than uses of other referential devices that require no thick identification. For instance, it may explain why my use of "I" in "I am silly" cannot fail in the way my use of "You" can fail in "You are silly", even when I use "you" to refer to myself (say I'm looking in a mirror at what I mistakenly take to be my own reflection).

The Indexical Reference View may capture the truth in Anscombe's remark that "with names, or denoting expressions (...), there are two things to grasp: the kind of use, and what to apply them to from time to time. With 'I' there is only the use" (1975: 59). Now, the proponent of the No Reference View might seize on the above comparison between "I"-ascriptions and indexical propositions to support her view in preference to the Indexical Reference View. The proponent of No Reference might reason as follows. The sharing of truth-conditions between a self-ascription such as "I am very tired" and other ascriptions does seem to require acknowledging that its truth-condition essentially involves a particular individual (DB), which individual can be referred to by genuinely referring expressions ("DB", "she", "the person to my left", etc.). But this does not require accepting that "I" is a component in the ascription with the distinct function of identifying some particular individual (in any sense of identification, however thin). On the contrary, a self-ascription such as "I have a toothache" is 'subjectless'. Though its truth-condition does essentially involve a particular individual, there is no component of it that refers to that individual; in that sense, the ascription as a whole is not about that individual. Applying the comparison to indexical propositions, we can think of "I" as receding in to the background, as it were, and functioning more like a true index on the whole proposition than like a singular referring expression.

I think the Indexical Reference View still has an advantage over this (reading of the) No Reference View. The Indexical Reference View allows us to preserve the logico-semantic continuity between "I"- and other ascriptions, and thus to respect the Generality Constraint. This is because the view respects the idea that "I"-ascriptions, just like referential ascriptions that are interchangeable with them in context *salva veritate*, genuinely involve singling out particular objects—are about them—and involve ascribing properties *to* them. What reflects this is the fact that the Indexical Reference View reserves a distinct component in the relevant ascription whose function is to pick out the particular individual. This component can be traded for other referential devices that serve to pick out that same individual—in whatever way, by others or by oneself, in conversation or in thought.

What is at issue between the (present reading of the) No Reference View and the Indexical Reference View is, then, whether "I"-ascriptions are about an individual subject—whether they contain a distinct component which genuinely refers to the individual whose features make the ascription true or false. In favor of the No Reference View, it might be insisted that genuine reference requires complying with Russell's 'knowing which' requirement: a subject can be said to be thinking about a particular object only if she knows which object it is she is thinking about. (See above, p. 61.) Yet, on the Indexical Reference View, the user of "I" can successfully single out the relevant individual even when she is not in a position to exercise even minimal (non-identificatory) abilities to track it. But then the Indexical Reference View does not explain how the user of "I" can be said to *know which* object she is thinking of, and thus how referring with "I" can be said to comply with Russell's requirement on reference.

The proponent of the Indexical Reference View might reply in one of two ways. She might insist that, even without exercising any tracking abilities, the user of "I" can still be said to know who she herself is, and thus which object she 'has in mind' when making the self-ascription. In the special case of knowledge of who oneself is, very little indeed is required for satisfying Russell's 'knowing which' requirement. The act of tagging or marking the speaker or thinker through the use of "I" may be sufficient for the "I"-user to make the right epistemic contact with the referent. No more epistemic effort is needed on her part. Alternatively, the proponent of the Indexical Reference View might cite referring through the use of "I" as a special case in which reference to a particular object does *not* require the user to know which object it is she is referring to. With Strawson, the proponent might say:

If someone has, and formulates to himself or herself, such a thought as 'I am feeling terrible,' . . . [she] will have mastered the ordinary practice of personal reference by the use of personal pronouns; and it is a rule of that practice that the first-personal pronoun refers, on each occasion of its use, to whoever then uses it. So the fact that we have . . . a user, is sufficient to guarantee a reference, and the correct reference, for the use. It is not in the least necessary, in order for the guarantee to operate, that the user know *who* he is. (Strawson 1994: 212)

In other words, the proponent of the Indexical Reference View might waive Russell's 'knowing which' requirement on reference for the special case of "I".[32] She might take that as the true upshot of recognizing that the user of "I" does not have herself as a target of reference, but rather marks herself as the source of her ascription. Either way, the Indexical Reference View preserves the idea that "I" is a genuinely referential device, a distinct component in "I"-ascriptions that allows them to be interchangeable with other ascriptions involving referential components *salva veritate*. And it does so without requiring "I" to refer to an immaterial Cartesian Ego.[33]

Earlier (see Chapter 2, pp. 35 ff.), I argued that it is hard to see how, if one took Cartesian Egos to be the referents of uses of "I", such uses

---

[32] The Indexical Reference view is, however, different from the view proposed by Strawson (1994), according to which the guaranteed reference of "I" is ultimately a matter of convention, and where "I" is used only for the benefit of others. I want to make room for the idea that, even absent linguistic convention, there can be a referential device (say, in a mental medium of representation) that functions in the way described by the Indexical Reference view.

[33] More needs to be said about the two alternatives as well as about the significance of the differences between the Indexical Reference and the No Reference Views. But I have to defer further discussion to another occasion.

could still be understood as hitting genuine targets of reference. I think we now have an alternative to the Cartesian way of guaranteeing reference for "I". On the Indexical Reference View, "I" is a genuinely referential device, which does not refer to any extraordinary object. Nevertheless, uses of "I" are guaranteed to single out the right referent, because using "I" is precisely *not* like hitting an independent target. We still could, if we like, think of the referent of "I" as a kind of target; but then it would be a target that is fixed to the muzzle of the "I"-gun of each user of "I", so to speak. If so, it is hardly a surprise that we cannot fail to hit the target of "I". Once we see it this way, the mystery about the guaranteed success of "I" as a referential device should disappear, and with it the need for inventing a special, infallibly recognizable referent for "I".[34]

## "I"-Ascriptions: The Semantic and the Epistemic

My overall aim is to explain Epistemic Asymmetry—the special security of certain kinds of "I"-talk (and thought)—without compromising Semantic Continuity—the various logico-semantic continuities and interconnections between "I"-talk and other kinds of talk, as well as continuities within "I"-talk. In presenting Epistemic Asymmetry, I have emphasized the fact that *not all "I"-ascriptions are equally secure epistemically*. This fact remains unexplained even if we accept the Indexical Reference View of "I" described above.

The Indexical Reference View seems to improve on the Reference Without Identification View in addressing the puzzle framed by Anscombe: viz., how could "I" be a genuinely referential device and yet be guaranteed to succeed in picking out the right referent, namely, the self-ascriber? The Reference Without Identification View does not explain the striking resistance of uses of "I" to semantic failure in cases where the user of "I" is unable to exercise even the non-identificatory abilities mentioned by Evans. The Indexical Reference View remedies this by reducing to a bare minimum the epistemic requirements

---

[34] The metaphor of a target fixed to the muzzle of a gun is due to Doug Long. See Bar-On and Long (2001: 315 n. 6), where the metaphor is used in the course of objecting to the Cartesian view of "I". Here, however, the suggestion is that the metaphor can be co-opted by my preferred, Indexical view "I". Thanks to David Robb for this suggestion.

on successful reference for "I". If acceptable, this view can explain the special guarantee of "I" as a referential device: the fact that uses of "I"—*all* uses of "I"—are guaranteed to have *a* referent, and the right referent at that. But while this may allow us to understand perceived contrasts between "I"-ascriptions and ascriptions to others, as well as ascriptions to oneself that do not employ "I", it does not enable us to understand epistemic contrasts *within* the class of "I"-ascriptions.

Recall Wittgenstein's distinction between uses of "I" as subject and uses of "I" as object. Shoemaker and Evans proposed that what is characteristic of the former uses is that they issue in ascriptions that are immune to error through misidentification (IETM), whereas the latter are not. As part of their effort to demystify "I"-talk, they further pointed out that "I"-ascriptions are not alone in being IETM. But we should now recognize explicitly that *the guaranteed success of "I" in referring is a separate phenomenon from the immunity to error through misidentification of "I"-ascriptions.* This is so because "I" enjoys the special guarantee of successful reference even when its use does not issue in an ascription that is immune to error through misidentification. *Even when "I" is used as object*, where the "I"-ascription as a whole is vulnerable to errors through misidentification, "I" seems guaranteed to refer to the person making the ascription.

Suppose that, upon looking at the doctor's chart attached to my hospital bed, I say, "I have a very high blood pressure today". Here, I am presumably relying on an identification procedure in picking out the subject of my ascription. Given the way I come by the ascription, it would make perfect sense for me to wonder, "Someone has a very high blood pressure today, but is it *me*?" My ascription relies on an identification judgment to the effect that I am the person whose medical information is on the chart. It is thus vulnerable to an error through misidentification, since the identification judgment could be false. I may *not* be the person whose medical information is on the chart. Now, suppose I am in such an error: the chart in fact records someone else's blood pressure. Still, the most natural interpretation of my ascription is one on which my use of "I" succeeds in referring to *me*, and the ascription is understood as saying something false of me. I will not be understood to be thinking of the other person (whose blood pressure is recorded on the chart) and making a true ascription of her. So, my ascription as a whole fails *due to an error of misidentification,* but my use of "I" still succeeds in picking out *me.*

This fact—that the guaranteed success of "I" as a referring expression can be pulled apart from its potential to issue in ascriptions that are immune to error through misidentification—can be appreciated if we recall that only a subclass of "I"-ascriptions enjoys immunity to error through misidentification. In addition to the blood-pressure case just considered, we may consider the following examples of perfectly ordinary "I"-ascriptions: "I have insufficient funds in my checking account," "I am 5′5″ tall," or "I have mud on my shoes." In each of these cases, the self-ascriber can sensibly raise the possibility that, at least in some sense, she is wrong about the identity of the subject of her predication, or has picked out the wrong individual. She can wonder, e.g., "*Someone* has insufficient funds in their checking account, but is it *I?*" and so on. In each case, the ascription has an identification component—a judgment of the form "I = r", where "r" stands for some way of representing herself to herself ("r") that the self-ascriber uses as part of her basis for judging that *she* satisfies the predicate used in the ascription. For instance, my ascription "I have insufficient funds in my checking account" may rely on my judgment that I am the one whose checking account balance is showing on the bank-teller's screen. Or my ascription that I have mud on my shoes will typically rely on what I see when looking down at my feet. But in all these cases the ascriptions would naturally be understood as involving reference to the self-ascriber, rather than to the person of whom the descriptions in the identification judgment are true. Indeed, successful self-reference is presupposed when we want to reject the ascriptions as false: "*You* don't actually have insufficient funds in your account; you have $300"; "*You* have no mud on your shoes; it's I who have mud on my shoes." We take the ascriptions to be *false of the self-ascriber,* rather than true of someone else who got picked out by the pronoun. And this presupposes that the self-ascriber successfully picked *herself* out as the subject of the ascription with her use of "I".

In fact, the separation between the phenomenon of successful reference and the phenomenon of immunity to error through misidentification could already be seen in the case of demonstratives. On the Reference Without Identification View, as we saw earlier, uses of demonstratives such as "this" and "that" can succeed in singling out a particular object, even when the user employs no identifying information or descriptive beliefs about it. And it was pointed out that the use of demonstrative devices, like the use of "I", can issue in ascriptions that are IETM (e.g., "That is moving fast," made when one is attending to some object nearby). However, the use of a demonstrative does not *always* issue in ascriptions that are IETM. At a clothing store, thinking I saw the salesperson place a red shirt on a certain shelf earlier, I might say to my friend, pointing to some shelf, "There's a really nice red shirt on *that* shelf". (For a similar example, see Shoemaker (1968: 558).) In this case, I rely on an identification judgment to the effect that *that* shelf is the one where the salesperson had put the nice red shirt earlier. I can sensibly wonder, "There's a nice red shirt on *some* shelf; but is it *that* shelf?" So the judgment is not IETM. However, my use of the demonstrative "that" will be most naturally understood as referring to the shelf to which I am pointing or attending. In that sense, my use of "that" succeeds in singling out the intended referent, despite my mistake in identifying it. So here too we have a split between successful reference and immunity to error through misidentification.

Let us consider a case where it may seem as though one's use of "I" does not refer to oneself. Suppose I am watching a home movie that I erroneously take to feature myself trying to play golf. I say (or think), "I am making a complete fool of myself." In this case, there is a positive identificatory false belief at work: namely, that I am that woman on the screen. My ascription clearly relies on an identification component, viz.: [I = *that* woman, or the woman on the screen, or . . .]. So the "I"-ascription here would not count as being IETM. I could sensibly wonder, "Someone is making a fool of herself, but is it *me*?" Now it might be suggested that, in this case, it is possible to understand the ascription as being about the woman in the movie, at least in the sense that she is the person I 'have in mind'.[35] I am passing judgment on the performance of *whoever* is on the screen. My use of "I" refers to her, because I mistake her for myself. (And maybe similar remarks can be made in other cases where the "I"-ascription is not immune to error through misidentification.)

---

[35] In the case of speech, we might put this by saying that the woman on the screen is my 'speaker reference'.

I do not wish to deny that we *could* understand the ascription that way (though I do not think this is a very natural reading of it). Instead, I wish to point out the following. First, even on this reading, we do not have here a case where "I" fails to refer to the *right* object, in the sense of picking out the object intended by the user. Whatever plausibility the reading has, it comes from taking the woman on the screen to be the one I *wanted* to single out in my use of "I". It is not that I used "I" to refer to myself and failed because the epistemic route I took led to someone else. Rather, I used "I" to refer to *whoever* is on the screen.[36] Secondly, suppose we do take the 'overt' use of "I" in "I am making a fool of myself" to represent a failure of "I" to refer to the right object. Still, the ascription in such a case must be taken to rely on a 'covert' use of "I" that *does* succeed in referring to me. I have in mind the use of "I" that is involved in the (erroneous) identification judgment which underlies my ascription: viz., that *I* am the woman on the screen. Absent this success, we cannot regard the ascription as involving a *mis*identification. The same is true whenever an "I"-ascription is not IETM.

It is time to re-evaluate the phenomenon of immunity to error through misidentification. I have emphasized throughout that not all "I"-ascriptions are IETM. Furthermore, even ones that are not IETM still enjoy the guarantees of semantic success that are characteristic of uses of "I". What this suggests is that a proper understanding of the phenomenon in question requires appealing to something beyond the semantics of referential devices, and beyond the observation that a subject can successfully refer to himself using "I" even in the absence of identifying information about himself, and even when unable to locate himself, etc. It requires attending to the way the relevant judgments are arrived at or grounded. To say of an "I"-ascription that it is IETM is to say that the self-ascriber's identification of herself as the subject to whom something is ascribed is not vulnerable to certain kinds of errors. But this is different from saying that her use of "I" is guaranteed to refer to herself. As we saw, explaining this guaranteed success of "I" is a matter of getting the right *semantic* account of how "I" refers, which, in my view, requires purging it of all unnecessary

[36] This can be seen as the reverse of what happens when I use a definite description to pick out someone in particular, rather than whoever uniquely fits the description I use—that is, when I use the description in what Donnellan calls the "referential use". (See above, p. 51, where Donnellan's distinction is mentioned.)

epistemic demands on the user of "I". Explaining the immunity to error through misidentification of "I"-ascriptions, on the other hand, requires attending directly to the *epistemology* of the relevant ascriptions, as opposed to the epistemic conditions on semantic success.

A full understanding of how an "I"-ascription can be IETM requires ceasing to focus narrowly on the subject component of the ascription and the way "I" refers, and thinking also about the ascriptive component and the way the predicate term is applied. More than that: it requires thinking about the basis for the ascriptive judgment as a whole. "I"-ascriptions that are not IETM are typically based on some kind of observation or evidence or inference regarding the subject. For example, consider the above example: "I have insufficient funds in my account." The device I use to pick myself out in this case—the pronoun "I"—may be direct, in the sense that its successful use to pick out me does not depend on my possessing any epistemic means or abilities for identifying, or recognizing, the referent. We might put this by saying (somewhat misleadingly perhaps) that my use of "I" is epistemically unmediated. However, the judgment that it is I myself who instantiates the relevant property *is* epistemically mediated.

Both Shoemaker and Evans emphasize that whether or not an ascription is IETM will depend on the *basis* on which the subject makes the relevant ascription. It is not simply a matter of the semantic content of the ascription. (The immunity feature, Evans says, "is not one which applies to propositions *simpliciter*, but one which applies only to judgments made upon this or that basis" (1982: 219).) Nor is the immunity in question produced through the mere employment of "I" as a referential device for picking out the subject of ascription. Rather, the immunity is relative to the ascriber's way of gaining knowledge that the relevant property is instantiated. My ascription "John is walking fast" will typically be based on some kind of perception or observation. And it will rely on the judgment that the person I observe to be walking is John. It will thus not be immune to error through misidentification. Similarly for the ascription "John has a toothache". But many of my self-ascriptions will also rely on some observation, or evidence, or inference, or memory. Among those are even "I"-ascriptions, such as that I have insufficient funds in my checking account, that I am five miles from downtown, that I am of such-and-such a height, and so on. In all these cases my judgment that the relevant property is instantiated is independent of the judgment that it is I who instantiates the property. So the ascription will rely on an identification of myself as the person about whom I am receiving certain information, say, through the bank-teller screen. Since I may be in error about my being that person, the "I"-ascriptions will not be IETM.

Of special interest are ascriptions such as "I am about to faint". Normally, such an ascription is not made on the basis of any ordinary evidence, or observation, or perception. At any rate, in the normal case, when I judge that I am about to faint, I have no basis for judging that the relevant property is instantiated—i.e., that *someone* is about to faint—other than whatever basis I have for judging that *I* am about to faint. However, a semantically identical ascription, "I am about to faint", *can* be arrived at in an atypical way. I may make that ascription on the basis of catching a glimpse in the mirror of a pale face that I take to be mine. My ascription will then depend on the identification of myself with the person whose face I see in the mirror, as well as on the separate observation of immanent fainting that I glean from the face in the mirror. My ascription will *not* be immune to error through misidentification. Similarly for the ascription "My legs are crossed". I may come to think my legs are crossed solely on the basis of looking down—say, if my legs are numb. In that case, my ascription will not be an instance of proprioception, but rather of an observational judgment, and it will not be immune to error through misidentification.

To sum up, whether an ascription is IETM or not depends on its epistemology, not on its semantics. It is a matter of the basis on which the ascription is made, and, in the specific case of self-ascriptions, it goes beyond the fact that the self-ascriber refers to herself using the epistemically unmediated "I" device. Many "I"-ascriptions are not IETM. Moreover, "I"-ascriptions that are normally understood as IETM, because they do not rely on any identification judgment, can be subject to errors of misidentification when made on an unusual basis. Now *all* "I"-ascriptions, not only those that are IETM, use "I" to refer to the subject of ascription. If I am right, the user of "I" is guaranteed to succeed in picking herself out with her use of "I". This is so because her existence at the moment of making the "I"-ascription is a necessary condition for her using "I", so the intended referent must exist and be present when she uses "I". Furthermore, for her to fail to refer to the intended object using "I"—namely, herself—she must ultimately make *some* successful use of "I" at least in thought. To explain this guaranteed success, I suggested that we think of "I" as functioning like an index. It refers not by hitting a semantic target, but by explicitly marking the source of an ascription. The epistemic demands on the use of such a device are very minimal indeed, much more minimal than those envisaged by the Reference Without Identification View. If this is so, then the use of "I" in an "I"-ascription can guarantee that one will be making an ascription to *oneself*. However, this by itself does not render the ascription IETM. An "I"-ascription will be IETM only if the subject of the ascription is not an *epistemic target* for the ascriber (as we might put it); that is, only if it does not rely on a judgment concerning the identity of the ascription's subject. This is so, as we have seen, only for a subset of "I"-ascriptions.[37]

## Avowals as Immune to Error through Misidentification

Our interest in the phenomenon of immunity to error through misidentification derived from the promise implicit in Shoemaker and Evans that a better understanding of the phenomenon would allow us to lay to rest the temptation to Cartesian dualism. We are now in a position to assess this promise. Typical present-tense "I"-ascriptions of current mental states—what I have called "avowals"—offer paradigm cases of ascriptions that are IETM. If I self-ascribe "I have a headache", "I am angry at you", "I think it's going to rain", my "I"-ascription does not rely on any identification of myself as the subject to whom I want to ascribe the relevant property. It is not as if I recognize someone in some way as being me, and think of that person that she instantiates the relevant property. My only basis for

[37] John McDowell (1997) makes several remarks concerning first-person reference that are quite congenial to the line I have been developing here. Since McDowell's remarks are made in the context of assessing Derek Parfit's reductionist view of personal identity, I have not undertaken to discuss them in the present context. (Thanks to Dylan Sabo for bringing McDowell's paper to my attention.)

thinking that someone has a headache, for example, is my thought that *I* do. And to tell that *I* instantiate the relevant property, I do not normally consult my behavior or otherwise observe myself. This is what renders the relevant judgment immune to error through misidentification.

Now Evans claims that the immunity to error through misidentification of mental self-ascriptions is not absolute. He asks us to imagine, for example, that I have reason to question my tactile information, and that my visual information is restricted to seeing a large number of hands reaching and touching nothing, except for one hand touching a piece of cloth. Here, "it makes sense for me to say 'Someone is feeling a piece of cloth, but is it *me?*' " (1982: 219 f.). Evans acknowledges that we "cannot produce this kind of case for mental predicates whose self-ascription is absolutely incorrigible". Presumably he has in mind cases like "I *seem* to be hearing a sound", or "I *appear* to be having a red after image". He dismisses such cases, saying, "But what is the interest of this fact?" (1982: 220). Quite possibly, the interest of such cases lies in the fact that they might tempt one to Cartesian dualism. So it may be important to give an account of their seemingly unique epistemic status, which is what I shall try to do later on.

Right now, what is more important than the question whether present-tense mental "I"-ascriptions are absolutely IETM is the question whether they are the *only* "I"-ascriptions that enjoy this immunity. For if they are not, then the phenomenon of immunity to error through misidentification will be of only limited interest for the purpose of understanding the special security of avowals.

On Evans's characterization, "I"-ascriptions divide into two different classes: the ones that are and the ones that are not IETM. As Evans observes, and as we have already seen, the class of ascriptions that share this feature is not restricted to present-tense *mental* "I"-ascriptions. There are at least two types of non-mental "I"-ascriptions that, when made in the normal way, exhibit the immunity feature as characterized so far. (See Evans 1982: sect. 7.3.) The first type of ascription includes bodily "I"-ascriptions such as "I am feeling a piece of cloth", "I am being pushed", "My legs are crossed", and so on. Such "I"-ascriptions are identification-independent. Normally, for me to have the information that the relevant property is being instantiated just is for it to appear to me that *I* instantiate the property (which is why it normally wouldn't make sense to say, "Someone is hot and sticky, but is it *me?*" or "Someone is being pushed—but is it *me?*", and so on). The second type of ascription includes ordinary "I"-ascriptions of position, orientation, and relation to other objects, based on one's perception of the world around one. If I self-ascribe "I am in the room" or "I am moving about" or "I am standing in front of a tree", it makes little sense, in the ordinary case, to say, "Someone is in the room, but is it *me?*" or "Someone is moving, but is it *me?*" or "Someone is standing in front of a tree, but is it *me?*"

But now it should become clear that, like Anscombe's view, the Shoemaker–Evans view spans the divide between *Wittgenstein's* uses of "I" as subject and those of "I" as object. For Wittgenstein put all bodily "I"-ascriptions, proprioceptive reports included, on the side of uses of "I" as object. Arguably, Wittgenstein was calling attention to the special security of *avowals*—i.e., to those self-ascriptions that ascribe occurrent *mental* states to self-ascribers—as what tempts us to Cartesian dualism. It seems that the Cartesian could accept that there are various bodily "I"-ascriptions that are IETM in Evans and Shoemaker's sense, but still insist on a *special* security to be associated more narrowly with avowals. If so, one may question whether Cartesian dualism can be completely laid to rest by attending to immunity to error through misidentification.

Evans himself thinks that Wittgenstein has misled us by giving as prime examples of immunity to error self-ascriptions of mental occurrences. He briefly considers the possibility that shifting attention to the predicative part of self-ascriptions would capture what Wittgenstein was concerned with in drawing the distinction between two uses of "I", but dismisses the significance of making the shift. This is because he thinks that "certain ways of gaining knowledge of ourselves *as physical and spatial things*", which *also* give rise to judgments that are equally IETM, play a constitutive role in explaining "what it is to think of oneself self-consciously". And this, he thinks, is "the most powerful antidote to a Cartesian conception of the self" (1982: 219 f.).

I agree that recognizing the relative epistemic directness of many non-mental self-ascriptions is an important step in weaning us away from Cartesian dualism. But I think it is insufficient for banishing its specter. As long as there remain apparently significant epistemic asymmetries between avowals and all non–mental self-ascriptions, which remain unexplained on a particular view on offer, dualism will continue to seem like a tempting option. (The history of the subject to date, I may observe, bears this out.) But even apart from any ambition to lay dualism completely to rest, the asymmetries in question may be sufficiently interesting and potentially important for our conception of mind, that they deserve serious attention and explanation. Or so I shall presume below, as I seek an account of the distinctively secure status of avowals.

# 4

# *The Epistemic Approach to Avowals' Security: Introspection and Transparency*

At the end of the last chapter, it was argued briefly that, despite its promise, the notion of immunity to error through misidentification cannot carry the full burden of separating avowals from other ascriptions. This is because, as observed earlier (see p. 16), the epistemic contrast class for avowals includes ordinary empirical ascriptions, past-tense "I"-ascriptions, and all ascriptions to others. It also includes certain present-tense non-mental "I"-ascriptions that enjoy immunity to error through misidentification (IETM).

As we have seen, bodily "I"-ascriptions such as "My legs are crossed" or "I am standing up" are similar to avowals in that they are not based on any inference, evidence, or ordinary observation. Furthermore, when made in the normal way, they do not involve an identification component; they are identification-free. Yet, unlike avowals, these non-mental "I"-ascriptions are completely and straightforwardly open to denial or correction by potential observers on the basis of *their* observation. Looking at me, you might simply say, "No, your legs are *not* crossed," or "You're not standing up, you're sitting down!" In general, avowals appear to be much more resistant to epistemic criticism than other "I"-ascriptions that are IETM. To be sure, avowals are themselves IETM; when avowing a mental state using "I", I cannot be in error through misidentification as to who is the subject of my ascription. But the security of avowals appears to go beyond this fact. For, when avowing, I enjoy in addition a special security in the ascription of the occurrent mental state to myself. And this security is of a kind I do not enjoy when making any non-mental "I"-ascriptions. I shall refer to this as the "ascriptive security" of avowals.

Authors generally unsympathetic to Cartesianism are still impressed by the epistemic contrast between avowals and non-evidential bodily "I"-ascriptions. Yet it is not easy to come by a satisfactory characterization of the contrast, let alone an explanation of it. Richard Rorty has proposed *incorrigibility* as marking the contrast. The avowals of a sincere, linguistically competent subject cannot be overridden, because "[w]e have no criteria for setting [them] aside as mistaken, . . . whereas we do have criteria for setting aside all reports about everything else" (1970a: 413). But this seems too strong. For although we do not simply set someone's avowal aside on the basis of our own straightforward observation to the contrary, we *are* sometimes prepared to challenge an avowal. For instance, you say, apparently sincerely, that you are not mad at me, and I wonder whether you really are not, since you seem to me pretty sulky and unfriendly. Or you say, apparently sincerely, that you're thinking hard about the objection I just raised to your argument, and I doubt it, because you seem to be very busy doing something else, and so on. In these cases, your behavior in context appears to give the lie to what you say, and I will not simply take your word. (This is not to say, however, that your word does not still carry significant weight: quite likely, if you persist in your avowals, I will defer to you, or at least reserve judgment.)

Crispin Wright suggests that a subject's avowals, unlike her proprioceptive reports, cannot fail in a systematic way. He says that there is no such thing as showing oneself "chronically unreliable" in one's avowals, whereas one's proprioceptive reports, for example, can presumably be subject to systematic failure (1998: 17).[1] Wright's idea here seems to be that one's avowals must at least be *by and large* taken as likely to be true, and are not *on the whole* subject to straightforward challenge on the ground that one has proved unreliable regarding one's own present mental conditions. Global doubts concerning the truth of *all* of a subject's avowals would seem to conflict with our taking the avowing subject to be a person, a subject who *has* mental states.[2] But there is a way in which this claim seems too weak. For, it seems to me that the strong presumption that avowals are true is more 'local' in character. It attaches to each avowal individually, and not

---

[1] This is not to say that Wright takes the security of avowals to be exhausted by this fact. See Wright (1998: 14–21) for his characterization of the security of avowals.

[2] See also Shoemaker (1968). Of course, there will be those who would claim that even the denial of the possibility of chronic unreliability is too strong. I come back to this issue in the next section.

merely courtesy of a global assumption that we make about subjects (although, as said before, the presumption can be overridden in certain circumstances). If so, then the contrast between avowals and other ascriptions can be pressed on a more case-by-case basis. But even apart from this, we want to understand *why* it is that we should take avowals as by and large true. We can agree with Wright's observation that subjects cannot be sensibly regarded as chronically unreliable in their avowals, and that this provides for a contrast between avowals and other ascriptions. But we may still seek to understand the source of this contrast.[3]

## Security through Introspection?

If we are no longer wedded to absolute incorrigibility as the mark of avowals, yet agree that avowals are governed by a strong presumption of truth, it may be tempting to play down the contrast between avowals and secure non-mental "I"-ascriptions. On a currently popular view the security of avowals should in fact be assimilated to the security of non-mental "I"-ascriptions. We can begin by recalling that certain bodily predicates, such as "crossed legs" or "is sitting down", exhibit an epistemic first-person/third-person asymmetry. Such predicates are applied on the basis of external observation in the third-person case, but on the basis of internal perception (or monitoring, or sensory feedback) in the first-person case. Likewise, we can think of "in pain", or "is angry at $y$", and so on, as predicates that are applied on different epistemic bases in the third- and first-person cases.[4] They apply on the basis of observation of behavior, or inference, or conjecture, in the third-person case, but, in the first-person case they apply on the basis of *introspection*.

Introspection, however, need not be understood in the Cartesian way, as an infallible faculty that reveals to each subject her own 'private' states, which no one else can access. On the contrary, *the*

---

[3] In his article, Wright considers the possibility that there is simply no explanation to be sought here, that the contrast is just a constitutive feature of mental concepts. This is the view he dubs the Default View. The Default View will be considered in Ch. 9.

[4] For nice illustrations of the many kinds of cases where there are systematically different ways of accessing a single state of affairs, and thus recognizing that a particular predicate applies, see Buckley and Hall (1999).

*materialist introspectionist* suggests that introspection is a faculty that reveals to us goings-on *inside* our bodies (more specifically, in our brains). On one story, it is speculated that the human brain is equipped with a special mechanism—a scanner—designed to deliver reliable higher-order judgments about our first-order mental states. My distinctive ability to tell what I am thinking right now, for instance, is due to my brain's ability to scan its own present operations so as to yield highly reliable, non-evidential judgments, which are then articulated (in speech or in thought) through self-ascriptions of mental states. There are two different versions of this view. On one version, known as "HOP" (for "Higher-Order Perception"), our scanning mechanisms deliver *perceptions* of first-order mental states. On the other, known as "HOT" (for "Higher-Order Thought"), they deliver *thoughts* about them. I do not think anything important in my discussion will hang on making the distinction, and my talk of higher-order *judgments* is intended to be neutral as between these two versions. On both these versions, introspective awareness consists in our passing a higher-order judgment (perceptual or conceptual) on some internal going-on. Co-opting the 'higher-order' view for present purposes, the materialist introspectionist might suggest that avowals can be seen as descriptive reports of these internal goings-on. Avowals would then be taken to represent the higher-order deliverances of the subject's inner scanning mechanisms, and the security of avowals would be taken to derive from the epistemic security of these deliverances.[5]

I should perhaps emphasize from the outset that my main concern in discussing the materialist introspectionist view is to argue that it does not offer an adequate explanation of commonsense intuitions about avowals' security. I will not be aiming to settle the question whether or not it is plausible to suppose that, as a matter of fact, our brains possess scanning mechanisms, which we put to use to obtain reliable judgments, and even knowledge, about our first-order mental states. Rather, my discussion will address the extent to which the materialist introspectionist view can accommodate the thesis I earlier called Epistemic Asymmetry in its full scope. Specifically, I will argue that the view cannot explain the systematic contrast ordinarily drawn between avowals and non-mental "I"-ascriptions. This will tell against

---

[5] See, e.g., Armstrong (1968: 323–38); Rosenthal (1986); Lycan (1987: 71–4; 1996: 13–43).

the materialist introspectionist view, insofar as a central philosophical (as opposed to neurophysiological) motivation for holding this view is its potential to explain in a non-dualist way the phenomena that may tempt one to Cartesianism.[6]

As I have indicated before, I do not take it to be part of the commonsense view of avowals that they are absolutely infallible or incorrigible. We do indeed sometimes take avowals to be false, and we do sometimes challenge or correct them. So far, then, we may agree with the materialist introspectionist. However, consider the form that challenges to avowals take when they occur in communicative settings: "You can't possibly feel hungry; you've just eaten a full meal!" Or: "How could you feel tired, after taking a two-hour nap?" Or: "I don't believe you really like this painting; it's hideous," and so on. Even when we are convinced, on whatever grounds, that the avower is not in the condition she ascribes to herself, we do not simply dismiss her self-ascription, as we might when denying a bodily self-ascription on the basis of our contrary judgment ("No, you are not bleeding" or "No, you're not sitting down, you're kneeling!"). We give considerable weight to the very fact that she avowed being in the condition. That this is so can be seen if we consider that we would eventually defer to a subject who persisted in avowing hunger, fatigue, liking the painting, etc. (assuming we did not question her sincerity).

The materialist introspectionist would have to insist that this aspect of our treatment of avowals simply reflects our acknowledgement of the fact that subjects are contingently better placed than their observers to perceive or track certain of their inner states. Our tendency to defer to subjects' avowals is something we could (and presumably would) give up, if we developed more direct ways of detecting people's mental states. Now, to lend credence to the materialist introspectionist view, these "more direct ways" would have to be understood as independent *both* of the subject's behavior *and* of her avowal. The idea would be that the internal goings-on reported by avowals simply *happen* to be available for ready and reliable, though perfectly fallible, scanning by their hosts. Being physical conditions inside the subject's body, there should be no reason why they could not in principle (even if not yet at present) be directly observed by others in ways that

---

[6] I return to this issue below, in the last section of Ch. 5.

require neither consulting the subject's own judgments nor studying her behavior.

Note that, on this model, it is not merely possible for a subject to issue a false avowal *on occasion*. If an avowal is a report that conveys how I take things to be inside me, given the deliverances of my scanner, then the possibility seems open that I could issue a false avowal due to a *brute local error*. Consider my sincere report that there is a cup on the table, or that I am bleeding. My perceptual and cognitive mechanisms may be perfectly in order, yet my report may be false, because, appearances to the contrary, in reality there is no cup on the table, or I am not bleeding. Similarly, on the present view I should be able to avow being in pain, or hoping for some rain, and my avowal may be false, even though I am sincere and my scanning mechanism is in perfect working order. For there is no reason why my scanner could not be 'fooled' into false detection. Moreover, it should also seem entirely possible that a subject might suffer *global systematic failure*. There should be no difficulty with the notion of someone who, though she *has* first-order sensations, thoughts, wishes, hopes, etc., and though she has the requisite higher-order concepts, like the rest of us, *never* 'gets it right' when she says—or thinks—that she is in one of these states. Clearly, someone could lose (or may never have had) the ability to see or hear, and someone could lose (or may never have had) the faculty of proprioception or kinesthesis (so she always gets it wrong when she tries to tell without looking, touching, etc. whether her legs were crossed, or whether she was sitting). Similarly, on the present view, someone could lose (or may never have had) the ability to tell by introspection what mental state she is in, so whenever she pronounces on it, she gets it wrong (or, perhaps, can only get it right when she uses evidence, inference, etc.).

There is a strong intuition that, where avowals are concerned, both the possibility of brute local error and the possibility of global systematic failure are more problematic than the materialist introspectionist view would allow. As regards the first possibility, note that, even when we are prepared to deny the truth of an avowal, there is an assumption that the avowal's falsity is due to some failure or irregularity on the part of the avower. Unlike the perceptual case, when we take someone to have issued a false avowal, we assume that there must be some psychological explanation for it. We take it that some psychological failing is at work—that something went wrong *with the subject*—as opposed to accepting that the subject might simply have been *fooled* into issuing a false avowal by an 'uncooperative' mental world.

The second possibility, of global systematic error, is the possibility of a subject to whom we are prepared to ascribe mental states, as well as the *concept of* a mental state, but whom we regard as 'chronically unreliable' in her avowals. Such a subject would not simply be wrong in her avowals of wants, fears, intentions, etc. She would be systematic-ally wrong in *all* her avowals, including those that ascribe present *thoughts* to herself, about herself or anything else! I am inclined to agree with Wright (and others) that "[w]holesale suspicion about my attitudinal avowals—where it is not a doubt about sincerity or understanding—jars with conceiving of me as an intentional subject at all" (1998: 17 f.).[7] Of course, we may question someone who avows, "I want to go home now". We might say, "Do you really? You seem like you're having a good time, and are not ready to leave." But suppose the avower retrenches and says, "Well, I *think* I want to leave." This can lend some credence to our doubting that the subject really wants to go home, by suggesting that the subject herself is in some doubt about what she wants, but only on the assumption that our subject tells us correctly what she *thinks* she wants. This also seems borne out by attempts to establish through psychological experiments some sys-tematic unreliability of avowals. Such attempts typically fall back on some avowals that are taken at face value and whose security is not questioned.[8] The same holds for therapeutic contexts, where it is assumed at the outset that the patient may be 'out of touch' with her motives, emotions, and so on, and therefore may issue many false self-ascriptions. Here too, it is only by taking at face value what a patient says she *thinks* or *believes* that we can question her self-ascriptions of intentions, wishes, etc. Thus, although the truth of avowals can be questioned in various contexts, this is so only against a background in which they are generally presumed to be true.

---

[7] For an interesting argument for the impossibility of "self-blindness" (as he calls it), see Shoemaker (1994: Lecture II). I briefly address this argument in Ch. 10 (p. 407 ff.).

[8] I am here alluding to the recently much-cited experiments on so-called blindsight (for references and discussion, see Weiskrantz (1986)). On one possible construal, these experiments try to establish that people can be systematically wrong about how things seem to them, since they apparently deny having certain visual experiences. This result, however, is obtained by taking at face value the subjects' avowals concerning what they *think* about their visual experiences.

It is instructive to re-examine in this context the contrast ordinarily drawn between avowals and, specifically, secure bodily self-ascriptions. Consider again my pronouncement that my legs are crossed. Here it does seem that, although I may rely on no evidence or inference or observation, so there is an epistemic third-person/first-person contrast in terms of the *basis* on which the pronouncement is made, still, my word is no better than that of an observer. On a given occasion, my body could clearly be in a state that my proprioceptive mechanism cannot distinguish from the state of my legs being crossed. I could also prove to be very unreliable in reporting my limb positions or bodily movements with my eyes closed. Furthermore, in addition to the possibility of an observer simply *looking* to see whether my legs are crossed (a possibility that is already in place), we can easily conceive of someone else gaining knowledge of my limb position proprioceptively (say, if her brain was so hooked up to my limbs as to receive direct information about their position). Such a person could have a non-observational facility for telling where my limbs are that is equal to mine. Under the circumstances, it seems that there would be no residual difference between the status of my pronouncements on my limb positions and hers.

But now suppose that someone else became able to ascribe to me reliably and correctly present mental states without relying on any observation or evidence. It does not seem as though this would suffice for her pronouncements to inherit the status of my avowals. For one thing, establishing her reliability in ascribing occurrent mental states to me would at least partly depend on finding a regular match between her ascriptions and my avowals. But, more importantly, so long as there was no question about my grasp of the language or my sincerity, it seems that my avowals would continue to have a much stronger *prima facie* claim to being correct. If disagreement broke out between us over what is now going on in my mind, her consistent past success in reading my mind would not be sufficient ground for taking her word over mine. It seems, rather, that we would take the disagreement as signaling the waning of her mind-reading powers. Similar remarks would apply to the imaginary scenario in which an external brain-scanner is set up to replace one's own self-scanning mechanism and render verdicts on one's present mental states.

Suppose our subject persistently denies feeling hunger, and there is no behavioral evidence that goes against her denials. That is to say, the subject's behavior and her no-hunger avowals line up. It seems that we would sooner question the reliability of the brain-scanner that appeared to register hunger sensation than reject the subject's denial. If so, then the special status normally assigned to avowals would seem to survive even as we envisage a brain science allowing observers to 'look inside and see'.

So far, I have tried to highlight features of the ordinary conception of avowals that the materialist introspectionist account does not readily accommodate. The account seems to allow for various possibilities that commonsense intuitions take to be problematic. It bears emphasizing that I have *not* aimed to offer a direct argument against these possibilities; nor will I attempt to produce such an argument in the rest of the book. My point has rather been that the materialist introspectionist view would require us to compromise rather than properly understand the ordinary view of avowals. The ordinary view is not sacrosanct, and it need not be thought to represent the last word on avowals' security. However, other things being equal, I think we should prefer an account of avowals' security that does not require commitment to possibilities that common sense would deem problematic, *unless* we can see why, or how, common sense should have gone awry.

So the question now becomes how well the materialist introspectionist can explain (or explain away) the commonsense intuitions regarding avowals' special security. Since the materialist strategy rests on assimilating the epistemology of avowals to that of secure bodily "I"-ascriptions, our question becomes how well such assimilation can be reconciled with perceived asymmetries between avowals and, say, proprioceptive reports. The materialist is likely to seize upon the fact that avowals concern states *inside* our bodies, whereas non-evidential bodily "I"-ascriptions concern bodily surfaces, orientation, posture, limb position, etc. A first suggestion might be that introspection is not vulnerable to the failings of outer perception. This may, of course, be true, as a matter of fact. Our brains may be much better at detecting states inside our bodies than conditions at our bodies' surfaces, or external states of our bodies. But this fact could hardly explain why, ordinarily, and absent any understanding of the workings of our brains, we should so strongly presume avowals to enjoy such a high degree of security. It would seem very odd to suggest that the ordinary treatment of avowals reflects a specific empirical conjecture regarding the relative reliability of our mental self-reporting system as compared to, say, proprioception.

A second suggestion would be that we ordinarily recognize (perhaps tacitly) that avowals, unlike proprioceptive reports, concern goings-on that are normally *hidden* from plain view, and are not readily observable by others. Perhaps this difference could suffice to explain the contrast we draw between avowals and secure non-mental "I"-ascriptions. But it is hard to see why we should suppose this difference to yield an increased degree of security for avowals. After all, we do *not* take subjects to be in a privileged position to pronounce on *non*-mental conditions inside their bodies (e.g., the condition of their livers or their hearts, and many conditions of their brains). On the contrary; if someone pronounced on some hidden chemical process taking place in their spleen, we would be very doubtful. Again, let us suppose that, as a matter of empirical fact, our brains are, for some reason, more reliable at detecting a certain subset of our internal conditions. Still, even setting aside the question of the natural delineation of this subset, the question remains why our pronouncements about some of the conditions hidden inside our bodies should be taken to enjoy unparalleled security.

The materialist introspectionist can perhaps offer us an empirically cogent account explaining how it might be *possible* for us to produce highly reliable reports about some of our internal states. *Assuming* with common sense that avowals enjoy an especially high degree of security, the materialist introspectionist account can answer the question how that could come to be. The answer is a very simple one: if avowals are indeed especially secure, it is because they are self-reports subserved by an especially reliable inner tracking mechanism. But *our* main question is not: How *could* avowals be more secure than our pronouncements? Rather, it is: *Why* are avowals ordinarily treated as more secure than all other pronouncements, including non-evidential bodily "I"-ascriptions? I submit that this question is not answered adequately by postulating the existence in us of a reliable mechanism that is designed to deliver largely true self-reports. Thus, if our concern is to explain Epistemic Asymmetry in its full scope, we should search for an alternative to the materialist introspectionist account.[9]

There are other reasons for seeking an alternative account. The idea of introspection—as inner gaze, or internal monitoring, or scanning—seems most inviting and compelling when we think of avowals of present sensations and feelings. States such as feeling hungry, thirsty, achy, relaxed, cold, angry, anxious, cheerful, and so on, each has associated with it a characteristic phenomenology. It is tempting to think of the phenomenology as the *appearances* displayed by some goings-on inside us: the special access each of us supposedly has to her present phenomenal states amounts to the ability to judge what is going on inside us *based on these appearances*. These appearances are what our internal introspective mechanism would be sensitive to, as it detects the presence of the relevant states in us.

Recall, however, that the distinctive status ordinarily assigned to avowals is not restricted to phenomenal avowals. It also covers intentional avowals: avowals of various intentional states. However attractive the inner perception or inner scanning model may seem in connection with phenomenal states, its prospects of explaining the special security of subjects' pronouncements about *what* they are thinking about, wishing for, hoping, are angry at, scared of, etc. do not seem promising. Explaining the security of intentional avowals requires explaining not only how it is that a subject can determine the presence of some state in her, but also how a subject can tell what her state is *about* (or *of*, or *for*, etc.). Unlike phenomenal avowals, intentional avowals explicitly relate subjects to objects and states of affairs outside their minds. They ascribe to the subject a state with intentional content. But it is not at all clear how the intentional content of a state could reliably be gleaned from an inward gaze at internal mental goings-on.[10]

---

[9] My thanks to Ram Neta for pressing me to offer the foregoing clarification of my main objection to the materialist introspectionist.

[10] On some views, all mental states, phenomenal states included, have representational content. See Shoemaker (1994). See also Anscombe (1965); Lycan (1996); and Dretske (2003). If this were so, the significance of the apparent differences between phenomenal and intentional states might be reduced. Still, phenomenal *avowals* are different from intentional avowals in that they do not *specify* the representational content of the ascribed state. And there seems to be no presumption that the avowing subject *knows* or can *tell* the representational content of her phenomenal states (if they have any); whereas there is a presumption that the person who says (or thinks) "I am hoping it's not too late to get tickets" or "I find this painting fascinating" knows or can tell the content of the intentional state she ascribes to herself.

The problem is not simply that beliefs, desires, hopes, etc., unlike thirst, hunger, fatigue, and so on, apparently do not in general have characteristic phenomenology. It is that the *intentional content* of an intentional state is not plausibly understood as an intrinsic feature it has, discernible by a mechanism that is sensitive only to the state's presence and quality. Suppose we grant that I could tell by looking inside whether I am feeling angry at, rather than enchanted by, $x$ right now, based on my internal state's characteristic features, which I can internally perceive. Still, how could I tell, by attending to the internally detectable features of my present state, that it is directed at $x$ rather than $y$? It seem implausible to suppose that for any $x$ and $y$ that I could have intentional attitudes about I must have distinguishing signs 'from the inside' that tell me whether, at a given moment, my attitude is about the one rather than the other. And the problem persists even if the strict analogy with sense perception is abandoned, as long as avowals are taken to articulate judgments or beliefs that are arrived at through the exercise of some mode of epistemic "tracking" or detection that is directed at first-order mental states only. For it is hard to see how any such tracking could yield especially reliable results concerning properties of intentional states that are essentially relational, since they relate one's state to objects, states of affairs, etc. outside the subject.[11]

## Avowals' Security as Due to 'Transparency-to-the-World'

We now turn to an alternative account of avowals, which can be found in Evans (1982). Evans recognizes that the Cartesian view is motivated by a seeming contrast between mental and non-mental "I"-ascriptions. But, unlike the materialist introspectionist, he does not seek to explain (or explain away) the contrast by appeal to a highly reliable, though fallible, faculty of introspection. Instead, he observes that our ordinary conception of ourselves, which accords

---

[11] For a critique of the perceptual version of the materialist conception of introspection along similar lines, see, e.g., Shoemaker (1994); Davidson (1987); and Heil (1988). See also Wright (1998) and Moran (2001: 12 ff.). MacDonald (1998) tries to develop a perceptual model of self-knowledge that circumvents some of the more standard objections to the perceptual model. For discussion of materialist alternatives to the perceptual model, see Fricker (1998).

avowals a special status, does not subscribe to *either* the Cartesian *or* the materialist model of *intro*spection. In arriving at mental self-ascriptions, Evans point out, we do not ordinarily engage in anything like inner perception at all. Following Wittgenstein, he suggests that the true remedy for Cartesianism is to abandon the idea that ordinary mental self-knowledge "always involves an *inward* glance at the states and doings of something to which only the person himself has access" (1982: 225). In a much-cited passage, he says:

[I]n making a self-ascription of belief, one's eyes are, so to speak, or occasionally literally, directed outward—upon the world. If someone asks me 'Do you think there is going to be a third world war?' I must attend, in answering him, to precisely the same outward phenomena as I would attend to if I were answering the question 'Will there be a third world war?' (1982: 225)

As I ascribe to myself a present belief, or thought, I direct my attention outward, not inward. I typically 'look outside', at the objects my belief or thought are about, rather than inspecting goings-on 'inside' *either* my immaterial mind *or* my material brain. Making a related point, but one pertaining more to the phenomenology of one's thoughts about one's own present thoughts, Loar says: "When one attends reflexively to one's thought that Freud lived in Vienna, it is difficult not to see it as pointing outwards, towards Freud and Vienna and the one's inhabiting the other. My thoughts appear transparent, as if I look through them towards their objects" (1987: 100).[12]

The kind of transparency at issue here is to be distinguished from the traditional notion of transparency, which had to do with the alleged clarity with which one can 'peer into' the contents, intentional objects, or intrinsic qualities of one's own mental states, when directing an 'inner gaze' toward them. For the sake of terminological clarity, I shall reserve the term "self-intimation" for the latter kind of transparency. I shall refer to the transparency with which we are now concerned as "transparency-to-the-world".[13]

---

[12] Notice, though, that Loar is still describing "reflexive attending" in perceptual terms, speaking of how I "see" my thought, how my thoughts "appear" to me, and of my "looking through them".

[13] For a recent example of the more traditional use of "transparency" see Wright (1998: 15). What I am calling "transparency-to-the-world" is pointed out by Collingwood (1940: ch. 11 and 12); Anscombe (1975: 55), and, more recently, Greenwood (1991); Blackburn (1995), Gallois (1996); Moran (1988), (1994), (1997), (2001); and Falvey (2000), among others. Moran's particular use of transparency-to-the-world to account for so-called first-person authority will be discussed below, pp. 128–46.

For present purposes, the interest of the feature of transparency-to-the-world lies in its potential for explaining the distinctive status and security of avowals. It certainly looks as though this feature can serve to capture an important contrast between intentional avowals and corresponding explanatory reports. Explanatory reports rely on observation, evidence, or inferences whose purpose is to identify the relevant individual's mental states, which can allow us to explain or predict his behavior. As observed earlier, sometimes our intentional *self*-ascriptions are similarly based, for sometimes we make them in an attempt to explain or predict our *own* behavior. Thus, I might come to ascribe to myself regret for leaving my job, for example, on the basis of psychological evidence that has unraveled during several therapy sessions—regret that I would not have come to avow, but for the therapy. Or, after spending some time at the cognitive science lab, I might come to attribute to myself certain motives or preferences I would not otherwise avow. Such self-ascriptions are *not* 'transparent-to-the-world'. And it is also true that they do not share in the secure status of intentional avowals. Their status is quite similar to that of ordinary descriptive reports. An ordinary descriptive report or judgment will be made on the basis of perception, observation, evidence, inference, conjecture, etc. and will be subject to familiar sorts of failings. 'Non-transparent' intentional *self*-ascriptions deploy similar epistemic routes in identifying one's contentful mental states, so it stands to reason that they should be vulnerable to various epistemic failures.

By contrast, distinctively secure intentional self-ascriptions—that is, intentional avowals—do not involve consulting evidence or making inferences about the ascribed state. They characteristically involve direct, or 'transparent', consideration of the objects or states of affairs they are about. Although Evans introduces the idea of transparency in connection with self-ascriptions of beliefs, I think his observation can be generalized to other intentional avowals. If asked whether I am hoping or wishing that $p$, whether I prefer $x$ to $y$, whether I am angry at or afraid of $z$, and so on, my attention would be directed at $p$, $x$ and $y$, $z$, etc. For example, to say how I feel about an upcoming holiday, I would consider whether the holiday is likely to be fun. Asked whether I find my neighbor annoying, I would ponder her actions and render a verdict. Considering whether I am scared of the dog,

I will think of the dog, and whether it is scary. In general, in addressing questions about what I think, believe, want, prefer, feel, and so on, I concern myself not with me and my states, but rather with the world outside myself. (To put it in Loar's terms, when I attend to my present feeling about the holiday, or anger at my neighbor, or fear of the dog, and so on, I inevitably 'look through' my state to its objects—going on holiday, the neighbor, the dog—as if I were to say or think, "*This* (going on holiday) is a great idea" or "*She* (the neighbor) is so annoying" or "*It* (the dog) is so scary".) I consider directly the intentional objects of my self-ascriptions, and employ my normal abilities and dispositions for acquiring desires and other intentional attitudes upon being confronted with objects and conditions in the world outside myself.

With this observation, Evans can capture a significant contrast between intentional avowals and intentional ascriptions to others. This contrast can be seen as structurally similar to the epistemic contrast between proprioceptive reports and reports on someone else's limb position. In both cases, *what* is ascribed in the first person is the same as what is ascribed in the third person (viz., "My legs are crossed" versus "DB's legs are crossed"; "I believe that *p*" versus "She believes that *p*"). But the first-person ascriptions are arrived at via a different epistemic route as compared with the truth-conditionally equivalent third-person ascriptions. For, in our own case, we have available to us different epistemic procedures for making the relevant ascriptions. And with this contrast at hand, we can even fund a contrast between intentional avowals and *grammatically identical* intentional "I"-ascriptions. For, just as one can report on one's *own* limb position on the basis of, say, looking at one's body, so one can issue an evidence-based intentional self-ascription. On the present proposal, the significant difference lies in the fact that the avowal, unlike the evidence-based self-ascription, is transparent-to-the-world.

I think the present proposal by Evans can best be understood by recalling his treatment of the special security of self-ascriptions that use "I" as subject (see previous chapter, p. 56 ff.). Evans and Shoemaker both point out that when one uses "I" as subject, one does not rely on an identification judgment concerning the subject of the relevant "I"-ascription. (That is to say, one's "I"-ascription in

that case is identification-independent—it does not rest on a judgment of the form "I = δ", where δ represents some descriptive means
of identifying oneself.) This can allow us to capture at least one aspect
of Epistemic Asymmetry. For, unlike ordinary empirical ascriptions,
which are identification-dependent, "I"-ascriptions that use "I" as
subject are not vulnerable to errors through the misidentifying
of their subject (they are IETM). Now, in keeping with what I have
called Semantic Continuity, and in conformity with what Evans
calls the Generality Constraint, Evans insists that we can still see
"I"-ascriptions that are IETM as *referring to* the self-ascriber, semantically speaking. This is because, even in the absence of descriptive
beliefs or identifying information about herself, the subject will
normally still be in possession of more epistemically minimal (non-
descriptive, non-identificatory) abilities and dispositions that allow
her to single herself out. So "I"-ascriptions that use "I" as subject represent a subject's thoughts *about* herself. Furthermore, though relying
on no identifying judgment, they can represent knowledge she has
that *she herself* is in some state. For, once again, though the subject may
have no identifying descriptive beliefs about herself, she is still exercising a capacity to gain knowledge that is specifically about herself.

Evans's construal of intentional avowals can be seen as following
the same pattern of accounting for Epistemic Asymmetry without
sacrificing Semantic Continuity. In this case, we can take Evans to be
portraying intentional avowals as self-ascriptions that are made on *a
different epistemic basis* from other intentional ascriptions—i.e., intentional ascriptions to others, as well as evidence-based ascriptions
of intentional states to oneself. Unlike these other ascriptions,
intentional avowals are transparent-to-the-world. In issuing them,
we employ *a distinctive epistemic procedure*, which does not depend on
recognizing or identifying (or hypothesizing about) a state inside us.
(Semantic Continuity in this case requires insisting that intentional
avowals, just like their semantic cousins, do involve genuine ascription
to individuals of mental states with particular intentional contents. So
in this case, too, Evans will need to explain how it is that one can still
manage to make a judgment *about* one's intentional state (i.e., a judgment to the effect that one has an intentional state with a particular
content). In addition, he needs to explain how it is that one can be
thought to gain genuine mental self-*knowledge*, even though one has

not employed any epistemic procedure for detecting the presence in oneself of a state with that content.[14])

Here is how Evans describes the distinctive procedure we use in making ordinary intentional self-ascriptions:

> I get myself in a position to answer the question whether I believe that p by putting into operation whatever procedure I have for answering the question whether p. (...) If a judging subject applies this procedure, then necessarily he will gain knowledge of one of his mental states: even the most determined sceptic cannot find here a gap in which to insert his knife. . . . [With this] method of self-ascription . . . we . . . have no need for the idea of an inward glance.

> We can encapsulate this procedure for answering questions about what one believes in the following simple rule: whenever you are in a position to assert that p, you are *ipso facto* in a position to assert 'I believe that p.' (1982: 225 f.)

With this procedure, Evans thinks he can make good on his promise to "avoid the idea of this kind of self-knowledge as a form of perception—mysterious in being incapable of delivering inaccurate results" (1982: 225). The procedure identified by Evans is not one of recognizing in oneself the presence of a state with that content, so we can continue to avoid the idea of "an inward glance". For the procedure involves only a direct consideration of the ascribed belief's *content* and requires only that the subject exercise her normal abilities and dispositions for forming beliefs about the world.

Now although, epistemically speaking, all one *has to do* in order to arrive at the self-ascription in avowing is to go through the "transparency procedure" (as I shall refer to it), "mastery of this procedure cannot constitute a full understanding of the content of the judgement 'I believe that p' " (1982: 226). A subject who ascribes the belief that p to himself is different from a subject who merely forms the belief that p; the former must possess "the psychological concept expressed by 'ξ believes that p,' which the subject must conceive as capable of being instantiated otherwise than by himself" (1982: 226).

---

[14]  Later (see p. 206 below), I distinguish two questions in this connection: the question how one can make a *genuine* ascription of an intentional state, and the question why one is assured of making a *correct* ascription. As I read Evans, he does not explicitly separate the two questions. The procedures he offers for explaining self-knowledge of intentional states seem to play the role of explaining both how one can think about one's intentional state at all, even though one is not directing attention at the state, and how one can obtain reliable self-knowledge regarding such states.

In other words, a subject who avows a belief has no need to employ the procedures we typically employ to ascertain that someone else has a certain belief. Still, if the subject is to be credited with making a genuine ascription of a belief to herself—i.e., with having a thought, or saying something that is *about* a contentful state she is in—she must conceive of herself as instantiating a certain kind of state with a certain kind of content. This is what Semantic Continuity (and the Generality Constraint) requires in its application to the ascriptive part of intentional avowals. It is the analogue of the requirement in its application to the subject part: namely, that an individual who thinks "I am (in) M" must have a conception of what it is for *someone*—not necessarily herself—to be (in) M, though she need not employ any thick epistemic procedure for recognizing an internal state of hers as a certain kind of state with a certain intentional content.

By invoking a special transparency procedure or method, then, Evans can capture the contrast between intentional avowals and other intentional ascriptions. But he can also capture a further contrast: between intentional avowals, on the one hand, and proprioceptive reports, as well as ordinary kinesthetic self-reports and reports on one's orientation, on the other. These latter kinds of report do utilize a distinctive set of abilities that we can employ only in our own case. However, the relevant abilities are different in kind from the distinctive ability we employ when issuing intentional avowals. Take the ability that underwrites proprioception, for example. This is an ability for own-body perception, which fits very well the materialist model of introspection as inner perception or internal self-scanning, as Evans himself notes (1982: 230 n. 42). By contrast, the procedure of "re-using the conceptual skills which one uses in order to make judgments about the world" does not require that we postulate any "special faculty of inner sense or internal self-scanning" (1982: 230 n. 42). This means that, in the case of intentional avowals, we have no need to exercise any special ability that is directed *either* at states of our immaterial Egos *or* at a subset of our internal bodily states. We simply engage the ordinary abilities and dispositions that result in our acquisition of first-order intentional attitudes about states and objects in the world outside us. Still, Evans suggests, though not *directed at* our intentional states, these abilities are apt to give *knowledge about* our own states.

To sum up, as I read Evans, he is offering an answer to the question that is part of our main concern: namely, what it is that renders intentional avowals distinctively secure (though, as we shall see, Evans does not want to commit himself to the security being entirely unparalleled). Having brought out immunity to error through misidentification as a distinctive form of epistemic security, Evans is first to note that avowals are not alone in being IETM. The class of ascriptions that are IETM also includes many non-mental "I"-ascriptions; yet avowals seem more secure than these non-mental "I"-ascriptions. If avowals were simply reports on our mental states that were based on the findings of an internal self-scanning faculty, then their seemingly additional *ascriptive* security would seem puzzling. The Cartesian is moved to suggest that ascriptive security is due to the special nature of *what* we are reporting when we introspect: namely, *non-physical* (or immaterial) states. Evans thinks this is unnecessary. Instead of funding the mental/non-mental contrast by appeal to the nature of the items scanned, he suggests that the difference lies in the epistemic method used in gaining knowledge about the relevant states. Whereas intentional ascriptions to others are based on observation of their behavior, and proprioceptive reports are arrived at by a method of internal own-body scanning, intentional avowals are arrived at through the use of the transparency procedure. We determine what we believe, think, hope, etc. not by studying our own behavior, *or* by examining the contents of our minds, but rather by putting ourselves in a position directly to consider the worldly objects and states of affairs that our thoughts, beliefs, etc. are *about*.

## Evans's Transparency View as an Epistemic View

As I presented it, Evans's procedure of 'looking outside' to the worldly objects and states that our ascriptions specify was offered as a viable alternative to the discredited introspectionist's method of 'looking inside'. Its apparent advantage is that it seems to point to a significant difference between avowals and (even) non-mental "I"-ascriptions that are IETM. However, when we try to understand Evans as offering an account of avowals' distinctive security, we can see that there is an important point of agreement between him and the introspectionist.

On Evans's Transparency View, when we self-ascribe intentional states in the ordinary way, we simply turn our gaze to the world outside us, and put our cognitive and conative mechanisms directly to work on the worldly matters themselves. We can tell whether we believe that *p* by simply trying to determine whether *p* is true; we tell whether we desire *x* by examining features of *x* itself, and considering whether it is desirable. Similarly with respect to whether we hope that *q*, are angry at *y*, afraid of *z*, etc. The directness and immediacy that mark intentional avowals, then, are not the directness and immediacy of inner sense perception, as introspectionist views would have it. Rather, they are whatever directness and immediacy are afforded by transparency-to-the-world. Now, if we take the mark of intentional avowals to be their transparency-to-the-world, then it seems reasonable to expect an explanation of their distinctive security in terms of this feature. Indeed, Evans clearly suggests that the transparency-to-the-world of ordinary mental self-ascriptions amounts to the use of a distinctive and very reliable *epistemic method*—the transparency procedure: "If a judging subject applies this procedure, then necessarily he will gain knowledge of one of his own mental states: even the most determined sceptic cannot find here a gap in which to insert his knife" (1982: 225). And we are to take the use of this method to *obviate the need for introspection traditionally understood*; for, with this "method of self-ascription . . . we . . . have no need for the idea of an inward glance" (1982: 225).

This means, however, that although Evans offers his Transparency View as an alternative to the introspectionist view (in both its Cartesian and materialist versions), his view actually belongs together with introspectionist views, at least in terms of the way it approaches the question of avowals' security. For, like the introspectionist, Evans seems to subscribe to what I refer to as the Epistemic Approach to avowals' security. On this approach, we are to explain the security of avowals by appeal to the security of the epistemic basis on which they are made. If avowals are especially secure, it is because they are (or express) *self-judgments* that are arrived at via an *especially secure epistemic route,* or by deploying an especially secure epistemic *method or procedure.* Importantly, what renders avowals especially secure is the very same feature that qualifies them as articles of self-*knowledge*.[15] If we

---

[15]  For a variety of views that fall under the umbrella of what I'm calling the Epistemic Approach, see Fricker (1998: 175–85). See Bar-On and Long (2001: sect. 1) for a brief critique of the approach.

understand Evans's view as falling under the Epistemic Approach, we can expect it to be subject to at least some of the difficulties raised for introspectionist views. In addition, arguably, Evans's transparency method fares worse than its introspectionist rival in some respects.

**The transparency method is too epistemically indirect.** One feature of avowals that we have noted before is the directness and immediacy of their production. Avowals, it is often observed, do not seem to be made on *any* basis. Yet, on Evans's Transparency View, we are to take them to be self-judgments that are arrived at on the basis of consideration of the relevant worldly items. This means that, appearances to the contrary, we should take our normal way of pronouncing on our mental states to be epistemically rather indirect. I tell what is going on in my mind *by way of* consulting the world around me, which seems even less direct than my way of telling whether I am standing, or where my limbs are. *These* things I presumably tell by inner own-body perception, which is causally more direct than even ordinary perception, and therefore (perhaps) less prone to error. By comparison, the method of looking outside to determine what one believes or feels about something seems much more "roundabout", as Evans himself puts it (1982: 225).

Insofar as we take the security of avowals to be related to their notable epistemic directness, the invocation of a relatively indirect method of determining the character of one's intentional state seems out of place. In keeping with Semantic Continuity, we want to preserve the idea that an intentional avowal is—semantically speaking— *about* the intentional state it ascribes and its content. But we need to avoid compromising the aspect of Epistemic Asymmetry that pertains to the comparative epistemic directness of avowals. In order to preserve the immediacy and directness of avowals, we need to find a way to close the 'epistemic distance' between the self-ascriber and her ascribed state. But, at least on one way of understanding how the transparency method is supposed to work, it operates at one more remove as compared with the introspectionist method. For, whereas the introspectionist appeals to inner perception (or detection) of one's first-order mental states, which is presumably at least causally more direct and immediate than sense perception, the transparency method seems to require one first to attend to the world, and then *figure out on that basis* what one is thinking, wanting, feeling, etc.

It may be objected that this way of understanding Evans is not true to the spirit of his discussion. That may be so. However, I think Evans does not make it at all clear how we ought to understand the use of his transparency procedure so that it *both* gives us a secure method of gaining knowledge about our present states *and* satisfies the desideratum of preserving the immediacy and directness of avowals.[16] In any event, the first difficulty I have raised can still serve to highlight the fact that, appearances to the contrary, the transparency-to-the-world of avowals does not by itself suffice to capture their epistemic directness or immediacy. If Evans's Transparency View is no worse off than introspectionism on this score, it is not clearly better off, either.

**As an epistemic method, transparency has only limited scope of application.** The distinctive method Evans invokes is applicable to a fairly limited range of avowals. The transparency procedure has the clearest application in those cases where we are asked explicitly whether we believe *p*, or like *x*, and so on. In such cases, it is plausible to suppose that we answer by attending to the relevant state of affairs or object, without examining our internal state. Perhaps this is so even in the case of questions such as "What do you think about the Republicans' victory?" or "How do you feel about Lisa?", where the putative intentional content is specified in the question, so one can still attend to it 'transparently'. Although in these cases it seems more evident that, as a method of determination, Evans's procedure is rather indirect. For here it is clear that the assessment of the relevant worldly state of affairs or object is in aid of *figuring out what state* we are currently in. (For example, if, reflecting on the fact of the Republicans' victory, I judge it to be distressing, I can conclude, "I am quite upset about it.")

But now consider spontaneously volunteered avowals such as "I'd really like a cup of tea right now", or "I am so worried about my dad" (declared unprompted), or "I am wondering what time it is" (said out of the blue). In this kind of case, no question is posed to me (by myself or by anyone else), which specifies a subject matter or object for my 'transparent' consideration. I simply pronounce on my current state of mind. While I agree that it is not fruitful to portray such

---

[16] Later on in this chapter I consider a use of the transparency idea that represents a more radical departure from introspectionism and involves an abandonment of the Epistemic Approach, which Evans still seems wedded to in his discussion.

avowals as the upshot of an 'inward gaze', I think it is equally implausible to suppose that they involve a look at the world outside us. Indeed, it is very unclear *where* in the outside world one would look to find out what one's state of mind is in this type of case.[17]

The transparency method does not have clear applicability even when avowals made in response to questions are concerned. Suppose we are asked, "How are you feeling right now?", or "What would you like to do most right now?", or "A penny for your thoughts". These questions are quite open-ended, inviting us to pronounce on our current mental condition. In these cases, *no* subject matter, no worldly fact or object, is specified about which our reaction is solicited and at which our attention can be directed. Rather, the request seems to be for a pronouncement on how things are with us at the given moment, and it ordinarily comes with no less strong a presumption that we are in a special position to offer a decisively correct answer. Yet no amount of gazing to the world beyond us would seem to help us answer such questions, much less explain the special security that our own answers are presumed to enjoy. Avowals made in response to open-ended questions, unlike spontaneous avowals, may more plausibly be thought to require some kind of gazing, but the more appropriate direction would seem to be inward. Indeed, consideration of such avowals is apt to draw us back to the idea of introspection as an internal 'search and find' method. But even if we were to resist this idea, it still does not seem promising to characterize what one *is* doing when avowing, let alone the *security* of one's avowal, in terms of an actual use of the transparency procedure.[18]

Evans might concede that when issuing an avowal spontaneously, or in response to an open-ended question, one does not *actually* engage in the transparency procedure. Still, he might point out that, in one's own case, that procedure is in principle *available* to one, as a way of *verifying* the truth of one's pronouncements.[19] So, if I say, "I'm

---

[17] Just in case the introspectionist and the transparency views seem to exhaust the available options, let me point out, in anticipation of later discussion, that we could think of spontaneous avowals as direct *expressions* of one's present mental states, rather than as upshots of some reflection or determination, whether inwardly *or* outwardly directed.

[18] Contrast open-ended invitations to avow with open-ended questions to report on one's perceptual state. If asked, "What are you noticing right now?" or "What can you see/hear/. . .?", it does seem helpful and correct to suggest that I turn my attention to the world outside (rather than 'look inside') in order to answer. (We come back to perceptual self-reports below.)

[19] Thanks to Keith Simmons for proposing this take on Evans's view.

worried about my dad", then, unlike you, I am in a position to ascertain the truth of the relevant ascription by attending directly to my dad's condition and deeming it worrisome. If I am asked, "What would you like to do right now?" and I answer, "I want to go see a movie," I can assure myself (and you) of the correctness of my answer by recognizing that, upon considering the possibility of going to a movie, I would deem it desirable. However, it is not clear to me that the mere availability in principle of the transparency procedure would be sufficient to explain the asymmetrically high degree of security that we ordinarily assign to avowals. We ordinarily presume that avowals are *actually* likelier to be true than other pronouncements, and less subject to epistemic criticism, not merely that subjects are in principle better placed to verify their truth, should it be questioned. Thus, the more liberal version of Evans's Transparency View, while it may allow him to capture some asymmetry between the first-person and the third-person case, would at most yield an explanation of the *potential* security of avowals. And this would place Evans's account at a disadvantage in comparison with the account offered by the introspectionist. It's also not clear how to apply the liberal version to one's response to a request such as "A penny for your thoughts!" No one seems as well placed as I am correctly to pronounce on my present thought. Now, suppose I answer, "I'm thinking of my aunt." It would seem very peculiar to suggest that the secure status of my reply is due to the fact that I, unlike others, can in principle consider my aunt directly and recognize her as the object of my thought.

**Phenomenal avowals do not seem good candidates for the application of the transparency method.** For the liberal version to work, it must still be assumed that in every case of avowals there is in the offing some potential state of affairs or object that the avowal is about, such that one could attend to that state of affairs or object to verify one's self-ascription. Yet not all avowals seem to meet this condition. Consider ordinary self-ascriptions of so-called *phenomenal* states—sensations such as feeling tired, thirsty, achy, uncomfortable, or non-specific emotional states such as simply feeling sad, calm, cheerful, anxious, irritable, and so on. It is characteristic of avowals of such states that they do not contain any specification of an intentional object or propositional content of the state. In the case of such avowals, there simply does not seem to be a ready worldly candidate— actual *or* potential—for the subject to consider directly by way of obtaining a secure self-ascription. The difficulty is not simply that it seems odd to suggest that I normally *tell whether* I am thirsty or sad by attending directly to some item or state of affairs outside my self. It's hard to see what worldly items or states I (in contrast to others) could possibly attend to by way of ascertaining the correctness of whatever phenomenal avowal I make.

Evans might fall back on the view, now accepted by many, that *all* mental *states*, phenomenal states included, have representational content.[20] So the potential candidate for transparent consideration would be supplied by the representational content of the ascribed phenomenal state. For example, suppose we take the state of thirst to be a subject's state when she perceives (or appears to perceive) her own body's dehydration. The avowal "I feel thirsty" can then be seen as reporting that representational state. Even if the subject does not actually tell that she is thirsty by considering whether her body is dehydrated or not, we may still have a candidate for the subject's transparent consideration: namely, the content *My body is dehydrated*. But are we to suppose that the security of the subject's avowal of thirst, which itself does not specify any intentional content, is due to the fact that she could verify her self-ascription by reflecting directly on the alleged representational content of the ascribed state?

There are several difficulties with this suggestion. First, in many cases, a subject will not be in any position to articulate or identify in any way the putative representational content of her ascribed state. Yet, we would normally suppose her to be in a special position cor- rectly to ascribe the state to herself. (I can securely self-ascribe "I feel furious", even if I cannot say what I feel furious *about*, and even though I would have no idea where to begin searching for the rep- resentational content of the state of non-specific rage, so as trans- parently to check my self-ascription.) Secondly, even in those cases where a subject does have an idea of what the ascribed state's putative content is, as in the case of, e.g., self-ascriptions of toothaches, it does not seem plausible that the security of one's self-ascription is due to

---

[20] See n. 10 above. Also, see Evans (1982: 230).

one's ability to consider directly what one's state represents. Not only do I not normally tell that I have a terrible toothache by attending to the condition of my tooth, but if I *were* to consider the condition of my tooth directly, it hardly seems that the security of my findings would suffice to ground the security that my pronouncement "I have a terrible toothache" seems to have. Finally, pinning the security of phenomenal avowals on the security of direct consideration of conditions of one's body (actual or potential) would result in an assimilation of phenomenal avowals to self-reports of internal bodily conditions. For example, the avowal "I feel hungry" will be a report on the condition of my stomach, which *I*, unlike others, can make without a medical examination, through a direct consideration of my stomach. But, presumably, for me to be able to obtain knowledge of my hunger in this way, I have to have a special, non-evidential access to an internal bodily condition of mine. This would seem to portray phenomenal avowals very much on the model offered by the materialist introspectionist. But the initial attraction of Evans's appeal to transparency was its promise to offer an alternative to the introspectionist model, in both its Cartesian and its materialist versions. This attraction would be diminished considerably if it turned out that his view ends up assimilating phenomenal avowals to bodily self-reports in this way.[21]

**Even where applicable, the transparency method does not seem apt to yield especially secure results.** In general, once the security of avowals is pinned to the security of an epistemic method, we want to understand why its use should issue in self-judgments that are systematically *more* secure than other self-judgments. Arguably, however, Evans's transparency procedure offers no more adequate

---

[21] For Evans's all-too-brief remarks on phenomenal self-ascriptions, see his (1982: 230). Ram Neta has suggested that an avowal such as "I feel thirsty" may be elliptical for (and have as its logical form) something like "I thirst for some liquid". I am doubtful that such a semantic analysis (which would require a claim of synonymy between the surface and the deep forms) can be made to work, though I don't have on hand an argument that rules it out. But I do not think it is clear how such an analysis would make room for a plausible application of the transparency method. Are we to suppose, e.g., that I should consider any liquid whatsoever and determine whether I 'thirst' for it, as a way of determining whether (or ascertaining that) I feel thirsty? Also, it is far from clear how this kind of analysis can be extended to all the relevant cases, including avowals such as "I feel anxious", "I feel so blue", etc. We often seem to be in a position to offer a secure self-ascription of a non-specific emotion, even though we are patently not in a position to pronounce, for any *given* item we would care to consider, whether we feel the emotion toward *it*.

answer to this question than the materialist introspectionist's procedure of 'looking inside' (though for different reasons). Thus, suppose we accept the idea that we attend to things outside us in order to determine what state we are in at a given moment. Then it is hard to see why avowing should not be expected to be riskier, epistemically speaking, than we take it to be. Consider, for instance, how prone to error we might be if we were really to determine whether we are in a given mental state by directly considering the worldly object of the state. Looking at the bulldog in front of me, I may judge it not to be scary—perhaps it is acting in a friendly manner, and I am informed that bulldogs are actually quite tame. Yet in point of fact, right now I feel rather agitated—no, downright terrified—by the dog, as my observers can tell by my bodily demeanor. Similarly for self-ascriptions of beliefs. I am really convinced right now that the Democrats will win the elections, perhaps for no good reason. But if I were to consider the question on its merits—*Will* the Democrats win the election?—I might, more reasonably, declare that I believe the Republicans will win. I will thereby be falsely ascribing to myself a belief I do not have. Even if such misascriptions do not occur too often, it may still seem puzzling why we should be prepared to assign greater ascriptive security to avowals than to proprioceptive reports.

Looking at the world, and directly assessing relevant states of affairs and objects, would seem to be a secure way of determining what is *to be* thought about *p*, whether *x* is *to be* desired, and so on. But, on the face of it, the question about avowals' security concerns our ability to tell what we are *in fact*—as opposed to what we *should be*—thinking, wanting, feeling. This is what the introspectionist, whether Cartesian or materialist, is trying to explain, and this is what Evans's transparency method should explain if it is to be a viable alternative to the method of introspection. (We shall return to this point below.)

**Evans's transparency method applies to some non-avowals.** It is instructive to examine a case in which a transparency procedure *can* offer a superior alternative to the introspectionist model. After discussing self-ascriptions of beliefs, Evans considers self-ascriptions of *perceptual experiences*—for example, a report such as "I see a tree". On Evans's analysis, such a report is based on an internal informational state that has a certain content—*that there is a tree around*. However,

Evans claims that to determine whether he is seeing a tree, a subject "does not in any sense gaze at, or concentrate upon, his internal state"; rather, "he gazes again *at the world* (thereby producing, or reproducing, an informational state in himself)" (1982: 227). Later, he says:

[T]hose inner states of the subject that we spoke of cannot intelligibly be regarded as objects of his internal gaze.... [W]hat we are aware of, when we know that we see a tree, is *nothing but a tree*. In fact, we only have to be aware of some state of the world in order to be in a position to make an assertion about ourselves.... Nothing more than the original state of awareness— awareness, simply, of a tree—is called for *on the side of awareness*, for a subject to gain knowledge of himself thereby. But certainly something more than the *sheer* awareness is called for: the perceptual state must occur in the context of certain kinds of knowledge and understanding on the part of the subject. (1982: 231 f.)[22]

It does seem plausible that we determine whether we are seeing a tree, or hearing a loud noise, not by looking into the contents of our minds, but rather by checking the world around us for the presence of a tree (*to be* seen), or a loud noise (*to be* heard). Although when I say "I (am) see(ing) a tree" (or "I (am) hear(ing) a loud noise"), I am saying something about a state I am in, I do not determine that I am in the state, thus verifying the truth of my self-ascription, by looking inside. Rather, I look transparently at the extra-mental world. In this case, the transparency procedure also seems highly reliable. Provided I use my eyes to determine whether there is a tree around (or my ears to determine whether there is a loud noise), my verdict on the worldly matter will systematically correlate with the self-verdict that concerns whether *I see* a tree (or hear a loud noise). If so, then we could appeal to the transparency procedure to explain the relative security of self-reports of sense perceptions.

However, we must note that, traditionally, reports of one's sense perceptions have *not* been regarded as sharing in the distinctive security of avowals. Indeed, Descartes initially funds the claim of epistemic asymmetry by contrasting reports such as "I see a tree" with self-ascriptions of visual (and other) sensations, as well as thoughts. And,

---

[22] Evans goes on:

No judgement will have the content of a psychological self-ascription, unless the judger can be regarded as ascribing to himself a property which he can conceive as being satisfied by a being not necessarily himself ... He can *know* that a state of affairs of the relevant type obtains simply by being aware of a tree, but he must *conceive* the state of affairs that he then knows to obtain as a state of affairs of precisely that type. (1982: 232, my emphases.)

intuitively, "I see a tree" seems in the same category as proprioceptive reports such as "My legs are crossed" and reports of my posture (such as "I am sitting down"). Such reports are made on a different basis in one's own case, but they are fully open to correction by observers on the basis of *their* (differently based) perceptions. Similarly, "I see a tree" seems as open to straightforward correction as the corresponding perceptual report (viz., "There's a tree"). You could deny my self-ascription by saying, "No, you do not." You could support your denial by pointing out, "There *is* no tree here," which is a perceptual report you make on the basis of your own perceptions.

So, if we accept Evans's brand of the Transparency View, we would have to conclude that, at best, avowals should be regarded as no more secure than self-reports of perceptual states.[23] This is a conclusion that Evans himself welcomes. Indeed, on the analysis he offers, "I *seem* to be seeing a tree" turns out to be no more secure than "I see a tree". And its security is due to the same reason: the fact that it rests on a (suitably modified) transparency procedure (1982: 228 f.). In both cases, as well as in the case of intentional ascriptions, Evans invites us to observe that, in determining the truth of the relevant ascription, we direct our attention transparently to the world, thereby engaging the same cognitive mechanisms that are causally responsible for our first-order states. This is what supposedly ensures the correctness of the self-ascriptions. The security of the self-ascriptions is then to be explained by appealing to the epistemic security of the transparency procedure they use. Thus, accepting Evans's explanation requires that we regard the apparent difference in security between avowals and perceptual self-reports as illusory.

Another case in point is that of memory reports. These too exhibit a first-person/third-person asymmetry, insofar as we make such reports on a different basis in our own case. And, indeed, it is plausible to suppose that we make these reports using Evans's transparency procedure. (To decide whether I *remember* that *p*, I will typically simply consider whether *p* happened.) But, again, memory reports have traditionally been contrasted with avowals in point of their security.[24]

---

[23] I say "at best" since earlier (see p. 118 f.) I raised a doubt about how secure avowals should be taken to be if we regard them as judgments that use the transparency procedure. And later on, I will argue that the feature of transparency-to-the-world is apt to characterize only *intentional* avowals, which involve explicit specification of intentional content. Yet the security of avowals has wider scope.

[24] The case of memory was suggested to me by Ram Neta.

If the security of avowals amounts to nothing more than what is obtained through the availability of the transparency procedure, avowals should share their security with many ascriptions that we are inclined to put in their contrast class.

Since Evans's transparency account applies to some non-avowals (such as perceptual self-reports and memory reports), it is too inclusive. But, in another way, it is too exclusive. As I explained above (p. 116 f.), the relevant notion of transparency is applicable only to intentional avowals—i.e., avowals that specify some intentional content, some object or state of affairs at which one's present state is said (or thought) to be directed. Since not all avowals are of this kind, any account that uses transparency-to-the-world as the central notion will fail to explain the security of all and only avowals (and this is regardless of whether or not it subscribes to the Epistemic Approach; see below).

I think we would do better to find an explanation of avowals' security that does not require us to compromise Epistemic Asymmetry in this way. As should be clear by now, I am very sympathetic to Evans's strategy of seeking an explanation of our relationship to our own minds that does not require us to invoke Cartesian entities. And I applaud his resistance to replacing Cartesian introspectionism with a materialist ersatz. However, I think that, in order fully to undermine the motivation for the Cartesian view, we must be better able to show how the Cartesian intuitions regarding avowals' character and status can be respected without going Descartes's way.

## Against the Epistemic Approach in General

For the most part, the difficulties I have raised so far for Evans's brand of transparency view have had to do with the particular kind of epistemic method he appeals to in explaining the distinctive security of avowals. I now want to offer some more general considerations against the explanatory adequacy of the Epistemic Approach to avowals' security, regardless of the particular character of the proposed epistemic basis.

We can think of the special status we ordinarily assign to avowals in terms of a special privilege granted to avowing subjects—what I shall refer to as "first-person privilege", to replace the more familiar label "first-person authority".[25] Our discussion so far has suggested that the privilege has a very distinctive and restricted domain: it applies only to *mental* states of mine, and only to states of my mind that are *contemporaneous* with my ascription. Further, the privilege has the following features. First, it is reflexively anchored to self-ascribers. It has to do with the fact that the states ascribed by my avowals are *my own*, and are ascribed to me *by myself* as *being my own*. Second, as the earlier discussion of the possibility of mind reading suggests, the privilege cannot be inherited by another person. It is *non-transferable*. Third, as suggested by doubts regarding the possibility of a subject who is 'chronically unreliable' in her avowals, the privilege cannot easily be 'detached' from subjects of mental states. So it is *inalienable*. My complaint regarding the Epistemic Approach, in a nutshell, is that it cannot adequately account for these features of our ordinary conception of first-person privilege.[26]

The Epistemic Approach begins with the idea that we possess some kind of special knowledge of our own minds, and seeks to characterize an especially secure way we have of knowing our own mental states. It then attempts to explain the security of avowals by appeal to the epistemic security of this special way of knowing. This means that what I have dubbed "first-person privilege" would have to be seen as reflecting our (perhaps tacit) recognition that self-ascribers have available to them this secure way of learning about their present intentional states. The Epistemic Approach, then, can be seen as construing first-person privilege as an *epistemic* privilege. Perhaps the most familiar model for epistemic privilege of this sort is the model

---

[25] The use of the label "first-person authority" is very prevalent, as can be evidenced by a cursory look at the articles in three recent collections: Cassam (1994); Wright *et al.* (1998); Ludlow and Martin (1998). Even authors who take themselves to oppose the introspectionist conception, such as Moran (2001) adhere to the idea that the special security of avowals is a matter of *authority*. Since authority is often understood in epistemic terms, in Bar-On and Long (2001), we introduced the notion of "first-person privilege" as a more neutral notion, which does not prejudge the question whether avowals' security is a matter of epistemic advantage.

[26] My criticism of the Epistemic Approach has points of contact with the discussions by Smith (1998) and by Wright (1998). I have borrowed the use of the terms "inalienable" and "non-transferable" in this context from Wright, who remarks: "the authority which attaches to [avowals] is, in a certain sense, inalienable. There is no such thing as showing oneself chronically unreliable in relation to . . . avowals" (1998: 17). And later: "the authority I have over the avowable aspects of my mental life is not transferable to others: there is no contingency . . . whose suspension would put other ordinary people in a position to avow away on my behalf, as it were" (1998: 24). Below, I am offering my own diagnosis of the main problem with the Epistemic Approach, which is partly based on discussion in Bar-On and Long (2001: sect. 2).

of expertise. Experts are people who 'know best'. They are individuals whom we take to have greater knowledge than most of us about certain matters, through having greater experience, training, or natural facility. When we take a trained botanist to be an expert about plants, for example, we take it that she is better placed than most of us to identify or analyze certain plants, for example. So whenever she pronounces on such matters, we presume that she is right. Now, the presumption that the botanist's claims about plants are correct is exhaustively explained by our recognition that she is well placed epistemically to convey more reliable information than the rest of us in that domain.

We are also familiar with the notion of "an authority" in some domains, such as the arts, where we may be less sure of the existence of 'hard facts'—i.e., facts that are independent of aesthetic judgments. But here too the idea of authority seems to be linked to that of expertise. Someone who is an authority on music is thought to be *relatively better placed* than most to pass judgment on musical matters, where it is assumed that the authoritative status is earned, and equally that it can be lost. Setting aside the idea that music critics have a *constitutive* role in deciding what is musically worthy, we think of the musical expert as someone who has *shown* herself capable of producing reliable judgments in the domain of music. (In the aesthetic cases, this *may* perhaps mean only that the expert's judgments are ones we could be brought to *agree* with.) In this way, ordinary assignments of epistemic authority to experts are responsive to perceived abilities or knowledge of specific individuals, and are typically contingent upon an empirically supportable assessment of the degree of an individual's reliability.

It is worth highlighting the fact that the ordinary notion of "an authority" as characterized above is bound up with the idea of someone who has an *establishable* claim to know certain facts that *any of us could equally come to know*, at least in principle. Even oracles are presumably taken to have a special ability to know in advance things that ordinary folks *will* (or at least *could*) in due course come to know equally well, though not through *fore*sight. The idea of assigning expertise to someone concerning matters that we suppose ourselves in principle unable to ascertain seems odd, even if not incoherent.

Now suppose that, with the Epistemic Approach, we explain first-person privilege as a species of epistemic authority. We say that, in one way or another, subjects are able to know best about their present mental states: they have some epistemically secure way of telling the facts in this domain (be it introspection, the transparency procedure, or what have you). As 'mental experts', they are epistemically better placed to pronounce on these matters. The difficulty I see is that this idea does not seem adequately to characterize, or exhaust, the special advantage that avowing subjects are supposed to have regarding, specifically, their *own present mental* states. As earlier discussion suggested, the assignment of first-person privilege does not appear to have the status of a defeasible generalization (or even supposition) that awaits our dealings with *individual* avowing subjects. Nor does it seem to reflect our assessment of subjects' relative facility in a certain domain of facts. Far from depending upon individual credentials, the presumption applies indiscriminately to the avowals of *any* avowing subject, so long as she is deemed linguistically competent and sincere. And it does not concern individuals' special reliability regarding a *specific* subject matter (viz., their minds), but rather their pronouncements about what goes on in their minds *at the time of avowing*. Furthermore, as suggested earlier, it is hard to imagine how one could attempt to substantiate the reliability *or* unreliability of particular (linguistically competent) subjects concerning their occurrent mental states without taking at face value many of the subject's avowals.[27] All this seems to go against the idea that our ordinary treatment of avowals is crucially similar to our treatment of expert reports. If anything, we seem to give avowals the role of *constraining evidence*, to which others' judgments about the avowing subject's mental states are answerable.

I should perhaps emphasize that my objection to the use of the model of expertise is *not* that there is no way for observers to establish the authority of a subject concerning her present mental states, because those states are "private" or inaccessible to the rest of us. It is interesting (and maybe surprising) to note that someone who did maintain the privacy of the mental could not readily explain our ordinary assumption of first-person privilege on the model of assigning authority to experts. This is because, on the supposition of privacy,

---

[27] Again, it is telling that even experiments designed to show that people are regularly confused about various matters of cognition, perception, and emotion depend upon taking subjects' pronouncements about their perceptions, thoughts, and judgments at face value. See, e.g., Nisbett and Wilson (1977).

no one (except God?) would ever be in a position to establish a subject's expert credentials, since no one could verify the correctness of her avowals. Thus, on the privacy supposition, we should never have any good reason to *take* subjects to know best their own present mind.[28] But I am objecting to the adequacy of the expertise model even on the contrary supposition that a subject's mental states *are* in principle accessible to others.

Thus, let us suppose, with the materialist, that mental states are internal physical conditions of our bodies, which are publicly accessible only in the sense that others *could* come to observe them. What would it take for us to think of "authoritative" subjects on the model of expertise? The earlier examples suggest that we ourselves would need to be in a position to have at least some independent knowledge of their mental states, so that we could see how good they are at telling what states they are in. If we could set up an external brain-scanner that detected a subject's mental states, and we could see that, in a sufficiently large number of cases, the subject's avowals agree with the results delivered by the external scanner, we would have reasons to regard the subject as an expert. Earlier (see above, p. 100 f.) I suggested that we would not be inclined to measure the subject's alleged authority against the scanner's verdicts. On the contrary, the external scanner's reliability (just like a human mind-reader's) would most likely be measured against the subject's avowals. Such is the ordinary notion of first-person privilege. Right now, however, I want to press a different point. We do not, as a matter of fact, have ready access to the internal physical conditions that constitute mental states on the materialist view, since we do not as yet possess the relevant theoretical means to identify them. So we cannot in fact establish the likelihood of the truth of subjects' avowals (and thus their reliability). This means that we are not currently in a position to declare subjects to be

---

[28] The proponent of privacy would have to maintain that, as a matter of fact, only subjects know about their own present mental states—first-person privilege simply consists in being *uniquely* placed to pass correct judgments on one's present mental states. I can enjoy this privilege even if no one else can establish that I have it. Note, however, that this (Cartesian) view does not offer an explanation of the ordinary assumption of first-person privilege or the security of avowals. This suggests that even a Cartesian may not readily construe the assumption of first-person privilege on the model of assignment of epistemic authority to experts.

I suppose that the proponent of privacy could maintain that we may have reason to assign expert self-knowledge to others by projection or analogy from our own case. This would require maintaining that each of us can have good reason to think that she herself has expert knowledge of her own present mental states.

experts on their own mental states. Yet we do assign to subjects first-person privilege. I think this tells against construing the ordinary assumption of first-person privilege on the model of expertise. If we assign special "authority" to avowing subjects, it is not simply because we make the empirical assumption that they are better placed than others to gain knowledge about (or have special epistemic access to) their present states of mind.

The application of the model of expertise to the case at hand would seem to require a view according to which the mental states of others are not even contingently (or at present) hidden from plain view. Ironically, the kind of view of mental states that fits this bill has traditionally been thought to involve an outright rejection of any genuine first-person privilege, and consequently a revision of the ordinary conception of avowals' special security. I have in mind views of the behaviorist variety, according to which the presence of a mental state of a certain type is in some way guaranteed by the presence of certain behavioral manifestations (either because a mental state is understood to be constituted by certain behavioral manifestations, or because it is understood to be *essentially* whatever causes such manifestations). On such views, it might be thought that we are, even at present, in a position to recognize that people are very good at telling what mental states they are in, and thus to declare them 'authoritative'. By the same token, however, such views would require rejecting, rather than explaining, the commonsense idea of a privilege that is essentially first-person, and that is at least relatively inalienable and non-transferable.[29]

Obviously, I have not addressed every imaginable brand of the Epistemic Approach. However, I hope I have said enough to point to a principled difficulty with the attempt to explain avowals' security and first-person privilege by appeal to the special epistemic where-withal of self-ascribers—a difficulty that is independent of the epistemic method postulated. That the Epistemic Approach has seemed attractive to philosophers with rather diverse views on the nature of mental states suggests a certain convergence on the explanatory task. I suggest that the convergence is due to conceiving the primary question concerning avowals' security and first-person privilege

---

[29] For relevant discussion, see Rorty (1970a). MacDonald (1998) tries to develop an epistemic view that addresses some of the difficulties I have raised.

to be: How is secure self-knowledge *possible*? Proponents of the Epistemic Approach plausibly answer this question by supplying different methods whose epistemic security could ground secure self-knowledge. However, I have tried to argue that their answers are not apt to address the following question, which the ordinary treatment of avowals raises, namely:

Why should it matter to the security of pronouncements about some contingent matters of fact that they concern the *very person* issuing the pronouncement, and specifically, her *occurrent mental states*?

It is with this question in mind that our search for an explanation of avowals' security continues.

## Transparency-to-the-World and the 'First-Person Perspective'

The feature I have labeled "transparency-to-the-world" has received much attention in contemporary discussions of self-knowledge. And rightly so, I think, since attending to it is potentially helpful in freeing us from erroneous pictures of our relationship to our own minds. However, combining the transparency idea with the Epistemic Approach has proved problematic and unsatisfactory. I would like to conclude this chapter with a critical examination of a different attempt to use transparency-to-the-world in understanding so-called first-person authority and the special status of avowals, an attempt recently made by Richard Moran.[30]

Beginning with the idea that we do indeed possess a special kind of self-knowledge, Moran seeks to characterize what is distinctive about this kind of self-knowledge and to explain its philosophical as well as psychological significance. He wants to establish that we possess a way of knowing our own minds that is "categorically different in kind and manner, different in consequences" from any way we have of knowing others' minds (2001: p. xxxi), and, further, "that it belongs to the concept of a person that he should be able to achieve knowledge of his attitudes in this way" (2001: p. xxx). Like Evans, Moran does not

---

[30] Moran offers his transparency view in (1988), (1994), (1994) and (1999), which form the basis of his (2001).

subscribe to the infallibility or incorrigibility of our ordinary self-ascriptions of mental states, and he too thinks that their character and status are not to be understood by appealing to a special form of inner perception. Moran also seeks to characterize the distinctive way we have of knowing our present beliefs, and other intentional states, in terms of what I've called the transparency-to-the-world of intentional avowals (see below). Like Evans, he frequently speaks of this distinctive way as constituting "a very different *basis*" on which self-ascriptions are made (1994: 157), and a kind of "*access to* what one believes" (1997: 143). He portrays it as one of "two *ways of coming to know the same thing*," (1997: 154), "two *routes* to knowledge of the same fact" (1994: 156 f.).[31]

Moran maintains that, in general, ascriptions of intentional states can be made from two different *perspectives*, or *points of view*, or *stances*: either third-person or first-person. Ascriptions made from the third-person perspective are typically made on the basis of inference or hypothesis about, observation or perception of, the subject's mental condition. By contrast, ascriptions made from the first-person perspective enjoy a certain epistemic immediacy as well as authority. A person does not ordinarily ascribe present mental states to himself on the basis of observing his own behavior, or on the basis of evidence or inference, yet there is a clear sense in which his own self-ascriptions count for more. But Moran does not think that what is distinctive about the first-person perspective is adequately captured by appeal to a form of highly reliable (and direct) access we have to our own mental states.

To bring out the distinctive character of the first-person perspective, Moran calls upon Moore's famous paradox, which involves asserting, e.g., "I believe that it's raining but it's not raining".[32] A striking feature of sentences of this sort is that they do not involve a formal contradiction. In each of them, one conjunct constitutes a claim about a first-order worldly state of affairs, and the other constitutes an ascription of a belief to oneself regarding that state of affairs. Clearly,

---

[31] The same language, which is highly suggestive of the Epistemic Approach, is retained throughout Moran (2001). However, as we shall see, it is probably more charitable not to take Moran to be trying to explain the security of avowals in terms of a highly reliable epistemic method that is used in issuing them (viz., the transparency method).

[32] For recent discussions of Moore's paradox, see Kobes (1995); Green (1999); and Falvey (2000). The paradox can also take the form "It's raining, but I don't believe it's raining".

there is no contradiction in the idea that someone's beliefs may fail to match the way things are; indeed, the very concept of belief seems bound up with the idea of such a potential gap. The paradox, then, must be seen as a consequence of the fact that we are dealing specifically with present-tense *self*-ascriptions of beliefs.

Seizing on this fact, one solution to Moore's paradox, sometimes attributed to Wittgenstein, proposes that the verb "believe" has a different meaning (or use) in the present-tense first-person case from its meaning in other contexts. Whereas in the third-person (or past-tense) use, we use "*x* believes that *p*" to ascribe to someone a particular psychological state, in its first-person present-tense use, the phrase can only serve to *present the relevant proposition*, in a guarded way perhaps. On this solution, the first-person component of a Moore sentence will not have the meaning of a self-ascription of a belief. Rather, it will be semantically equivalent to claiming the opposite of what its other component says (viz., "it's raining"). If this is so, then, as Moran notes, the paradoxical utterances will, after all, involve a contradiction: asserting *p* (perhaps with some hesitation) and at the same time denying it.[33] Moran rejects this solution for reasons closely related to those we have grouped under Semantic Continuity and Evans's Generality Constraint. He thinks we ought to preserve the idea that, at least in certain situations, one may wish to make a genuine assertion (or judgment) about one's own belief "*as* a fact about oneself" just as one does when talking about others. It is implausible to claim that "while you can talk and think about the psychological life of other people, you are peculiarly barred from doing so in your own case" (1997: 145). We should thus be suspicious of any solution to Moore's paradox that simply rules out the possibility of making genuine psychological ascriptions to oneself, for 'grammatical' or other reasons.[34]

Now consider the self-ascriptive part of the Moore sentence: "I believe that it's raining". On Moran's proposal, we could understand it from two different perspectives. Understanding it from the third-person perspective, we could regard it as an empirical claim about

---

[33] See Moran (1997: sect. II), and compare Moran (2001: 69 ff.).

[34] Another solution to the paradox dismissed by Moran is the pragmatic solution (also attributed to Wittgenstein sometimes), which portrays the paradox as an artifact of the commitments involved in the *speech*-act of asserting that *p*, which are violated by the conflicting self-ascription. Moran rightly points out that *thinking* to oneself that *p* but not believing that *p* is as problematic as asserting it in speech (2001: 70).

someone's beliefs—someone who happens to be oneself. We can then appreciate that the Moore sentence as a whole involves no formal contradiction. But it is natural to understand self-ascriptions of beliefs as offered from the first-person perspective. In its ordinary use, "I believe" serves "to declare one's view of how things are, out there in the world beyond oneself". The paradoxical appearance of the utterance can then be seen as due to the fact that we naturally read the self-ascriptive part of the Moore sentence as declaring one's belief that *p*; yet its other part is a denial of *p*'s truth. (Presumably, Moran thinks one can 'declare one's view' in thought, and not only in speech.)

Appreciating what makes Moore sentences appear paradoxical can thus serve to confirm Evans's observation that ordinary self-ascriptions of belief exhibit transparency-to-the-world. Following Evans, Moran points out that, ordinarily, if a question is posed to me (by others or by myself) about my *own* present beliefs or thoughts regarding some worldly matter, I will respond by directing my attention "transparently" to the relevant worldly matter rather than "scan the interior of my own consciousness". And Moran takes this to be characteristic of the first-person perspective. Ascriptions of belief to oneself from the first-person perspective—belief *avowals*—meet the Transparency Condition, which says that "I can report on my *belief* about X by considering (nothing but) X itself" (2001: 84), and that "in ordinary circumstances a claim concerning one's attitudes counts as a claim about their *objects*, about the world one's attitudes are directed upon" (2001: 92).

## The Limits of Transparency

In what follows, I will argue that, even apart from appealing to transparency as a secure epistemic procedure or method, what is distinctive about avowals traditionally so-called—i.e., ordinary present-tense self-ascriptions of occurrent states of mind—cannot be adequately captured by appealing to their transparency-to-the-world. For, as we shall see, this feature is characteristic only of a certain subclass of avowals. I will further argue that, while Moran may be able to account for a *kind* of first-person authority, he does not explain the privileged status of the basic sort of self-knowledge that we ordinarily associate with avowals; he fails to address what we here understand by first-person privilege. Thus, as a viable alternative to introspectionism, Moran's brand of the transparency view holds no more promise than does Evans's.[35]

**Some non-avowals are transparent-to-the-world.** Let me begin by noting that there are two kinds of ascriptions that could qualify as transparent-to-the-world, but which do not share the security of avowals. The first kind was mentioned in the discussion of Evans's transparency view: it is the class of self-reports of perceptual states (such as "I see a tree" or "I hear a loud noise"). Such reports appear to meet Moran's Transparency Condition. Paraphrasing: "I can report on my [perceptual state involving] X by considering (nothing but) X itself"; and "in ordinary circumstances a claim concerning one's [perceptual state] counts as a claim about [the presence of] its *objects*, about the world [one's state] is directed upon" (see above, p. 131). Asked whether I see *x*, I will consult the world around for *x*'s presence—I will check whether *x* is there *to be seen*. I treat a question that is about me and my state as though it were a question about the world. (Similar remarks would apply to memory reports, such as "I remember going to the movies last night".) We saw that Evans is quite happy to place avowals in the same epistemic category as self-reports of perceptual states, since he thinks that the Cartesian view, which keeps them separate, rests to some extent on an illusion of incorrigibility. But although Moran does not discuss the status of perceptual self-reports, I suspect that he would want to treat them as epistemically different from avowals. Yet it is not clear what in his view would allow him to do so.

The second kind of ascriptions to be considered are ordinary, non-theoretical ascriptions of intentional states to others. Moran repeatedly

---

[35] At least some of the difficulties I raised for Evans's use of transparency apply equally to Moran's (although one would need to recast them in terms appropriate to Moran's exposition, which I have not done here). The general criticism leveled against both concerns the *scope* of the transparency feature: the feature is not one shared by *all and only* avowals (ordinarily understood). In later chapters, I will present the transparency-to-the-world of (a subclass of) avowals as a consequence of another feature that *is* shared by all avowals and is *not* shared by ordinary reports, including some that *are* transparent-to-the-world.

On a charitable reading (which I will be following below), Moran's view has resources for addressing the charge that transparency is a feature shared by some non-avowals. However, once these resources are put to explicit use, it becomes clear that the view is not apt to explain what is sometimes called "*basic* self-knowledge"—the kind of self-knowledge that concerns the introspectionist, and which is represented by a wide range of distinctively secure avowals.

points out that intentional self-ascriptions are not made exclusively from the first-person point of view. (Another way of putting this: not all such self-ascriptions constitute avowals.) We sometimes do ascribe to ourselves intentions, beliefs, desires, and such, from what he describes as the third-person, or theoretical, perspective. But Moran *also* thinks that intentional ascriptions to others are not made exclusively from the theoretical perspective. Like many who oppose the so-called 'theory'-theory in the philosophy of mind, he does not think that our psychological ascriptions to others are all made in light of "the purely third-person project of explaining and predicting their behaviour" (1994: 170). Just as, when trying to understand ourselves, we may "bracket" the question of the truth of our beliefs and be concerned with explanations of our behavior, so when interacting with others, we may be directly concerned with the truth of their beliefs rather than with the explanatory and predictive adequacy of our belief ascriptions.

This means that often, when ascribing beliefs (and other intentional attitudes) to others, our gaze is also directed at the world outside, not at inner mental workings. To use a familiar example from the 'simulation' literature, we see that our friend who is ahead of us on the trail is scared, we look ahead to see what he sees, and noticing the big scary bear, we say (or think), "He thinks he's about to be attacked by the bear," or "He's scared of the bear." We do not focus on whatever internal states might best explain and help predict our friend's behavior. We attend instead to the world around, and project onto the friend an intentional state that we would ascribe to ourselves, as we try to see things through his eyes. Our question is *not* the third-person theoretical question, "What is going on inside him?", which is to be answered by finding the best causal-predictive explanation of his behavior. Rather, we ask the world-oriented question, "What is one *to* think/feel now?", which is to be answered by transparent consideration of the world.[36] But if this is so, it becomes important to understand what is distinctive about transparent *self*-ascriptions—i.e., about avowals.

In order to understand how Moran would separate avowals from other transparent ascriptions, we should consider his opposition to

---

[36] See Gordon (1986); Goldman (1989); Heal (1989); and Moran (1994). See also Loar (1987) and Blackburn (1993).

understanding first-person self-knowledge in terms of special epistemic access. Much in the spirit of our earlier attack on the Epistemic
Approach, he argues that no amount of theoretical expertise, and no
degree of privacy or special reliability—not even 'mind reading as
applied to oneself' or 'self-telepathy'—could yield the distinctive
kind of self-knowledge afforded by the first-person stance. Moreover,
unlike Evans, he does not seem to think of conformity to the
Transparency Condition in terms of employing an epistemically
superior method for gaining knowledge about what intentional state
one is in. First-person self-knowledge, he maintains, is *avowable*

knowledge, where "the connection with the *avowal* of one's attitudes
would not be established by the addition of any degree of such epistemic ingredients" (2001: 93). This is because, as he understands it,
avowing is not a matter of aiming at a correct identification of the
mental states one is in. Correspondingly, our primary concern when
considering—as an audience—a subject's avowals is not with the
subject's own better view of, or 'take' on, those facts.

If meeting the Transparency Condition does not yield any straightforward epistemic advantage, how does it help to account for the
distinctive status of avowals? Moran's answer is that we must see "the
claim of transparency [as] grounded in the *deferral* of theoretical
reflection on one's state to *deliberative* reflection about it" and recognize "the primacy of the deliberative stance within the first-person"
both philosophically and "in the life of the person". Conformity to
this condition represents a "*normative* demand"; it is not a matter of
adopting a reliable epistemic procedure. (See Moran (2001: p. xvi), my
emphases.) In a key passage, he offers the following summary:

[T]he first-person perspective, and the authority of the first-person, has two
distinct aspects that normally run together but can in principle come apart,
and only one of them fits the traditional understanding of a purely epistemic
capacity. One aspect is the familiar feature of epistemic immediacy; . . . [the
other is] that in ordinary circumstances a claim concerning one's attitudes
counts as a claim about their *objects*, about the world one's attitudes are
directed upon. It is part of the ordinary first-person point of view on one's
psychological life both that evidence is not consulted, and that, for example,
the expression of one's belief carries with it *a commitment to its truth*. What
we have been calling the Transparency Condition is equally a feature of
ordinary first-person discourse. But . . . it is no more than ordinary, and

when endorsement fails, then so does transparency, for *without endorsement the person cannot declare his belief through avowal of it*. He might still, however, retain a kind of immediate epistemic access to it. (2001: 91 f.), all emphases but the first are mine)

Thus, transparency as Moran sees it is essentially tied to the *commissive* character of avowals. When I ascribe to myself a belief that *p*, for example, I *commit* myself to *p*'s truth. By contrast, when I ascribe a belief to another, even if I base ascription on a transparent consideration of the world, my ascription only offers what I take the *other's* commitment to be. Presumably, the same applies to other intentional ascriptions. When I ascribe to myself wanting *x*, or being mad at *y*, I commit myself to *x*'s being desirable, and to *y*'s being maddening, respectively. But when ascribing desires, etc. to someone else, I can fully distance myself from such evaluative judgments. From the first-person perspective, there is an "unavoidable . . . connection between the question about some psychological matter of fact and a commitment to something that goes beyond the psychological fact" (1997: 147–8). Unlike ascriptions that simply cite the objective facts about someone's present mental states, first-person self-ascriptions of intentional attitudes—intentional avowals—are declarations of one's commitments.

It is important for Moran to insist that not all intentional self-ascriptions are commissive. We do sometimes ascribe intentional states to ourselves with an eye to reporting a purely psychological fact about ourselves, using evidence, behavioral observation, theory, or self-interpretation. However, Moran thinks that such self-ascriptions are in an important sense alienated, and that the kind of self-knowledge they represent is "merely attributional". The limitations of the purely theoretical or empirical point of view on oneself can be appreciated when we reflect on psychoanalytic contexts, where one may acquire reliable information about one's hidden wishes, fears, or beliefs. In the course of therapy, a patient may become thoroughly convinced, for example, that, deep down, she believes her brother has betrayed her. Such theoretical realization, however, is not what the therapeutic process primarily aims at. It is only when the patient becomes able to avow, "I believe my brother has betrayed me," that the therapy will be declared successful. At that point, the patient no longer accepts the self-ascription as a merely theoretical hypothesis about her beliefs that best explains her behavior and other mental states. She now expresses her commitment to—or endorsement of—the claim that her brother has betrayed her. Until she can do so, she will remain alienated from her own belief, and the therapeutic process cannot be seen as complete.[37]

That the crucial contrast Moran sees between avowals and other ascriptions is not to be captured *simply* through the contrast between ascriptions that are transparent-to-the-world and those that are not can be seen when considering the way Moran contrasts his own view of first-person authority with his opponent's:

[T]he primary thought gaining expression in the idea of 'first-person authority' may not be that the person himself must always 'know best' what he thinks about something, but rather that it is *his business* what he thinks about something, that it is *up to him*. In declaring his belief he does not express himself as an expert witness to a realm of psychological fact, so much as *he expresses his rational authority over that realm*. (2001: 124 f., last two emphases mine)[38]

The dimension of endorsement is what expresses itself in one aspect of first-person authority, where it concerns *the authority of the person to make up his mind, change his mind, endorse some attitude or disavow it. This is a form of authority tied to the presuppositions of rational agency* and is different in kind from the more purely epistemic authority that may attach to the special immediacy of the person's access to his mental life. (2001: 92, my emphases)

The crucial contrast for Moran, then, is between ascriptions that employ the theoretical (or empirical) perspective and those that play a *practical*, or *deliberative*, role. And although Moran is not concerned to deny that there *are* objective facts about one's states of mind, his appeal to transparency is in aid of capturing the deliberative character of avowals, rather than their status *qua* uniquely secure pronouncements on a certain range of facts. Once this is appreciated, however, I think it can be argued that Moran's account is in a different explanatory business altogether from that of the Epistemic Approach. This claim will gain support once we see the limited applicability of Moran's transparency-as-commitment as the mark of avowals.

**Many avowals are not commissive.** The notion of commitment or endorsement has the clearest application to the case of avowals of

---

[37] See Moran (1988: 142 f.; 1997: 152, 156) and compare (2001: 83 ff.).
[38] See also Moran (2001: 55 ff., 77 ff.).

present beliefs. One does not, in the ordinary case, avow believing that $p$, without thereby committing oneself to $p$'s truth. We can perhaps find commitments whenever there is an identifiable cognitive component in the self-ascription. An avowal of a desire for $x$ could perhaps be seen as an expression of the judgment that $x$ is desirable, and thus as one's endorsement of $x$. The avowal of an intention can be seen as expressing a resolution to do something, and thus as undertaking the commitment to do it. In the case of avowals of fear, anger, shame, etc. we could perhaps point to whatever commitments are involved in the corresponding judgment—e.g., that some worldly item is frightening, maddening, shameful, etc.[39] But what commitments would be involved in avowing hunger, thirst, non-specific rage or joy, pain, and so on? None, it seems. Avowing "I have a terrible headache", for example, *may*, at least under certain circumstances, incur a practical commitment to take actions necessary to relieve the headache, if possible. But this commitment is one that is connected to the fact that one is indeed in the state that the avowal ascribes to one. It is clearly not the kind of rational or practical commitment that Moran connects with the transparency-to-the-world of avowals. For it is not "commitment to something that goes beyond the [relevant] psychological fact", and which is given by what the ascribed psychological fact is said to be *about*.

The problem is symptomatic of a general difficulty with using transparency-to-the-world to mark the class of avowals. We have already seen aspects of this difficulty earlier, when criticizing Evans's appeal to transparency as an epistemic method (see above, pp. 114–16). The criticism was that the transparency method has application only where there is some intentional content (some propositional content or intentional object) that one could attend to, in lieu of attending to one's internal intentional state. Now, the key idea of transparency-to-the-world survives even if we set aside transparency as an *epistemic procedure*. It is an idea that Moran still adheres to: namely, that in the first-person case one can trade a question that is about one's mental state for a question that is about the objects or states of affairs that the state is said or thought to be about. Such trading would seem to require that the relevant self-ascription involve a *specification* of some

---

[39] See Moran (1988: 138).

intentional content. Yet not all avowals involve such specification. The category of avowals as delineated both traditionally and by pre-theoretical common sense includes many non-intentional avowals—i.e., avowals that ascribe a present mental state without assigning to it or specifying any intentional content. Recalling some of our earlier examples, we often say things like "I'm feeling so uncomfortable", "I am furious!", "I feel very sad", "I feel hungry/thirsty/tired/achy". Such avowals seem at least as secure as intentional avowals.[40] When made in either speech or thought, they are taken (both traditionally and intuitively) to represent things we are in a special position to pronounce on. Yet they do not seem to meet Moran's Transparency Condition. Indeed, they do not seem to be pronouncements made from a deliberative stance at all.[41]

Worse still, even when it comes to intentional self-ascriptions that *do* involve a specification of content, it does not seem that the idea of commitment or endorsement is always to the point. I often ascribe to myself a thought or wish that *p*, or a desire for or fear of or disgust at *x*, with an eye to declaring my view on the world (viz., that *p* is or should be the case, or that *x* is desirable or frightening or disgusting). But this is not always the case. "I really want that piece of candy," I say (or think). I know the candy would be terrible for my teeth; as I look at it, I think it's pretty gross, and so on. Still, my avowal stands. Or, thinking of the therapeutic context again, at the analyst's office I declare, gasping, "I feel like I can't breathe." It would be a poor therapist who saw his job done once he could get me to see (and even be committed to the claim) that my air passages are clear, there's plenty of air *to* breathe, and so on. And there are also avowals of present thoughts passing through one's mind: "I'm just thinking about my good friend Jim." In these kinds of cases, it looks for all the world as though it is crucial for the production as well as the uptake of one's avowal that it concerns one's present mental state. And it seems that the security of one's avowal—its presumed correctness and relative

---

[40] Indeed, it is not uncommon for philosophers to take so-called phenomenal avowals as more paradigmatic of first-person authority. Thus, in his summary of the traditional view of avowals, Wright (1998: 14–15) presents phenomenal avowals as enjoying "strong authority": a sincere, competent subject's making the avowal provides a guarantee of its truth, whereas 'attitudinal avowals' enjoy only weak, presumptive authority.

[41] See n.10 for the point that, even if one maintains that all mental states have representational content, one can still recognize a difference between intentional avowals, which *specify* intentional content, and phenomenal avowals, which (often) do not.

epistemic unassailability—must have *something* to do with one's privileged position with respect to that state (however non-epistemically characterized). Commitment and endorsement regarding whatever that state is about seem beside the point, or at best of secondary importance.

Moran seems aware of the limited applicability of his notion of transparency-as-commitment. In a section defending the connection between first-person self-knowledge on the one hand and agency and responsibility on the other, he explicitly contrasts sensations with beliefs and other attitudes. "A sensation of pain or vertigo really is something one may be passively subject to, something that just happens"; "[b]eliefs and other attitudes, on the other hand, are stances of the person to which the demand for justification is internal" (2001: 114). This demand is essentially linked to the characterization of the first-person stance as deliberative, and of first-person authority as the authority of an autonomous and rational agent. However, the link is severed not only in the case of sensations, but also in the case of the attitudes. For, Moran observes:

Some desires, such as those associated with hunger or sheer fatigue, may be experienced by the person as feelings that simply come over him. They simply happen. . . . The person's stance toward such desires, and how he deals with them, may be little different from his stance toward any other empirical phenomenon he confronts. From this angle, a brute desire is a bit of reality for the agent to accommodate, like a sensation, or a broken leg, or an obstacle in one's path. (2001: 114 f.)

Moran refers to brute desires as "unmotivated" desires, which (following Nagel) he distinguishes from what he terms "motivated", or "judgment-sensitive", desires. These latter are desires whose persistence in the agent depends on the sustaining of certain justificatory or evaluative beliefs.

For the person himself . . . his motivated desire is not a brute empirical phenomenon he must simply accommodate . . . as a 'judgment-sensitive' attitude, [it] owes its existence (as an empirical psychological fact) to his own deliberations and overall assessment. (2001: 115 f.)

This means that, even among avowals that do specify an intentional content for the ascribed state—avowals of desires and other intentional attitudes—Moran's account is intended to apply *only* to those avowals that ascribe 'motivated', or 'judgment-sensitive', states. In the preface to his book, Moran mentions that he will be concentrating on "the knowledge a person may have of his own attitudes: beliefs, desires, intentions, and various emotional states", setting aside questions about "whether a person can be said to *know* his qualitative sensations in a way that is essentially unavailable to another person and if so, how such 'knowing' is to be understood" (2001: p. xxxiii). But it now turns out that even as regards one's own attitudes, the domain for Moran's account of first-person authority and self-knowledge is restricted to self-ascriptions of attitudes the very existence of which is subject to change through one's deliberation.

**Even where the notion of rational authority is applicable, its connection to what we have called first-person privilege is not clear**. Suppose we focus, with Moran, on commissive self-ascriptions of 'motivated' attitudes. It still remains unclear how the transparency-as-commitment account helps to explain the special security ordinarily assigned to such pronouncements and the commonsense intuition that subjects are in a privileged position to make them. If it does not, then it can be charged that rational authority is different in kind from so-called first-person authority, and that it is not apt to illuminate *basic* self-knowledge (the sort of self-knowledge we ordinarily take avowals to represent).

The idea of commitment can help fund a sharp first-person/third-person asymmetry. But one must tread carefully here. Utterances of "I promise to do the dishes tonight", or "I hereby take you to be my lawful husband", or "I name this ship 'Martha'", contrast sharply with their third-person analogues precisely in point of the commitments involved. In suitable circumstances, the first-person utterances in each case involve expressing certain commitments, whereas their third-person analogues represent mere reports of commitments undertaken by someone else. In these kinds of cases, there is *also* a certain kind of authority granted to the utterer. Given the right background, the one who says "I promise" is granted the authority to make the promise; the one who says "I name this ship 'Bertha'" is authorized to christen; and the one who says "I pronounce you husband and wife" is authorized to marry. But this is the authority of *authorship*. It is granted to the utterers in virtue of their being the legitimate agents of certain performative acts—agents who, in the act of utterance, are in a position to *bring certain states of affairs into existence.*

It is possible to defend this 'legislative' or 'constitutive' view in the case of self-interpretation of certain of our emotions and propositional attitudes. Thus, Charles Taylor has argued that "formulating how we feel, or coming to adopt a new formulation, can frequently change how we feel", where the change is not merely causal but logical. "When I come to see that my feeling of guilt was false, or my feeling of love self-deluded, the emotions themselves are different," so "our understanding of [certain emotions] or the interpretations we accept are constitutive of the emotion" (1985: 100–1).[42] This may have plausibility in some cases. If I take a question about how I feel about something as an invitation to *make up my mind* how *to* feel about the matter, then it makes sense to suggest that the authority I have over the answer is of the 'constitutive' type. For presumably, in such a case, there is no antecedent fact of the matter about my feelings; or if there is, it is not what I aim to pronounce on.

On the constitutive model, avowals would be seen as performative acts which bring into existence the relevant states of affairs, acts of *forming* an intention, *deciding* what *to* want, believe, hope for, etc. This seems a far cry from the naïve conception, according to which avowals are pronouncements on the self-ascriber's present mental state, a state which others (and she herself) may also be able to report from the third-person point of view. Among what we would normally consider to be avowals are self-ascriptions of occurrent states (whether of intentional or phenomenal states) that we in some sense find ourselves in— feeling pain, joy, rage, momentary sadness, thinking about lunch, wanting to touch our friend's hand, intending to finish the chapter, etc. And we naïvely think of our avowals as in some way reflecting these states we are in, not as in any way bringing them into existence. When it comes to such avowals, our saying does not seem to make it so.

We have seen that Moran wants to insist that the first-person perspective gives us a "route to knowledge" or "a way of coming to

---

[42] Quoted in Moran (1988: 136). Taylor's constitutive view is the subject matter of that paper (which is the basis of ch. 2 of Moran (2001)). Moran attempts to articulate "the restricted sense in which the facts about a person's mental life are bound up with how he interprets them" (1988: 135). Tanney (1996) offers some interesting cases to which the constitutive view plausibly applies.

know" *the same facts* that can be depicted from the third-person perspective (see above, p. 129). Construing first-person authority on the above constitutive model seems to conflict with regarding avowals as pronouncing on facts about one's mental states that are objective, at least in the sense of obtaining independently of anyone's judgment that they obtain, and being equally accessible using other routes. Thus, Moran understandably distances himself from this model.[43] But it is not clear how Moran's own portrayal of first-person authority as rational authority avoids some of the pitfalls of the constitutive model.

**Like the constitutive view, Moran's view cannot compete with epistemic accounts of avowals' security.** Consider a self-ascription of a present motivated desire: "I want to finish this chapter tonight." Let us grant that the ascribed desire itself is judgment-sensitive in Moran's sense; it depends for its justification on various beliefs I have, and losing the justification for it would make a difference as to whether I *continue* to have it (see (2001: 115)). What are we to make of the alleged authority I have regarding my self-ascription of this desire? Could it be exhausted by the fact that I have rational control over the desire itself—the unique power to change it in consequence of direct reflection on what justifies it? Doesn't crediting me with this power require supposing that I am able securely to *tell*, at least at some point, that I actually *have* that desire? Don't we have to suppose that I am in a position to tell what my desires *are*, if we take it that I am able to exercise that power effectively? If so, then it would seem that the assignment of rational authority depends on the presumption that avowals are secure, and presupposes what I have called first-person privilege. Even if the appeal to the transparent-cum-commissive character of avowals and to rational authority can help us mark a significant first-person/third-person contrast, it cannot play the requisite explanatory role in an account of avowals' distinctive security and of privileged self-knowledge.

---

[43] See especially (2001: 42 ff.), where Moran distinguishes a more radical from a more modest version of the "self-constitution" idea. He rejects the former, but clearly has sympathy for the latter, which he later expounds in terms of connections to deliberation, rationality, and autonomy. I think that some of the reasons Moran himself offers in rejection of the more radical version still tell against his own characterizations of the first-person view as essentially practical, or deliberative, and his portrayal of first-person authority as rational authority. In his (1997: 145 ff., 157 f.) it seems clear that Moran himself is sensitive to this tension. What is less clear is how he offers to resolve it. But I cannot here undertake to discuss such exegetical matters. (My present interest in Moran's view, recall, is as a potential alternative to epistemic views of avowals' security and first-person privilege.)

It can be agreed on all sides that, in the realm of his own beliefs and desires, a person has the kind of authority Moran is speaking of, which no one else has. In a sense that may be essential to being a rational and practical agent, what a person thinks, believes, intends, wants, prefers, and chooses is 'up to him', and is 'his business'. This is the kind of authority that one can assert with respect to one's attitudes, as one "speaks for" (as Moran often puts it) one's opinions, preferences, etc. Following Kant and Sartre (among others), we can accept that genuine rational and practical agency actually requires that we have this kind of authority, and that there is a deep connection between at least one kind of self-knowledge—reflective self-knowledge—and freedom, or autonomy.[44] Still, it seems that rational authority can be separated from another kind of authority that we can be said to have as avowing subjects. This is the authority—or privilege (as I prefer to refer to it)—of someone in a special position correctly to tell and pronounce on what her present thoughts, desires, preferences, etc. *are*. Acknowledging that we have this latter kind of privilege, of course, does not require subscribing to certain accounts of it. In particular, it does not require adopting the Epistemic Approach. However, Moran's construal of first-person authority as rational authority does not seem apt to explain this privilege.

The main criticism leveled against the Epistemic Approach earlier in this chapter was that it fails to provide an account that respects Epistemic Asymmetry in its full scope and captures the distinctive character of first-person privilege. Moran clearly shares my opposition to the Epistemic Approach. However, it emerges that what Moran takes to be distinctive about first-person perspective is *not at all* a matter of our being in a better position to pronounce correctly on our present state of mind. Correlatively, his characterization of avowals as transparent is *not* in aid of explaining why avowals, understood as pronouncements on our present states of mind, are especially apt to be true, or more protected from certain epistemic errors, or less vulnerable to correction. This suggests that Moran is engaged in a different explanatory project from proponents of the Epistemic Approach. If this is so, then, whatever its merits, Moran's transparency

---

[44] Moran elaborates on these connections in (2001: 138 ff.), citing, in addition to Sartre and Kant, Korsgaard and Nagel.

view cannot be seen as a viable alternative to the epistemic accounts we have considered so far.

In the next chapter, I will begin to introduce the alternative I myself favor. So it will be useful to conclude this chapter by indicating briefly how Moran's view, as well as the other views canvassed in this chapter, fails to meet what I consider to be desiderata on an adequate account of avowals' security. As a reminder, in Chapter 1 (p. 20), I mentioned the following desiderata:

**D1.** The account should explain what renders avowals protected from ordinary epistemic assessments.

**D2.** It should explain why avowals' security is unparalleled: why there are asymmetries in security between avowals and all other empirical ascriptions, including (truth-continually-equivalent) third-person ascriptions and non-mental first-person ascriptions.

**D3.** It should explain the non-negotiable character of the security— the fact that it is 'non-transferable' and 'inalienable'.

**D4.** It should apply to *both* intentional and non-intentional avowals alike, and allow us to separate avowals from other ascriptions in terms of their security.
(Meeting D1–D4 would amount to accounting for Epistemic Asymmetry in its full scope.)

**D5.** It should accommodate the continuities in semantic and logical structure between avowals and other ascriptions. In particular, it should present avowals as truth-assessable.
(Meeting D5 would amount to accommodating Semantic Continuity.)

**D6.** It should avoid portraying avowals as absolutely infallible or incorrigible.

**D7.** It should avoid appealing to Cartesian dualist ontology.

**D8.** It should allow for the possibility that avowals represent privileged self-knowledge.
(Meeting D8 would make room for a non-deflationary view of self-knowledge.)

Both the materialist introspectionist view and Evans's view are put forth with an eye to meeting D5 and D7. On both views, avowals represent one's judgments on certain of one's present states, which can be interchanged in context with other judgments *salva veritate*, and do not require supposing that the judgments are about states of an immaterial Ego. (The materialist introspectionist explicitly begins with the idea that mental states are states of our brains.) Neither view maintains the infallibility or incorrigibility of avowals. So they adhere to D6, as well. However, I have argued that neither view is apt to explain why avowals should be more resistant to epistemic criticism and correction than, specifically, non-mental self-ascriptions that are immune to error through misidentification; so these views do not adequately meet D1. The materialist introspectionist requires denying the non-negotiable character of avowals' security (D3) and accepting the possibility of brute as well as global error. At best, this view would allow us to meet a very modest version of D2, compromising the idea that avowals' security is unparalleled. Evans's account, on the other hand, is able to offer a distinctive epistemic method of ascription (the transparency procedure), so he goes some way toward meeting D2. But his method is not applicable to all avowals, and *is* applicable to some non-avowals. Neither the materialist introspectionist nor Evans is able to meet D4; thus they both fail to respect Epistemic Asymmetry in its full scope. As for D8, both views may be said to allow for the possibility of genuine self-knowledge as represented in avowals, though its privileged character is qualified. Finally, the Epistemic Approach in general can be accused of misconstruing first-person privilege on the model of epistemic authority or expertise.

This last criticism is one that Moran clearly escapes. On his construal, first-person privilege is not a matter of epistemic access and expertise. By way of avoiding the expertise model, Moran offers a characterization of avowals as self-ascriptions that are distinctively first-person. He often denies that avowals are incorrigible or infallible (D6), and he explicitly portrays the first-person perspective from which they are made as a different 'route' to knowledge of the same facts knowable in other ways, suggesting that he aims to respect D5. Also, his account in no way appeals to Cartesian dualist ontology (D7). (It may be worth noting, however, that he does ground the claim that we have rational authority in the claim that such authority is necessary for autonomous deliberation and free agency. There are those who think we could not possess genuine autonomy and freedom if we were nothing over and above our physical bodies. And there will be those who would balk at the idea that the ordinary assumption of basic self-knowledge rests on commitment to the weighty assumption that we are free agents.)

Now, Moran argues that the ability to make first-person self-ascriptions is essentially linked to being a person, and the kind of self-knowledge they represent is both philosophically and psychologically indispensable. To that extent his view seems able to meet D1–D3. However, I argued that, although Moran's notion of transparency-as-commitment allows him to characterize *a* class of self-ascriptions that both are distinctively first-person and genuinely contrast with other ascriptions, it does not enable him to provide a suitably general account of avowals' security that captures Epistemic Asymmetry (while respecting Semantic Continuity). By the same token, while he may have identified *a* kind of authority that only we ourselves enjoy with respect to (some of) our mental states, this is not the kind of broad and basic authority (read: privilege) we attribute to people with respect to their occurrent mental states. So Moran fails to meet D4, and ultimately does not succeed in respecting Epistemic Asymmetry as I have understood it. Finally, as regards D8, Moran's view accommodates the kind of privileged self-knowledge we can have of what we *shall* believe, or desire, or intend, as we transparently deliberate, *qua* rational or practical agents, on the reasons for our beliefs, desires, and intentions. To the extent that this is the *only* kind of privileged self-knowledge he would make room for, his view of ordinary self-knowledge would seem deflationary; so we may question how well he meets D8.

Both Evans and Moran are motivated by a search for a non-Cartesian view of avowals and self-knowledge. They both seize on the transparency-to-the-world of avowals by way of rejecting the inner theatre spectator's view of our relationship to our own minds. As we shall see in the next chapter, I agree that the spectator's view is apt to lead us astray in this domain. However, I do not think that either of these authors is able to provide an account that is broad enough to constitute a true rival to the Cartesian introspectionist view. Yet I believe that, until we have such an account, the specter of Cartesianism will continue to haunt us.

# 5

# Content Externalism, Skepticism, and the Recognitional Conception of Self-Knowledge

In the previous chapter I argued against the adequacy of several attempts to explain what I have called the *ascriptive security* of avowals. I considered two major representatives of the Epistemic Approach: the materialist introspectionist view and the transparency view offered by Evans. The two views contrast sharply. Evans rejects the introspectionist idea that a subject who ascribes a mental state to herself must somehow inspect her own mind to determine the presence of the state in herself. Nonetheless, we saw that his own positive account still relies on the idea that mental self-ascription involves the use of an epistemic method or basis. Thus, Evans can be seen as adhering to the core idea of the Epistemic Approach that if avowals are especially secure, it is because they represent well-founded judgments concerning subjects' own present mental states. I argued that, in general, this way of conceiving avowals' security does not do justice to the distinctive, non-negotiable character of first-person privilege. I also considered a non-epistemic version of the transparency view (offered by Moran) that is designed to do that. I concluded that Moran's transparency view, like Evans's view, focuses too narrowly on intentional avowals—ones that explicitly assign intentional content to the self-ascribed state. (In addition, Moran's account in terms of rational authority turns out to be engaged in a different explanatory project from epistemic accounts, and so cannot serve to replace them.) If the security of *non*-intentional avowals is not plausibly understood in terms of their transparency-to-the-world, then we have not yet found a viable alternative to the introspectionist account.

In this chapter I focus on one aspect of the ascriptive security of intentional avowals: the security of content ascription. When avowing an intentional state such as a thought *about* or wish *for* something, or fear *of* or anger *at* someone, and so on, one is presumed to be in an especially good position to know, or tell, the propositional content or the intentional object ("intentional content" for short) of one's state. This is an aspect of avowals' security that world-directed views would initially seem better placed to handle than introspectionist views, since they do not suppose that we should be able to glean what a state we are in is *about* by 'looking inside' and considering only the state itself. However, there is a recently much-discussed puzzle regarding our ability to have secure, privileged knowledge of the content of our thoughts and other mental states, which the transparency, or world-directed, views considered thus far have left untouched. The puzzle is how such security can be reconciled with *externalism about content*— i.e., the view that the contents of our thoughts, beliefs, and other contentful mental states are determined by the presence and nature of extra-mental elements, of which we may, as thinkers, be ignorant.

The puzzle regarding the compatibility of content externalism and ordinary self-knowledge of content is of special interest to us for several reasons. First, as hinted above, the puzzle of content externalism and self-knowledge can be raised in a way that cuts across the divide between inner gaze and world-directed views. World-directed views maintain that to determine whether we, e.g., believe that $p$, or desire $x$, or are afraid of $y$, we direct our attention not inward but outward, to the worldly states and objects mentioned in the content-clause of the relevant self-ascription. But the question remains how we can know that we are assigning the *right* content to our state in our self-ascription in the first-place.[1] A close examination of the puzzle can thus help to support my claim that none of the views we have considered thus far holds the key to our understanding of avowals' special security. Secondly, it has been argued that, if content externalism is true, then we may have to face a form of *skepticism about content*, analogous to the more familiar

---

[1] Considering $p$ directly may be the best thing to do to decide whether I (am to) believe, or want, or hope that $p$; but it seems powerless to determine that $p$ is indeed the content of a present state of mine (which seems in a way to be a prior question). The transparency-to-the-world of avowals can thus be exploited only once we have settled on a particular content for the ascribed state. (The puzzle arising from content-externalism is not addressed by Evans; Moran mentions the puzzle, but sets it aside (2001: p. xxxiii, 15 ff.).)

skepticism about the external world. Such skepticism would pose a challenge to one aspect of the commonsense view of avowals' security: the idea that our ordinary claims about the *content* of our present thoughts, wishes, and other intentional attitudes are more epistemically secure than everyday claims about the external world. Uncovering what goes wrong with this skeptical challenge will help clarify and deepen our understanding of the commonsense view. Finally, examining how content externalism can be reconciled with ordinary self-knowledge can also serve to motivate more directly the view of avowals' security and self-knowledge that I shall be developing in subsequent chapters.

I begin with a comparison between skepticism about our knowledge of content and external-world skepticism, which fuels the incompatibility argument. I then argue that the content skeptic who enlists content externalism must tacitly rely on a *recognitional conception* of our knowledge of content in particular, and of self-knowledge more generally. Yet, on this conception, skepticism about knowledge of content may be inevitable, *even if we abandon content externalism.* This should give us good reason to reject the recognitional conception itself. The question then arises: What can we put in its place? In the next chapter, I propose that ordinary self-ascriptions of contentful mental states, even if not absolutely infallible or incorrigible, are protected from skepticism about content precisely because they do *not* represent recognitional self-judgments. To anticipate, I argue that, when ascribing an intentional state (and, more generally, occurrent mental states) to oneself in the ordinary way, one's self-ascription is no more grounded in recognition of some internal state as being of a certain kind or possessing a certain intentional content than it is grounded in recognition of some individual as being oneself. Thus, intentional avowals (and avowals more generally) enjoy *ascriptive immunity to error*—a notion I model after the notion of immunity to error through misidentification discussed in earlier chapters.

## External-Content Skepticism Meets External-World Skepticism

As I am sitting at my desk in front of my computer, a thought crosses my mind: there's water in the glass. The thought has a particular content: *that there is water in the glass*. And, if all is well, there is indeed water in the glass; that is, my thought is true. According to *external-world skepticism*, I still do not *know* that there is water in the glass, because for all I know, I may only be under some kind of illusion that there is water in the glass; this is not something that my way of telling what is in front of me allows me to rule out. So my belief that there is water in the glass, even if true, is not sufficiently warranted to constitute knowledge. According to *content skepticism*, we can construct a skeptical challenge to the idea that we know the contents of our own present thoughts that is parallel to the external-world skeptic's. The content skeptic claims that I cannot know I am *thinking* that there is water in my glass, even if in fact that is what I am thinking. This is because, for all I know, I may be under some kind of illusion that I am thinking there's water in the glass; my way of telling what I am thinking does not allow me to rule this out. So, if I have a belief that I'm thinking that there's water in the glass, then this belief, even if true, is not sufficiently warranted to constitute knowledge.

As common sense would have it, though, self-ascriptions of contentful thoughts, etc. represent remarkably secure knowledge—much more secure than the knowledge we have of our extra-mental world. The commonsense view regarding our knowledge of content can be summarized as follows:

**CSK** (Content Self-Knowledge): When avowing contentful mental states, we securely assign content to our states without relying on any inference, evidence, or observation. Our assignments of content are not taken to be subject to brute error and are presumed to be correct. They are also not subjected to requests for reasons or ordinary epistemic criticism. Nevertheless, they represent genuine and privileged knowledge we possess of the contents of our present mental states.[2]

CSK is fairly modest. It does not imply absolute infallibility or even incorrigibility; nor does it imply self-omniscience regarding one's present mental states. I think this is in keeping with the commonsense view. The crucial idea CSK aims to capture is that each of us can tell knowledgeably *what* she is now thinking, hoping, feeling, wanting, fearing, etc. with unparalleled, if not absolute, security. Ordinary

---

[2] This formulation of CSK is somewhat different from the one offered in Bar-On (2004a). The differences merely reflect conformity to previous discussion in the present work.

content self-knowledge is privileged at least in the sense that we can each have it with respect to our own, and only our own, present mental states, and the self-ascriptions representative of this knowledge enjoy a special warrant. Can the commonsense confidence about ordinary knowledge of content be sustained in the face of a skepticism that proceeds by analogy to external-world skepticism?

Suppose I now say, or think:

**EW**: There is water in the glass.

The external-world skeptic invites me to question whether EW represents something I actually know. When doing so, I may at least initially take the presence of the external-world belief and its content (viz., *that there is water in the glass*) as somehow given to me. Moreover, although the challenge issued by the Cartesian external-world skeptic is supposed to generalize to all of our external-world beliefs, it is not supposed to culminate in doubts about those beliefs that concern the contents of our present states of mind. In fact, Descartes himself, who articulated a dominant form of external-world skepticism, thought that beliefs of the latter type ultimately *could* not be open to the kind of doubt to which beliefs about the extra-mental world can be subjected. This is because, he argued, one cannot so much as doubt that $p$ without thinking that $p$, since doubting is a species of thinking. And this is something each of us can recognize by going through the *cogito* reasoning.

Full symmetry would require the external-content skeptic to invite me to doubt that I now have a thought with content $p$ while at the same time holding fixed, or at least not questioning, my belief that $p$. But it is not clear how I am to proceed. How can I confidently affirm that there is water in the glass, even as I doubt that I am now thinking that there's water in the glass? Am I to think, "There's definitely water in the glass. But, for all I know, I may not now be *thinking* that there's water in the glass"? This seems like a version of Moore's paradox.[3] Just as I cannot doubt $p$ without thinking that $p$, so I cannot affirm $p$ without thinking that $p$; and this too is something I can easily recognize. Explicitly entertaining a doubt about whether some external-world proposition that I believe is true, as well as expressing confidence that such a proposition is

---

[3] I discuss Moore's paradox above, Ch. 4 (pp. 129 ff.)

true, is inconsistent with simultaneously entertaining a doubt about whether I am thinking that $p$. But this suggests that external-content skepticism cannot proceed in a way that is fully parallel to the way (Cartesian) external-world skepticism proceeds. Each of us can 'internalize' the external-world skeptic's challenge, and pose it in the form: as I am thinking that $p$ is the case, for all I know, $p$ may not be the case. Yet it seems we cannot pose to ourselves the external-content skeptic's challenge in a parallel form: viz., as I am thinking that I am thinking that $p$, for all I know, it may *not* be the case that I'm thinking that $p$.

Another notable feature of Cartesian external-world skepticism is its fairly innocent first-person character. The alternatives that are supposed to threaten my knowledge of the external world are alternatives I can appreciate as threatening from my own perspective, as I reflect on what I know. I am already familiar with the possibilities of dreaming and of sensory illusions. All the skeptic needs to do is convince me that I have no conclusive ways of ruling out these possibilities in particular cases in order to pose a threat to the epistemic security of my external-world beliefs in those cases. Moreover, I myself could perhaps appreciate that the threat would affect all of my external-world beliefs, even though it doesn't spread to my beliefs about my own states of mind.

Relatedly, external-world skepticism need not rely on any particular view of the nature of the external world, except perhaps the negative idea that the existence and nature of external objects is not, in general, dependent on our impressions and thoughts of them. Thus, regardless of what I believe about the nature of water, or of chemical substances in general, I can appreciate that there may be explanations for my thinking there's water in the glass that are radically different from the one I naïvely hold—namely, that I am in the presence of a real glass of water. It is these different explanations that furnish the alternatives I am presumably unable to rule out. For this reason, it seems natural to try to combat external-world skepticism by arguing either that I can, after all, rule out these alternatives, or that I do not need to be able to rule them out in order to be warranted in my belief, at least not in every context. Either way, it can be argued that the external-world skeptic is relying on unreasonably demanding, or at least ordinarily inapplicable, standards for non-deductive, empirical knowledge.

The situation seems different with content skepticism. A typical subject is not normally in a position to appreciate the kinds of alternatives that would support a skeptical doubt concerning what she is currently thinking. She has to be brought to that position by some philosophical stage-setting or reasoning. To generate a skeptical doubt that is analogous to the Cartesian doubt about the external world, the content skeptic needs to present us with alternatives that would be distinct in reality but appear indistinguishable to us. The commonsense notion of the content of a mental state does not readily furnish us with such alternatives. Of course, at a given moment, I *could have had* the thought that there's gin in the glass, or that the sky is blue, instead of the thought that there's water in the glass. But that is no reason for me to worry that, for all I know, the thought I am entertaining right now may have one of these other contents. (Just as the mere fact that, right now, there *could* have been here a glass of orange juice, or a small brown ladder, instead of a glass of water, is no reason for me to worry that, for all I know, I am in the presence of one of those things.)

To get the right analogue of external-world skepticism, then, the content skeptic must find a way of presenting us with alternatives that threaten our conviction that we can *tell* what we are presently thinking—alternatives that would be distinct in reality but appear indistinguishable to us. This is precisely what the view called *externalism* (or anti-individualism) about content is supposed to have provided.[4] The thesis of content externalism says, roughly:

**EXT**: The contents of our thoughts (and other mental states) depend for their individuation on the nature of our physical or social environment. Whether an individual is in a mental state with one content rather than another depends in part on relationships between that individual and her extra-mental environment.[5]

The precise character and extent of the dependence will vary with the specific version of externalism one adopts. I will be using

---

[4] There are other ways to generate skepticism about knowledge of content, derivable from familiar arguments in ch. 2 of Quine (1960) and in Kripke (1982). In my (1990) I compare and contrast Quinean meaning skepticism and external-world skepticism. The incompatibility between content externalism and self-knowledge is often pointed out by way of reducing content externalism to absurdity. My concern here, by contrast, is to examine critically the idea that, if content externalism is accepted, then a certain skepticism about self-knowledge could be generated.

[5] The *loci classica* are Putnam (1975) and Burge (1979). Putnam presents the thesis as one about the meaning of terms; Burge defends the externalist thesis with regard to the contents of mental states.

throughout a rather strong version of externalism according to which, at least in the case of thoughts about natural substances, one cannot, e.g., harbor any *water*-thoughts if one has never been in any causal contact, direct or indirect, with the chemical substance water (i.e., $H_2O$). So a person who spent all her life on Twin Earth (a planet that is just like Earth, except that what appears like water there is, chemically, not $H_2O$ but XYZ), and who had no contact with people who did possess the concept *water*, could not have any *water*-thoughts. Such a person could only have *twater*-thoughts.[6]

Armed with EXT, the external-content skeptic may try to generate a skeptical doubt regarding our ordinary knowledge of content, a doubt that is analogous to the Cartesian doubt regarding ordinary knowledge of the external world as portrayed by CSK above. But it should be noted that content externalism, as represented by EXT, is a metaphysical doctrine concerning the nature of the facts that determine whether an individual's thought has one content rather than another.[7] By contrast, the claim that we have knowledge of the contents of our present mental states as summarized by CSK is an epistemological claim concerning the epistemic status of certain of our self-ascriptions. If there is a conflict between these two claims, then it must be because for some reason, if the facts about content are as EXT maintains, we could not have knowledge of contentful states of the kind CSK attributes to us.

The intuitive worry is this. My ascription of contentful states to myself can constitute privileged knowledge only if I can be in a special position to tell what content my states have. But if what makes it the case that my states have the particular contents they have has to do with features of my environment of which I may be completely ignorant, how can I achieve knowledge—let alone especially secure and privileged knowledge—of my states' contents? This problem breaks

---

[6] I use this strong version both for the sake of simplicity, and also because the arguments I will be considering seem most persuasive when this version is assumed. I am not assuming that all content externalists subscribe to the stronger version. The externalist doctrine is sometimes characterized in terms of the negative claim that facts about what concepts an individual possesses (and thus what thoughts she can have) do not supervene on the individual's internal constitution and organization, or on her phenomenology, at least insofar as those are understood to be independent of any facts about the individual's physical or social environment. For relevant discussion, see Brueckner (1992).

[7] Content externalism is sometimes taken to present a claim about a *logical* or *conceptual* dependence. (See, e.g., McKinsey (1991) and Brown (1995).) I agree that the dependence in question is not merely causal-psychological. However, I think the content externalist doctrine is more plausibly represented by speaking of metaphysical dependence; and I believe its main exponents have intended it that way, though I cannot discuss the issue here.

down into two questions. First, How can I be said to achieve *any* kind of knowledge of my mental states' contents, given content externalism? But, second, How can I achieve self-knowledge as understood by CSK—i.e., knowledge that is *especially secure* and *privileged* (in the sense that only I can have it, and only with respect to my own present mental states), given content externalism? The second question points to a certain disanalogy between the external-content and the external-world skeptic's respective tasks. The external-world skeptic is typically taken to raise a doubt about any of us having *any* knowledge of the extra-mental world. On the other hand, the external-content skeptic who challenges CSK can be taken to raise a more specific doubt about each of us having *especially secure, privileged* knowledge of the contents of our own present mental states. Since the external-content skeptic's challenge is more limited, it may seem easier to raise and more difficult to answer. However, in what follows, I will be paying considerable attention to the first question. This is because I think that misconceptions concerning what would constitute a satisfactory answer to the first question may mislead us when we try to answer the second.[8]

Suppose I make the following self-ascription of a contentful state:

**SAC**: I am thinking that there's water in the glass.

For SAC to constitute a piece of knowledge that I have about myself, it must, of course, be true that right now I am thinking that there's water in the glass. EXT entails that for this to be true, I must meet certain conditions—e.g., I must have had some causal contact with water (or have acquired my concepts from others who have had such contact). EXT clearly does not require that I myself be in a position to know or ascertain that I satisfy these conditions in order to satisfy them. However, if SAC is to constitute something I know, it is not enough that it be true. I must also be somehow warranted in holding SAC true. And it may seem that this does require that I somehow be able to ascertain that I satisfy the environmental conditions for thinking that there's water in the glass. This, in turn, does seem to be

---

[8] MacDonald (1998) claims that the second question is the difficult one to answer. Davies also thinks that the first question (which presents what he calls the "achievement problem" for content externalism) "does not pose any insuperable problem for first-person authority" (1998: 342). He thinks the more difficult problem is what he calls "the consequence problem". (I address the latter problem elsewhere (2004).) Though I agree with MacDonald and Davies that "the achievement problem" is not insuperable, I think that solving it takes some doing. I should clarify that my complete answers to both the epistemological questions will not be given until Ch. 9.

something I can only do through a study of my relations to my extra-mental environment. Yet, according to CSK, my self-ascription of the thought relies on no such study. (Intuitively, I do not have to check whether I am in an environment containing water to know whether I am having a *water*-thought.) Unlike others, I use no ordinary inference, evidence, or observation in ascribing to myself a thought with a particular content. So we may wonder what could possibly warrant me in my self-ascription.

So far, however, I do not think a clear or special problem for the externalist view of content has been identified. As suggested earlier, the external-content skeptic's doubt is not supposed to rely on a doubt about the extra-mental world. So the alleged problem for CSK that is based on EXT should not be taken to follow from a more general skeptical problem concerning our ability to know ordinary extra-mental propositions. Thus, consider my claim that the shirt in front of me is red, or that the person next to me is George, or that there's water in the glass. Under normal circumstances, and not assuming global external-world skepticism, such claims would presumably count as things I know. But how can this be? After all, whether or not the relevant claims are in fact true depends on facts that I have not ascertained (regarding wavelengths and light reflectance, biological origin, and chemical structure, respectively). My knowledge in these cases is obtained through more or less direct perception, and relies on my routine acquaintance with the relevant items or features, rather than on my theoretical knowledge of their underlying nature. But then we may wonder why things should be any different with respect to knowledge of mental content. Granted, if EXT is true, contents have essential features—a kind of nature, if you will—that are not immediately available to us purely in virtue of being thinking subjects; they admit of theoretical understanding. But this by itself does not rule out the possibility of knowing that our thoughts have particular contents without possessing such theoretical understanding. If the external-content skeptic allows that I can know I am drinking water, even in ignorance of chemistry, why is it that I cannot know that I am *thinking* that I am drinking water, even in ignorance of the correct theory of content?

This leads directly to a further observation. If theoretical knowledge of the (metaphysical) determiners of content were required for all knowledge of content, this would spell trouble for the ordinary knowledge that *others* are often enough supposed to have of the contents of our mental states. Ordinary folks are not philosophers of mind; nor are they chemists. As you ascribe to me wanting to have some water, or thinking that George is boring, though you (unlike me) rely on some evidence, your evidence directly concerns my verbal and non-verbal behavior, not the causal history of my concepts or the underlying nature of the items that my mental states are about. Of course, one could raise a skeptical doubt about the possibility of obtaining any genuine knowledge of content—of one's own states *or* those of others—in the absence of proper ascertaining of the obtaining of the relevant conditions. But such a doubt would have nothing especially to do with either content externalism or with knowledge of the contents of one's own present mental states.

I take the upshot of the above considerations to be this. As we consider whether ordinary content self-knowledge is compatible with content externalism, or whether the content skeptic can usefully enlist externalism, we should avoid tacit appeal to requirements on knowledge that would equally rule out ordinary knowledge of the extra-mental world, on the one hand, and suggest that *non*-externalist views of content are also unable to accommodate content self-knowledge, on the other hand. We should bear this lesson firmly in mind as we continue to examine the relationships between externalism, content self-knowledge, and external-content skepticism.

## Is Externalism Compatible with Self-Knowledge?

So far I have pointed out that in general, for any range of truths, there may be different ways of knowing those truths, not all of which involve a theoretical probing into the underlying nature of the known items. However, in the absence of such theoretical understanding, if someone is said to know some truth $p$, it is because she has some positive way of telling that $p$ is the case; and that *seems* to imply that she must go by some features of the relevant situation that are somehow correlated—and reliably so—with the obtaining of $p$. Thus, if I can be said to know that this man is George, even though I have conducted no DNA tests, this is because my way of telling that this is

George—i.e., visual recognition—represents a reliable method for correctly identifying people. Similarly for knowing that there's water in the glass, or that the shirt is red. The world being the way it is, we can in many cases tell who is who, and what is what, going by looks and other perceptible qualities; we do not need to conduct elaborate theoretical investigations. By the same token, recognizing the content of one's own thoughts would be possible even without a study of one's environment, if there were 'certain signs', however untheoretical, by which to tell what our own thoughts are about.[9]

It might be thought, however, that the truth of EXT would make it especially hard to see how we could obtain immediate knowledge of content. For, on the externalist hypothesis, it seems that there can be no 'certain signs' by which we could recognize contents 'from the inside'. Content externalists often hold that my duplicate on Twin Earth and I could have *phenomenologically identical experiences* at a given moment and yet be entertaining thoughts with different contents. While I may be thinking that there's water in the glass, she may be thinking that there's twater in the glass. It follows that thought contents do not wear marks of their hidden nature on their perceptible sleeves, so to speak. So how can I be warranted in ascribing to myself the thought that there's water in the glass?[10]

Presenting the problem in this way suggests that the externalist view plays directly into the hands of content skepticism. The thought experiments that are supposed to support content externalism are often couched in terms of the possibility of differences in thought contents that are not reflected in what is accessible to a thinker 'from the inside'. This suggests the possibility of 'identical twin contents': distinct types of contents that would appear to be the same to a thinker, and thus be indistinguishable from her own perspective. This

---

[9] The present suggestion has obvious affinities with what is known as Reliabilism, which is usually presented as an externalist view of knowledge. It has often been observed that content externalism can (perhaps must) be coupled with epistemological externalism in order to avoid the charge of incompatibility with self-knowledge. I have avoided the label "Reliabilism" here, since I am not certain that the proposal I am working with qualifies as a purely externalist proposal. (See discussion below.)

[10] Ram Neta has suggested (following McDowell (1982) ) that the content externalist could claim that, given our environmental differences, My twin and I do differ also in terms of how things appear to us introspectively; one's phenomenology, too, depends on relations to one's extra-cranial environment. This view is not without its difficulties, but I cannot discuss it here. For present purposes, it seems dialectically appropriate to suppose that my twin and I share phenomenology. (Later on, I begin to develop what I take to be a more attractive option by denying that our knowledge of content, and of present mental states more generally, is a matter of recognition by characteristic internal signs.)

possibility, in turn, undercuts the proposal that the immediate knowledge we have of the contents of our own states of mind could rely on features of content that are uniquely discernible by us. Yet this proposal seems to offer the most promising rebuttal of the charge that content externalism is incompatible with content self-knowledge.

Bearing in mind our earlier lesson, however, we should reflect on the fact that we do ordinarily credit people with perceptually based knowledge of individuals and substances in their environment, even in the face of the fact that perceptual recognition is not apt to rule out all logically possible counterfeits. I can be said to know that there is water in the glass, even though, logically speaking, there are liquids— e.g., twater—that would fool me. How so? Again, ordinary knowledge attributions seem to be concerned with actual abilities to tell. To know some truth $p$, we must have some reliable epistemic access to the worldly conditions that render $p$ true; but it is not clear that, in order for us to have knowledge, this access must afford us *counterfactual discrimination*. If there is no twater, but only water in my environment, can I not know that there is water in the glass, even though *had* I been confronted with a glass of twater (or a tlass of water, or . . . ), I might have been fooled? If so, why could I not know that the thought I am having is that there's water in the glass, even though, had circumstances been different, I might have been fooled into thinking that that's what I was thinking?[11]

Note that skepticism about the external world can proceed even without trading on an implicit counterfactual discrimination requirement. The Cartesian external-world skeptic invites us to consider alternatives that may *in fact* obtain for all we know, ones that (so the challenge goes) we are unable to rule out. Such an inability to rule out alternatives is supposed by the skeptic to undermine our claims to know external-world propositions, for it shows a diminished capacity for discrimination in actual, and not merely counterfactual, situations. And such diminished capacity does seem to bear on epistemic warrant. If I am to have perceptual or recognitional knowledge that this man is George, or that the liquid in my glass is water, for example, I must be able to tell George apart from other individuals I know, and water from other liquids, respectively. Such discriminative abilities are

---

[11] For relevant discussion of what I am calling "counterfactual discrimination", see Dretske (1999).

necessary if I am to *know which* individual is George, or which liquid is water, which in turn seems to be a precondition of my being warranted in thinking that this man here is George, or that the liquid in the glass is water.[12] Of course, how good my ability to discriminate must be in order for me to be warranted is open to debate. The safe answer for present purposes would be: good enough so that it is not a sheer coincidence that I hold the relevant claim true, but not so good that it would allow me to rule out counterfeits in all imaginable situations. As it happens, I am quite good at discerning George by his looks, voice, manner, etc., and am quite adept at telling water apart from other liquids by its color, smell, and taste (or lack thereof). But now suppose that George in fact has an identical twin brother, or that Twin Earth is discovered, and we begin to import Twin Earth's twater (XYZ) to Earth. My world in such cases encompasses actual candidate counterfeits. If I still cannot tell George apart from his twin, or water apart from twater, could I still be warranted at times in thinking that I am looking at George, or that I am drinking water? Arguably not. And if not, then the external-world skeptic can legitimately mount a challenge to our knowledge of the external world by trying to offer actual alternatives that we cannot rule out.[13]

To preserve the analogy with external-world skepticism, the external-content skeptic would either have to challenge CSK without relying on the counterfactual discrimination requirement, or to explain why the requirement must be met in the case of content self-knowledge, even if it need not be in the external-world case. The external-content skeptic needs to persuade us of the following possibility. As I ascribe a thought with a certain content to myself, there are, perhaps unbeknownst to me, *counterfeits* of that thought: i.e., thoughts I now may in fact or could be having which differ in content, and which I could not tell apart from the thought I take myself to be having. In other words, the external-content skeptic must show that it is possible for me to be fooled by (actual or counterfactual) imposters of my present thought into merely being under the false impression

---

[12] Earlier (Ch. 3, p. 61), we saw that Russell proposed a 'knowing which' requirement as a requirement on having a *thought* about an individual. We also saw Evans's construal of this requirement in terms of an ability to discriminate the object of judgment from other things. Here our concern is with a requirement on *knowledge* of certain propositions involving individuals. It would be interesting to consider the relationship between the two requirements, a matter I cannot take up here.

[13] Whether the dream hypothesis and the evil demon/brain-in-the-vat hypotheses qualify as legitimate, such alternatives can of course also be debated. For relevant discussion, see Goldman (1976).

that I'm having that thought. But this is not as straightforward as the task facing the external–world skepticism.

Thus let us go back to the self-ascription

**SAC**: I am thinking that there's water in the glass.

Given EXT, whether or not SAC is true will depend, roughly, on whether I have acquired the relevant concepts on earth or on Twin Earth. If conditions were sufficiently different, so that I would not possess the concept *water*, what SAC says would be false. Under those conditions, I could not be thinking that there's water in the glass (since having that thought requires possessing the concept *water*). But the external-content skeptic cannot simply envisage a situation in which the relevant conditions are indeed different. This is because the very conditions that would render SAC false in that situation would *also* prevent me from making the self-ascription given in SAC, in the first place. To keep the analogy with external-world skepticism, the external-content skeptic needs a situation in which I do manage to ascribe to myself a *water*-thought, but where it is possible, for all I know, that I am having a *twater*-thought.

The trouble is that if my present situation is one in which there is (and has always been) only water around, then I can only have *water*-thoughts, and so I cannot go wrong by ascribing to myself a *twater*-thought. And any situation in which I can only have counterfeit *water*-thoughts, because I fail to meet the conditions for having genuine *water*-thoughts, will be a situation in which I cannot so much as *think* that I am having a *water*-thought. By contrast, a situation involving counterfeit glasses of water is not one in which I cannot merely think (or believe, or be under the impression) that there is a glass of water. Now, if I cannot have *water*-thoughts, then, of course, SAC, being a self-ascription of precisely a *water*-thought, would be false, so it could not constitute something I know about myself. But it would also be false that I (falsely) *think* that I'm having a *water*-thought, thereby ascribing to myself that kind of first-order thought. I could of course say to myself the words used in SAC, but under the circumstances that would not constitute ascribing to myself a *water*-thought. If I can have no *water*-thoughts whatsoever, I can be in no position even to *ascribe* to myself such thoughts. (The analogue in the case of external-world skepticism would be that, if it were the case that there was a glass of twater in front of me, rather than a glass of water, then for some reason I could not so much as believe that there was a glass of water there, so I couldn't be fooled in that situation.)

The point is quite general, and fully appreciable from a first-person perspective. It is not possible for me to entertain a doubt about the contents of my present first-order mental states that is analogous to the Cartesian doubt about my external-world beliefs *simply* on the basis of the kinds of content differences that are thrown up by EXT. EXT envisages changes in worldly conditions that would issue in changes in our cognitive repertoire—in what thoughts we are able to have. But such changes would affect both our first-order contentful states and any self-ascription in which we specify the contents of those states. If EXT is right, a necessary condition of my having intentional states involving the concept of water is that I have had some causal contact with water ($H_2O$). Still, as I self-ascribe the belief/hope/wish . . . that there is water in that glass, it cannot be a possibility open to me that perhaps my state is about twater (XYZ) rather than plain old water. For, unlike in the case of an ascription to someone else (or certain ascriptions to myself), my assignment of intentional content to my own present states is bound to draw ingredients from the same conceptual pool as the ascribed intentional states themselves. If my first-order intentional states cannot involve the concept *twater*, since I have never been in contact with XYZ, then none of my self-ascriptions of intentional states can involve *twater*, either. In this way, the contents of my self-ascriptions are locked onto the contents of the ascribed states. And for this reason, alternative assignments of contents that are not in my cognitive repertoire cannot be used to generate skepticism about my knowledge of what I am thinking, hoping, wishing, etc.[14]

---

[14] The 'locking' of the contents of first-order and self-ascriptive thoughts has been used by several authors to explain how externalists can block the threat to content self-knowledge (see, e.g., Davidson (1987); Heil (1988); Brueckner (1992); Burge (1988) and (1996); Peacocke (1996); Bernecker (1998) ). The diagnosis I am offering here is designed to bring out more clearly the contrast between external-content skepticism and external-world skepticism. It is also designed to show the limitations of this line of defense (see below).

It is sometimes suggested that the locking of contents is due to the fact that the content of the first-order state is literally part of the self-ascription; see, e.g., McLaughlin and Tye (1998). In the next chapter, I explain what I take to be the truth in this observation. It can also be suggested that the locking of contents is limited to a very small subset of self-ascriptions: so-called self-verifying self-ascriptions, of the form "I am now entertaining the thought that *p*". I have deliberately presented the point in a way that brings out the generality of the locking. I discuss self-verifying self-ascriptions at some length in Bar-On (2000), and below, Ch. 6.

To generate such skepticism based on content externalism, we must envisage situations in which one's self-ascriptive thoughts will remain the same while one's first-order thoughts shift (or vice versa). Suppose, as before, that twater is brought to Earth. Confronted with a glass of twater, I will presumably still believe—falsely—that there's a glass of water in front of me. But while such a change in my environment can clearly lead to a change in the truth of some of my external-world beliefs, and may threaten my claim to know that there's water in the glass, it will not automatically render false my belief that I am thinking there's water in my glass.[15] I do not cease to have *water*-thoughts, or begin to have *twater*-thoughts upon the introduction of twater into my environment, or even upon first encounters with twater. Indeed, the very claim that, as I am presented with a sample of twater, I will form the false belief that there's water in the glass, presupposes that I'm still entertaining *water*-thoughts. Similar remarks apply when we envisage a situation in which I am suddenly transported to Twin Earth unbeknownst to me. Such a switch will not result in a change in the contents of my first-order thoughts. For, simply moving me to Twin Earth will not automatically result in my beginning to have *twater*-thoughts, instead of *water*-thoughts. When I undergo a 'fast switch' to Twin Earth, I will still be thinking that there is water in my glass. Since there is no water on Twin Earth, my thought is bound to be false. But my self-ascription to the effect that that is what I am thinking will still be true.

Now suppose that I undergo a 'slow switch': I am transported to Twin Earth and stay there long enough to have acquired the concept *twater*. (We may then imagine that I travel between earth and Twin Earth with some frequency, as in Ludlow (1998).) Note that we must not conceive of this situation as one that results in a total *replacement* of my old concept *water* with a new concept *twater*. For, whereas a fast switch is incapable of bringing about enough of a change, a slow

---

[15] The contents of so-called object-dependent thoughts may vary with sudden shifts in environmental conditions (see, e.g., Davies (1998) ). But EXT, as I understand it, is not intended simply to present a special case of object-dependent thoughts. The paradigm of object-dependent thoughts is that of thoughts involving an indexical or demonstrative component (e.g., "this"/"that", "here"). The content of a singular thought such as "That is moving fast" is said to be object-dependent in that the thought's having content at all (and the individual's having any thought at all) supposedly depends on the presence of the object referred to by the demonstrative component of the thought. I think it is at best misleading to assimilate the environment dependence of the content of thoughts such as "There's water in the glass" to the object dependence of the content of demonstrative thoughts.

switch that resulted in conceptual replacement would bring about a change that is too sweeping: it would affect my cognitive repertoire across the board, leading to a displacement of all my former *water*-thoughts, self-ascriptive thoughts included, by *twater*-thoughts. I would now be able to have first-order *twater*-thoughts, but I would no longer be able to make self-ascriptions of *water*-thoughts, since I would have lost the conceptual wherewithal for making such ascriptions. So we must consider instead a situation in which, having been transported to Twin Earth, I stay there long enough to acquire the concept *twater*, but I do not thereby lose my concept *water*.

At this point it seems to me that there is a certain avenue that is open to externalists, but which to my knowledge has not been exploited. Content externalism, at least as it is formulated in EXT, lays down only a *necessary* condition on the possession of (some of our) concepts. It tells us that standing in certain relations to one's natural and/or social environment is required for the possession of those concepts. EXT remains silent on what kind of involvement with relevant parts of the environment would be *sufficient* for concept possession. This means that it is open to the externalist to insist that my possession of the concept *water* is not exhausted by standing in the right relations to water (or to other thinkers who possess the concept). I may, for instance, also be required to have some discriminatory abilities appropriate to the environment in which I regularly exercise the concept. By the same token, if I am to acquire the concept *twater*, it may not be enough for me to hang around the substance twater for a while. (The externalist should not be saddled with a model of concept acquisition whereby acquiring a new concept is like contracting a disease through exposure to a virus.) Maintaining this in no way conflicts with the key externalist claim, which is that I and my *doppelgänger* could share all of our discriminatory dispositions understood in abstraction from our (external) relations to our respective environments, yet still possess different concepts. But it does allow us to press the question of what it would take for a *single* individual to acquire the concept *twater* as a new concept, absent any ability to distinguish water from twater. In the slow-switching case described above, we may legitimately wonder what reason there might be to suppose that I have acquired a new concept, *twater*, that is both distinct from and coexists with my old concept *water*. Why not suppose instead that my old concept has been replaced by a new one, or, perhaps, that my old concept has expanded so that it now has a broader extension that includes both water ($H_2O$) and twater (XYZ)? The fact that the old discriminatory abilities served me rather well on Earth, and *would* have served me well had I always lived on Twin Earth, does not mean that they are sufficient to sustain possession of two distinct concepts such as *water* and *twater* side by side.

What is at issue is not whether I can *tell* that I have acquired a new concept or not, but whether I now satisfy both the necessary and the sufficient conditions for possessing a new concept, *twater, in addition to* my old concept *water*, simply through my having spent long enough in the new twater environment. We may continue to suppose, with the externalist, that *what* concepts I possess depend partly on external factors of which I may be ignorant, and, further, that there is an objective matter of fact as to which concepts I possess at a given time. But this still leaves open the question as to what will make it the case that, at a given time, I possess two distinct concepts (both *water* and *twater*), as opposed to a single one (either *water* or *twater* or *water-cum-twater*). And the present point is that the externalist can consistently maintain that this depends not only on what substances I have been around, but also on my acquiring certain cognitive abilities or dispositions pertaining to them, which is a matter of changes that are reflected in my cognitive organization. Admittedly, if I am completely unaware of there being distinct liquids on Earth and Twin Earth, and furthermore, have no way of telling whether I am on Earth or Twin Earth (so that I might potentially defer to different sets of individuals in my uses of the terms), it is far from clear what the relevant different cognitive abilities or dispositions could be. But this may give reason for the externalist to deny that I will acquire *twater in addition* to *water* with the result that, after moving to Twin Earth, I have two distinct, coexisting concepts (*water* and *twater*) in my cognitive repertoire.

I am thus suggesting that the externalist can draw a distinction between what goes into the *identification* of an individual's concepts and what goes into their *enumeration*. *Which* concept someone has may well depend on relations between the individual and her environment. But this does not mean that whether one's conceptual repertoire has changed, or *how many* (externally individuated) concepts one has, is independent of factors internal to one's cognitive organization.

The content externalist may maintain the possibility of an individual who is phenomenologically indistinguishable from me who could have a concept that is distinct from mine (in virtue of being differently 'environmentally ensconced'). But, so far as I can see, it does not follow from this that there could be a *single* individual who actually possesses two distinct concepts that are in no way distinguishable except by reference to the individual's environment.

The upshot of the foregoing for our discussion is this. Adverting to additional conditions necessary for possession of twin concepts, the externalist might be able to deny that slow-switch cases allow the external-content skeptic to raise a skeptical doubt analogous to that raised by the external-world skeptic. For, if we have not yet managed to describe a situation in which I might be in possession of twin concepts such as *water* and *twater*, then by the earlier reasoning, we do not have a situation in which there could be a mismatch between the content that my first-order thought actually has and the content I ascribe to it.[16]

Suppose, however, that I do somehow manage to satisfy the necessary and sufficient conditions for having both the *water*- and the *twater*-concept. Would the external-content skeptic then have the makings of a situation in which, for all I know, though I believe that I'm in a mental state with *water*-content, I may be in a mental state with *twater*-content (or vice versa)? If my cognitive pool could be expanded, so that both types of thoughts become available to me, then, at a given moment, I could indeed be having either a *water*- or a *twater*-thought. So why could I not ascribe to myself a state with one type of content yet, for all I know, actually be in a state with another type of content? Let us suppose that I now make a self-ascription such as SAC. I ascribe to myself a *water*-thought. This means that in my self-ascription, I exercise my *water*-concept. However, could it not be, for all I know, that as a matter of fact, my first-order thought is *that there's twater in the glass*—that is, could I not be exercising my concept *twater* rather than *water* in my first-order thought? If this were indeed the

---

[16] For relevant discussion, see Burge (1998b). Burge maintains that it *is* possible to understand slow-switching cases as involving the acquisition of an additional concept, rather than the replacement of the old concept, or the expansion of one's old concept into an "amalgam" concept with an extension that includes that of the old concept as well as that of the twin concept. It may be plausible to suppose that the old concept is retained, because "the old abilities will normally still be there; and there are situations . . . that can bring these abilities into play" (1998b: 357). Burge does not, however, specify what are the relevant (new) abilities, if any, that would be additionally necessary for the possession of the two "disjoint" concepts (as he refers to them). See my discussion below.

case, then I would be issuing a self-ascription that would be false. But if I cannot rule this out, how could my self-ascription count as something I know, let alone know with special security?

As against the external-content skeptic, it might be argued that, even in cases where the individual's cognitive repertoire contains both concepts, it is still not possible for the content of the self-ascription of a thought and the content of the self-ascribed thought to pull apart. Thus, Tyler Burge has claimed that, even in slow-switching cases, "there is no possibility of counterfeits":

No abnormal background condition could substitute some other object in such a way as to create a gap between what we think and what we think about. Basic self-knowledge is self-referential in a way that ensures that the object of reference just is the thought being thought. If background conditions are different enough so that there is another object of reference in one's self-referential thinking, they are also different enough in that there is another thought. The person would remain in the same reflexive position with respect to this thought, and would again know, in the authoritative way, what he is thinking. (1988: 659)

However, if we keep in mind the analogy with external-world skepticism, we may wonder what allows Burge to insist on the locking of contents in those situations where the candidate twin contents both belong to the individual's actual, active cognitive repertoire. If my external world contains both water and twater, then when I think there's water in my glass, what is in my glass could, for all I know, be twater. So, if my internal world contains both *water-* and *twater-* thoughts, then when I think I'm having a *water*-thought, why could I not, for all I know, be having a *twater*-thought? To break the analogy, we need to understand what it is about basic self-knowledge which makes it "self-referential" in a way that rules out the possibility of counterfeits or imposters, and ensures that the content of the ascribed thought and the ascribing thought will still interlock.

Burge himself makes some suggestive remarks about this question, to which I will turn in the next section. In concluding this section, however, I would like to point out that the question is not automatically answered or obviated by abandoning externalism in favor of content 'internalism'—i.e., by insisting that the contents of our thoughts are fully determined by (in the sense of metaphysically supervening on) facts about what is 'inside our heads'. To secure content self-knowledge in the face of a skeptical challenge, it is not enough to maintain that contents depend for their identity only on facts 'internal' to the individual. One has to be assured that the relevant internal facts are somehow *immediately available* to the subject who has contentful mental states. But the mere acceptance of internalism about content does not provide this assurance. It is true that the internalist may deny that inability to tell apart *water*-thoughts and *twater*-thoughts poses no threat to an individual's knowledge of content. Still, content internalism is not immune to the possibility of twin thoughts that a subject may be unable to distinguish immediately, without studying her internal organization. Let me explain.

Content externalism presents us with a view of content on which at least some of the conditions necessary for harboring states with a given content may elude individuals who in fact harbor those states. But content externalism is not alone in this. As long as what makes it the case that someone has states with certain contents includes some objective facts about them that are not directly available to her, then, regardless of whether those are 'inside' or 'outside' her head, we will have the makings of an appearance/reality gap with respect to content *even in one's own case*. Where there is such a gap, there is a possibility of imposters in the mental realm: mental states that appear to a subject to have contents that are different from the contents they actually have. It is this possibility that is relevant for generating content skepticism on the model of external-world skepticism. Thus, consider, for example, the view that the content of a thought is fully determined by its inferential role, where this is understood purely in terms of certain cognitive processes 'inside the thinker's head'. On such a view, it may always be in principle possible for me to determine the content of a given thought I have without examining anything other than my own thought processes. Still, surely, as I ascribe to myself a thought with a particular content, I do *not* tell that it has that content by ascertaining that it has the relevant inferential links. Furthermore, if being able to tell what content my thought has indeed required that I somehow latch onto some underlying objective truths about such links, then it would seem that there is no reason why, on any given occasion, I could not be fooled by an imposter.

On any objective theory of content, the presence in an individual of a mental state with a particular content will depend on the actual obtaining of certain conditions, be they conditions involving relations between the individual and her extra-mental environment, or conditions involving only the individual's internal psychological and/or physiological organization. If being warranted in holding true a claim such as SAC always required ascertaining that one has satisfied the conditions for having the self-ascribed thought, then this would seem to go against the uniquely non-evidential, 'effortless' character of self-knowledge. Thus, regardless of whether the relevant conditions are external or internal, we need to understand how ordinary content self-knowledge as portrayed by CSK is to be accommodated. Simply insisting that content is fully determined by (or supervenes on) conditions internal to subjects' organization does not guarantee that subjects will always be in a position to know effortlessly whether they satisfy those conditions. And it does not guarantee protection against counterfeits.[17]

Earlier, I recommended a certain caution in developing content skepticism. On the one hand, the content skeptic must not tacitly appeal to requirements on knowledge that would rule out ordinary extra-mental knowledge. Such appeal would betray that the content skeptic is mounting a doubt that is not merely parallel to, but is rather *parasitic on*, external-world skepticism. On the other hand, the content skeptic we have envisaged attempted to develop a doubt that is parallel to the external-world skeptic's doubt by enlisting a specific view of content: that offered by content externalism. Yet the considerations of this section suggest that, to the extent that the external-content skeptic *can* mount a challenge to ordinary self-knowledge, it is a challenge that not only externalist views would have to face. It remains to be seen whether externalist theories are less well placed to meet the challenge than internalist theories.

## Content Self-Knowledge and the Recognitional Conception

How could a thinker know what content her present thought has, if it is possible for her to assign a counterfeit content to it? This problem, I argued earlier, can arise for any view of content—be it externalist or

---

[17] A similar problem would face various philosophical accounts that offer theoretical analyses of content-clauses in terms of, e.g., their truth-conditions. For relevant discussion, see Bar-On (1995) and Higgenbotham (1998). The problem has to do with the theoretical character of the *analysans*.

internalist—that took the determiners of content to be objective conditions that are not themselves gleaned directly through introspection. I now want to argue that if this problem appears especially intractable for the externalist, this is because discussions of the relationship between externalism and self-knowledge are often tacitly informed by a certain conception of content self-knowledge in particular, and of self-knowledge generally. It is this conception that makes it appear as though accommodating CSK requires abandoning content externalism.

Recall that, according to CSK, in self-ascribing present contentful states, I do not make any use of ordinary observation, evidence, or inference, in order to ascertain the content of my state. Ordinary self-ascriptions made in that way—what we have been calling "avowals"—are thus special, in that they do not rely on the use of ordinary epistemic means. On what we may describe as *the recognitional conception*, it is thought that, if such self-ascriptions are nonetheless thought to constitute some kind of knowledge, then they must be grounded in our ability to tell through our recognition of distinctive features of a present mental state what content it has. Moreover, for me to be able to *tell* that a state of mine has a certain content $c$, I must be in a position to *tell apart* states with content $c$ from states with other contents that are available to me by latching onto something that reliably correlates with having *that* content, as opposed to any other. And, in keeping with CSK, this method must be especially secure and unique to me.

Central to the recognitional conception is the idea of a recognitional judgment: a judgment made as I attend to features of my state accessible 'from the inside', which represents my taking it to have content $c$, rather than any other content that is available to me as a thinker, and on which my self-ascription of a state with content $c$ rests. The key idea of this conception is that even if I am not required to ascertain whether I satisfy the metaphysical conditions for being in a state with content $c$, I must nevertheless have (and use) a 'discriminative' method that is in some way attuned to those conditions, so that using the method allows me reliably to tell that a present state of mine has content $c$, rather than some other content it could potentially have.

This "recognitional requirement", as I shall call it, may be inspired by considering familiar cases of non-theoretical knowledge of the extra-mental world. As remarked earlier, I can often be said to know various things about the world around me, even in the absence of theoretical investigation or specialized study. I can indeed know that this man is George, even when I haven't checked his DNA, and know that there's water in the glass, even when I have not conducted chemical tests. But this is only because I have certain recognitional abilities with respect to the relevant items, which allow me to tell them apart from other items through their appearance. To satisfy the recognitional requirement in the case of content self-knowledge, we would similarly have to postulate some ability I have to identify—presumably *not* through observation of my own behavior—what content a present mental state of mine has, which would enable me to recognize it as *that* content, as opposed to some other candidate. Perhaps I latch onto the way the contentful state appears to me as I look inside, as introspectionist views would have it. Or perhaps I can instead attend to the world outside me, as some transparency views would have it.[18]

We can now see why extraordinary situations in which an individual actually harbors in her cognitive repertoire twin contents that are distinguishable only by reference to certain conditions in the individual's environment pose a threat to the externalist's way of accommodating content self-knowledge. It seems that the 'mental world' of such a thinker is in fact inhabited by imposters which she has no way of ruling out on the basis of the way things appear to her from the inside. But, in the imagined cases, it seems that even attending directly to the world outside would be of no help, since the thinker lacks the wherewithal to discriminate the relevant worldly conditions as well. (By hypothesis, the protagonist in Twin Earth thought experiments could not tell the twin substances apart by their appearances.) So this thinker fails to satisfy the above recognitional requirement, and could not have content self-knowledge. Content externalism thus may seem able, after all, to furnish us with alternatives that can play the relevant role of counterfeits, at least in those situations where a thinker has come to possess twin concepts.

How does this bear on ordinary situations, where the individual does not harbor twin contents, so there are no actual counterfeits in her mental world? Wouldn't the external-content skeptic have to

[18] These are views considered in the previous chapter as representatives of the Epistemic Approach.

show that we *are* in fact in a twin-concept situation in order to raise her skeptical doubt? At this point, I think the dialectics becomes rather tricky. As far as defending content externalism is concerned, it may be enough for the content externalist to argue that content skepticism poses a threat to content self-knowledge (given external-ism) *only if* extraordinary situations (e.g., slow switching) are indeed possible, and only when such situations in fact obtain. In ordinary situations, we can and do know the contents of our thoughts.[19] But some content externalists may still want to insist that content self-knowledge would *not* be threatened even in extraordinary ('dual-concept') situations of the above sort. And this may be necessary if we want to insist not only that content self-knowledge is possible, but that it enjoys an especially secure status.

In a recent article, Burge explicitly considers cases in which an "individual has undergone a conceptual change that is unknown to the individual . . . [due to] his inability to distinguish [the two substances and] . . . cannot explain or articulate a distinction between the concepts in the first and second environment". He insists, however, that

the individual will commonly have immediate, non-empirically warranted self-knowledge of the form *I think (believe, judge) that p*, where *that p* included the relevant concept. . . . In relevant self-attributions, the individual simulta-neously uses and self-attributes concepts (in the reflexive, that-clause way). In these cases the individual cannot get *the content* wrong. For the attributed intentional content is fixed by what the individual thinks.

He immediately adds:

It [the content] is not something that he identifies independently.

Much of the literature on this subject deals with problems that arise from the assumption that we need to *identify* the content of our thoughts in such a way as to be able to rule out relevant alternatives to what the content might be. [T]his assumption is not acceptable on my view. One's relation to one's content, when one is non-empirically self-attributing in the reflexive, that-clause way is not analogous to a perceptual, identificational relation to which alternatives would be relevant. In present-tense self-attributions of the relevant kind, alternatives are irrelevant. (1998*b*: 354 f.)[20]

---

[19]   This is a line taken by Ludlow (1998).

[20]   I take it that by "attributions of the relevant kind" Burge means present-tense contentful self-ascriptions that are made in the *ordinary* way—what I have been calling "avowals"—which are to be contrasted with "alienated" or "theoretical" self-ascriptions, made on the basis of evidence, inference, therapy, cognitive science experiments, etc.

As I read him, Burge is here denying that telling what content one's present state has is a matter of telling apart the content from other potential candidates in a way analogous to ordinary recognitional identification. Twin alternatives do not threaten content self-knowledge, because normal content self-ascriptions do not need to comply with what I called the recognitional requirement. In other words, Burge is recommending a rejection of the recognitional conception of content self-knowledge. But if this is so, then reconciling the theses we have dubbed EXT and CSK is not simply a matter of a proper understanding of the externalist view. It requires in addition a positive understanding of the character of content self-ascriptions—in particular, it requires understanding what qualifies our assignments of content to be securely knowledgeable.[21]

## A Non-Epistemic Alternative to the Recognitional Conception: Davidson's Line

Burge is not alone in suggesting that we ought to reject the recognitional conception in the course of defending externalism against content skepticism. A very similar suggestion is made by Donald Davidson in the context of trying to explain how so-called first-person authority is not compromised by content externalism. Davidson undertakes to answer the following question, which he formulates in the (by now) familiar terms of an asymmetry between ordinary mental self-ascriptions and ascriptions to others:

Why should there be ... asymmetry between attributions of attitudes to our present selves and attributions of the same attitudes to other selves? What accounts for the authority accorded first person present tense claims of this sort, and denied second or third person claims? (1984: 101 f.)

---

[21] McGeer (1996) notes that content externalism presents a *prima facie* problem for our pre-theoretical intuitions about first-person authority only so long as we continue to adhere to what I have called the "recognitional conception" of self-knowledge. But McGeer concludes that what should be given up is the idea of self-knowledge as involving second-order beliefs about first-order states, and proceeds to advocate an alternative picture of first-person authority as commissive. In Ch. 4 (pp. 136ff.), I argued that the commissive view is not satisfactory. My goal in what follows is to develop a "middle way" of understanding avowals and self-knowledge, which avoids thinking of the security of avowals in terms of the epistemic security of higher-order judgments about first-order states, while preserving the intuition that they represent genuine and privileged knowledge of facts about one's own mental states.

Davidson is careful to emphasize that what he terms "first-person authority" does not amount to the infallibility or incorrigibility or indubitability of certain self-ascriptions. We *can* make mistakes about our own thoughts, beliefs, wants, etc.; others *can* have evidence that could overthrow our avowals; we *can* doubt our self-ascriptions. But this cannot be the general case, and "even when a self-attribution is in doubt, or a challenge is proper, the person with the attitude speaks about it with special weight" (1984: 103). There is a presumption of correctness that attaches to self-ascriptions which, though defeasible, is of a special character, and demands an explanation.

The puzzle becomes more pressing, Davidson thinks, when we reflect on what content externalism teaches us regarding the essential dependence of the contents of our thoughts and other propositional attitudes on the nature of our environment. If the contents of our thoughts are determined by things about which we can be seriously wrong, why should we be in a privileged position to tell what the contents of our thoughts are? The key to solving the puzzle, Davidson thinks, is to rid ourselves of the Cartesian conception of our relationship to our own mental states. The externalist view of content can give rise to skepticism regarding our special knowledge of the contents of our propositional attitudes only on the assumption that knowing what one believes requires knowing in some way the causal determiners of the contents of those attitudes. But this assumption must be rejected. It rests on the erroneous supposition that one's relation to what goes on in one's mind (including what thoughts, beliefs, etc. one harbors) is analogous to one's relation to what goes on in one's surroundings.[22]

Davidson's rejection of the erroneous assumption is in keeping with our earlier rejection of the recognitional conception. But the question is what he can offer in place of this conception. As I understand his positive proposal, Davidson thinks that first-person authority over propositional attitudes, which is traditionally thought to be epistemic in character, should be reduced to what may be described as the *semantic authority* we have as speakers of our own language regarding the contents of our attitudes. The reduction goes as follows. Davidson points out that if we focus on linguistic beings, the question

---

[22] See Davidson (1987) and also Burge (1988) and Boghossian (1989: sec. III).

why we have a special warrant for self-ascriptions of propositional attitudes can be restated as the question why our pronouncements regarding our own propositional attitudes enjoy a special, privileged status. Why is my self-ascription "I believe that Wagner died happy" to be favored over your report to the same effect? For our respective ascriptions to be true, both of us must know *that* I hold-true the content sentence—i.e., the sentence specifying the content of the belief "Wagner died happy" (where holding-true is the Davidsonian *ersatz* for believing). And both of us must know that *I* know *what* it is that I hold-true—i.e., what the content sentence says. So far, there seems to be no asymmetry. The difference is, though, that on these two assumptions, *I can be presumed to know authoritatively what I believe, while you may not* (cf. 1984: 110).

Davidson suggests that this latter presumption boils down to the presumption that *I* know what I mean by my words, whereas you need not. The presumption is that I know (or am in a position to know) *what* it is I believe in holding-true the content sentence, whereas you may not. Davidson's proposal, then, is that the first-person/other-person asymmetry in propositional-attitude ascriptions reduces to the asymmetry between speakers and interpreters' knowledge of what a speaker's utterances mean. He then offers to explain *this* asymmetry by showing in what way a speaker's knowledge of his own words' meanings is privileged—"why there must be a presumption that speakers, but not their interpreters, are not wrong about what their words mean" (1984: 110). One's first-person authority over the contents of one's attitudes becomes a matter of one's *knowledge of what one means* by the words which serve to specify the contents of one's attitudes.

Now, Davidson thinks that there is an obvious fact differentiating speakers from their interpreters: "the interpreter must, while the speaker does not, rely on what, if it were made explicit, would be a difficult inference in interpreting the speaker" (1984: 110). Interpreters must base their interpretations on complex evidence concerning the speaker's behavior, her relation to her environment, etc. and on various inferences.[23] The same is not true of the speakers themselves.

---

[23] Davidson makes this point about the predicament of interpreters initially in the context of discussing radical interpretation. But he wants to carry it over to ordinary language understanding, which seems highly implausible to me. (See, e.g., Davidson (1973), (1974).)

But this, again, could serve only to highlight the asymmetry, not to explain the speaker's privileged knowledge of meaning. In two key passages, Davidson invokes two (apparently different but related) claims to explain the speaker/interpreter asymmetry in knowledge of meaning:

The speaker, after bending whatever knowledge and craft he can to the task of saying what his words mean, cannot improve on the following sort of statement: "My utterance of 'Wagner died happy' is true iff Wagner died happy." An interpreter has no reason to assume this will be his best way of stating the truth-conditions of the speaker's utterance. (1984: 110 f.)

The best the speaker [in a radical situation] can do is to be interpretable, that is, to use a finite supply of distinguishable sounds applied consistently to objects and situations he believes are apparent to his hearer. . . . It is . . . obvious that the interpreter has nothing to go on but the pattern of sounds the speaker exhibits in conjunction with further events (including of course, further actions on the part of both speaker and interpreter). It makes no sense in this situation to wonder whether the speaker is generally getting things wrong. His behavior may simply not be interpretable. But if it is, then what his words mean is (generally) what he intends them to mean . . . There is a presumption—an unavoidable presumption built into the nature of interpretation—that the speaker usually knows what he means. So there is a presumption that if he knows that he holds a sentence true, he knows what he believes. (1984: 111)

To sum up, Davidson's treatment of first-person authority comes in two stages. The first stage involves construing first-person authority as semantic, rather than epistemic, authority. The relevant authority is grounded in special knowledge that speakers have concerning what they mean by the words that serve to specify the content clauses of their attitudes. The second stage involves portraying speakers' knowledge of meaning in a rather deflationary way. One's privileged knowledge of what one means, which serves to ground one's semantic authority over the contents of one's attitudes, is simply a matter of being an interpretable *user* of the relevant terms. Knowing what you mean by your words does not require having theoretical knowledge or any stable information *about* the words in your repertoire. Importantly, it does not require knowing—let alone knowing with epistemic authority—the necessary causal preconditions that determine what your words mean. It requires only being a competent user of words with those meanings—which means *satisfying* the relevant preconditions, rather than *knowing that* they are satisfied. To think otherwise, Davidson suggests, is erroneously to assimilate knowledge of meaning to knowledge of ordinary objects—it is to take meanings to be objects 'in front of the mind's eye' (or maybe configurations in one's brain) which one inspects and whose intrinsic and relational features one must determine, in order to have knowledge of them.[24]

Davidson thus suggests that we can understand the notable first-person/other-person asymmetries in propositional attitude ascriptions, if we reduce knowledge of the contents of one's propositional attitudes to semantic knowledge, and reduce semantic knowledge, in turn, to competent language use. On this proposal, the relevant asymmetries ultimately boil down to the fact that, at least in a radical interpretation situation, an interpreter must interpret the speaker, but all the speaker has to do—indeed, all he *can* do—is *be* an interpretable speaker, using words competently in a variety of circumstances. Now, although I think this proposal has some force against the challenge posed by the external-content skeptic, it must be recognized that its explanatory scope is rather limited, as I shall now explain.

Suppose it is granted that, as a speaker, I have an undeniable semantic authority, in the sense that I am in a better position than anyone else to know the meanings of sentences in my idiolect. On Davidson's construal, my being in this better position is not a matter of my having any distinctive epistemic advantage; it simply amounts to my being a competent user of those sentences. Thus understood, my semantic authority can help to explain in a non-epistemic way my privileged position concerning the contents of my present states, by assuring us that I have the last word on the meanings of sentences that *could* serve to specify the contents of my propositional attitudes. It is ultimately *my* use of words that determines the correct specification of the contents of my propositional attitudes. So even though I do not have a special epistemic access to the conditions that determine a self-ascription such as SAC to have one content rather than another, I can be said to know that it is a *water*-thought rather than a *twater*-thought, inasmuch as my linguistic repertoire, whose character is determined by *my* use of words, contains no term meaning *twater*.[25] But now

---

[24] See Davidson (1987), and compare Burge (1988) and Heil (1988). See also Smith (1998).

[25] Note that this account would have to be couched in terms of my use of concepts if it is to generalize beyond self-ascriptions made in speech.

we must notice that CSK goes beyond this; it concerns my being better placed to tell that I am currently entertaining a thought (or have a wish, etc.) with a *particular* content, from among all the contents available to me. According to CSK, given any sentence in my semantic repertoire, I am in a much better position than others to tell whether *right now* I have an attitude *with that content* (as well as what attitude I possess toward it). Appeal to my semantic authority over the meanings of sentences in my repertoire may allow us to explain how twin contents are 'screened off', so that we can meet the challenge posed by external-content skepticism. But we are still left with the question how, given all the sentences that *are* in my repertoire, with their meanings taken as fixed by *my* use, I can tell what sentence correctly specifies the content of a present state of mine. Given my semantic authority as understood by Davidson, we can be assured that *whatever* thought I now have, the question whether it may be a *twater*-thought is moot. But we have still not been told why it is that I am better placed than others to issue correct present-tense contentful self-ascriptions.[26]

A key idea in Davidson's response to external-content skepticism is the claim that content externalism does not threaten first-person authority, because this authority should not be taken to rest on authoritative knowledge of the causal determiners of the contents of those attitudes. Being in a privileged position to tell that you are having a thought that is *about* water cannot require being able to distinguish whether you are on Earth or Twin Earth; nor does it require that you know the chemical constitution of the stuff you refer to by the term "water". This would be asking too much of knowledge of content. However, even if we relax these requirements, we may still want to know how it is that we do achieve secure knowledge of what content our present thoughts have. Although Davidson's response to external-content skepticism takes a correct first step in showing us how we can depart from the recognitional model on which this skepticism rests,

---

[26] As an *ad hominem* we might also point out that the Davidsonian account risks severing certain first-person/third-person continuities. On his proposed account, we are to take my authoritative knowledge of what I believe to consist solely in my being a competent user of the terms (concepts) of the clause specifying the content of my belief. But, presumably, your knowledge of what I believe will still be taken to consist in your possessing a justified true belief about a belief that I have. By Davidson's own lights (see Davidson (1984) ), this should make us question whether we are talking about the same thing when we ascribe *knowledge* to both of us.

like Burge's response, it still leaves untouched key questions regarding content self-knowledge.[27]

## The Recognitional Conception of Ordinary Self-Knowledge

The limitations of the response to external-content skepticism offered by Burge and Davidson can be further appreciated by considering that external-content skepticism is but a special case of a more general skepticism that does not have to do specifically with content. This general skepticism, too, can be seen as directly fueled by the recognitional conception of self-knowledge. Once this is appreciated, we can see that, even in the case of content skepticism, adequate remedy requires more than improvement in our understanding of externalism; it requires a proper positive understanding of ordinary self-knowledge. Thus, in the remainder of this chapter, I want to consider the recognitional conception as it applies broadly to our knowledge of the presence and character of our present mental states, including those states whose ascription involves no specification of content.

In its most general form, the analogue of external-world skepticism in the case of our knowledge of our own present minds takes the following form:

When I self-ascribe a present mental state M, is it not possible, for all I know, that I am in a different mental state M'?

M could be a state such as thirst, or hunger, or malaise, whose ascription does not involve the assigning of content.[28] If the ascription does

---

[27] Burge is quite explicit that he does *not* consider the task of explaining the special status of self-ascriptions of thoughts, etc. to be complete by establishing what he calls the "environmental neutrality" of self-knowledge (1988). As I see it, Burge (1988) seeks to defend content externalism from skepticism in a way that is rather similar to Davidson's, by showing that it rests on a misunderstanding of the status of twin alternatives. Whereas in (1996) and (1998a), he addresses more directly the special epistemic status of our judgments about our own thoughts and attitudes. There he offers a Kantian argument to the effect that our nature as critical reasoners requires a special entitlement to self-knowledge. We shall return to Burge's view in Ch. 9.

[28] I have allowed that *all* mental states, including so-called phenomenal states, have representational content. (See above, Ch. 4, n. 10.) Even if this is correct, it is still true that not all mental ascriptions involve the specification of intentional contents.

involve assigning content, then we have the further question: Is it not possible, for all I know, that my state has a different content, $c'$, from the one I ascribe to it? This question arises not only for *twin* contents, but also for 'normal' distinct contents such as *that there's water in the glass* versus *that there's gin in the glass*.[29]

Now suppose that knowing what state one is in requires making a recognitional judgment. In paradigm cases of recognition, one is typically confronted by an individual, a substance, or a state of affairs, which one takes to be someone, some kind, or some way. For example, when I say (or think), "There's George" or "There's water in my glass", my statement relies on a judgment to the effect that the man I see, who appears to me a certain way, *is* George, or that the liquid I see in the glass, which appears a certain way, *is* water, respectively. Analogously, on the recognitional model, my self-ascription "I am in M" would rely on an independent judgment to the effect that a present state of mine that appears a certain way to me *is* M.

If this were so, then answering the internal-world skeptic would seem to require some assurance that *either* mental states and their contents cannot appear to be what they are not, as one tries to identify them, *or* that although they could, this does not threaten everyday self-knowledge, as we ordinarily understand it. The Cartesian philosopher embraces the first option, for she denies the possibility of imposters in the mental realm. As thinking subjects, we are endowed with a special faculty of introspection, which, unlike perception, is not vulnerable to illusion. If we ask *why* it is that we cannot be fooled by counterfeits in the mental realm, the Cartesian answer is ultimately that the relevant *objects* of mental self-knowledge (i.e., mental states) are of a special sort. What we know through introspection are states of our immaterial Selves; and such states are by their nature infallibly recognizable by their 'hosts'. The Cartesian strategy can thus be seen as rejecting skepticism by denying that there is any epistemic distance between appearance and reality for introspective recognition to traverse.[30]

---

[29] There is also the question: Is it not possible, for all I know, that it is someone else, not me, who has the ascribed state? This question would not arise if the self-ascription is immune to error through misidentification. (See above, Ch. 3 (pp. 56–60).) For a classification of the different aspects of security in terms of different questions that can be raised regarding the self-ascription, see Ch. 1, p. 4.

[30] Applied to the case of content, the move would be to postulate a special kind of content that is necessarily available for introspection. (Some versions of the "narrow content" view may fit this bill.) Georgalis (1994) tries to characterize a notion of content that is by its nature knowable in the way characteristic of effortless content self-knowledge.

The Cartesian can be seen as offering a hypothesis about the special nature of *what* we know when we have ordinary knowledge of our own minds, as the best explanation of the special security of such knowledge. The Cartesian in effect maintains that in the case of our own mind, unlike in the case of the extra-mental world, indiscernibles must always be identical. But there are good reasons not to accept this strategy, some of which we have already seen (in Chapter 2). Here I will point out only that doing so would seem to undermine the very use of the recognitional model in explaining self-knowledge. The recognitional model is tailor-made for cases where we are confronted with some object whose identity is determined independently of our recognition of it, and where we form beliefs about its identity based on the way it appears to us. It is a poor model on which to understand a recognitional faculty that is immune to all illusions because the objects it tracks must by their nature be what they seem and seem what they are.

As we saw in the previous chapter, many contemporary philosophers of mind embrace the idea that we possess a special faculty of introspection, while discarding the Cartesian notion that introspection is *in principle* invulnerable to recognitional mistakes. In opposition to Descartes, they believe that mental states possess an objective nature that *can* elude us. Still, they believe that the ordinary knowledge we possess about the presence and character of mental states in us is similar in important respects to ordinary recognitional knowledge of the extra-mental world (even if it is relatively more secure). These philosophers vary in their views about the objective conditions that must obtain for being in a given mental state. What bears emphasizing, though, is that anyone who understands introspection on the recognitional model must confront directly the possibility of counterfeits in accounting for our special *knowledge* of mental states. This is so regardless of whether they are externalists or internalists regarding the *nature* of such states.[31]

Suppose one holds that being in a mental state M supervenes entirely on facts internal to the individual; the individuation of the

[31] Davidson (1987) argues that we should reject the introspectionist picture for reasons similar to the ones given here. "The only object that would satisfy the twin requirements of being 'before the mind' and also such that it determines the content of a thought," he says, "must, like Hume's ideas and impressions, 'be what it seems and seem what it is'. There are no such objects, public or private, abstract or concrete" (Davidson 1987: 457). For a sustained criticism of the "inner sense model" of self-knowledge, see Shoemaker (1994).

state (viz., whether it is an M-state or an M′-state) then depends not at all on the individual's relations to her environment. (Perhaps it is a matter of the individual's functional internal organization understood 'narrowly'.) Still, unless the relevant facts are immediately recognizable without any theoretical self-examination, we still have to face the skeptic's challenge. If my normal way of telling that I am in M does not involve determining facts about my internal organization, how is it that I can be immune to being fooled by counterfeits—states that appear to me to be what they are in fact not? As long as whether or not I am in M at a given moment is thought to be an objective fact about me, and as long as my normal way of being apprised of this fact is understood on the recognitional model (i.e., as involving my telling that it is M I am in rather than M′ by the way it appears to me), this question must be confronted.[32]

One might try to address the question regarding knowledge of our own mental world by adopting certain proposals that have been made in connection with our knowledge of the extra-mental world. All empirical knowledge is knowledge in the face of possible counterfeits. And the knowledge we normally have of our own minds is but a special case of empirical knowledge. What allows us to have such knowledge is not the ability to rule out mental state imposters, but rather simply the *de facto* reliability of our internal introspective mechanism in tracking the presence, character, and content of the mental states we are actually in. Notice, first, that if we allow this route to securing self-knowledge in general from the threat of skepticism, externalist views of content, specifically, and of the nature of mental states more generally, should no longer seem in special trouble. For, on the present Reliabilist proposal, I could still be said to know that I am in a state M with a certain content $c$, even if, for all I know, I could be in a different state, M, or in state with a different content, $c'$. This would be so, as long as my self-ascriptions reliably track my first-order states and their contents, and even if I could not tell apart M and M′ (or $c$ and $c'$) on the basis of the way they appear to me. However, secondly, this pure reliabilist proposal itself represents a departure from the recognitional model. For, on this proposal, I can

---

[32] Crispin Wright (1989) speaks in this vein of the problem of the "theoreticity" of mental states. See also Goldman (1993). Goldman proposes that we can tell we are in a given state through its qualitative features, thereby reaffirming his commitment to the recognitional model.

know *that p* even in the absence of an ability to tell apart *p*-states of affairs from alternative ones that could obtain on the basis of their appearances. And this suggests that we no longer insist on the recognitional requirement.[33]

In any event, it is clear that the Reliabilist proposal just canvassed is designed to treat the possibility of counterfeits in the case of knowledge of our own mind on a full par with the possibility of counterfeits in the case of ordinary empirical knowledge. Thus, the proposal can at most accommodate a tempered version of the commonsense view of ordinary (or 'basic') self-knowledge. Perhaps it could allow that we are in an epistemically privileged position with respect to our own minds, but only in the sense that we are somehow epistemically better off in the case of our own minds than we are in the case of the extra-mental world. Yet there is a persistent Cartesian intuition that the security of ordinary self-knowledge is of a different *kind* from whatever security our knowledge of the extra-mental world can have. As I self-ascribe a present mental state in the normal way, it seems as though it isn't only that I am more likely to 'get it right' than when I make a perceptual judgment. Even if my self-ascription is not absolutely infallible, it does not seem open to brute error of the sort that may occur when the world (or someone) simply plays tricks on me.[34] In the normal case, there seems to be *no room* for the idea of a simple illusion of a sort similar to the sensory illusions that are possible when I have beliefs about the external world. Indeed, it may be thought that part of the idea that we possess an especially secure and privileged form of self-knowledge is the fact that, when it comes to ordinary mental self-ascriptions, the notion of a possible counterfeit is entirely out of place. If this is so, then it is not sufficient to be assured that we could have secure knowledge of our present states of mind consistently with any given view about the nature of those states; we need to understand the distinctive and unique character of such knowledge.

---

[33] This is not to deny that one could adopt some other Reliabilist proposal that continued to embrace some version of the recognitional requirement, yet insisted that the skeptic's alternatives are irrelevant.

[34] As explained in Ch. 1 (pp. 9 f.), ordinary perception is subject to brute errors in the sense that a subject's perceptual and conceptual faculties may be perfectly in order, normal conditions for proper functioning of her perceptual faculties may obtain, and yet she nevertheless makes a mistake about what she perceives. I can have my eyes open, my vision can be perfect, the light conditions may be perfectly normal, and yet I can judge that there is a cat in front of me when there isn't, simply because I have been presented with a fake cat.

Contemporary proponents of the 'inner sense' view may simply deny what I am calling the persistent Cartesian intuition. They may claim that the appearance of special security is an illusion. To do so would be to reject the explanatory project in which we have engaged. This is, of course, a possibility. But even if we are willing to accept that common sense is simply wrong about the special security of avowals, we may still want an explanation for the mistake. Why is it that present mental self-ascriptions *appear* more secure than ordinary claims about the external world? And why should internal-world skepticism *seem* so much less plausible, or threatening, than external-world skepticism? Simply rejecting the intuition does not allow us to answer these questions. In any event, it seems to me that here, as elsewhere, we should not embrace the eliminativist option, unless we have seen good reason to give up the search for an explanation.

The persistent Cartesian intuition about self-knowledge is not only the lore of common sense. It is accepted by many philosophers who hold significantly divergent views on the nature of mental states. Naturally, different philosophers offer different ways of capturing the intuition, as well as different explanations of its source. A proponent of the inner sense view could perhaps accept a tempered version of the Cartesian intuition. He could suggest that, although there is a difference in security between certain mental self-ascriptions (i.e., avowals) and ordinary empirical claims about the extra-mental world, once we reject the Cartesian claim of infallibility, there is no good reason to treat the difference as a difference in *kind*. All we need to allow is a difference in the *degree* of security. And this difference in degree is something that can be accommodated on the inner sense view. It is to be explained by the fact that inner sense is in fact more reliable and less vulnerable to the kinds of failures that afflict the outer senses.[35]

Understood in terms of the recognitional conception that has occupied us in this chapter, the claim would be that we are in fact better at telling mental imposters apart by their appearances than we are at telling apart extra-mental imposters by their appearances. But why should this be so? Why should the conditions under which inner

---

[35] For discussion of the idea that the high security of ordinary self-knowledge is simply due to the fact that introspection is more reliable than extra-mental perception (and for references), see above, Ch. 4 (pp. 95 ff.).

recognition operates be any more favorable than those under which outer recognition operates? More importantly, given that in everyday commerce with fellow human beings we are normally entirely unaware of the way their introspective mechanisms work, how could we pin the relatively high degree of security of their mental self-ascriptions on the assumed reliability of these mechanisms? For the purpose of the present point, we may grant that we do possess highly reliable inner mechanisms for recognizing our mental states, and even allow that these mechanisms deliver self-judgments about those states. While this could explain how highly secure self-knowledge is *possible*, it seems inadequate for explaining the ordinary treatment of the putative deliverances of inner recognition. If *all* there is to the security of self-knowledge is the *de facto* reliability of inner recognition, then, given our obvious ignorance of the workings of inner recognition, it becomes a mystery why we should regularly presume so strongly (as we do) that people's pronouncements about their own present states of mind are much more secure than all their other pronouncements. It also remains unclear why we should take basic self-knowledge to have such a different status from knowledge of the extra-mental world.[36]

It is worth emphasizing that I am *not* claiming that the recognitional view of self-knowledge is internally incoherent, or that it cannot be true. Furthermore, my criticism here is *not* that this view portrays self-knowledge as merely contingently privileged, whereas the privileged status of self-knowledge must be seen as somehow necessary. Rather, I am complaining that the recognitional conception of self-knowledge simply fails to explain our ordinary treatment of avowals and our commonsense intuitions about the character and status of self-knowledge. If we want such an explanation, if we are still in search of an account that meets the desiderata I have earlier spelled out, we must turn away from the recognitional view.

Accepting the Cartesian intuition does not require accepting Cartesian infallibility. Now suppose (as I am inclined to think) that although ordinary mental self-ascriptions can be false, when they are, this is always due to the presence of unusual background conditions,

---

[36] The present point echoes a point made in the previous chapter in criticizing the expertise model of first-person privilege. (See above, pp. 124 ff.)

or some kind of psychological failure on the part of the subject. In other words, suppose that such ascriptions, unlike perceptual judgments, are not open to brute error. I think this would give some credence to the Cartesian intuition. At the same time, it would tell against adopting the recognitional model of ordinary self-knowledge. I think the Cartesian intuition is part and parcel of the commonsense view regarding ordinary mental self-ascriptions and basic self-knowledge. The Cartesian intuition may also explain the strong expectation that environmental changes of the sort imagined in Twin Earth switch cases should not matter to the individual's basic self-knowledge, even though such changes would obviously affect the individual's knowledge of the extra-mental world. This expectation is precisely what the opponent of content externalism trades on when trying to reduce the view to absurdity by showing that it entails that environmental changes *would* affect self-knowledge. Thus, I think we should respect the Cartesian intuition, even as we reject the Cartesian doctrine of infallibility (as well as Cartesian dualism).

Let us take stock. Earlier, I tried to argue that raising a skeptical doubt about content that is analogous to the doubt raised by the external-world skeptic requires invoking a recognitional conception of self-knowledge. On this conception, I argued, it is not just content externalism that would have to face the skeptical challenge, but any view that admitted the possibility of counterfeit contents. Once this is appreciated, we can see that the problem generalizes beyond content: any view of the nature of mental states in general which allows for a gap between appearances and reality in the mental realm, and which treats the ordinary knowledge we have of our present states of mind on the recognitional model, will have to reckon with skepticism about self-knowledge that is analogous to external-world skepticism. This should not come as a surprise. For skepticism thrives wherever we combine an appearance/reality distinction with a conception of knowledge as epistemic access mediated by some recognitional ability. Thus, someone who takes us to possess a specially secure and privileged knowledge of our present states of mind must *either* reject the appearance/reality distinction as it applies to our own mind *or* reject the idea that ordinary self-knowledge is knowledge based on how things in our 'mental world' appear to us. I myself do not see how to embrace the first option. But, in any event, I think we have seen reason enough to go with the second option, and reject the recognitional conception of ordinary self-knowledge. I regard the rejection of the recognitional conception as a crucial element in addressing external-content skepticism, as well as a necessary step on our way to a positive account of ordinary self-knowledge. However, taking this step is not sufficient by itself for providing such an account. We still need to see what can be put in place of the recognitional conception which would account for our seemingly special ability to make secure and knowledgeable pronouncements about our present mental states. This will be my task in the next chapters.

# 6

# *The Distinctive Security Of Avowals: Ascriptive Immunity to Error*

In the previous chapter, I argued that the skeptical challenge to our ordinary knowledge of content that is based on externalist twin alternatives relies on a recognitional conception of self-knowledge. I provided some reasons for rejecting that conception. In conformity with the commonsense doctrine of content self-knowledge (CSK), I argued that a plausible alternative to the recognitional conception should allow us to maintain that our knowledge of the content of a present state of ours can withstand the skeptical threat. It remains to be seen what we can put in place of this conception. But now recall the three questions regarding avowals and self-knowledge, which I separated earlier on (see Chapter 1, pp. 11 f.):

  (i)  What accounts for the unparalleled security of avowals?
 (ii)  Do avowals serve to articulate privileged self-knowledge?
(iii)  Avowals aside, what allows us to possess privileged self-knowledge?

I have recommended that we begin by investigating the distinctive security of avowals, without prejudging the question whether avowals represent a form of privileged self-knowledge, and if so, what is the source of its privileged character. In keeping with this recommendation, in this and the following two chapters, I turn to what I take to be the prior task of developing a positive account of avowals' security. The discussion of self-knowledge will wait till a later chapter.

I begin this chapter by explaining why the security that is of interest to us here—the security that makes for the asymmetries between avowals and all other ascriptions—goes beyond protection from a skeptical threat based on externalist twin alternatives. Moreover, we will see that the relevant security cuts across avowals that involve an assignment of intentional content to one's state and ones that do not. If so-called intentional avowals are not vulnerable to skeptical doubts based on content externalism, this is because they enjoy a more general security, which I have referred to as *ascriptive security*, where ascriptive security pertains to the part of an avowal that ascribes to the avower a certain present state, whether intentional or not. I will be proposing a particular take on ascriptive security. The ascriptive security of avowals, I will suggest, should be regarded as a matter of immunity to error that is over and above their immunity to error through misidentification. I will be motivating this characterization by considering a case of the same kind as the case that featured in my discussion of externalism and content skepticism in the previous chapter: the case of self-ascribing a present thought. In some ways, this represents a special case of avowals. However, I believe that key features of this case can be generalized to other avowals.

Identifying the distinctive security of avowals as immunity to a certain kind of error will serve a dual purpose. First, it will give us an alternative to the idea that avowals' security is a matter of epistemically secure access, method, route, or basis. (This idea, recall, was definitive of the Epistemic Approach rejected in Chapter 4.) Secondly, it will allow us to recover a key insight of a view that is very often contrasted with epistemic views: namely, the *expressivist* view of avowals, which maintains that avowals directly express, rather than report, the states they ascribe. The task of subsequent chapters will be to show how the expressivist insight can be appropriated without incurring the liabilities standardly associated with expressivist views. In this way, the present chapter marks a transition between my earlier rejection of other views of avowals and self-knowledge and the development and defense of my own positive view.

## Beyond Security in Content Assignment

When I self-ascribe a mental state in the ordinary way, I seem to produce my self-ascription effortlessly, without reliance on evidence or conjecture; yet I seem able to tell with a high degree of security what state I am in, as well as what its content is. Indeed, I think we should see the security of content assignment that concerns defenders of externalism as but a special case of the more general ascriptive security of avowals, which (as I indicated earlier) is shared by intentional and non-intentional avowals alike. At the end of the last chapter, I pointed out that this broader security still remains to be explained, even after we have successfully defended content self-knowledge against external-content skepticism. On the other hand, understanding the nature of the broader security may reinforce the arguments that such skepticism is misplaced.[1]

As a first pass, we can think of the security of avowals as a joint product of two separable securities: one pertaining to the subject part and one pertaining to the ascriptive part. As regards the first security, I have examined the idea that avowals are immune to error through misidentification (IETM) (see Chapter 3). A subject who avows is not vulnerable to a certain kind of error—an error of misidentifying the subject of her ascription. However, I argued that while this idea goes some way toward explaining the security of avowals, it still does not allow us to explain the asymmetries between avowals and other, non-mental "I"-ascriptions that are also immune to errors through misidentification—most notably, proprioceptive reports and the like. I shall now turn to the additional security of avowals, the one that pertains to their ascriptive part. My proposal below will be that this additional security can be regarded as a matter of a special, additional immunity to error.

When I proclaim, say, a desire for a glass of water, it is not just that my self-ascription is secure as regards its being water, rather than twater, that I want. My self-ascription is also secure as regards its being water, rather than gin, that I want. Here we have *ordinary* alternative thought contents—$c$ versus $c'$—where both $c$ and $c'$ are in my conceptual repertoire at the same time, and where the difference between my thinking $c$ and my thinking $c'$ is something that I do presumably understand and

---

[1] I thus disagree with Dretske (1999) that while we are practically infallible in the assignment of content to our present states, we know that we are in a given mental state (or in any mental state at all) only by using normal channels of obtaining knowledge, and the knowledge we have is no more secure than ordinary empirical knowledge.

Note that showing content self-knowledge to be protected from skeptical doubt generated by twin alternatives falls short of establishing that we can tell with a special security what kind of mental state we are in. It also falls short of explaining the security with which we tell that a contentful mental state we are in has one content rather than another, non-twin content.

could, in principle, verify. Still, it does not seem plausible to suggest that the relative superior security of my self-ascription as regards content rests on my being able to recognize $c$ as the content of my thought through some characteristic signs available to me but not to anyone else. It is true that, as I ascribe to myself a present state with content $c$, doubt as to whether it is indeed $c$ that is the content of my state, rather than $c'$, seems out of place. When I self-ascribe an intentional state in the ordinary way, the correct intentional content of the self-ascribed state is not up for grabs as it might be when I interpret someone else's utterances. But I would argue that this is not because I am so much better able to ascertain that my state has this rather than that intentional content. To suppose that this *is* the reason is to suggest something that seems implausible: namely, that even in the ordinary case, I have grounds for taking myself to be in some intentional state or other that are separate from whatever grounds I have for thinking that I am in a state with a particular intentional content, as though having somehow recognized that I am in a state of believing, or being angry, or wanting, I independently need to determine what content to assign to it.

For that matter, it also seems to me implausible to suppose that the security with which I seem able to tell *what state* I am in, in ordinary circumstances in which I avow my state, depends on my unique ability to recognize the presence and character of the state through some identifying marks. Again, the recognitional model has clear purchase in the case of mental ascriptions to *others*. In the case of others, it may be plausible to suggest that we recognize someone to be in, say, a state of fear, or anger, or puzzlement, independently of identifying the intentional content of their state. Quite possibly, the degree of security with which we can tell whether someone wants something (as well as what they want), or is angry at or afraid of someone, and so on, depends on the extent to which we are able to recognize characteristic signs of her being in the relevant state as well as of the state having the particular intentional content. But this does not seem to be an appropriate model for understanding the security with which we ordinarily tell that we ourselves are in a certain mental state, or what the state's content is. What seems wrong is the suggestion that, as I normally ascribe to myself hoping or thinking that $p$, or being angry with $x$, or wanting $y$, I am in the following epistemic position: I have recognitional grounds for the judgment that I am in *some* state or other, which state I take to have some content or other, independently of whatever grounds I have for thinking that I am in the *particular* contentful state I ascribe to myself. Perhaps I could be in this epistemic position—say, if I could *not* tell what state I was in at a given time, and set myself the task of figuring it out. Then I might use various clues, observe my own behavior, listen to my therapist, consult my friends, and so on. I could then recognize through characteristic signs, or come to the conclusion based on my evidence, that my state is that of, say, anger; and I may then also be left with the further task of figuring out who the object of my anger is. But that is decisively not my situation when I simply proclaim feeling angry at *x*.

If so, then in seeking to understand the special relative security of avowals, it may not be fruitful to search for an especially secure kind of recognition reserved for one's own present mental states. Instead, we might consider the following possibility. We have seen how the security of uses of "I" as subject can be understood by appeal to the immunity to error through misidentification of "I"-ascriptions that instantiate such uses. In a similar way, we could understand the ascriptive security of avowals by appeal to their *immunity to error through misascription*. Just as the former appeal obviated the need to invoke infallible recognition of one's Self, so the latter appeal may obviate the need to invoke infallible, or even just highly secure, recognition of one's present mental states and their contents.

## Ascriptive Security as a Species of Immunity to Error

Recall Shoemaker's characterization of the notion of *immunity to error through misidentification* (discussed at length in Chapter 3):

The statement "I feel pain" is not subject to error through misidentification: it cannot happen that I am mistaken in saying "I feel pain" because, although I do know of someone that he feels pain, I am mistaken in thinking that person to be myself. . . .

If I say "I feel pain" or "I see a canary," I may be identifying for someone else the person of whom I am saying that he feels pain or sees a canary. But there is also a sense in which my reference does not involve an identification. My use of the word "I" as the subject of my statement is not due to my having identified as myself something of which I know, or believe, or wish to say, that the predicate of my statement applies to it. (1968: 557– 8)

We saw that Shoemaker and Evans both offer the following intuitive test for immunity to error through misidentification. When a self-ascription of the form "I am F" is IETM, then, although I may fail to be F, so my self-ascription may be false, there is no room for me to think: "*Someone* is F, but is it *me*?" If I come to think in the usual way, "I have a toothache", or "I'm standing in front of a tree", or "I see a canary", I cannot sensibly doubt whether it is *me* who has the relevant properties without doubting that *someone* has them. This is because in such cases I have no grounds for thinking that *someone* has the relevant properties over and above, or separately from, any grounds I might have for thinking that *I* have them. With respect to many self-ascriptions I do have such independent grounds. For example, I often learn how much money I have in my bank account by consulting a bank-teller's screen. If in fact the screen is giving information about someone else's account, I would be right to think that *someone* has, say, $500 in her account, though wrong to think that *I* have $500 in my account.

Now consider the ascriptive part of avowals. In the normal case, as I say or think, "I am feeling terribly thirsty", it would seem as out of place to suggest, "I am feeling *something*, but is it thirst?" as it would to question whether it is *I* who am feeling the thirst. Or take an avowal with intentional content, such as "I'm really mad at you". "I am mad at *someone*, but is it *you*?" and "I'm in *some* state, but is it being mad?" would both be as odd as "*Someone* is mad at you, but is it *I*?" when I simply avow being mad at you (as opposed to making a conjecture about my own state of mind, for example). Similarly for avowals of propositional attitudes, such as "I am wondering whether it's time to leave". "I am wondering *something*, but am I wondering *whether it's time to leave?*", as well as "*Something* is going on in me, but is it a *wondering?*", seem out of place, as I ascribe the wondering to myself in the normal way. By contrast, both "I am doing *something* with my arm, but am I resting it on the chair?" and "I am resting my arm on *something*, but is it a chair?" could make perfect sense even as I think, "I'm resting my arm on the chair" in the normal way.

There is a related intuitive linguistic test for immunity to error we can consider, one suggested to me by Ram Neta. The test can be used to determine whether a component of an ascription rests on what I have called recognitional judgment. When it does, we can without anomaly append, "It appears (to me) that . . . " to the relevant component. Thus, consider the anomaly of saying, "It appears to me that *I* am the one who is raising her arm". It's not that one cannot sensibly say that. But if one did, the obvious implication would be precisely that one is *not* offering a *proprioceptive* report. (For example, it would not be odd to say that if I am looking in a mirror, or watching a video film. But in such a context, the embedded ascription "I am raising my arm" would be an ordinary perceptual report.) By contrast, there is no anomaly in saying, "It appears to me that *my legs are crossed* (not stretched out)," even as I am offering a proprioceptive report. But in the case of avowals, when I avow, "I'm so happy to see you", *both*, e.g., "It appears to me that *I* am the one happy to see you" and "It appears to me that I am *happy* to see you (not annoyed)" or "It appears to me that I am happy to see *you* (not my sister)" seem anomalous. To clarify, I am not claiming that "It appears to me that I am *happy* (rather than annoyed) to see *you* (rather than my sister)" is grammatically ill-formed, logically contradictory, or otherwise inherently anomalous. It *can* be sensibly said (and thought). But if one were to say it, the contextual implication would be that one is offering a third-person conjectural report on one's present state, rather than avowing it.[2]

Unlike non-mental "I"-ascriptions, then, ordinary mental "I"-ascriptions pass intuitive tests for immunity to error not only with respect to their subject part, but also with respect to their ascriptive part. I dub this additional immunity "immunity to error through misascription" (ascriptive immunity to error, for short). As we ascribe mental states to ourselves in the ordinary, everyday way (i.e., not on the basis of therapy, consultation with others, self-interpretation, or cognitive test results, etc.), our self-ascriptions are no more vulnerable to recognitional mistakes regarding the ascribed state than they are to mistakes of identification of the subject of our ascription. In the case of avowals of intentional states, we can think of ascriptive immunity to error as breaking down further into immunity regarding the presence

---

[2] At this point, I don't want to commit myself on the precise nature of the implication. I also want to stress that the implication is not purely a conversational matter. Similar remarks would apply to self-ascriptions made in thought. As we consider someone who thinks to herself, "It appears to me that I am happy (not sad)," it is natural to understand the self-ascription as some kind of a third-person, evidential self-report (made to oneself), rather than an avowal.

and character of the ascribed mental state and immunity regarding the state's intentional object/propositional content (intentional content, for short). This combined immunity can serve to mark a significant contrast between avowals and all non-mental "I"-ascriptions, even those that enjoy immunity to error through misidentification of their subject. While I may be immune to errors of misidentifying the subject of certain of my bodily self-ascriptions, I am not immune to errors of misidentifying or mischaracterizing the bodily condition I am in, even as I use the normal way of gaining that type of information about myself. But when I avow a mental state, I am immune to errors of mis-ascribing a state of mind to myself, as well as mis-assigning an intentional content to my state.

To say that avowals enjoy this combined immunity to error is *not* to deny that one could sincerely and competently make a self-ascription such as "I feel angry, but I'm not sure who I feel angry at" or "I don't know how I feel about you". We may even take such self-ascriptions to be avowals. We can think of them either as avowals of certain indeterminate states of mind or as avowals of a (determinate) state of doubting, or wondering, whose content concerns one's own present state of mind. I am not questioning the possibility of such avowals. My claim is rather that, as I make an avowal that does ascribe to me a determinate state with determinate content, it would make as little sense for me to question the character or content of the state I am avowing as to question the identity of the individual to whom I am ascribing the state. It is this feature of avowals that is relevant to the intuitive tests for ascriptive immunity to error.

In understanding my suggestion that we regard avowals as enjoying ascriptive immunity to error, we should keep in mind the following features highlighted in my earlier discussion of immunity to error through misidentification of certain "I"-ascriptions (see above, Chapter 3). First, "I"-ascriptions that are said to be IETM are not in general incorrigible. "I see a canary", "I am sitting down", "My legs are crossed", can all be plausibly said to be IETM, yet no one would be tempted to regard them as incorrigible.[3] Second, when an ascription is IETM, then, even if it can be mistaken, it is not open to a certain kind

---

[3] We noted in Ch. 3 that being immune to error through misidentification is not even unique to "I"-ascriptions. Both Shoemaker and Evans think that demonstrative thoughts such as "This is moving fast", though clearly not infallible or incorrigible, are immune to error through misidentification.

of error: an error of mistaking one object for another because of a mistaken identification. Third, whether or not an "I"-ascription is IETM depends not on its semantic content, but rather on its 'epistemic pedigree'. An "I"-ascription that is IETM when issued in the normal way can become vulnerable to error when made on the basis of an identification judgment. (If I tell that I am sitting down by seeing in a mirror, or on a video screen, someone who is sitting down and whom I take to be me, my "I"-ascription "I am sitting down" will *not* be IETM, even though it would be IETM when it is made in the normal way.) Fourth, if I issue an ascription of the form "I am F" that is IETM, then my ascription can properly be said to be *about* me, and I can legitimately be said to be ascribing some property or state to *myself*. Finally, I can be said to be able to tell that it is I myself who has the property F, even though my ascription does not rest on a judgment that identifies me as the 'right' subject of my ascription.

This last feature bears emphasis. Having immunity to error through misidentification implies being protected from a certain *kind* of error—the error of misidentifying *who* it is that is said to be F. But it does not reflect a special success in recognizing someone as being the right individual of whom to predicate F. Quite the opposite. Immunity to error through misidentification reflects the *absence* of recognitional identification. When I say or think in the ordinary way, "I see a canary," it is not as though I recognize someone as seeing a canary, and take that someone to be me. If I cannot go wrong in identifying myself as the correct subject of my ascriptions, it is precisely because my ascription does not rest on any judgment that identifies me with anyone. As mentioned in Chapter 3 (p. 68), there is a thin sense in which I do identify myself as the subject of the ascription, for I do manage to *refer* to myself, and referring is picking out, and picking out is a form of identifying. But my ascription does not rest on a recognitional judgment of the form "I = r" (where "r" stands for some identifying description or demonstrative representation of an individual).[4]

---

[4] It may be useful to distinguish between the *referential* notion of identifying (a semantic notion) and the *recognitional* notion of identifying (an epistemic notion). Compare Evans: "The word 'identify' can do us a disservice here. In one sense, anyone who thinks about an object identifies that object (in thought) . . . It is quite another matter . . . for the thought to involve an identification component—for the thought to be identification-dependent. There is a danger of moving from the fact that there is no identification in the latter sense (that no criteria of recognition are brought to bear, and so forth) to the conclusion that there is no identification in the former sense" (1982: 218).

On the above analysis, it is the absence of an independent *recognitional judgment* to the effect that someone is me that renders a self-ascription of the form "I am F" immune to error through misidentification. In some cases, I make judgments of this form when I have no grounds for thinking that *someone* is F that are independent of my grounds for thinking that *I* am F. Similarly, I suggest that in the case of immunity to error through misascription, the relevant ascription "I am in M (with content *c*)" is not grounded in an independent recognitional judgment concerning the character of my present state or its content. I can be said to ascribe to myself being in state M with content *c*. But I have no grounds for thinking I am in some state or other (or for thinking it has some content or other) that are independent of my grounds for thinking I am in state *M* (with content *c*). In other words, I am not in the epistemic position of judging that I am in some state with some content and making the judgment that the state is M and its content is *c* based on recognizable features of the state.

Now, in the case of ascriptions that are *only* IETM, such as "My legs are crossed" (as ordinarily made), there *is* an independent recognitional judgment that one can fall back on regarding the state of one's limbs (i.e., my legs are in some position, though they are not crossed—bent, perhaps?). Hence, one can sensibly entertain the possibility that one is in some state, though not the one ascribed—whereas I am claiming that avowals contrast with such ascriptions in that there is no similar judgment to retreat to regarding the ascriptive part of the avowal. As I shall put it, when avowing, one has no epistemic grounds for the ascription of some mental state or other (or for the assignment of some content or other) that are independent of whatever grounds one has for ascribing a particular mental state with a specific content to oneself. (One also has no epistemic grounds for thinking that someone is in the mental state that are independent of whatever grounds one has for thinking that one is *oneself* in the state.) Moreover, just as one's normal proprioceptive *self*-ascription is not grounded in what Evans describes as a 'thick' identification of oneself, so I maintain that the ascription of a particular mental state to oneself that's involved in avowing is not underwritten by a recognitional judgment regarding the character or content of some state that one takes oneself to be in. This is what I mean by claiming that avowals are immune to error through misascription in addition to being immune to error through misidentification.

The idea of ascriptive immunity to error can be elaborated further by contrasting it with the central idea advocated by the Epistemic Approach. On my proposed characterization, the distinctive security of avowals is not a matter of recognitional success, which then invites an epistemic explanation. It is rather a matter of invulnerability to certain kinds of epistemic errors, correction, or criticism, which is understood in terms of the *absence* of a certain kind of epistemic grounds. Suppose I avow wanting a cup of tea, as opposed to ascribing this state to myself on the basis of inference or evidence. On the Epistemic Approach, it will still be the case that there is some epistemic basis or grounds for my ascribing to myself the state of wanting (as opposed to some other attitude) and for taking *cup of tea* (as opposed to something else) to be the intentional object of my attitude. On the introspective view, the basis will be some characteristic signs that are internally perceived or scanned. Other epistemic views will substitute their preferred bases. By contrast, on my proposed analysis, avowals are not epistemically grounded in any recognitional judgments. Just as an ordinary report such as "I am sitting down" is not epistemically underwritten by a judgment to the effect that someone, whom I identify as myself, is sitting down, so my avowal "I want a cup of tea" is not epistemically underwritten by a judgment that I am in some state, which I recognize to be a state of wanting a cup of tea. For, when avowing, I have no epistemic grounds for thinking that I am in *some* mental state or other (and that it has *some* content or other) that is independent of my simply thinking that I want a cup of tea. Yet if my avowal were epistemically based on internal recognition (as introspectionists would have it), then I might very well have a reason for thinking I am in some state, which only *appears* to me to be that of wanting a cup of tea.

My suggestion is that if it is not up for grabs what state an avowing subject is in, or what content it has, this is at least in part because one's ascription of a state to oneself and the assignment of content to it are *not* mediated by recognitional judgments regarding the state's character or its content. And I am offering the fact that avowals' ascriptive part is as epistemically unmediated (or 'thin') as their subject part as a distinctive feature of avowals. Portraying avowals as enjoying ascriptive immunity to error has several advantages. We have seen how pointing to an ascription's immunity to errors of misidentification obviates the need to invoke a secure way of knowing who I am in order to explain the special security of uses of "I" as subject. Similarly, recognizing avowals as having ascriptive immunity to error may help us explain their ascriptive security without invoking some epistemically secure form of determination or ascertainment of the mental state one is in (or its content), or some epistemically secure recognitional judgment on which they rest. By the same token, portraying avowals as immune to error of misascription (as well as immune to error through misidentification) should allow us to avoid the temptation to invoke infallibly knowable Cartesian entities to explain the special security of avowals. Recall that Evans and Shoemaker offer the notion of immunity to error through misidentification in part as a way of avoiding the need for postulating the Cartesian Ego as a referent for "I". However, once we focus on the ascriptive security of avowals, we might be tempted to invoke the Cartesian Ego again, only this time to serve as a 'substratum' for the securely knowable mental properties or states ascribed in avowals. Or we might invoke directly knowable mental particulars—sense-data—to serve as the singular referents of mental terms in avowals. But if we no longer regard the ascriptive security of avowals as a matter of special recognitional success, the need to invoke such specially recogniz*able* Cartesian entities to explain it may disappear.

Succinctly put, then, the proposal I am making at this stage is this:

Avowals are not only immune to error as regards *who* it is that is in the relevant contentful state (that is, immune to error through misidentification), but are also *immune to error through misascription*. When ascribing a present mental state M to myself in the ordinary way, I am not vulnerable to recognitional errors regarding the presence, character, or content of my state. And this is because my self-ascription does not rest on an independent judgment that I am in some state or other, coupled with a recognitional judgment to the effect that the state is M (rather than M′), or on the judgment that my state has some intentional content or other, coupled with a recognitional judgment to the effect that the content is *c* (rather than *c*′).

As I see the general notion of immunity to error, it is essentially a negative notion. Possessing immunity to error clearly does not signal the presence of a highly secure epistemic basis. Neither does it signal absolute infallibility or the presence of a special guarantee of truth (see below). A person who is immune to error in some domain does not go astray in her pronouncements. But this is not because she knows her way around so well, or has a special route to the truth, but because she simply does not go down certain paths. If she is not victim to certain kinds of epistemic error, it is because there are certain epistemic risks she does not take. So it is in this negative way that epistemic errors are crowded out. Correlatively, if she is protected from epistemic criticism, it is not because she has followed impeccably safe epistemic protocol, as it were, but because, given the character of her self-ascription, it is inappropriate to subject her to such criticism.

## Ascriptive Immunity to Error: Epistemic Asymmetry and Semantic Continuity

We can already see how the idea that avowals enjoy ascriptive immunity to error can help capture, and account for, important aspects of Epistemic Asymmetry. Seeing avowals as immune to ascriptive error can explain why, unlike proprioceptive reports, for example, they are not seen as open to brute errors of ascription. A brute error, recall, occurs when one is simply fooled into thinking that things are a certain way not through any perceptual or conceptual failing on their part. A person makes a brute error when she *mistakes a* for *b* or something F for G, albeit not through a perceptual or conceptual failure. But, on the view I am proposing, when avowing being in state M' with intentional content *c*, I cannot be regarded as *mistaking* M' for N (or *c* for *c'*) the way I can mistake a fake cup for a real one, since I cannot be regarded as *taking* some state of mine to be M rather than N in the first place. To repeat, when I avow being in state M with content *c*, I have no grounds for thinking that the state I am in is a state of *some* kind (though perhaps it isn't M) or that my state has *some* content (though perhaps it isn't *c*), *other than* whatever grounds I have for thinking I am in state M with content *c*. With judgments that are IETM, I cannot question the identity of the state's bearer without questioning whether *anyone* is in the relevant state. With judgments that enjoy, in addition, ascriptive immunity, I cannot question the character or content of the state while still retaining the judgment that someone is in *some* state (maybe $M'$) with *some* content (maybe $c'$). Thus, my claim that avowals do not represent recognitional judgments concerning either the bearer of the state or the character and content of the state can help explain the intuition that there is no room for brute error in the case of avowals.

Furthermore, we can also see why, unlike ascriptions to others, as well as non-mental ascriptions to oneself (or even mental "I"-ascriptions in the past tense), avowals are so resistant to epistemic challenge or criticism. If my mental self-ascription "I am in M (with content $c$)" represents no recognitional judgment on my part, then it makes little sense to ask me to offer reasons or to question my justification for saying (or thinking) that I am in M (with content $c$). Just as it would be out of place to ask me, "Why do you think it's you whose legs are crossed?," when it is obvious that I am offering a proprioceptive report, so it would be out of place to ask me "Why do you think it's hunger you're feeling?" when it is clear that I am simply avowing my hunger. Thus, the lack of epistemic mediation that attends immunity to error seems to capture nicely the epistemic immediacy and invulnerability that we ordinarily associate with avowals.

Epistemic invulnerability does not imply infallibility. To say that epistemic errors are crowded out is *not* to say that truth is guaranteed. With common sense, I maintain that avowals *can* be false. Here again we can call on the model of immunity to error through misidentification. The issuing of an ascription that is immune to error of misidentification does not, in general, guarantee its truth. As we have seen, even when a subject issues a self-ascription such as "My legs are crossed" in the normal way, the ascription may be false. Its immunity to error of misidentification just means that, *if* I make a mistake, it is not a mistake of misidentifying the subject, since the ascription in no way rests on an identification judgment. Similarly, I want to suggest that when avowing, say, "I hope Emma will come soon", it is possible for me to be saying something false. But since I do not ascribe the hope to myself on the basis of any kind of recognition of my current state for what it is, my failure will not be the *epistemic* failure of *mistaking* one state for another, or mistaking one content for another, any more than it will be due to mistaking one individual for another as the subject of the ascription.[5] By the same token, if my avowal is true, the success will *not* be due to my correctly *taking* a state of mine (or its content) for what it is. This is part of regarding the avowal as immune to errors of misascription. (The analogous point about self-ascriptions that are IETM was that when I falsely say, e.g., "I am raising my arm", my error is not one of mistaking myself for someone else of whom I judge that she is F, or thinking that someone is F and erroneously taking it to be *me* who is F. And, correlatively, when my self-ascription is true, my ability to tell that this is so is not due to success in correctly identifying some individual as myself.)

The epistemic invulnerability afforded by ascriptive immunity to error does not imply incorrigibility, either. Even if we do not take an avowing subject to be guilty of any mistaking (of herself, of her state, of its content), we still can, and do, sometimes find reason to suppose that an avowal is false. As we shall see later (in Chapter 8), our judgment that someone's avowal is false does not require that we see their failure as an epistemic failure. It need not be backed up by an *epistemic* explanation that attributes to them errors of judgment.

Finally, we should recognize that ascriptive immunity to error in no way implies self-intimation. To say that when one avows, one's self-ascription is immune to errors of misascription is not to say that, for any mental state one is in at a given moment, one is guaranteed to know, or even to believe, that one is in that state. This should be fairly obvious, since immunity to error attaches to judgments or ascriptions as these are *made*. The claim that avowals are immune to errors through misascription just means that *if* one issues an avowal, then one's self-ascription enjoys ascriptive immunity to error. It leaves open that one could be in a mental state without judging one is in it, or without issuing any self-ascription, in speech or in thought, whether immune to error or not.

There is a question, which I take up in later chapters, whether avowing involves making any kind of self-judgment, or expressing any belief about oneself. In the next chapter, I will argue that insofar as we take avowals to express a present belief one has about oneself, we should not regard the distinctive security of avowals as coming

---

[5] In Ch. 8, I will be discussing the various ways in which avowals can fail, and will offer a non-epistemic explanation of such failures.

from the epistemic security of the belief. One way to see my main point in this chapter so far is as follows: I deny that avowing involves a certain *kind* of judgment—a recognitional judgment that grounds the ascriptive component of the relevant self-ascription. I take this to be a crucial point of contrast with epistemic views, since they seek to explain the security of avowals by appeal to the epistemic security of the recognitional judgments on which they rest. Thus, on the Epistemic Approach, if my avowal "I am tired" is especially secure, it is because I have a foolproof way (or at least a highly reliable way) of recognizing my present mental state for what it is, which I have put to use in issuing the avowal. Whereas I am claiming, on the contrary, that avowals not only do not involve drawing an inference, or consulting evidence; they are also not mediated by recognitional judgments concerning the character (or content) of one's self-ascribed states.

I regard the acknowledgement of avowals' ascriptive immunity to error as a crucial step in explaining Epistemic Asymmetry. But if, in keeping with Semantic Continuity, we take avowals to be genuine ascriptions, which can be true or false, we will need, in addition to understanding what protects avowals from certain kinds of epistemic errors and criticisms, to understand why it is that avowals are so strongly presumed to be *true*. This will be my task in a later chapter. Right now, I want to turn to a prior issue: the status of avowals as genuine, true or false ascriptions. On my view, recall, the success of any account of avowals' security is to be measured not only by how well it can capture Epistemic Asymmetry in its full scope, but also by whether it can preserve Semantic Continuity. If avowals are to be semantically continuous with other ascriptions, we must regard them as genuine ascriptions, which tell us something about the self-ascriber and her present state. But Semantic Continuity is not something we can assume; it must be earned.

Let me spell out, in a somewhat abstract way, what is involved in achieving Semantic Continuity. To begin with, we must insist that a typical avowal will have the logical form "I am (in) M", where "I" (or whatever "I"-device it uses) refers to the self-ascriber, and "M" picks out a kind of mental state.[6] Semantically speaking, an avowal will have

---

[6] For simplicity of exposition, I will be talking in terms of a genuine mental ascription requiring reference to a relevant (kind of) mental condition. But the requirement is intended to be neutral as between the property versus adverbial construal of mental predicates.

as its content the proposition that a certain individual—the self-ascriber—is in M at the time the avowal is made. And it will be *true* just in case the self-ascriber is indeed in the state ascribed. At the same time, to explain the distinctive status of avowals, we may need to make room for the notion that the way one ascribes a particular mental state when making an avowal may be different from the way one does so in ascriptions to others, or in evidential self-ascriptions. In our discussion of "I", we saw that one's lack of epistemic means of identifying the subject of an "I"-ascription does not impugn one's thinking *about* or referring to a particular individual, namely oneself. Recognizing this allowed us to avoid the No Reference view of "I". The analogous claim regarding the ascriptive part of avowals will be that one's failure to apply the mental term to some condition of oneself on the basis of the way one's 'internal scene' appears to one, or on some other epistemic basis representing what one *takes* one's state to be, need not impugn one's genuinely ascribing to oneself being in the relevant mental state.

This suggests that a crucial part of preserving Semantic Continuity is avoiding an analogue of the No Reference view of "I" for the ascriptive part of avowals. The analogue would be a No Ascription view of avowals, according to which avowing involves *no* genuine ascription of a mental state to a subject, no saying or thinking *that* the self-ascriber is in such-and-such a state. This view may seem tempting, given the special ascriptive security of avowals (just as the No Reference view seemed tempting in light of the special security of "I"). For it might seem that no genuine ascription could possibly exhibit the ascriptive security of avowals. Specifically, portraying avowals' security as (in part) a combination of immunity to errors of misidentification and immunity to errors of misascription seems to have the consequence that, when I avow being in state M (with content *c*), I cannot go wrong as regards either its being *I* who am in state M, or its being state *M* that I am in (or whether it is content *c* that it has). But then we may wonder what to make of the idea that I am genuinely ascribing to myself being in state M (with content *c*).

Let me put this in a different way, using earlier terminology. When discussing the special security we enjoy when using "I" as subject, I suggested that the user of "I" does not have the subject of her ascription (namely, herself) as an epistemic target—as someone she seeks to identify, in the thick sense. Still, I argued that she does make genuine reference to herself. She can be a semantic target for her ascription, without being an epistemic target.[7] Similarly, I think we should abandon the idea that a subject who produces an avowal has her mental state as an epistemic target—something whose presence, character, or content she seeks to ascertain. (This is by way of denying that the security of her self-ascription is the epistemic success of a well-grounded judgment concerning her present state.) Avowing no more involves epistemic targeting of the ascribed mental state or its intentional content (when it has one) than it involves epistemic targeting of oneself as the appropriate subject of the ascription. But, to avoid the No Ascription view, I must explain how, even in the absence of such epistemic targeting, one's mental state can still be the semantic target of one's ascription.

In other words, we need to see how avowals can be *about* the relevant mental states, and thus involve genuine self-ascriptions of particular mental states. This requires that expressions such as "thinking/wishing/hoping/etc., that *p*", or "feeling angry at/scared of/etc. *x*", or "being thirsty", etc., as they are used in avowals, genuinely refer to the relevant mental states, even though they are not applied on the strength of recognitional judgments concerning those states. Furthermore, we must require that the very mental states that subjects ascribe to themselves when avowing could be equally referred to by individuals other than the subject, and by the subject at other times. We also want the properties or states ascribed in avowals to be ascribable to individuals other than the subject. Otherwise, we would face problems analogous to those facing the No Reference view in the case of "I". Specifically, it would be hard to see how avowals could remain within the purview of the Generality Constraint (see above, Chapter 2, pp. 49f.).

Now, when trying to explain the special security of "I" without resorting to a No Reference view, it was necessary to explain both how one can make *any* semantic reference (in speech or in thought) to some individual, and how one can succeed in referring to the 'right' individual (namely, oneself ), despite making use of no recognitional

---

[7] I wish to emphasize that this point is distinct from a point about the way "I" refers that I made when criticizing Evans's and Shoemaker's treatment of "I" (see above, pp. 77f.). The latter point was that if we are to capture the distinctive guaranteed success of "I" in referring, we may need to recognize that, *semantically* speaking, "I" does not function as a device that 'hits a target', but rather as a device that marks the source of an ascription. (This is what I called the Indexical Reference view.)

means of identification. Similarly, when trying to explain avowals' ascriptive security without resorting to a No Ascription view, we need to address two questions. In the absence of any recognitional judgment regarding one's present mental state, there is, first, the question how one can succeed in making any reference *at all* to any kind of mental state. And, second, there is the question how one can succeed in making a *correct* ascription of the mental state to oneself. Our task is twofold:

**(i)** We need to explain how it is possible for a subject to make a *genuine ascription* of a mental state to herself, in the first place, without relying on a recognitional judgment concerning the presence or character (or content) of her state.

**(ii)** We need to explain what makes avowals, as genuine ascriptions that can be true *or* false, especially apt to be *true*, and less open to correction than other ascriptions (as well as not requiring justification, and not being subject to ordinary epistemic criticisms).

A No Ascription view would allow us to avoid this twofold task. If, in avowing an intentional state, I do not make a genuine self-ascription at all, then the question of how I can be thought to make a *true* self-ascription does not even arise.[8] (The analogous point regarding the No Reference view of "I" considered in Chapter 2 was that if in using "I" I make no reference at all, then the question of how I can succeed in picking out myself as the subject for my ascription does not arise.) Our commitment to Semantic Continuity, however, prevents us from taking this easy way out, for it requires us to see avowals as involving genuine ascriptions of mental states to particular subjects. This means we incur the additional explanatory obligation described in (ii).[9]

In the remainder of this chapter, I shall try to show that the epistemic immediacy that attends ascriptive immunity to error is no bar to achieving both genuine and correct self-ascription. I shall do this by considering, first, a special case of avowals: self-verifying avowals of presently entertained thoughts. I will then argue that this case exhibits some key features that are shared by all avowals. My next task will be to understand how avowals might be seen not only as protected from

---

[8] In the next chapter, I consider a prominent example of the No Ascription view and examine its weaknesses.

[9] For simplicity of presentation, from now on I will adhere to the separation between (i) and (ii) only where it clearly matters.

various epistemic errors and criticisms, but also as especially apt to be true. This will be accomplished by connecting the idea that avowals enjoy ascriptive immunity to error with the more familiar idea that avowals serve to *express* subjects' mental states, rather than *report* them. In the next two chapters, I will offer my Neo-Expressivist account, which features this idea, but which avoids the difficulties that are thought to beset expressivist views of avowals. This will complete my non-epistemic explanation of avowals' special security. I will then be arguing (in Chapter 9) that my non-epistemic take on the character and source of this security still makes room for the idea that avowals can represent genuine and privileged *knowledge* of one's mental life; thus it is consistent with a non-deflationary view of basic self-knowledge.

## The Security of Self-Verifying "I"-Ascriptions: Referring to Content by Articulating It

Consider the following special case of avowing, the Cartesianly inspired self-ascription:

**SVSA**: I am thinking that maybe I am being deceived by an evil demon.

Understood as ascribing to myself the mere entertaining of a thought about being deceived by an evil demon, as opposed to asserting or affirming that I may be so deceived, SVSA cannot fail on any of the scores we have identified. In making it, I cannot fail to refer to myself; I cannot misidentify myself as the subject of ascription; I cannot fail to ascribe to myself some thought or other that is crossing my mind; and I cannot fail to ascribe to myself a thought about the possibility of my being deceived by an evil demon. SVSA is *self-verifying*; it makes itself true. Setting aside slips of the tongue (or their analogues in thought, if there are such), any time I sincerely and competently ascribe to myself the entertaining of a thought with a certain content, while withholding affirmation or assertion of its truth, my self-ascription is bound to be true. To clarify: I intend SVSA to be understood differently from SAC, which featured in the previous chapter, in the following respect. SAC ("I am thinking that there is water in my glass") could be understood, for all I said there, as ascribing to me a present affirmative judgment, or occurrent belief, that there is water in my glass. And it did not matter to what I had to say about SAC that it be a self-verifying self-ascription, since my focus was on the question whether I could be secure in my assignment of a particular content to any type of my mental states—whereas here I am initially focusing on a feature special to the self-ascription of one particular kind of contentful mental state: the entertaining of a thought.[10]

In a discussion of self-ascriptions of intentional states, Brian Loar has proposed that self-ascribing a presently entertained thought is in this respect like *deciding* to think about the thought. In the normal way of doing it, Loar suggests, you cannot decide to think about the thought that Freud lived in Vienna without thereby entertaining that very thought.

Attending to a thought introspectively is quite different from attending to a sentence one has written down. When you *display* a sentence you do not thereby *use* it. But when you display a thought in order to attend to it, you do "use" it, for you *think* it, not necessarily by asserting it but at least by entertaining it. (1987: 100)

The distinction between our relation to a thought we are thinking and a sentence we have written is well taken, though I would prefer not to put it in terms of introspective attending and display. Loar is here drawing our attention to a certain feature of 'attending' to an entertained thought that is crucial for understanding the self-verifying character of self-ascriptions of such thoughts. Burge identifies the feature as follows:

When one knows that one is thinking that *p*, one is not taking one's thought (or thinking) that *p* as an object. One is thinking that *p* in the very event of thinking knowledgeably that one is thinking it. It is thought and thought about in the same mental act. (1988:654)

Self-ascriptions of entertained thoughts have a certain 'reflexive' element. But it's very unclear how this element could be captured, if we adhere to the introspective model that Loar is alluding to. If we took avowals such as SVSA simply to be the results of introspective attending to inwardly displayed items, then the differences between

---

[10] Note that SAC *could* be understood along the same lines as SVSA. Indeed, in (2004) I use SAC in that way, and treat it as an example of a self-verifying self-ascription. So it should be clear that the difference between SAC and SVSA that I am pointing out here is a matter of the difference not in the content clause, but rather in the way we understand the self-ascriptive component, i.e., "I am thinking that . . ." —whether we take it to refer to an episode of merely entertaining a thought or to an episode of affirming, or judging true, the proposition introduced by the "that"-clause.

our relationship to a self-ascribed entertained thought, on the one hand, and to a displayed sentence, on the other, would seem to vanish. Our relation would be precisely a matter of taking the self-ascribed thought as an object. And it would be entirely unclear why one's position as regards one's present self-ascribed thought should be any different from one's position as regards a thought ascribed to another. Specifically, it would seem puzzling how avowals such as SVSA could enjoy an absolute guarantee of truth—why they should be self-verifying. What the introspective model does not bring out or explain is Loar's idea that "when you display a thought in order to attend to it, you do *use* it" and Burge's idea that "[w]hen one knows that one is thinking that p, . . . [o]ne is thinking that p in the very event". The model of introspective attending to an inwardly displayed item does not, by itself, do anything to help capture or explain this idea. Yet the idea seems to be key to understanding how avowals of presently entertained thoughts are self-verifying.

What is striking about avowals of entertained thoughts is that, although they do not present logical or conceptual necessities of any kind, but rather represent contingent truths about a given subject's present state of mind, one's success in making a true self-ascription is guaranteed simply by the act of avowing. When one makes a self-ascription of an articulated entertained thought (with sincerity and comprehension), one thereby makes a true self-ascription of that entertained thought. This is because, as one makes the relevant self-ascription, one *ipso facto* entertains a thought with the ascribed content. The very act of making the thought ascription summons up the ascribed thought, as it were. It inevitably involves the thought 'passing through' one's mind, thereby rendering the ascription true. The act of articulating the content itself yields an instantiation of the ascribed state: viz., an episode of entertaining a thought with that content. And the content of the ascribed state cannot pull apart from the content that is assigned to it in the ascription; it is fully 'locked onto' it. This fact about the character of self-ascriptions of this kind is what explains their absolute security—their being self-verifying. (We can take this to be an analogue of the absolute guarantee against reference failure enjoyed by "I", where success in referring to the self-ascriber is guaranteed by the very fact of using "I".) Note that a correlative of this fact is that an act of thinking to oneself, "I am *not* now thinking

(= entertaining the thought) that *p*"—just like an act of saying, "I am not now saying (= uttering) 'p' "—will be self-defeating.

Avowals of entertained thoughts are special in being self-verifying. They also belong to a special subclass of avowals: i.e., avowals that explicitly specify an intentional content for the ascribed state. However, a proper understanding of the self-verifying character of avowals of this kind will, I believe, help us to identify a key feature they share with all avowals. This feature, in turn, will enable us to understand the source of the ascriptive immunity to error of avowals.

In explaining the self-verifying character of avowals of entertained thoughts thus far, I have simply assumed that they represent genuine ascriptions of thoughts with particular contents to particular individuals. This is in conformity with Semantic Continuity and the Generality Constraint. The Generality Constraint implies that I can be credited with a genuine self-ascription of an entertained thought only if I conceive of the situation described in my self-ascription in general terms, as one in which *someone* is *entertaining a thought* with *a certain content*. It must in principle be possible to substitute the different components of the ascription—subject, state, content—with relevant items in the self-ascriber's cognitive repertoire so as to formulate a possible thought for the subject. We can put this more explicitly (if somewhat more awkwardly), as follows. If a subject is to be credited with making a genuine self-ascription of a contentful state, then she must (at least) be disposed to conceive of the relevant situation as one in which one of the individuals of whom she can think is in one of the states she is capable of ascribing, and the state has one of the contents she is capable of assigning.

Let us go back to the self-ascription "I am thinking that maybe I am being deceived by a demon" (SVSA). The foregoing considerations suggest that to take it to be self-verifying is to regard it as *truly* ascribing to a particular individual (me) a present thought with a particular content: *that maybe I am being deceived by a demon*. But this means we must regard SVSA as being (in part) *about* this content, in the sense of referring to it, or singling it out. If so, then part of the explanation of how SVSA can be self-verifying will involve answering the question:

**(i)** When making SVSA, how do we succeed in singling out the content *that maybe I am being deceived by a demon*?

Once we answer this question, we should address the further question:

**(ii)** How is it that SVSA succeeds in assigning to our thought the *right* content—i.e., the content it actually has?

These questions are particular instances of the two questions we separated earlier regarding avowals (see above, p. 206). Question (i) concerns the status of SVSA as a *genuine* ascription, which picks out a particular content, whereas question (ii) concerns its status as a *true* ascription, which correctly identifies the content.

We noted above a certain reflexive element in SVSA: it involves an explicit (though not necessarily spoken) articulation of the very content assigned to the self-ascribed state. In response to question (i), I submit that explicit articulation is a perfectly legitimate way of referring to intentional contents. When one avows a presently entertained thought, one does not need to identify the content one ascribes to the thought in any epistemically rich sense in order to single out that content. One's reference to the content need not be mediated by some way of representing the content to oneself, which, moreover, must be correct, if one is to succeed in picking out that content. Even if one does not use any means of identifying the content as the one content wishes to assign to one's thought, one's ascription can still latch onto (and be semantically about) that content, simply in virtue of the fact that one articulates *that* content. Indeed, a subject who ascribes to herself an explicitly articulated entertained thought can even be credited with *knowing which* thought she is ascribing to herself. For, we can think of spelling out the thought content in the ascription as being sufficient for putting one in epistemic contact with the articulated content. The ability to spell out the content could then be seen as the analogue for content of the kind of practical abilities Evans thinks we put to use when referring to individuals using devices such as demonstratives and indexicals. Thus, suppose one thinks there is a version of Russell's 'knowing which' requirement applicable to the content component of intentional ascriptions (viz., that in order for one to be able to think about that content, one must know which content it is that one is thinking about). My suggestion is that putting to use one's ability to articulate the content (in speech or in thought) may qualify as a way of satisfying the requirement, just as putting to use one's ability to track an object perceptually, for example, can qualify for knowing which object one is thinking of, and thus for having a thought about that object.[11]

The directness in the assignment of intentional content is a feature that is not unique to self-verifying ascriptions of entertained thoughts. It is shared by intentional avowals quite generally. When avowing an occurrent belief, hope, preference, etc., I typically single out the content of the ascribed state directly, by articulating it in the very act of avowing. A typical avowal of a hope will involve 'going through' the relevant state's propositional content (in speech or in thought) in the very act of avowing: "I hope *she gets here on time.*" A typical avowal of a desire will involve an explicit mention of its intentional object: "I want *a cup of tea.*" This, in contrast with 'oblique' self-ascriptions such as "I hope for the same thing I hoped for yesterday", or "I want what you want", where the relevant intentional content is not itself made explicit in the self-ascription. In these latter cases, we do pick out the content indirectly, through some description or thick identification of it. But when avowing an intentional state, we do not; we single out the intended content (the content we want to assign to the ascribed state) simply by spelling it out. Thus, there is as yet no need to insist that if I issue an avowal that seemingly ascribes to me a state with a specific intentional content, my assignment of content must be epistemically mediated. On the contrary, I have argued that the assignment of content in avowals is epistemically immediate.

## Articulating Content as a Way of Expressing One's Intentional State

My proposal thus far can be summed up as follows:

When ascribing to myself a state with content *c* in the ordinary way, there is no need for any recognitional identification on my part of *c* as the content I wish to assign to my state. I can thus assign a particular content to my state in an epistemically immediate way. I single out *c*

---

[11] For discussion of the requirement in connection with reference to individuals, see Ch. 3, pp. 61ff.

It is a substantive question what the conditions are for possessing knowledge of content in general, one that I cannot take up here. And it may well be that there are different conditions on possession of concepts, on the one hand, and on mastery of linguistic expressions, on the other hand. For relevant discussion of linguistic understanding, see Dummett (1991: esp. essays 4–6 and 14–15). See also Bar-On (1996) for additional discussion and references. For relevant discussion of the mastery of concepts, see Peacocke (1992).

simply by *explicitly articulating c*, rather than some other content, in the course of articulating my state's content (in speech or in thought).

When I assign content to a present thought, as I do when issuing SVSA, I do not quote my own words, as I might when reporting some-one else's speech. I do not specify my thought's content by mentioning or displaying a sentence with the relevant content. Rather, I exercise my ability to *use* the relevant content, in speech or in thought, by meaningfully speaking the relevant terms, or competently deploying the relevant concepts. This is what is distinctive about explicit articu-lation, as opposed to other modes of referring to content.

Having proposed explicit articulation as a legitimate way of refer-ring to intentional contents, I want to point out that its use is not restricted to avowals. We commonly assign intentional content to others' intentional states by spelling out the assigned content ("She thinks that it's raining outside"; "He's annoyed by that noise"). When doing so, we put to explicit use elements from our own cognitive repertoire so as to latch onto a particular content that we wish to ascribe to their states. So in these cases, too, we pick out the content *not* by identifying it in some indirect way (as in "He is thinking about what I was just thinking"), but rather by explicitly articulating it ("He is thinking about the dinner he's about to miss"). This is just to say that intentional ascriptions both to oneself and to others may succeed in being semantically *about* (referring to, singling out) the intentional content they assign to the ascribed state by explicitly articulating the content, rather than picking it out in some indirect way.[12]

However, when we ascribe an intentional state to someone else, observers may straightforwardly challenge the correctness of our ascription. Specifically, they may question whether the content we have assigned is the *correct* content to assign to other's state. As noted before, intentional ascriptions to others contrast with avowals in terms of ascriptive security. Avowals exhibit a special security, com-pared to mental ascriptions to others, in that we are normally much more inclined to take them at face value. In particular, there is normally

---

[12] On one influential view of attitude ascriptions, known as "the paratactic view" (see Davidson (1968–9) ), an ascription such as "John believes that Superman is powerful" is to be parsed as a conjunc-tion: "John believes that. Superman is powerful," where the "that" is understood as a demonstrative refer-ring to the second sentence, which is a sentence in the ascriber's repertoire, and the ascriber is understood as using that sentence to specify the content of the ascribee's belief.

a strong presumption that the content one assigns to one's present state when avowing is the *right* one. This is one crucial aspect of Epistemic Asymmetry as regards the ascriptive part of avowals, which requires explanation. Having seen how avowals can involve genuine ascription of content to one's state (viz., through explicit articulation); we now need to explain the distinctive success of avowals in making *true* self-ascriptions of contentful states (thereby answering question (ii) formulated above, p. 206).

Let us examine the case of SVSA first. Borrowing terminology from Chapter 2, we can maintain that, to the extent that a self-ascription is semantically *about* an episode of entertaining a particular thought, there is *semantic distance* between the ascription and the ascribed state. This just means that there is no logical or conceptual bar to the ascription's being false. Now, there are two separable reasons why the self-ascription could fail to be true. I could correctly ascribe to myself a thought but incorrectly specify its content; or I could incorrectly ascribe a *thought* to myself, never mind its content. What is interesting about SVSA is that it is somehow guaranteed success on both these counts. When I avow a presently entertained thought, the act of articulating the thought content seems to secure my success in correctly ascribing to myself being in the state of entertaining *some* thought, while at the same time correctly singling out the right *content* for my thought. This success is not plausibly understood as due to some special epistemic access or method I employ for determining either the state's character or its content. Though I am genuinely ascribing a thought with a particular content to myself, *neither* the content *nor* the state need be in any way an epistemic target for me. (We might say that although there is a semantic distance between me and my state, there is no epistemic distance; my self-ascription is epistemically direct, or immediate.)

By contrast, when I ascribe an entertained thought to someone else, the state the other is in (and its content) *is* an epistemic target for me. This is so even if I do not make the ascription on the basis of hypothesizing on the internal causes of the other's behavior, but rather do it more directly, by projecting onto him an explicitly articulated thought of my own. For, in general, projection is still an epistemic method designed to enable us to determine what mental state the other is in, and what content it has (if any). Among psychological birds of a feather, it is a most practical and often indispensable method, and a very reliable one at that; but when it fails, its failure is typically one of mistaking one mental state for another. So there is an epistemic difference between ascribing a present thought to another and ascribing a present thought to oneself. In the case of ascription of a thought with a particular content to a subject other than oneself, the articulation of content merely serves to demonstrate the content one is prepared to assign to the other's ascribed state by presenting it explicitly. One still needs some basis on which to judge that the other is currently entertaining a thought, and that the thought has *that* content. Whereas in one's own case, the articulation of the thought's content obviates the need to use *any* epistemic method for determining what content one's state has *or* what state one is in.

Now we should ask: *How* exactly does one achieve correct ascription of both content and state when avowing an entertained thought? If I do not recognize, or determine in some epistemically robust way, my state as being that of entertaining a thought, and its content as being $c$, what is it that enables me to tell what state I am in and what its content is?

I think we already have in place the makings of an answer. In the case of self-ascriptions such as SVSA, where the state ascribed is simply one of entertaining a certain thought (as opposed to affirming its content), all I need to do, epistemically speaking, in order to succeed in making a genuine *and* true self-ascription of the entertaining of the thought that $p$ is to entertain the thought that $p$. But this I am bound to do as I ascribe the thought explicitly, by articulating its content. So explicit articulation of the thought suffices for making the self-ascription true. I can tell *that* a certain thought is crossing my mind as well as *what* content the thought has simply by telling it—i.e., *that* content. I submit that this is because, in my own case, *articulating the content serves directly to give voice to my present state; it constitutes expressing the very thought I am ascribing to myself.* Thus, in this special limit case, success in spelling out a particular content, in speech or in thought, is sufficient by itself for making a genuine self-ascription with a particular content, as well as for correctly ascribing to oneself a present state with that content.

Earlier, I pointed out that if we are to abide by the Generality Constraint and adhere to Semantic Continuity, we must explain how we can succeed in latching onto the right intentional content when issuing intentional avowals, despite their epistemic immediacy. Now, when discussing the referential success of "I", I proposed that no epistemic mediation is necessary for a subject to single herself out as the subject of ascription. For she can refer to herself *indexically*, thereby introducing herself as a subject for discourse, or thought (see Chapter 3, pp. 77f.). This feature of "I" allowed us to see how "I"-ascriptions that enjoy immunity to error through misidentification could still succeed in singling out the self-ascriber. A parallel proposal can now be made regarding the ascriptive part of avowals: viz., that no epistemic mediation is required for a subject to succeed in picking out the right content for the state she ascribes to herself. For she can single out the state's content *expressively*, by articulating it as she gives voice to the ascribed state itself.

In his "Language as Thought and as Communication", Sellars distinguishes three senses of expression.[13] We have:

**EXP₁** the *action* sense: a *person* expresses a state of hers by intentionally doing something.

**EXP₂** the *causal* sense: an *utterance* or piece of behavior expresses an underlying state by being the culmination of a causal process beginning with that state.

**EXP₃** the *semantic* sense: e.g., a *sentence* expresses an abstract proposition, thought, or judgment by being a (conventional) representation of it.

In the next chapter, we shall consider at length the first two types of expression. For now, it suffices to point out that $EXP_1$, unlike $EXP_2$, requires the performance of an intentional action. An involuntary twitch in my eye may express my discomfort in the causal sense, without *my* having expressed discomfort by it. It should be noted also that in its causal sense "express" is a success verb: an utterance or piece of behavior of mine cannot be said to express₂ fear, or anger, or joy, or whatever, without my actually being in those states. By contrast, in its semantic sense "express" is 'generic': an utterance of mine can express₃, e.g., regret without expressing *my* regret. In this same sense, the linguistic

---

[13] Sellars (1969). I here follow Sellars in speaking of three *senses*, though I should prefer to think of them as three *kinds* of expression, since I don't think the word "express" is really three-way ambiguous. As we shall see later on, I believe that there are interesting connections among $EXP_1$–$EXP_3$. See the next two chapters for an extensive discussion of expression. In the present context the distinction is brought in for the purpose of explaining the self-verifying character of SVSA.

locution "Regrettably *p*" expresses regret, though on a particular occasion it may not be used for—or may not succeed in—expressing the *utterer's* regret. (Whether or not in the action sense "express" is a success verb is a matter I shall take up later, in Chapter 8.)

Simple declarative sentences of English can be seen as conventional vehicles for the (semantic) expression of thoughts. Put in the present terms, in the special case of self-ascribing an entertained thought that *p*, the intentional *use* of a sentence that expresses in the semantic sense *the thought* that *p* suffices for giving expression to *one's thought* that *p*— i.e., expressing that thought in both the causal and action senses. This is because it is not possible to articulate an entertained thought intentionally without the articulation being causally connected to the entertaining of that very thought. The articulation may be the culmination of a process (however brief) that begins with the entertaining of the thought, or it will at least involve the entertaining of the thought in the course of articulating it. To give explicit semantic expression to a thought intentionally is *ipso facto* to express, in both Sellars's causal and action senses, a certain mental state of mine: the state (or episode) of entertaining that thought. If I intentionally issue a self-ascription of that state to myself, the self-ascription will inevitably involve an expression of the entertained thought in Sellars's causal sense, and so one will succeed in expressing *his* state of entertaining that thought in Sellars's action sense.[14]

Thus we can take the case of self-verifying thoughts to illustrate the following idea. Articulating, or spelling out, the content of a self-ascribed state—giving expression to a particular content in the *semantic* sense—can amount to giving voice to an intentional state one is in— giving it expression in the causal and action senses. This idea, I shall now argue, may be generalized beyond the special case of self-verifying avowals, to all intentional avowals.

Consider first avowals of beliefs. Saying (or thinking) "I believe John is angry with me" is not self-verifying. Still, if it is a case of avowing, the point of issuing the self-ascription seems to be at least in part to give direct voice to my (first-order) belief—that John is angry

---

[14] "Inevitably" provided only that one is using the content component on the occasion of issuing the self-ascription intentionally and sincerely. One can, of course, merely utter words (or have words run through one's head) parrot-style, which would clearly not be sufficient for expressing the relevant thought in the causal or action senses.

with me. If so, this could help explain the anomaly of Moore sentences such as "I believe that John is angry with me, but John is not angry with me", of which we spoke earlier. The sentence does not involve an overt contradiction. Its two conjuncts semantically express propositions that are mutually compatible. However, if we consider an *utterance* of the Moore sentence, we get some conflict. Given the right background conditions, a sincere utterance of a sentence which semantically expresses the proposition that $p$ will typically count as expressing$_1$ (as well as expressing$_2$), *one's belief* that $p$. So, when uttering the second part of the Moore sentence ("John is not angry with me"), I will typically be taken to express$_1$ my belief that John is not angry with me. But now suppose that we take the first part of the pronouncement to be an avowal, rather than a third-person theoretical report on my cognitive economy. Then, on my proposed account, we can see it as *also* expressing$_1$ my belief that John *is* angry with me. So we get an *expressive conflict*: in one act I am expressing$_1$ two conflicting beliefs, even though, semantically speaking, the sentence I utter does not express$_3$ a contradiction.[15]

Note that unlike the explanations of Moore's paradox mentioned in Chapter 4 (pp. 129–31), the above explanation requires supposing that the self-ascriptive part of the Moore utterance serves directly to express (in the causal and action sense) one's first-order belief itself, as opposed to, or at least in addition to, expressing the higher-order belief that one has the first-order belief. Now, there are other kinds of Moore sentences which take a different form from the one mentioned above: e.g., "$p$, but I don't believe $p$". And one may wonder whether the above explanation would account for their anomaly.[16] The difficulty is that while it is still natural enough to take the second conjunct as an avowal, "I don't believe $p$" would be a 'negative' avowal. On its face, such an avowal does not seem to involve expressing a particular belief which could stand in conflict with the belief expressed by the first conjunct (viz., $p$). I will discuss negative avowals briefly in Chapter 8. To anticipate, it seems to me that an avowal of the form "I don't believe (think) that $p$" can be systematically understood

---

[15] More needs to be said about the notion of expressive conflict at work here. A full account of this notion would, I suspect, require linking it to the study of practical reason and rationality. My present aim, however, is to show how the idea that avowals serve to express the state they ascribe can help explain the seeming paradoxicality of Moore sentences, as well as identify the kind of conflict involved.

[16] For the variety of forms that Moore sentences can take, see Green (1999).

in two different ways. The more natural interpretation, I would argue, is one on which the avowal is a cautious, or less blunt, way of expressing the avower's belief that not-*p*. On that reading, we get the same type of conflict as with "I believe that *p*, but not-*p*" (except that "*p*" and "not-*p*" are reversed). The more literal interpretation is one according to which the second conjunct simply expresses the avower's uncertainty or complete agnosticism regarding *p*. (A more natural way of expressing this attitude would be to avow "I'm not sure whether *p*" or "I have no opinion about *p*".) This means we have a subject who, in a single utterance or thought is expressing an attitude of confident affirmation of *p* (positively believing *p*) and an attitude of uncertainty, indifference, or complete agnosticism regarding *p*. So even on this interpretation we still get an expressive conflict (though, again, no contradiction).

We can regard intentional avowals more generally, whether of beliefs, or of hopes, desires, angers, fears, and so on, as playing (in part) an expressive role as described above. A typical self-ascription such as "I hope John will come" or "I'd really like some water!" or "I'm mad at you, Mom" will play the same role as is played by more direct expressions of one's own intentional states, such as saying, or thinking, "John will come, won't he?" *hopefully*, or "Water!" *eagerly*, or "Mom!!" *angrily*, and so on. The point of articulating the state's intentional content in avowing is directly to express one's self-ascribed intentional state in the very act of avowing. (Speaking of a 'point' here should not be taken to suggest that there is necessarily a deliberate plan on the part of the self-ascriber to use the avowal for a certain purpose.) If so, we can expect an anomaly of non-doxastic conjunctions analogous to the anomaly of Moore sentences. And indeed, conjunctive utterances such as "I hope it doesn't rain, but please, God, make it rain", or "I like this painting a lot, but it's horrible", or "I am really excited by this meeting, but it's very boring" do seem anomalous, and the anomaly is naturally explained by their expressive character. Such conjunctive utterances exhibit as much expressive conflict or dissonance as do Moore sentences. (Note, too, that Moore-type conflicts can be generated without producing any explicit self-ascriptions. Consider, for example, "Ouch! This doesn't hurt at all" or "[Yawn] this is really interesting"; "[Laughter] this joke is not funny at all".)

The generalized idea, then, is this. When issuing an intentional avowal, we explicitly articulate some content: we use (in speech or in thought) a vehicle which semantically expresses that content. What distinguishes this use in the case of avowals is that it is made in the service of expressing in the action sense a present mental state of ours. Now take the avowal "I am hoping it doesn't rain tomorrow", for example, and suppose, for simplicity, that it is made in speech. The avowal considered as a self-ascription, being a declarative sentence, expresses in the semantic sense the proposition (thought, judgment) that someone (me) is hoping that it doesn't rain. Typically, we take the sincere intentional utterance of a declarative sentence that semantically expresses($_3$) a given proposition $p$ to express$_1$ *one's* belief that $p$. Thus, we would expect that when issuing the avowal I express$_1$ *my higher-order belief (or judgment) that I am hoping that it doesn't rain tomorrow*. And perhaps I do. (We will return to this issue in Chapters 7 and 8.) My present point, however, is that we should *also* regard it as expressing$_1$—i.e., in the action sense—my (first-order) hope that it doesn't rain. It is in this way that avowing "I am hoping it doesn't rain" is like saying or thinking "It doesn't rain" hopefully.

On the present proposal, the point of avowing an intentional state is not to provide a descriptive report of it, but rather to share it, or air it, or give it voice, or just to 'vent' it. I think that once the expressive character of all avowals is properly understood, we will be able to see why avowals in general, and not only self-verifying avowals, are more secure than mental ascriptions to others, as well as being more secure than 'alienated' self-ascriptions of mental states (e.g., ascribing to myself hating my brother on the basis of what the therapist convinced me of). In offering my account of avowals' special security, I will thus be focusing on the fact that acts of avowing serve directly to express the ascribed state, rather than on whatever (if any) role avowals have as descriptive self-reports, made on this or that secure epistemic basis, or issued from a certain perspective *on* the state.

In the next chapters, I will be developing my Neo-Expressivist account, which features this idea. Right now, however, I want to turn to a piece of unfinished business. I have proposed that we extend the idea of explicit articulation of content from self-verifying avowals to intentional avowals more generally. However, we must not forget that intentional avowals in general are *not* self-verifying. So we need to understand why. My explanation is as follows. As I said earlier, in the special case of avowing an entertained thought, merely spelling out of the thought that *p*—whether to others or to oneself, whether in language or in some other medium or representation—suffices for *being* in the relevant state: viz., the state of entertaining the thought that *p*. In other words, in this special case, giving (semantic) expression to *p* suffices for expressing the thought that *p* in the causal and action senses; it secures success in expressing *one's* thinking that *p*, thereby making true the self-ascription. This does not hold in general, however. Merely spelling out of the propositional content or intentional object of one's hope, wish, fear, etc. does not suffice for being in a state of hoping that *p*, wishing for *x*, being afraid of *y*, etc. So, while the point of articulating content when avowing hoping, or wishing, or fearing, may still be to express one's first-order intentional state, the articulation by itself does not guarantee that one will succeed in expressing one's hope that *p*/wish for *x*/fear of *y* etc.; so the avowal is not self-verifying. Thus, as we shall later see (in Chapter 8), it is possible for avowals to be false. However, as I mentioned earlier, this possibility of falsity does not imply that avowals must be vulnerable to *epistemic* errors. If, as I have suggested, avowals are immune to errors through misascription, they would be protected from errors of *mis*-taking the ascribed state simply because they do not involve any 'taking' of it in the first place.

## Ascriptive Immunity to Error and the Expressive Character of Avowals

Putting together the fact that avowals in general are not self-verifying with the fact that they are nonetheless more secure than other ascriptions may seem to provide further ammunition for the Epistemic Approach, which explains avowals' security by appeal to the security of the epistemic basis on which they are made. On the one hand, when I avow "I hope Emma will come soon", the mere articulation of the hope's content does not guarantee the truth of my self-ascription. This may suggest that, in the general case of non-self-verifying avowals, more epistemic work is required on the part of the self-ascriber in order to succeed in making a true self-ascription. It may seem that one who avows a particular hope, unlike one who self-ascribes the mere entertaining of a thought, must use some epistemic means for determining her current condition to be that of hoping, rather than, say, believing. She may also need to have some epistemic method for ascertaining that the state has the content that she spells out in the self-ascription, rather than some other content available to her. She can at least in principle go wrong in identifying her state (or its content), and this explains why intentional avowals in general are not self-verifying. On the other hand, since intentional avowals still seem relatively more secure than ascriptions of similar states to others, as well as more secure than bodily self-reports such as "I'm sitting on a chair", it may seem that we must invoke an especially reliable epistemic mechanism for finding out about our own intentional states, or an especially secure epistemic basis on which intentional self-ascriptions are made.

This is a line of thought I have sought to resist. In opposition to the Epistemic Approach, I have offered the idea that avowing subjects enjoy immunity to epistemic errors of ascription, in addition to immunity to errors of misidentifying the avowal's subject. In expounding the idea of ascriptive immunity to error, I have followed closely the Shoemaker Evans model for explaining ascriptions that enjoy immunity to error through misidentification. In particular, I have seized on the following features of such ascriptions:

(i) Though not absolutely infallible, they are not vulnerable *to a certain kind or error and doubt.*
(ii) When the relevant ascriptions fail, this is not due to a *mis*-taking, or a failed recognitional judgment that represents how the ascriber takes things (viz., taking someone to be herself).
(iii) Though the ascriptions do not rest on recognitional judgments, and are epistemically immediate in relevant respects, they do have genuine semantic aboutness (viz., they involve genuine reference to myself).

Several comments are in order. We could say that, in general, an ascription is immune to error in a certain respect insofar as *the subject* issuing it is immune to error in the relevant respect, because she has not engaged in certain kinds of 'epistemic efforts'. In this vein, I have spoken of the fact that, for example, a subject who makes a proprioceptive report does not employ any thick means of identifying the subject of her report, and an avowing subject does not deploy any procedure for discovering, determining, or ascertaining that the relevant state (and its content, when it has one) is the right one to ascribe to herself. It should be emphasized, however, that the notion of immunity to error that primarily occupies us here concerns the epistemology of ascriptions, not their etiology or psychology. What matters is not what goes through the self-ascriber's head as (or right before) she makes her self-ascription. Rather, what matters is the *epistemic grounding* of the ascription (or lack thereof). It is probably true to the phenomenology of avowals to say that they involve no ascertainment (not even quasi-perceptual) of the presence, character, or content of the ascribed state. But that is of secondary importance. What is more important is the recognition that when one avows, one has no *reason or grounds* for thinking that someone is in some mental state and that the state has some content other than whatever reason or grounds one has for making the judgment that is semantically expressed by the avowal: namely, that the avower is in state M (with content $c$). Avowals, I maintain, do not have any epistemic grounding in recognitional judgments directed at the ascribed state or its content (any more than they have epistemic grounding in an identification judgment of the form I $= \delta$).

At this stage, I think we can remain relatively neutral on the question whether when I avow "I want some tea", say, I express$_1$ my judgment that I want some tea, *in addition to* expressing$_1$ my desire for some tea. Maintaining that my avowal enjoys ascriptive immunity to error opens up the possibility that if I do express$_1$ my higher-order self-judgment, it need not be epistemically grounded in some recognitional judgment concerning the presence, character, or content, of the state. In fact, I think I can even allow that the higher-order self-judgment I express$_1$ (if I do) must itself have *some* kind of basis or grounds. (Perhaps it is simply grounded in the first-order state itself.[17]) Still, what I would insist on, in opposition to the Epistemic Approach, is that even if I do make, and express$_1$, a higher-order self-judgment, the special security of my avowal does *not* come from whatever *epistemic* security that the higher-order self-judgment has.[18]

It is also worth reiterating that immunity to error is not a notion that pertains to the *semantics* of ascription. Semantically identical

---

[17] This is a view I shall consider in Ch. 9.
[18] Thanks to Ram Neta for urging me to clarify this important point. In Ch. 8, I explicitly discuss the question whether when avowing, one expresses$_1$ a self-judgment, as well as the ascribed condition.

ascriptions can vary with respect to whether they enjoy this or that kind of immunity to error. The separation of the epistemology of avowals from their semantics is crucial for my account of their security. The idea that avowals enjoy a special immunity to error holds promise because it allows us to combine protection from epistemic error with genuine semantic aboutness. In its extreme form, protection from error can come at the price of Semantic Continuity, a price I think we must not be prepared to pay. But, as I have taken pains to show, the kind of immunity to error that avowals enjoy is compatible with Semantic Continuity. Beginning with the special case of self-verifying self-ascriptions, I explained how avowals could be genuine ascriptions, which are semantically about the states they ascribe and their contents, even though they enjoy both immunity to error through misidentification and immunity to error through misascription. I pointed out, however, that if, in opposition to the No Ascription view, we maintain that avowals involve genuine ascriptions, we have the further task of explaining what renders the ascriptions especially apt to be correct or *true*. The strong presumption of truth governing avowals, which is an important aspect of Epistemic Asymmetry, is not immediately explained by their (combined) immunity to error.

Now, in the special limit case of avowals of entertained thoughts, recognizing the expressive character of such avowals allowed us to explain *both* how they can involve genuine ascriptions and what makes the ascriptions self-verifying, and thus true. I drew a connection between the epistemic immediacy of avowals and the fact that avowing subjects express in the action sense (express$_1$) the very conditions they self-ascribe—i.e., the conditions semantically picked out by the self-ascription they issue. As I generalize the expressivist idea beyond this special case, I will argue that it can help to explain the ordinary presumption that *all* avowals, even those that are not self-verifying, are apt to be true in a way that other ascriptions are not.

I have portrayed avowals as serving to express in the action sense (express$_1$) one's first-order mental state. But it is important to recognize that not every act of expressing$_1$ one's first-order mental state will involve a genuine self-ascription. We want to preserve a conceptual distinction between what I shall call *ground-level expressions* of one's state—e.g., expressing your belief that it's raining by saying "It's raining"—and *self-ascriptive expressions*—expressing your belief that it's raining by saying "*I believe* that it's raining".[19]

Echoing Evans (see above, p. 120), we could say:

Nothing more than the original state of belief—belief, simply, that it's raining—is called for *on the epistemic side* for a subject to make an ascription of that belief to herself. (Specifically, no epistemic grounding in a recognitional judgment concerning the state or its content is required.) But certainly something more is called for conceptually: the self-ascription must occur in the context of certain kinds of knowledge and understanding on the part of the subject. To have the content of a mental self-ascription, the self-ascriber must be regarded as ascribing to herself a property that she can conceive as being satisfied by a being not necessarily herself. She must be disposed to conceive of the relevant state of affairs as one of precisely that type.

The claim is that in the context of certain conceptual and epistemic abilities, very little epistemic work may be needed for a subject to be able genuinely to ascribe an intentional state to herself (in speech or in thought). With the right background conditions in place, all that is required for genuine ascription is that the subject be directly giving voice to her state using vehicles that semantically pick out that kind of state.

Portraying avowals as self-ascriptive expressions of one's first-order mental states, which enjoy special immunity to epistemic error and are especially apt to be true, will allow us to offer a non-epistemic account of their special security. But bear in mind that it will not suffice by itself for explaining what (if anything) renders avowals instances of genuine self-*knowledge*. Once we have achieved a proper understanding of avowals' security (Chapters 7 and 8), we shall still have to determine whether and how avowals can represent genuine, privileged self-knowledge (Chapter 9).

---

[19] This distinction will feature prominently in the development of my account later on.

# 7
# Avowals: 'Grammar' and Expression

In Chapter 6, I began to develop my alternative, non-epistemic account of the security of avowals. On my account, avowals are assigned a special, ascriptive security not because they represent self-judgments that are made on an especially secure epistemic basis, but in part because they are seen as immune to errors through misascription, as well as immune to error through misidentification. The key idea behind the characterization of avowals as enjoying the additional immunity to error can be presented as follows. When avowing, as opposed to issuing a mental self-ascription on the basis of evidence, inference, analysis, or self-interpretation, a subject has no reason, or epistemic grounds, for affirming the various components of the self-ascription other than whatever reason or grounds she has for issuing the self-ascription as a whole. When I avow feeling concerned that I'm overstaying my welcome, say, I have no more reason for thinking that *someone* (though perhaps not me) is concerned that . . . , or that I'm feeling *something* regarding overstaying my welcome (though perhaps not concern), or that I'm feeling concerned about *something* (though perhaps not about overstaying my welcome), than whatever reason I have for thinking, simply, that I'm feeling concerned that I'm overstaying my welcome. And, as I sometimes put it, my self-ascription does not rest, epistemically, on a 'judgment of appearances' regarding the bearer of the self-ascribed state, the presence or character of the state, or its intentional content.

The characterization of avowals as enjoying a distinctive ascriptive immunity to error seems to me to provide a suitably tempered interpretation of the claim that avowals are incorrigible and indubitable, an interpretation which does not require invoking either Cartesian privileged access or any distinctively secure epistemic basis on which avowals supposedly rest. Though on my alternative characterization avowals are not portrayed as absolutely incorrigible or indubitable, we can see why, and in what way, they are ordinarily protected from epistemic challenge, doubt, and criticism, unlike other empirical ascriptions. The characterization also gives a more precise sense to the intuition that avowals are epistemically more immediate or direct than other ascriptions. A proper identification of the source of the ascriptive immunity of avowals will thus enable us to explain important aspects of Epistemic Asymmetry that I have emphasized throughout.

In the second part of the last chapter, I suggested that the epistemic simplicity and immediacy of avowals can be explained by their being *expressions of subjects' self-ascribed mental states*. Beginning with the case of avowals that involve spelling out the content of the ascribed mental state explicitly, I pointed out that spelling out a state's intentional content can serve to give articulate voice to the ascribed state itself. I also suggested that this idea can be extended from self-verifying self-ascriptions to intentional avowals more generally. But I think we can generalize this idea even further, to cover so-called phenomenal avowals, such as "I'm so uncomfortable!", "I'm really thirsty", "I feel very achy/hot/irritable/anxious/etc.", which do not involve any explicit articulation of intentional content.[1] The generalized claim will be:

Avowals in general, whether intentional or phenomenal, are expressive acts in which subjects directly give voice to, by way of sharing, airing, or simply venting, a self-ascribed mental state.

The core expressivist idea that I shall adopt is that avowals—whether phenomenal or intentional—can be seen as pieces of expressive behavior, similar in certain ways to bits of behavior that naturally express subjects' states. The idea is a familiar one, and has also encountered familiar problems. The burden of this chapter will be to explain what I take to be correct about this idea and expound the use I want to make of it in my non-epistemic Neo-Expressivist account of

---

[1] To reiterate, for my purposes, I can remain neutral on the question whether phenomenal *states* have intentional content. (See above, Ch. 4, n. 10) Even if all mental states, including states of fatigue, hunger, anxiety, malaise, etc., are determined to have intentional content, I think it is uncontroversial that typical avowals of such states do not involve explicit *specification of* their intentional content. (More controversially, perhaps, I would argue that any self-ascription that did specify the intentional content such states are alleged to have would probably not qualify as an avowal, as it would probably be made on the basis of theory. But nothing in what I shall have to say hangs on establishing this stronger claim.)

avowals' special security. I shall first briefly present and criticize the more traditional expressivist account often attributed to Wittgenstein. This account, which I will refer to as the Simple Expressivist account, explains the special status of avowals by assimilating them very closely to natural expressions. I shall then begin to introduce a new express-ivist account of avowals designed to avoid the pitfalls that stand in the way of the more familiar account. On my Neo-Expressivist account, there is indeed a similarity between avowals and natural expressions. But the account does not imply that avowals express subjects' states in the same way as do natural expressions. Understanding the similarity will be crucial to my overall aim of capturing Epistemic Asymmetry without resorting to an epistemic account of avowals' security, whereas understanding the differences will be crucial to avoiding the mistakes of the Simple Expressivist account and respecting Semantic Continuity.

## Avowals as Expressive Acts, Take I: The Simple Expressivist Account

At the heart of the Simple Expressivist account is the idea that avowals are to be sharply contrasted with ordinary descriptive reports, and that their character is to be understood through a close comparison to natural expressions. When I sincerely utter "I am in pain", I am doing something very different from what you are doing when you say of me "She is in pain". Your ascription represents an attempt to report objectively some present mental state of mine, whereas my avowal is just like a grimace or a cry. I use words, but I might as well have used other vocalizations, or facial expressions, etc., since *all* I am doing is simply expressing a present (painful) state of mine. My avowal is also very different from utterances such as "There is a chickadee on our bird-feeder" or "My finger is bleeding". These latter utterances can be seen as perceptual reports that involve describing presently perceived states of affairs. Avowals, on the Simple Expressivist account, do no such thing. (As Wittgenstein puts it: "[T]he verbal expression of pain replaces crying and does not describe it" (1953: §244).)

It is useful to contrast the Simple Expressivist account with accounts that adopt the recognitional conception discussed earlier (in

Chapter 5). According to such accounts, subjects can form non-theoretical judgments as to whether, e.g., they are feeling pain, rather than a tickle. Just as one can tell red patches from green ones, by how they look, so one can distinguish pains from tickles—by the way they feel. And one can then go on to report one's findings, by saying, e.g., "I have a pain (not a tickle)". Avowals of sensations can then be seen to enjoy a security that is proportional to the security of our recognitional ability as regards our sensations, which includes our ability to distinguish among various sensations. By contrast, the Simple Expressivist account denies the relevance of any recognitional abilities to the perceived security of avowals. Indeed, on this account, there is really no room for the idea that we recognize the presence or character of a present sensation at all. Nor is there room for the question how we can tell what we feel. We are tempted to raise such questions because we are misled by the surface grammar of avowals. They seem like ordinary reports of certain goings-on, and such reports are normally subject to various epistemic assessments. However, the temptation should disappear once we appreciate the radical differences of 'logical grammar' between avowals and ordinary descriptive reports. (Again, as Wittgenstein puts it: "It can't be said of me at all (except perhaps as a joke) that I *know* I am in pain. What is it supposed to mean—except perhaps that I *am* in pain? Other people cannot be said to learn of my sensations *only* from my behaviour,—for *I* cannot be said to learn of them. I *have* them. The truth is: it makes sense to say about other people that they doubt whether I am in pain; but not to say it about myself" (1953: §246).)[2]

Avowals, on the Simple Expressivist account, are to be understood on the model of *natural expressions* of sensations, such as moans and groans, grimaces, giggles, etc. We naïvely think of natural expressions of sensations as spontaneous reactions that are in some important way characteristic of the subject's relevant states.[3] A subject in pain naturally groans, or cries out, or grimaces, or clutches the painful part. A subject being tickled will typically squirm and giggle. And natural expressions are not limited to sensations. There are natural expressions characteristic of emotions and feelings such as fear, anger, excitement,

---

[2] For exposition of the Simple Expressivist view as well as relevant references to Wittgenstein, see especially Ginet (1968); Fogelin (1976); Hacker (1993); and Wright (1998).
[3] Below, I offer an extended discussion of natural expression.

joy, etc., as well as of wants.[4] What is crucial about natural expressions of all these kinds is that they are in no way thought to represent or be epistemically grounded in a subject's *judgment* or *belief* about some state of affairs. It is not plausible to think of a subject's smile as either resting on, or in any way representing, the subject's judgment *that* she is pleased; instead, we think of it as giving expression to the pleasure itself. Correlatively, we do not expect the person who smiles or cries in pain to justify or give *reasons* for her smile or cry; we do not normally doubt, query, or challenge a gasp of fear, or a sigh of relief, and so on (except perhaps when we think they are 'put on').

Wittgenstein himself draws a comparison between avowals and natural expressions in the context of arguing against the idea that sensation terms refer to Cartesian private objects.[5] In Chapter 2, I offered a reading on which the invocation of such private objects is in aid of preserving Epistemic Asymmetry, given a commitment to Semantic Continuity coupled with a face-value understanding of the surface grammar of avowals. The Simple Expressivist account can be seen as offering to explain Epistemic Asymmetry by breaking away from the face-value understanding of avowals' grammar. As a first step, the account maintains that, despite surface appearances, avowals of sensations have the same 'logical grammar' as natural expressions of sensations. If so, then *'grammatically' speaking*, an avowal such as "I have a toothache" should not be understood as a descriptive report about an inner state whose presence and character are recognized by the subject. Instead, it should be regarded simply as a subject's way of crying, or moaning. As a second step we can then

---

[4] Compare Hacker: "A child who wants a toy reaches for it and tries to get it. The child's anger is manifest in striking out, contorted features, and screams of rage. . . . if he is frightened, he blanches, cries, and runs to Mummy" (Hacker 1993: 88).

[5] See e.g. the following passages (1980):

§244: How do words *refer* to sensations?—There doesn't seem to be any problem here; don't we talk about sensations every day, and give them names? But how is the connexion between the name and the thing named set up? This question is the same as: how does a human being learn the meaning of the names of sensations?—of the word 'pain' for example. Here is one possibility: words are connected with the primitive, the natural, expressions of the sensation and used in their place. A child has hurt himself and he cries; and then adults talk to him and teach him exclamations and, later, sentences. They teach the child new pain-behaviour. "So you are saying that the word 'pain' really means crying?"—On the contrary: the verbal expression of pain replaces crying and does not describe it.

§245: For how can I go so far as to try to use language to get between pain and its expression?

§246: In what sense are my sensations *private*?—Well, only I can know whether I am really in pain; another person can only surmise it.—In one way this is wrong, and in another nonsense. If we are using the word "to know" as it is normally used(. . .), then other people very often know when I am in pain.—Yes, but all the same not with the certainty with which I know it myself!

realize that, *epistemically speaking*, it is misguided to regard the special status of avowals as a consequence of a special recognitional access that subjects have to their own states of mind, and there is no need to seek any secure epistemic basis on which avowals are made. If avowals are not vulnerable to doubt, and are not open to query, or correction, this is not because of the security of their epistemic basis, but because they do not serve in any way to describe or tell of the avower's present condition in the first place. Like natural expressions, they merely serve to express subjects' mental states, and so they belong in the wrong 'grammatical' category for any epistemic assessment. It is as inappropriate, conceptually speaking, to assess their epistemic credentials as it would be to assess a moan or a cry or a laugh in terms of its evidence, correctness, or reasons. And this can serve to explain the asymmetries between avowals and other ascriptions. But with this explanation of Epistemic Asymmetry, we can see that, *ontologically speaking*, there is no longer any need to invoke Cartesian entities to play the role of especially accessible mental items that are referred to by sensation terms.

Against this background reading, it is natural to see the proponent of the Simple Expressivist account as offering a No Ascription account of the ascriptive part of avowals, analogous to Anscombe's No Reference account of "I".[6] The No Reference account of "I", recall, attempted to preserve Epistemic Asymmetry between "I"-ascriptions and others by rejecting the presupposition that "I" refers. Similarly, the Simple Expressivist account can be seen as attempting to save Epistemic Asymmetry in its application to the ascriptive part of avowals by rejecting the presupposition that mental terms as they are used in avowals have the semantic function of picking out mental states and ascribing them to individuals (which is the analogue of the presupposition that "I" refers). On this account, since avowals do not involve any reference to subjects' mental states, they *ipso facto* cannot involve genuine—let alone true—ascription of mental states to avowing subjects. Rather, they *only* express those states, as do cries, or winces, or joyful hugs. But if avowals do not involve genuine self-ascription—if they do not in any way *tell* us of the avowing subject's state—then it would be entirely inappropriate to ask someone who

---

[6] See, e.g., Peacocke (1982) and Foot (1982). Also see above, Ch. 2 (pp. 52f.) and Ch. 6 (pp. 204ff.).

avows, e.g., being in pain how she knows it, or to require her to supply reasons or cite a basis for what she says. It would also make little sense to challenge or question the avowal (unless, of course, we suspect that the subject's expressive behavior is faked). If we accept the No Ascription view, a subject who avows "I am in pain" is to be regarded just like one who spontaneously lets out a cry: such a one cannot be legitimately corrected, questioned, or challenged.

The Simple Expressivist view understood along the above lines succeeds in offering an explanation of Epistemic Asymmetry without resorting to private Cartesian entities that could serve as specially accessible referents for mental terms. However, there is a general consensus that this view faces serious difficulties.[7] Very briefly, if avowals do not involve genuine, truth-evaluable ascriptions of mental states to particular individuals, then they cannot have truth-conditional equivalents with which they can be legitimately interchanged in certain contexts, and they cannot serve as legitimate premises in logical inferences. This means that we would have to abandon Semantic Continuity. It also means that avowals could not be subject to the Generality Constraint of which we spoke earlier, since they could in no way be regarded as expressing any judgment that some individual (i.e., oneself) is in some state. Furthermore, we could not hope to recover the idea that avowals may represent things that subjects *know*, and can tell others, about themselves. Avowals would turn out to be invulnerable to error and incorrigible—indeed, absolutely so—but only in the degenerate sense of belonging to the wrong grammatical category. As glorified moans and groans, grunts and grimaces, avowals would be protected from epistemic assessment, but only by not representing any epistemic *or* semantic achievement. Thus, if the Simple Expressivist idea requires adopting the No Ascription proposal, it would purchase Epistemic Asymmetry at a very high price, analogous to the price that the No Reference proposal regarding "I" had to pay.[8]

---

[7] Crispin Wright, who has recently attempted to revive the expressivist proposal, concludes: "[T]he expressivist proposal flies rather further than is usually thought. But it is a dead duck all the same" (1998: 38).

[8] Using earlier terminology, the Simple Expressivist account (understood as implying No Ascription) closes the epistemic distance between avowing subjects and the states they avow by eliminating all semantic distance between avowals and the states they are said to express. For it will turn out that avowals no more semantically represent sayings or thoughts about subjects' mental conditions than do their groans and grimaces.

## The Simple Expressivist Account versus Ethical Expressivism

In its suggestion that avowals involve no reference to relevant mental states, but only serve to express them, the Simple Expressivist account is reminiscent of the emotivist view put forward by Ayer (1946) and Stevenson (1944) to analyze ethical discourse. On the emotivist view, ethical terms (such as "good/bad", "just/unjust", "virtue/vice", etc.) are not descriptive terms which serve to designate genuine properties of things, but are rather terms of approbation or disapproval (like "Hooray!" and "Boo!"). And utterances involving such terms really just are expressions of certain emotions or preferences, rather than genuine assertions that describe objective states of affairs and admit of truth-values.

Over the years, the emotivist view has come under severe attacks. Of the greatest interest to us right now, though, is the criticism that emotivism cannot take account of crucial features of ethical discourse. In particular, it cannot accommodate the fact that ethical terms, just like ordinary descriptive terms, can occur in all sorts of grammatical contexts. With respect to some of these contexts, the emotivist claim would appear highly implausible. For instance, suppose we were to accept that to say "Helping the poor is good" is only ever to express a pro-attitude toward helping the poor. Still, it is difficult to accept that the sentence is used that way when embedded in the context of a conditional: "If helping the poor is good, then we should tax the rich and give the money to poor people." In such a context, it seems as though the sentence makes a semantic contribution that is not properly captured by the emotivist analysis.

This point against emotivism, originally due to Peter Geach (1965), can perhaps be handled by the emotivist. First, we can note that the kinds of contexts which seem to cause trouble for the emotivist proposal have a certain distinctive feature: they function so as to strip utterances of *all* illocutionary force. Take, for example, an utterance of an indicative sentence: e.g., "It usually rains here at this time of the year." Suppose the utterance is made in the appropriate circumstances with an uncontroversially assertoric force. Still, if we embed this sentence in a conditional—"If it usually rains here this time of the year, then it would be unwise to hold the party outdoors"—it loses its status as an assertion. It also loses its status as an assertion if we embed the uttered sentence in the context "It is not the case that . . . ". (And similarly for propositional attitude contexts: "John thinks/doubts/suspects that it usually rains here . . . " will not constitute an assertion of the embedded claim.) What this means is that from the possibility of embedding an indicative sentence in a force-stripping grammatical context, we cannot infer anything about the illocutionary force that is standardly associated with it when it is uttered on its own. This should not come as a surprise, given the familiar separability of force and surface grammar. "I'd like to know what time it is", for example, is an indicative sentence that is standardly used to ask a question, rather than to make an assertion about oneself. But now it can be pointed out on behalf of the emotivist that, at most, the Geach point establishes that sentences containing ethical terms do function (grammatically and logically) like ordinary indicative sentences. They must then have whatever semantic features allow sentences to function in that way. However, that is consistent with their being systematically used to express one's attitudes, rather than to make an assertion or offer a descriptive report.[9] The fact that ethical sentences, like other indicative sentences, can be embedded in force-stripping grammatical contexts does not tell against the expressivist claim that the standard function of ethical utterances is to express attitudes or feelings, rather than to make assertions about the world.

In a discussion of the Geach point, Crispin Wright argues that while the Geach point "is powerless to determine that the standard use of a locution is to assert [truth-evaluable] content", it still signals the presence of such content. The main force of the Geach point against ethical expressivism comes from the positive contribution to truth-conditions that ethical sentences seem capable of making in force-stripping contexts. Thus, Wright thinks that Geach's observation does raise a serious challenge for the ethical expressivist. For it shows that "everyday moral thought . . . requires . . . that truth-evaluable moral contents exist" (1998: 36), something the expressivist must presumably deny. Wright here seems to presuppose that indicative

---

[9] This point about the Geach point is nicely made in an unpublished paper by Andrew Mills.

sentences must have what he calls "truth-evaluable content", *and* that the only way a sentence can have such content is by having the kind of truth-conditions possessed by ordinary empirical descriptive sentences. But these presuppositions could be rejected. The Geach point by itself is not sufficient to establish that indicativeness requires truth-evaluable content in a sense which the expressivist must reject, or that only sentences with subject–predicate form, where the subject term picks out an individual, or class, or substance, etc., and where the predicate term denotes a genuine property (whatever that amounts to), can possess such content. It is true that an expressivist owes us a story about how to prize apart indicativeness from truth-evaluability, or else explain how, even if ethical terms do not denote genuine properties, ethical sentences might still possess truth-evaluable content. But it is not clear that the expressivist is left without answer. Appealing to the familiar separation between meaning and indicative form, on the one hand, and illocutionary force, on the other, the expressivist could point out that features pertaining to the kind of act performed in producing an utterance pull apart from their grammatical and semantic features. If, furthermore, she can show how ethical sentences can earn indicative grammatical form, as well as make systematic contributions to truth-conditions when embedded in truth-functional contexts, even in the absence of a moral realm of facts, then she can meet the objection based on the Geach point. For she could then maintain that an ethical sentence may lose its expressive function while still retaining the syntactic and semantic features that would allow it to be embedded in truth-functional contexts, just like ordinary indicative sentences.[10]

Now, going back to avowals, the Geach point would also seem to hold against the Simple Expressivist account of avowals. The charge would be that it is impossible to reconcile the claim that avowals merely serve to express the self-ascriber's mental states, and in no way constitute assertoric reports about them, with certain grammatical facts about avowals. For instance, the sentence "I'd like some ice cream" can be embedded in constructions such as negation and conditionals just like other indicative sentences which are normally used

---

[10] For the separation between grammatical form and propositional content, on the one hand, and illocutionary force, on the other, see Austin (1961). For attempts by ethical expressivists along the lines I am suggesting, see, e.g., Blackburn (1984), (1993), and Alan Gibbard (1990). Obviously, more needs to be said here, but doing so will take us too far afield.

to make assertoric reports. Yet, in "If I'd like some ice cream, then it would be nice for you to get me some", the sentence in the antecedent would not normally be taken to express a desire for ice cream. (Similarly for "Rachel thinks that I'd like some ice cream".) So it seems as though we must associate with the mental self-ascription as much truth-evaluable content as with, e.g., "I am six feet tall". And that may seem to give the lie to the Simple Expressivist account.

So far, the response offered above on the emotivist's behalf can serve the proponent of the Simple Expressivist view just as well. The Geach point cannot be used to force an assertoric reading on a class of sentences. At most it can show that they can function like ordinary indicative sentences. From the fact that "I'd like ice cream" can be unproblematically embedded in force-stripping grammatical contexts, all that follows is that it must possess whatever features are required for a sentence to take indicative form. It does not follow that it must always be used to make assertions or descriptive reports about oneself, or that it cannot serve only to express, but not report, one's desire outside force-stripping contexts.

However, there is a difficulty for the Simple Expressivist account that does not face ethical expressivism. The difficulty has to do with the fact that the Simple Expressivist view attempts to capture a contrast that arises within a single area of discourse—i.e., mentalistic discourse. This is the contrast between avowals, on the one hand, and, most notably, mental ascriptions to others, as well as past-tense mental self-ascriptions, on the other. Whereas the (alleged) contrast that the ethical expressivist proposes to capture is between ethics and other, straightforwardly 'factual' areas of discourse. The ethical expressivist claims that ethical statements, unlike ordinary empirical statements, are not factual statements, made true or false by the facts in the relevant domain. In the ethical case, the relevant separation is achieved by combining

(a) the positive, *expressivist claim* that ethical proclamations regularly serve to express pro- and con-attitudes, rather than to make assertions about objective states of affairs, with

(b) the negative, *'non-cognitivist' claim* that, in general, since ethical terms do not refer to properties of things in the way that ordinary descriptive terms do (since there are no ethical properties to refer to), ethical utterances are *never* apt to represent genuine truth-evaluable ('cognitive') judgments.

If the expressivist can show how ethical utterances can nevertheless earn indicative form and make systematic contributions to truth-conditions, she will have succeeded in offering a systematic, alternative conception of ethical discourse on which ethical utterances need never be construed as ascribing ethical properties to some individual, or act, or state of affairs. By contrast, the scope of the Simple Expressivist proposal is presumably limited to a certain range of mentalistic utterances: it encompasses (at most) those utterances that involve apparent ascriptions of mental states to oneself in the present tense.[11] The expressivist proposal here is that such utterances—avowals, as we have been referring to them—are mere expressions of subjects' present mental states. They do not represent assertoric reports about the subject's present mental states, and they involve no reference to those states. However, this proposal is at risk of prizing mentalistic self-ascriptions too far apart from other ascriptions within a single (i.e. mentalistic) discourse.

Let me explain. We have noted before (under the rubric of Semantic Continuity) that there are logico-semantic continuities between avowals and other ascriptions that use the *same* mentalistic vocabulary. If I avow "I'd like some ice cream", you could presumably use my avowal to infer: "She (DB) would like some ice cream." And I could later conclude, remembering my avowal, "Earlier, I wanted some ice cream." Semantically and logically speaking, these three sentences are transformations of each other, which can support valid inferences and chains of reference. However, on the Simple Expressivist account as fashioned after ethical expressivism, we are to combine the idea that avowals serve only to express subjects' mental states with the negative claim that the mental terms contained in avowals never refer to properties of things the way ordinary descriptive terms do, so avowals are not apt to represent genuine truth-evaluable ('cognitive') judgments. But it is very hard to see how to reconcile the negative claim with the logico-semantic continuities between avowals and other mentalistic ascriptions. The difference is that the

---

[11] I say "at most", because we have noted that some present-tense mentalistic self-ascriptions—viz., ones made on the basis of evidence, inference, testimony, or reflective self-interpretation—are plausibly to be regarded as descriptive self-reports. See below.

ethical expressivist is offering an account on which ethical terms do not refer to genuine properties *wherever they occur.*Thus, *if* she can explain how ethical utterances can earn propositional form and content, even though ethical terms do not refer to genuine properties, her work is done. The proponent of the Simple Expressivist account, on the other hand, needs to explain how an avowal such as "I have a toothache", which involves no genuine true or false ascription of a state or condition to an individual, can still be truth-conditionally equivalent to non-expressive, assertoric utterances which do involve such ascription.

I have in mind here utterances of three types. First, we have third-person reports (e.g., "She/DB would like some ice cream"). Second, we have tense transformations (e.g., "I wanted some ice cream earlier"). And third, we have mental present-tense self-reports (e.g., the admittedly unusual but nevertheless possible "I want some ice cream" made on the basis of evidence or inference). In his discussion of an expressivist treatment of mental self-ascriptions, Wright lists the fact that such self-ascriptions submit to tense transformation, along with the fact that they can be embedded in conditionals/negation under the heading "the Geach point".[12] I think the second case, of tense transformation, should be grouped together with the first and third cases just mentioned—of truth-conditionally equivalent third-person ascriptions and of present-tense mentalistic self-reports—which are omitted by Wright. The reason for my grouping is that I take the three cases to illustrate how, *pace* Wright, the Simple Expressivist treatment of avowals as presented so far is in a greater *prima facie* difficulty than the expressivist treatment of ethical discourse.

It may seem that, in response, the Simple Expressivist could follow the ethical expressivist's lead and adopt a more thoroughgoing non-referential account of mentalistic discourse, according to which mental terms are *never* taken to refer to mental states. The idea would be that, when making mentalistic ascriptions, all we ever do, whether in the first person or the third person, whether in the present or past tense, is express various subjective conditions. So, for instance, saying of another "She is in pain" would be like emitting a sympathetic cry,

---

[12] See Wright (1998: 35 f.) Wright also adds two facts: the fact that avowals can stand in logical relations to other statements (so from "I am in pain", we can infer "Someone is in pain") and the fact that they can be embedded in knowledge ascriptions (so we get "He knows that I am in pain", which seem to attribute to someone knowledge of some state of affairs that is apparently described, and not merely expressed, by the embedded sentence).

thereby expressing one's pity for her, as when a parent exclaims "Ouch!" upon seeing her child hurt. Notice that this non-referential account goes beyond the familiar claim that mentalistic discourse requires special treatment, because it differs from non-mentalistic discourse in being subject to various normative constraints.[13] It also goes beyond the No Ascription account we canvassed at the end of the previous section. For the account we are considering now requires maintaining that terms such as "is feeling pain" or "is afraid of the dog" or "is thinking about Vienna" simply do not serve to pick out conditions of individuals in *any* of their uses, first-person *or* third-person, present or past. Thus, an utterance such as "DB has a headache" would be understood as (only) expressing your sympathetic attitude toward me and not at all as referring to a state of mine.

It should be clear that an account along these radical lines is not sustainable. The difficulty most relevant to us here can be seen by considering how we can consistently maintain that mentalistic terms do not refer, while at the same time holding that mentalistic attributions serve to *express states of mind*. For it seems clear that this claim itself requires quantifying over states of mind. If mental terms do not refer in any context, and sentences involving such terms never serve to represent truth-evaluable judgments about mental states, what are we to make of the Simple Expressivist account itself? The trouble for the mentalist expressivist who opts for a thoroughgoing No Ascription account is that her alternative account of mentalistic discourse must appeal to items of the very same kind she takes to be questionable: namely, mental states. Claiming that, even when ascribing mental states to others, we never report or describe those mental states, but only express our own attitudes and mental states, still requires acknowledging that there are mental states to *be* expressed. (This, of course, leaves open various accounts of what the nature of those states might be.) By contrast, claiming that when we make ethical pronouncements, we never report or describe moral properties of things—people, acts, states of affairs—but only express our own pro- and con-attitudes toward things, only requires acknowledging that there are pro- and con-attitudes to be expressed; it does not require acknowledging that there are moral properties.

---

[13]  See, e.g., Davidson (1973 and 1994) and Dennett (1987: *passim*).

Even if the radical No Ascription account of mentalistic discourse as a whole could somehow avoid this last problem, it should be recognized that it is not an attractive option in the context of explaining the special security of avowals. Recall one of our criticisms of Anscombe's No Reference account of "I" (in Ch. 2). Such an account would not allow us to explain the differences in status between different kinds of "I"-ascriptions. How can denying that "I" ever refers help to explain why *some* "I"-ascriptions are more secure than others? Similarly, a thoroughgoing No Ascription account of mentalistic terms would undermine the Simple Expressivist attempt to account for the asymmetries between avowals and other mental ascriptions. If *all* mental talk is expressive rather than descriptive or reportive, and if mental terms do not refer in *any* ascriptions, what will remain of the distinctive character of avowals? As presented earlier, the central idea of the Simple Expressivist account was that when *I* ascribe a mental state to myself (at least when avowing), I do something different in kind from what others do when they ascribe a mental state to me. This contrast would disappear once the expressivist idea is generalized to cover all mentalistic discourse.

## Avowals as Expressive Acts, Take II: A Neo-Expressivist Account

The evident weaknesses of the Simple Expressivist account should not blind us to the correct insight it has to offer us. The insight lies in the expressivist *positive* claim: namely, that avowals are expressive of the conditions they apparently ascribe. And I believe that at least some of the major weaknesses can be avoided if we see how the positive, expressivist claim can be decoupled from the negative, 'non-cognitivist' claim that is often assumed to be definitive of expressivism.[14]

---

[14]  The Neo-Expressivist account I will be offering here has roots in Bar-On and Long (2001), where we sketch what is there labeled the 'Modified Expressivist Account'. I wish to thank Doug Long for many discussions that informed my earlier thinking about expression. More recently, I have benefited from reading Mitchell Green's unpublished manuscript 'Self-Expression' and from many illuminating conversations with him. I am also greatly indebted to Ram Neta for some specific helpful suggestions, which I have incorporated into the account I develop below. For some earlier discussions of avowals and expression, see Alston (1965), whose view will be discussed below, as well as Fleming (1955); Gasking (1962); Bradley (1964); and Aune (1965).

To anticipate: on the Neo-Expressivist account I will be offering, although avowals, like natural expressions, serve to express the self-ascribed mental states, unlike natural expressions, and like various mental reports, avowals represent genuine ascriptions (or 'truth-evaluable judgments'). My main task is to defend the expressivist positive claim and explain how it can be combined with a 'cognitivist' view of mental discourse (avowals included). With this combination in hand, we will be in a position to understand the special security of avowals as captured by Epistemic Asymmetry without compromising Semantic Continuity. (And later on, in Chapter 9, I will go on to explain how avowals might also be said to represent genuine and privileged knowledge.)[15]

Consider a paradigm case of expressive behavior: a small child, Jenny, eagerly reaching for a teddy bear. Jenny simply wants the toy, and her reaching for it directly reveals her desire, quite independently of any judgment on her part to the effect that she wants the teddy. Using previous jargon, we might say that there is no epistemic distance between Jenny's behavior and her desire for the toy. Her present state is in no way an epistemic target for her; she simply gives vent to it. And in normal circumstances, her audience will be directly responsive to the state they perceive her to be in; barring contravening reasons, they will simply hand her the toy.

But now consider another episode in which Jenny emits a certain sound ("Uh!"), or calls out "Teddy!", as she reaches for the toy. And finally, consider an episode in which she avows "I want Teddy", perhaps with no reaching at all. Intuitively, the verbal emissions, just like the reaching behavior, which we would consider a natural expression of Jenny's desire, may all 'come directly from' the child's desire. They seem equally 'pressed out' from her, and they appear no more driven

---

[15] The two claims are presented above, pp. 236f. It is interesting to consider to what extent ethical expressivism could also benefit from decoupling the positive and negative claims. The idea would be to maintain that ethical utterances have as their primary function the expression of subjects' pro- and con-attitudes, rather than the description of ethical reality. In addition, the ethical expressivist could maintain that there is no mind-independent ethical reality that could make ethical judgments true or false. But this does not mean that one could never make a genuine ethical judgment possessing of truth-evaluable content. What would *make* such judgments true or false in the absence of ethical reality is a matter for ethical metaphysics to determine. The important thing is that, ordinarily, when we engage in first-order ethical discourse, we are not (or not primarily) concerned with the 'truth-makers' of ethical judgments. In "Ethical Neo-Expressivism" (tentative title), a paper in progress, Matthew Chrisman and I try to develop this view.

by a prior deliberation, consideration, or determination regarding how things are presently with her. The verbal utterances seem to be equally expressive of her desire for the teddy. Granted that when saying "I want Teddy!", Jenny makes intentional use of conventional verbal means that are acquired. If her saying "I want Teddy" itself constitutes expressing her desire, the expression will not be a natural one (at least in one sense of the term). But notice that the same would hold of her saying "Daddy!" to express her happiness at seeing her dad, or her saying "Ouch!" to express her pain. Very early on in our lives, we begin to use acquired, conventional means—both words and gestures—to give expression to our states. (Much will be made of this point later on.)

To give some more intuitive purchase to the expressivist idea, let me focus attention first on a special subclass of avowals, which includes in addition to Jenny's "I want Teddy!" also avowals such as

"I feel so hot!" uttered as one is walking into an over-heated room.
"I hate this mess!" emitted as one walks into her apartment.
"I'm wondering what she'll do next", said as one is intently watching someone's unusual movements.

In this subclass, we have verbal acts in which a subject volunteers a present-tense mental self-ascription spontaneously and unreflectively, not in response to an invitation to describe their state, nor even (we may suppose) with the aim of informing their audience of what is going on in them. We also have in this subclass self-ascriptions produced in utter silence, and not in the presence of any (real or imaginary) audience, as when someone says to herself "Boy, I can't stand him". Following Bar-On and Long (2001), I shall refer to avowals in this subclass as "avowals proper".

As I understand them, avowals proper do not plausibly represent the self-ascriber's opinion, or carefully formed judgment, that she is in the ascribed mental state. They are not reasonably regarded as the culmination of the subject's inwardly directed truth-targeting reflection. Furthermore, avowals proper are not acts that subjects deliberately undertake to perform with a specific audience-directed goal in mind, such as convincing, informing, pleasing, etc. Like many non-verbal expressive acts, they may not even have any communicative point. Just as one can smile to oneself in amusement, or kiss the photo of one's beloved in the solitude of one's room, so one can think to oneself: "I hate this mess" or "I hope this ends soon". And even when one says out loud, "I can't stand this!", the point of one's verbal act may be none other than to give vent to a present feeling or emotion that one 'finds oneself in'. Thus, for all their articulate, self-ascriptive, linguistic form, as behavioral performances, avowals proper seem on a smooth continuum with less articulate, or non-self-ascriptive verbal emissions such as "Yuk!", "Ugh, so hot!", or "What a mess!". And these, in turn, seem continuous with acts of sighing in exasperation, letting out a cry, gasping in surprise, making a face, etc. As we consider these various performances in context, it is natural to regard their agents as 'doing the same sort of thing'. Given this continuity, I think it is very plausible to regard at least avowals proper as a species of behavior or doing, overt or covert, which serves to *express* the mental state they ascribe to the subject.

Intuitively speaking, when a subject issues an avowal proper, the point of the subject's use of words is not to offer a descriptive report of her state, or to provide evidence for its presence, or to inform someone about it. The subject's act of self-ascription may have no other point than to vent her frustration, shout for joy, give voice to her fear, air her idea, articulate her thought, let out her anger, and so on. The avowing subject does what people who are in the relevant mental state very often do; for verbal creatures like us, suppressing an avowal proper may be as unusual or 'unnatural' as suppressing a wince or a sigh. A subject who issues an avowal proper, like one who says, "This is great!" or "How gross!" or "God, please no!", simply *speaks from* her state, instead of giving a non-verbal, natural expression to her state. The crucial point is not that the speech comes directly from the state, without the mediation of the subject's judgment that she is in that state—though that may be true enough. Rather, what's important is that, although the avowal proper tells us that the self-ascriber is in some state, just like a report of that state (by someone else or by the avower herself), in the circumstances, it plays the same expressive role as a natural expression of it. Though the avowal proper "I'm so sick of this" may not display the subject's exasperation as would her stomping her foot, it may equally have no other point than that of voicing her present feeling.[16]

Interestingly, there is a special place reserved in the law for a notion that I believe to be a close relative of my notion of an avowal proper. The "rule of hearsay" deems testimony based on hearsay inadmissible evidence in a court of law. The idea behind the rule is, presumably, that if the witness is reporting what someone else said or thought, what we are receiving is a second-hand report on what the witness takes someone else's opinion on some matter to be. And the resulting report is too indirect, too mediated by interpretation, to serve as reliable testimony. However, there is an exception to that rule: a witness may invoke in her court testimony an "excited utterance" he or she has heard from someone else. An "excited utterance" is an unreflective responsive utterance emitted in immediate reaction to something. For example, a witness may call on her memory of someone screaming "Stop it! You're killing me!" Without much of a stretch, I think we can understand the idea behind this exception as follows. When I report someone else's excited utterance, as opposed to (what I take to be) her opinion, it is as though I serve as a vehicle for transmitting to the court something that directly delivers what the other person actually perceived, thought, or felt, unmediated by interpretation or gloss. Assuming I am not lying or misremembering (both of which are, of course, possible in the case of any witness), my report of someone else's excited utterance can be seen as offering to the court an unfiltered, interpretation-free reflection of the other person's state of mind, for it reproduces an utterance that, in turn, serves directly to give voice to that state of mind.[17]

What renders avowals proper a good entry point for my expressivist account is the fact that in terms of behavior, as well as phenomenology, they exhibit features characteristic of non-verbal, or verbally less articulate, expressive behavior. They are spontaneous, reactive, unreflective, and need not (though they can) serve any communicative purposes. At the same time, they share features characteristic of typical

---

[16] There may well be psychological purposes that are served by our ventings, both 'natural' and verbal. But this does not mean that, in venting, we intend to achieve those purposes, or that the relevant acts have them as their point. Moreover, there may be good reasons why, on particular occasions, subjects use verbal rather than natural forms of expression. Still, a verbal act, like a non-verbal one, may have no other point than venting.

[17] For discussion of excited utterances as exceptions to the "hearsay rule", see Strong (1992: ch. 26).

linguistic reports. An avowal proper shares syntactic and semantic properties with other ascriptions. It shares surface propositional form with genuine ascriptions of mental states to subjects. As a linguistic act, the avowal proper may stand on its own, without the accompaniment of any gestures or special tone of voice, etc., which serve to display or exhibit the state expressed. A person may walk into a room and simply say "I'm sick of this mess" with no affect. Also, she may simply *think* to herself, "I'm sick of this mess."

On the face of it, a purely linguistic act (as well as a silent mental act) of issuing a self-ascription, unaccompanied by any non-linguistic expressive behavior, may seem rather different from an act of smiling, or wincing, or shaking one's head. In what sense can such an act serve to express a subject's present state of mind? One strategy for answering this question is to try to offer a full-blown theoretical analysis of the notion of expression that establishes avowals as a special case. Given the focus of this work, and given space limitations, this is not a strategy I can pursue here. Instead, I will examine more informally some reasons we might have for regarding avowals as fundamentally different from uncontroversial cases of expression, including so-called natural expressions, and identify the aspects of similarity that matter for my Neo-Expressivist account. This, while bearing in mind, in full keeping with Semantic Continuity, that avowals, unlike natural expressions, share logical and semantic properties with assertions, statements, reports, and the like. As will become clear, what is most crucial for my Neo-Expressivist explanation of Epistemic Asymmetry is to understand avowing on the model of intentionally giving expression to one's mental state *using language* (or its analogue in thought). My explanation will neither presuppose nor require a uniform analysis of expression that is fully applicable to all acts of giving expression to one's mental states. Nevertheless, in the course of my discussion, I will venture to identify relevant aspects of resemblance between natural expressions and avowals, as well as other linguistic acts of expression.

In a paradigm case of avowal, a subject uses language, in overt speech or *sotto voce*, to ascribe a present mental state to herself. How, or in what sense, can such an act serve to express the self-ascribed mental state? In his article "Expressing" (1965), William Alston argues that there are two distinct senses of "express": one reserved for natural

expressions, the other reserved for intentional linguistic acts. He
thinks that "there is a fundamental difference between *expressing* a
feeling by saying something (interjectional or declarative) and showing, demonstrating, or manifesting, a feeling by a 'facial expression' "
(1965: 18). As Alston carves things up, we can speak of "facial expressions and the like as expressing something or other". So we can say,
"Her face expressed great determination"; "His every movement
expressed his indignation". But he claims that "[t]he presence of a certain facial expression or a certain demeanour is not a sufficient ground
for saying that *the person* expressed determination or indignation, while
having said something of an appropriate sort would be" (1965: 18).
Someone does not express his enthusiasm by "throwing his hat in the
air, dancing a jig, emitting squeals of delight, or 'lighting up' one's eyes"
(1965: 17). Thus, what philosophers often take to be paradigm examples
of expressions of feelings and attitudes—cries, groans, squeals, looks,
tones of voice—are representative of only one sense of "expressing", a
sense distinct from that in which one expresses one's feelings or attitudes in a linguistic utterance. With naturally expressive behavior, etc.,
"one might be said to have shown, demonstrated, evinced, or betrayed
enthusiasm, but not to have *expressed* it" (1965: 17). On the other hand,
Alston thinks "that it is just in the same sense of 'express' that a feeling
is expressed by an interjection or by a declarative sentence in the first
person present tense" (1965: 17). Thus,

> I can express my enthusiasm for your plan just as well by saying 'I'm very
> enthusiastic about your plan', as I can by saying 'What a tremendous plan!',
> 'Wonderful', or 'Great!' I can express disgust at X just as well by saying 'I'm
> disgusted', as by saying 'How revolting!', or 'Ugh'. I can express approval as
> well by saying 'I completely approve of what you are doing' as I can by say-
> ing 'Swell', or 'Good Show'. And I can express annoyance as well by saying
> 'That annoys me no end' as by saying 'Damn'. (1965: 16)

It is worth emphasizing that Alston is not denying that what I am
calling avowals can properly be said to express the very state the subject avows. On the contrary: he thinks that *only* in the case of linguistic expressions—avowals, as well as "interjections"—can we properly
speak of *a person expressing* her state, as opposed to merely engaging in
behavior that 'evinces' or 'betrays' it. So Alston would be sympathetic

to the letter of the positive expressivist claim. However, since the expressivist wants to highlight a certain similarity between avowals and natural expressions, whereas Alston is concerned to draw a sharp line between all linguistic expressions and natural expressions, Alston may seem unsympathetic to the spirit of the expressivist idea.

Alston is motivated to draw a sharp line between natural expressions and linguistic expressions by his opposition to the ethical non-cognitivism defended by emotivists such as Ayer and Stevenson. He agrees with these philosophers that linguistic utterances can properly be said to express attitudes and feelings, but disagrees with them that such expressive utterances are, for that reason, non-cognitive, or involve no assertions. This is why it is important for him to give a lot of weight to the contrast between linguistic expressions and natural expressions, on the one hand, and to show that "there are only minor differences between expressing a feeling (linguistically) and asserting that one has it", on the other hand (see 1965: 17). However, as I pointed out earlier, the Neo-Expressivist need not be wedded to a non-cognitivist view of mentalist discourse. Unlike the emotivist, she can happily accept Alston's claim that linguistic expressions are similar, in certain crucial respects, to ordinary assertions or reports. Indeed, her commitment to Semantic Continuity requires her to capture the similarity in some way. Also, on a suitably weak understanding of assertion, we can at least agree that one can express one's feeling, thought, etc., even when making an assertion. (There is a correspondingly weak understanding of the notion of a statement or a report.) However, if we understand assertion as a specific kind of speech-act, with a relatively well-defined point or purpose and felicity conditions, on a par with making a request, issuing a command, asking a question, then we may insist that at least some acts of expressing one's feeling, thought, etc. in language are not acts of making an assertion, issuing a statement, or delivering a report. (See below.) For this reason, I think the opposition to non-cognitivism is better cast in terms of the insistence that the relevant class of utterances do involve expressing judgments or making claims.

In a little while, we will see how we can preserve Alston's intuition that linguistic expressions are importantly like assertions. But first I want to take issue with the above way of separating linguistic and natural expressions. Recall the distinction I invoked earlier among three senses of expressing:[18]

EXP$_1$ the *action* sense: a *person* expresses a state of hers by intentionally doing something.

For example, when I intentionally give you a hug, or say, "It's so great to see you," I intentionally do something so as to give expression to my joy at seeing you.

EXP$_2$ the *causal* sense: an *utterance* or piece of behavior expresses an underlying state by being the culmination of a causal process beginning with that state.

For example, one's unintentional grimace or shaking hands may express in the causal sense one's pain or nervousness, respectively.

(EXP$_3$) the *semantic* sense: e.g., a *sentence* expresses an abstract proposition, thought, or judgment by being a (conventional) representation of it.

For example, the sentence "It's raining outside" expresses in the semantic sense the proposition that it's raining at the time of the utterance in the utterer's vicinity.

Of special concern to us right now will be the distinction between EXP$_1$ and EXP$_2$. For one way to capture Alston's sharp separation between linguistic and natural expressions is to maintain that only linguistic expressions fall under EXP$_1$, whereas natural expressions all fall exclusively under EXP$_2$. I think, however, that it is implausible to suggest that all cases of natural expression involve expressing only in the causal sense. Consider again Jenny's reaching for the teddy, which seems as good a case as any of naturally expressive behavior. Jenny's reaching behavior is not merely directly caused by her desire for the teddy; it is an intentional act on her part that serves to give expression to her desire. It seems artificial to deny that *Jenny* is expressing$_1$ (in the action sense) her desire for the teddy by reaching. Similarly for many so-called natural expressions, such as rubbing one's temples or eyes,

---

[18] See above, Ch. 6 (p. 216). The distinction is to be found in Sellars (1969). I do not wish to suggest, however, that Sellars would endorse my reading or use of this distinction. (For a recent discussion of the distinction, see Rosenberg (2002: 72 ff.).) I have provisionally followed Sellars in talking about three *senses* of expressing, though I hope my discussion below will reveal at least certain continuities among EXP₁, EXP₂ and EXP₃.

squinting, letting out a cry, smiling, frowning, giggling, or Alston's throwing one's hat in the air and dancing a jig. Unlike reflex movements, such behavioral manifestations are typically under the voluntary control of the subject, to the extent that they can be suppressed, or at least minimized or exaggerated. Alston himself warns against treating "A did $x$ intentionally" as requiring that A's overt activity be "accompanied by a covert mental commentary or preceded by a conscious act of resolution" (1965: 24 n. 1). But then it isn't at all clear why we should deny that a subject can express$_1$ her feeling or attitude through non-verbal means just as much as through a verbal utterance. We may grant that not all cases of so-called natural expression fit this bill. The sudden white complexion on your face may only express$_2$ your nervousness; the trembling hands may only express$_2$ your fear; the blush may only express$_2$ your embarrassment; and the sudden instinctive shift of your eyes may only express$_2$ your state of being startled. But instances of so-called natural expression encompass a much wider array than these. At the same time, it seems arbitrary to require of expressing in the action sense (as Alston seems to) that it involve the use of specifically linguistic means—means governed by linguistic rules. This seems especially arbitrary if, with Alston, we acknowledge that "[i]n calling a facial expression a 'natural sign' of a feeling, we are not implying that it is natural or innate, as opposed to learned or acquired as a result of conditioning" (1965: 24).

Following a suggestion made to me by Ram Neta, we could perhaps explicate the distinction between EXP$_1$ and EXP$_2$ by appealing to a familiar distinction in the theory of action between rational and brute causation. A person can be said to express$_1$ a mental state M through a bit of behavior, provided that the behavior is an intentional act on the person's part, and M is the reason (or 'rational cause') for the act. By contrast, a bit of behavior (whether intentional or not) can be said only to express$_2$ a mental state M, provided that the behavior is caused by M, but does not provide the person's reason for it. Two qualifications are in order. First, to accept the distinction between brute and rational causes is not to commit oneself on the question of whether reasons are causes. If reasons are causes, they constitute a special subset of causes: the subset of causes apt to *rationalize* action. The term "rational causes" will then refer to that subclass. Secondly, note that what I am concerned with here are reasons for *action*, not reasons for belief. The present suggestion is not that a non-cognitive mental state, such as pain or desire, can be one's reason for *believing* that one is in the relevant state (though I shall consider this view in Chapter 9, when we discuss the question of how avowals could constitute items of self-*knowledge*). Rather, I am proposing that various self-ascribed mental states (including states that are not beliefs or judgments) can constitute one's reasons for intentionally behaving in certain ways or for doing certain things. One can accept this, even if one maintains that only beliefs can serve as reasons for other beliefs.[19]

If we understand Sellars's distinction between EXP$_1$ and EXP$_2$ in terms of the distinction between brute and rational causes, it will become quite clear that natural and linguistic expressions do not map neatly onto cases of expressing in the causal sense only and cases of expressing also in the action sense, respectively. One's squinting one's eyes and rubbing one's temples is not merely caused by one's headache. The headache is not merely the brute cause of the non-linguistic expressive behavior; it also provides the reason for it. The relevant behavior is something the person engages in, or allows to occur intentionally, and through which she can be said to express her present state of mind. Thus, *contra* Alston, I believe that it can be perfectly appropriate to speak of a person expressing$_1$ her state by intentionally producing a bit of naturally expressive behavior—a gesture or bodily movement or sound, etc.—and also by just letting such bits of behavior occur (that is, by not stopping them from occurring, even when one can). If so, then we should not be moved to separate sharply linguistic from natural expressions on the grounds that only linguistic expressions express in the action sense.[20] (On the other hand, we can imagine cases of linguistic behavior that is only caused brutely by some underlying mental state. Turret's syndrome comes to mind here. But even more familiar and common are cases in which, for example,

---

[19] For the distinction between brute and rational causation, see McDowell (1982). Thanks to Dylan Sabo for prompting the two qualifications.

[20] For a congenial notion of behavior, see Dretske (1988: ch. 1). Dretske's treatment makes room—plausibly, I believe—for a notion of a doing, or an act, that is broader than the notion of an intentional action (understood as an action done from a (prior) intention or with an (explicit) intention to do what one is doing). The broader notion has, among others, the advantage that it is applicable to natural expressions, as well as to 'silent' expressions (i.e., expressive mental acts). See also Bratman (1989).

a nasty expletive escapes one's lips involuntarily, much to one's embarrassment and dismay.)

## Avowals as Acts and as Products

Clearly, as we consider the respects in which avowals may resemble natural expressions, we should be focusing on natural expressions that fall under $EXP_1$—where the relevant mental state is the rational cause of, or reason for, one's expressive behavior. Furthermore, as we consider these cases, I think we must distinguish between the *act* of expressing and its *product*. In what follows, I will be arguing that the important similarities between avowals and other intentionally produced expressions (intentionally produced natural expressions included) require thinking of *avowals as acts*, whereas the salient dissimilarities come to the fore when we think of *avowals as products*. This will prove crucial to the Neo-Expressivist attempt to explain Epistemic Asymmetry while preserving Semantic Continuity, as it will allow us to capture different dimensions along which to compare and contrast avowals and other expressions.

Like other nominals in English (and other languages), such as "statement", "assertion", "ascription", "report", as well as (NB!) "expression", etc., "avowal" admits of two different readings. It can be read as referring to someone's act of avow*ing*, which is an event in the world with a certain causal history and certain action properties. But it can also be read as referring to the result or product of such act—a linguistic (or language-like) token, an item with certain semantic properties. The product of an act of avowing, unlike a smile or a wince, or even a verbal cry such as "Ouch!", is a semantically articulate self-ascription, an item with semantic structure and truth-conditions. It is a product whose properties allow it to serve, and be caught up, in other kinds of distinctively linguistic (and mental) acts. Importantly, avowals, understood as products, express$_3$ (in Sellars's semantic sense) self-ascriptive propositions, to the effect that the avower is in some state. And the mentalistic terms that constitute parts of avowals semantically represent the relevant states. Natural expressions understood as products—facial expressions, gestures, bodily movements, demeanor, inarticulate sounds, however produced—do not express$_3$

anything. There are no semantic conventions in virtue of which laughter represents amusement, no linguistic rules in virtue of which a hug signifies, or refers to, joy at seeing the person hugged, or a cowering demeanor stands for feeling threatened. Thus there are notable differences between avowals and acts of natural expression in terms of their products.

The significance of these differences should not be exaggerated. As even Alston admits, there are many intermediate cases of non-linguistic expressions. Like linguistic expressions, many gestures, gesticulations, and facial expressions (e.g., raising one's eye-brows, turning up one's nose, tipping one's hat, saluting, shaking hands, showing the middle finger) are generated or governed by cultural/societal rules and conventions. And interjections such as "Ugh", "Damn", "Bully", unlike terms such as "nausea", "happy", "thinking", and so on, though they are linguistic expressions by Alston's lights, and are linked by rules or conventions to the states they express$_1$, do not semantically represent those states. (See Alston (1965: 25 ff.) And some cases that Alston would (plausibly) count as linguistic expressions of speakers' mental states also do not involve semantic representation of those states— e.g., "This is gross!", "How awful!", "You look so pretty!" But, in any event, I think that the expressivist insight regarding avowals should be understood, in the first instance, as a claim about the relevant *acts*, not about their products. The claim is that there are notable similarities between acts of avowing a state and the act of giving it a (so-called) natural expression—e.g., between acts of saying "I really like this!" (or, alternatively, "This is wonderful!" or "Yippee!") and the act of giving an ear-to-ear smile or a firm handshake. And this claim could be true, even if there were systematic differences between the products of acts of avowing, and other linguistic acts, on the one hand, and the products of naturally expressive acts, on the other.

In the specific case of avowals proper, at least, it may be further suggested that the relevant utterances are produced through a *process* that is very similar to the process we typically associate with natural expression. Thus, consider a scenario in which you see something exciting. There are countless ways you could give expression to your excitement. Consider, in particular, the following. You could clap your hands enthusiastically, emit a "Yea!", say "This is great!" or avow "I'm so excited". Pre-theoretically, there seems to be very little to distinguish the different acts in terms of the process they involve. In point of phenomenology, the non-verbal clapping, the interjection, the descriptive exclamation, and the self-ascriptive avowal proper all seem to issue directly from your excitement, without the intervention of an inward reflection on, or even recognition of, your condition. And, if we are after a commonsense explanation of the subject's behavior, there seems to be no more reason to appeal to the subject's self-assessment in the case of the avowal proper than in the case of the other performances. These considerations may speak in favor of a *prima facie similarity in the process involved* in all these performances. This similarity of process, moreover, is consistent with the fact that the performances use very different *expressive vehicles*. The hand clapping constitutes a visual display of one's excitement, whereas the verbal performances may stand on their own, with no accompanying display or even special tone of voice. And among the verbal performances, "Yea!" is a semantically inarticulate sound, and only the avowal speaks directly of one's excitement. (The differences will occupy us in what follows.) Still, the performances, we may assume, are all intentional acts on the subject's part. And if we ask after the subject's reason for engaging in the respective behaviors, it seems that the answer may well be the same in each case. Thus, if we were to ask the subject, "Why did you clap your hands?", "Why did you say 'Yea!'/'This is so great!'/'I'm so excited'?", a natural and appropriate answer to all these questions would be: "Because I was excited."[21]

In general, when a subject reaches for a toy, yawns, grimaces, sighs, gives a happy smile, and so on, there is normally no temptation to suppose that the subject's expressive behavior is psychologically mediated by a higher-order judgment about the condition that her behavior expresses. Though the expressive behavior is understood as intentional, we think of its relation to the condition expressed as importantly similar to the relation of unintentional bits of naturally expressive behavior, such as trembling hands or a blushing face, to the conditions they express (one's fear, or one's embarrassment, respectively).

---

[21] Alston concedes that an utterance of "Damn", though linguistic, "is more like a frown than it is like a [linguistic] utterance" in being "more spontaneous, less deliberate, more explosive" (1965: 26). He takes these features to point to some contrast between interjections and self-ascriptive utterances (whose significance he proceeds to downplay). But surely one's utterance "I'm so mad at you" need be no less spontaneous, no less explosive, no more deliberate or preceded by reflection, than an utterance of "Damn!" or an exaggerated frown.

How should the similarity be characterized? As suggested earlier, the intuition is that a reaching behavior, like a blushing face, may 'comes directly from' the relevant condition. Yet the former behavior, we are assuming, represents an intentional doing on the part of the subject. It is not something that simply happens to her. Doesn't the intentionality of the act implicate some kind of psychological mediation? Perhaps. But if so, this would suggest that we should not understand the directness or immediacy that is seemingly shared by intentional and unintentional acts of natural expression in terms of the absence of psychological mediation.

We should also note, however, that even if we did so, this would point to a dissimilarity between cases of intentionally produced and unintentional, natural expressions (and thus, perhaps, between expressing$_1$ and expressing$_2$); it would not directly undermine the claim of similarity between linguistic and non-linguistic acts of expressing$_1$. Yet it is the latter similarity that is the crucial one for the Neo-Expressivist account. For, as hinted above, what is crucial for the account to establish, even more narrowly, is a similarity between avowals and other intentional *linguistic* acts in which a subject expresses$_1$ her attitude, feeling, etc. Thus, strictly speaking, the explanatory potential of the expressivist idea does not depend on there being a univocal notion of expression binding together intentional and unintentional expressions, or even linguistic and non-linguistic intentional acts of expressing. Although in later sections I shall explore the possible basis for such a univocal notion, I don't think the plausibility of the Neo-Expressivist account depends on the existence of such a basis.[22]

Behind the effort to distinguish sharply between linguistic and natural expressions may lie a certain philosophical prejudice. This is the supposition that a speaker who makes intentional use of an indicative, truth-evaluable sentence (unlike someone who makes a gesture, a face, or a noise) *must* be offering a descriptive report, or making an assertion, or issuing a statement, about what the sentence semantically expresses. In particular, it is assumed that if a speaker intentionally utters a sentence that semantically represents a present mental state of hers, the state she self-ascribes must be something she aims to report or describe correctly, in order to inform her audience of the relevant

---

[22] Ram Neta has suggested to me that a basis for a univocal notion of expression could be found in the analysis of expression offered by Nelson Goodman (1968: 85 ff.).

state of affairs. (In its application to thought, the prejudice is that if a subject has made a mental self-ascription in thought, then she must have at least some implicit assertive purposes, such as stating to herself how things are with her, perhaps in order to draw some inferences, or at least making a mental note of her present state 'for her own record'.) Given this prejudice, it will seem natural to assume that a subject who issues a self-ascription of a present mental state must be at least tacitly attempting to line up her self-judgments with the relevant mental facts, and thus must have some epistemic reasons or grounds for the self-ascriptions she produces. It will then seem natural to explain, with proponents of the Epistemic Approach, that such security as the self-ascription enjoys must be due to the epistemic security of the basis on which it is made.

It is important to understand my appropriation of the expressivist insight against the background of my rejection of the Epistemic Approach. For I want to invoke the insight in my explanation of avowals' immunity to errors of misascription, and later in my explanation of the asymmetric presumption of truth governing avowals. My claim is that we would be able to understand these aspect of avowals' special security better if we recognized the expressive role played by avowals in context—a role similar to that played by certain nonverbal performances, as well as some verbal performances that are not self-ascriptive.[23]

To reiterate, the suggestion I have made is that avowals are similar to natural expressions in terms of the *acts* that avowing subjects perform; but their products are different. Avowals as products have semantic structure. Of the product of an act of avowing (i.e., a self-ascription of a present mental state) we can say that it expresses$_3$ the proposition or thought that the subject is in a certain state. For the avowal-as-product is a conventional representation of that thought. And a component of it—viz., the mental term—conventionally represents the relevant mental state. Not so in the case of natural expressions. A natural expression (as product) does not semantically express the proposition that the expressing subject is in the relevant condition, regardless of whether the natural expression expresses$_1$ or only

---

[23] Speaking of an expressive role played in context should not mislead us into thinking that the account to be offered here is limited to avowals made in conversation, or at least in speech. I will continue to try to make clear how my expressivist account cuts across avowals made in speech and in thought, though for ease of initial exposition I often focus on examples of spoken avowals.

expresses$_2$ the condition. Though the natural expression indicates the presence of the relevant condition, it includes no semantic representation of the condition (or its presence).[24] So we can agree with Alston that, in some sense, linguistic utterances perform and achieve their expressive function in a different way from natural expressions. To vary the example, a linguistic utterance such as "It's so good to see you!", which typically serves to express$_1$ the speaker's joy, does so with an expressive vehicle that expresses$_3$ the proposition or thought that it is very good to see one's hearer, again, in virtue of the rules of English. If, as I maintain, one can also express$_1$ one's joy by avowing "I am so glad to see you!", this would involve using a sentence which, in virtue of the rules of English, expresses$_3$ the proposition or thought that the speaker is very glad to see her hearer. By contrast, the product of an act of giving your friend a cheerful hug is not governed by any syntactic or semantic rules of English, and it does not express$_3$ anything. The expressivist claim is that, despite the differences in products, a speaker may be performing the same kind of act—i.e., expressing her joy at seeing someone—in all three cases.

Several points need to be made. First, for my purposes, I do not have to understand the above claim as entailing anything as strong as that avowals involve the same (or even very similar) causal-psychological processes as other acts in which a subject expresses a first-order mental condition.[25] Whether or not my verbal utterance "I am so excited" is issued through a psychological process that is similar in all crucial respects to that behind the behavior of clapping my hands, it may be plausible to identify the respective behaviors as belonging in the same category of acts. The classification of behaviors into acts is not, in the first instance, a classification in terms of the psychological processes involved, any more than it is a classification in terms of bodily movements.[26] Thus compare an unintentionally produced excited facial

---

[24] Below, I shall discuss in more detail the question of how natural expressions express relevant conditions. As we shall see, although natural expressions do not express the presence of mental states in Sellars's semantic sense, they do exhibit a certain kind of articulation, which makes them convenient candidates for replacement by semantic expressions.

[25] Establishing such a similarity of processes would require an empirical psychological study. Though I think it is plausible to expect such a study to reveal interesting similarities, we may also expect some psychological differences, given the involvement of 'speech centers' in the production of avowals. For some suggestive psychological evidence favoring an expressivist approach to first-person claims, having to do with autism, see McGeer (2001).

[26] I take the question of individuation of behavioral performances into actions to be, in the first instance, a matter for a theory of action. It may or may not afford ready translation into a purely psychological question.

expression with an intentional, but spontaneous, clapping of hands. I am inclined to think that, in point of being expressive of one's excitement, the two are on a par. But I think we would be hard pressed to isolate key psychological ingredients that make for the expressive character of the two 'performances'. Again, we may be inclined to say that both come directly from the excitement. But it isn't clear what this amounts to over and above the claim that in both cases you are not engaging in the behavior for some specific purpose or reason, and that the behavior is produced without any prior deliberation on, or assessment of, or even recognition of, your excitement.

To say this is to offer a negative characterization, similar to a characterization of, e.g., sincerity in terms of the absence of any intention to deceive or dissimulate. Notice, however, that the negative characterization of expressiveness could apply equally to a verbal performance—to an excited interjection "Yea!", to an utterance of "This is great!", or, finally, to a self-ascriptive avowal proper like "I'm so excited!". For the verbal performances may be equally immediate in the sense just explained. Bearing this in mind, we can see the case of avowals proper as helping to diminish the plausibility of the prejudice of which we spoke earlier. We can begin to see that it may be a mistake to think that as soon as linguistic behavior is involved, or at least when it takes the form of a self-ascriptive utterance, epistemic mediation by recognitional judgments is mandatory.

In my discussion of avowals proper, I have highlighted the familiar interchangeability (in context) of avowals and other articulate linguistic utterances with various expressive non-verbal acts, as well as with semantically inarticulate interjections. But I do not mean to discount the various pragmatic differences between non-verbal and verbal performances, or to deny that subjects may have various reasons or be under various pressures to prefer one type of expressive vehicle over another in a given context. Rather, I want to suggest that acts of self-ascription may sometimes be performed with no more of a special communicative or other further purpose than paradigmatic non-verbal acts of giving vent to one's present state. (Note, however, that to say of a bit of behavior that it is performed with no special communicative or other further purpose is not to deny that behavior is *purposive*.) Moreover, there may be no more reason—other than philosophical prejudice—to postulate the presence of an intervening recognitional self-judgment in the case of acts whose products are self-ascriptions than to do so in the case of corresponding (intentional) non-linguistic expressive acts.

However, a second point I want to make is that even the similarity suggested by the negative characterization of expressive immediacy is not what ultimately matters to the Neo-Expressivist account. What ultimately matters is that, when issuing an avowal proper, a subject's *epistemic* position vis-à-vis her own mental condition may be in important respects similar to her position when she expresses her state through smiling, sighing, or cheering. Though she is using a semantically articulate, self-ascriptive expressive vehicle, her present self-judgment—*even if we suppose she makes one*—is beside the point. It is no more obligatory to regard her avowal "I am so excited" as resting, epistemically, on her judgment about how things are with her at the moment, than it is obligatory in the case of her saying "This is great!". What matters to the Neo-Expressivist account primarily is not the absence of a self-judgment mediating between the mental state and the avowal, but rather the irrelevance of any such judgment to the treatment of the avowal as a secure performance, protected from epistemic criticism or correction. Thus, my opposition to the Epistemic Approach does not even require denying outright that avowals somehow involve recognitional self-judgment. It is sufficient for my purposes to offer an explanation of the distinctive security of avowals that does not appeal to the epistemic security of such a self-judgment. This is what I aim to achieve by establishing that acts of avowals, like paradigm intentional acts of expressing$_1$, simply serve to vent, air, or voice the subject's first-order (and self-ascribed) mental condition.[27]

Before turning to the role played by the expressivist insight in my alternative account of avowals' special security, I would like to make a third point. The idea that an avowal such as "I am very excited about this", even unaccompanied by any special facial expression, or gesture, or tone of voice, can be said to express the subject's excitement often meets resistance. I think the idea is most jarring if we hold as our paradigm of expression winces, cries, sighs, tears, and so on. But

---

[27] This second point will become important when we turn to the general case of avowals (ones that are not avowals proper). In the next chapter I take up the question whether or not avowals do express self-judgments as well as the self-ascribed conditions.

I think it is important to bear in mind that, avowals aside, both in philosophy and in everyday commerce, we very readily speak of verbal utterances of a great variety as expressing subjects' feelings, attitudes, and so on. We are often prepared to say, in a perfectly ordinary, seemingly innocent sense, that someone has expressed her frustration by saying "Darn!", or her disgust by saying "Yuk!" or "Gross!", or her annoyance by saying "This is so annoying", and so on. Philosophers of language often speak of the performance of certain speech-acts as expressing certain states of mind (e.g., a speaker making a request is said to be expressing her desire for the thing requested). Emotivists claim that we express various pro- or con-attitudes when saying (or thinking) things such as "He is a good man", "Abortion is wrong", "You shouldn't have abandoned that dog". Finally, it is standard practice to take it that a sincere utterance of a declarative sentence, such as "There's a cardinal on the bird-feeder" or "I've lost three pounds" or "The phone bill is overdue", serves to express the speaker's belief or thought or judgment.

What kind of expression is involved in these kinds of cases? What are said to express the speakers' mental states in such cases are intentionally produced linguistic utterances. But the words produced do not themselves express a proposition that semantically represents the speaker's state of mind. Expletives and interjections do not express$_3$ (i.e., express in Sellars's semantic sense) propositions at all. And the propositions expressed by semantically more articulate utterances (such as "This is gross", "The phone bill is overdue") are not self-ascriptive; they concern individuals or things other than the speaker or matters external to her. In these cases, we take the speaker to be intentionally using verbal means—an expletive, an interjection, *or a* more or less articulate ascription—to express in the action sense her state of mind. Although the verbal utterances would presumably not count as natural expressions of the relevant states—after all, they involve use of conventional, acquired means—there is no *prima facie* reason to suspect a radical shift in the notion of expression at work. There doesn't seem to be any hidden equivocation in the claim that the person who waves a fist at you and the one who says "You're going too far!" have both expressed their anger at you.

Although I have mainly used examples from speech behavior, I think the kinds of expressive utterances I have discussed have their analogues in thought. Instead of waving a fist at you, a person might think to herself silently, "You're going too far!". As regards such expressive mental acts, we need not take it that the thinker is intentionally producing the expression in thought; it suffices to suppose that the expressive articulation in thought is something the thinker allows to happen. Sometimes, of course, there is nothing one can do to stop thinking "That bastard!" in response to someone's particularly egregious behavior. It still seems natural to me to think of "That bastard!" produced *sotto voce* as expressing one's annoyance or outrage. (If you think this kind of case does not qualify as a case of expressing one's state in the action sense, since no intentional act is performed, it still seems possible to regard it as a case of expressing one's state in the causal sense.)

The foregoing is intended to draw attention to the fact that we do have in place an ordinary notion of expression that applies readily to non-verbal and verbal expressions alike, whether in speech or in thought, which notion carries over into philosophical discussion. This ordinary notion is all that the Neo-Expressivist account needs to invoke. The commonsense notion we can avail ourselves of is that of an act, whether linguistic or non-linguistic, involving speech or not, whose point is not to offer a descriptive report, make an assertion, or provide someone with information about the speaker's present thoughts, feelings, emotions, or attitudes. Such acts can be performed with no particular purpose, and for no other reason than to put forth, or air, or give vent to one's present state. As we have seen from our examples, the notion of expression in question seems applicable even when the expressive means are not 'natural' but, rather, are introduced in some conventional way, and are acquired. And it is applicable to acts performed in the absence of an audience, as when someone spits at a photograph or caresses a souvenir while alone, as well as to mental acts such as saying to oneself "Oh my God!" or "That bastard" or "What a mess!". The Neo-Expressivist account maintains that avowals should count among such expressive acts. Just as an ascription such as "This dog is scary" is semantically about some dog and a characteristic of it, but can be used to give voice to the speaker's fear, so a self-ascription such as "I am scared of this dog" can be semantically about the subject and a state of her, but can nevertheless also be seen as giving voice to the speaker's fear. (Notice that in both cases we may want to ask whether, in addition, the utterance expresses the speaker's belief that things are as her utterance semantically represents them: i.e., that the dog is scary, that she herself is scared of the dog, respectively. We shall return to this issue in the next chapter.)

The observation that is crucial for the Neo-Expressivist account is that, in point of its potential to express a subject's present state of mind, a self-ascription such as "I am so annoyed at you" (produced in speech or in thought) is no different from, e.g., "This is very annoy-ing", or "Enough!", or even "Ugh!". I think it is further plausible that these latter expressions can be expressive of a subject's mental state in the same sense as intentional acts of natural expression, such as letting out a sound or making a face or a gesture, that are not conventional. In other words, I think there is a continuum of expressive behavior that progresses roughly as follows:

- natural expressions (vocal sounds, facial expressions, bodily demeanor or gestures, and so on, whose connection to the relevant states is set up by nature);
- acquired, conventional non-verbal expressions (tipping one's hat, shaking hands, showing a finger, as well as various sounds and facial expressions, etc.);
- verbal emissions (expletives, interjections, as well as semantically articulate, explicit linguistic utterances that are not about the sub-ject or her state, but still serve to express this or that emotion, atti-tude, feeling, or thought);
- avowals proper and avowals more generally.

But the Neo-Expressivist account can survive even if it is somehow established that there is a significant break somewhere along this con-tinuum, as long as we can retain the uncontroversial sense in which a whole variety of acquired, conventional expressive devices can be said to serve in the intentional expression of subjects' mental states.

I shall have more to say about the continuity between avowals and non-self-ascriptive verbal expressions, as well as acquired and conven-tional non-linguistic expressions, later on. But right now I would like to explain how acceptance of this continuity in expressive character can contribute to our understanding of the special security of avowals. As part of my attempt to develop an alternative to the Epistemic Approach, I have offered a characterization of avowals whereby they contrast with all other ascriptions in being immune to errors of misascription, as well as misidentification. I connected the idea of ascriptive immunity with the absence of epistemic distance or epistemic targeting as regards the state that an avowal self-ascribes. I think the foregoing discussion allows us to see these features of avowals as tied to their expressive character.

Consider again what I have called "avowals proper" as these are made in speech. When issuing an avowal proper, a subject uses an expressive vehicle that ascribes a mental state to herself, but the subject is not putting forth the self-ascription by way of offering a descriptive report about the state, or providing evidence for its presence, or informing someone about it. When issuing an avowal proper, one has no purpose other than that of venting one's frustration, shouting for joy, giving voice to one's fear, spelling out one's thought, airing one's idea, letting out one's agony, sharing one's anxiety, and so on. A subject who issues an avowal proper, like one who says "This is great!" or "How gross!", or "Please, God, no!" simply speaks from her condition, *in lieu* of making a gesture, or a face, or grunting, etc.

At least when it comes to avowals proper, we can see how this affords the unique, combined immunity to error characteristic of avowals (on my account). When issuing an avowal proper, as when issuing a proprioceptive report, a subject does not have herself as a target of recognitional judgment. She has no reasons or grounds for thinking that someone is in M that is independent of her thinking that *she* herself is in M. But, in addition, she does not have her present state as a target of recognitional judgment, either. She has no reasons or grounds for thinking that she is in some state or other, independently of simply thinking she is in M. And she may have no reasons for self-ascribing M over and above her simply being in M. She issues a self-ascription of a mental state in the course of speaking directly from her present condition, rather than reporting her finding regarding her present state of mind. Unlike the person who grunts, or smiles, she is *speaking* her mind—that is, she is using articulate verbal means to express her state of mind. And unlike the person who says "Darn it!" or "How awful!" or "This is great!", she is speaking *self-ascriptively*. Even so, the self-ascription equally serves as a vehicle for giving voice to her present mental state.

If we regard an avowing subject as simply speaking her mind, then one major component of Epistemic Asymmetry should seem less surprising. To the extent that we regard a subject as simply giving voice to the condition she self-ascribes, rather than, say, providing an evidence- or recognition-based report on her own self-findings, it should indeed seem inappropriate to ask after the reasons she has for the different aspects of the self-ascription she produces when avowing. To do so would be to betray a misunderstanding of the character of her performance. Appreciating the expressive character of avowals should also help us see why avowals seem protected even from the kinds of epistemic assessment and criticism that are appropriate to ordinary perceptual reports. Insofar as we take someone's linguistic utterance (or its analogue in thought) as simply presenting or evincing ('putting on the table') her present state of fear, anxiety, joy, disgust, etc., asking for reasons for, or taking issue with, her self-belief or self-judgment—even assuming she has one—would seem entirely out of place. On the present account, though avowals employ semantically articulate self-ascriptive vehicles, *as acts* they are on a par with acts of linguistic expressions that are not self-ascriptive. Just as someone who says "This is disgusting" may be speaking from her state of disgust, rather than offering a descriptive report of something, so someone who says "I am disgusted" may be speaking from her disgust rather than offering some kind of a perceptual or recognitional self-report (though, semantically speaking, only the latter is self-ascribing the relevant state). To vary the example, if a self-ascription such as "I am annoyed by your reaction" is issued as an expression of one's state, then it is as inappropriate to raise questions about the epistemic grounding of the self-ascriber's *judgment that* she is annoyed or of various aspects of it as it would be to ask such questions of a person who utters "Your reaction is so annoying" or "Darn!" (or, for that matter, of a person who stomps her foot, or makes some other non-verbal annoyed gesture or vocal emission).

We can thus see avowals' distinctive ascriptive immunity to error as a consequence of their expressive character. Furthermore, as I shall explain later, the relative incorrigibility of avowals and the supposition that subjects are much better placed than others to pronounce on their present mental states can also be explained by appeal to the expressivist idea. On the present account, to regard someone's self-ascription as an avowal is to take her to be expressing her self-ascribed state. But then it makes little sense to contradict or correct her self-ascription. For, to take it that she has indeed expressed her state just is to take it that she *is* in the relevant state (and that she has successfully given it voice).[28]

I shall later argue that the above explanation can be generalized beyond the case of avowals proper. Even in the case of present-tense mental self-ascriptions that are offered in response to questions or upon reflection, or ones made with some communicative or reportive purposes, I will argue, there is still room for the expressivist idea. To anticipate: I will be suggesting that *insofar as* we think of all avowals as enjoying a special security, a security that goes beyond the epistemic security of well-grounded or highly reliable self-reports, it is *because, or to the extent that*, we regard them as (at least in part) serving to express the very conditions they ascribe. Recognizing an expressive element in all avowals should thus contribute to the explanation of the distinctive security of all avowals. For in the case of all avowals, it will still be true that, to the extent that we take the avowing subject to be expressing her present mental state, any epistemic reasons she might have for the judgment that she is in that state will be beside the point. It is worth emphasizing again, however, that portraying avowals as acts of expressing one's first-order mental states is intended only in aid of explaining Epistemic Asymmetry. The appeal to the expressivist idea is by way of explaining the additional immunity to (ascriptive) errors of avowal, which makes for their distinctive resistance to epistemic assessment. This explanatory goal can be achieved without supposing that the products of avowals are semantically similar to smiles, frowns, or groans. (Nor is it necessary to assume that avowals and natural expressions are produced through the same psychological processes.)

## Natural Expressions as 'Transparent-to-the-Subject's-Condition'

The core claim put forth by Neo-Expressivist account is this:

When avowing, a subject performs an act of expressing₁ a present mental state. In point of the act performed, a subject expresses her

---

[28] Importantly, on the Neo-Expressivist account, acts of avowing, like other expressive acts, can succeed or fail. A successful avowal will have as its product a true self-ascription, whereas a failed avowal will have as its product a false self-ascription. In the next chapter, I explain how the possibility of false avowals can be reconciled with the expressivist explanation of the presumption of truth.

mental state through an avowal such as "I feel so mad at him" just as she might express her belief that $p$ when she sincerely asserts $p$, or her approval of something when she says "This is excellent", her anger at someone when she says "He's such a jerk!", or her annoyance when she utters "Darn!". What separates avowals from other expressive acts is the fact that the product of an avowal is a self-ascription of a present mental state, where the self-ascription expresses$_3$ the presence of very same state that the avower expresses$_1$ in issuing the self-ascription.

As I pointed out earlier, strictly speaking, the core claim requires only invoking the same commonsense notion of expression that is readily applicable to a variety of intentionally produced bits of behavior, both linguistic and non-linguistic, that are associated with the relevant states or attitudes by convention, rather than by nature. In other words, for purposes of my Neo-Expressivist account of avowals' security, the reader need only allow that there is a legitimate sense in which subjects can express their present mental states using a variety of acquired, convention-governed expressive vehicles or means. The core claim is that *in that sense* an avowal, too, can be said to be expressive of one's present mental state. And, as far as that claim goes, it can be left open to what degree that sense of expression is the same as, or continuous with, the sense in which an unintentional grimace expresses one's discomfort, or even the sense in which a person expresses$_1$ her pain when intentionally producing so-called natural expressions.[29]

However, in this section I would like to venture beyond what is strictly necessary for the core claim, and explore the extent to which the wide spectrum of cases which fall under the commonsense notion of expression are held together in some way. I shall be examining, albeit in a preliminary and intuitive way, whether there is, after all, a univocal notion of natural expression, which is applicable regardless of whether the expressive behavior is intentionally produced or merely caused by underlying conditions, and the extent to which that notion, in turn, carries over to all intentional acts of expressing, regardless of whether the expressive means are natural or conventional. I hope this discussion, though incomplete and speculative in

[29] Thus, the Neo-Expressivist account of avowals' security allows that acts falling under the heading of expressing in the action sense separate into different kinds, depending on whether the expressive means are 'natural' or not. Moreover, it seems that it does not depend on there being a uniformity of sense between expressing in the action sense and expressing in the causal sense.

parts, will help us gain a better understanding of the commonsense notion of expression in its various applications, an understanding which should serve us well when we return to the core expressivist claim later on.

I begin with some reflections on the commonsense notion of a natural expression. Alston suggests that we could think of natural expressions as simply a species of natural signs. When we regard something as a natural expression, this is just like "any case of taking one thing to be a natural sign of another, for example taking a certain noise in an engine to be an indication of an improperly seated valve" (Alston 1965: 21).[30] The production of a natural expression is underwritten by causal regularities in nature; it is a natural, reliable indicator of the relevant psychological state. Now, I think it's true that, like natural signs, natural expressions can be regarded as indicative of the presence of certain conditions; for there is a reliable correlation between the behavior that constitutes the expression and the presence (and perhaps some features) of the expressed condition. Furthermore, it is plausible to regard the correlation between the behavioral manifestations and the states they express as set up by Mother Nature, and to take the manifestations to be relatively direct causal upshots of the states they express. In these respects, the correlations between, e.g., being embarrassed and blushing, being nervous or alarmed and turning white, being upset and crying, being scared and having a trembling voice or shaking hands, and so on, may seem quite similar to the correlations between having a cold and sneezing, or having a migraine and having dilated pupils. Nevertheless, I think that the purely causal construal of the notion of a natural expression fails to capture our ordinary notion of a natural expression. I want to suggest that the commonsense notion of natural expression is intended to capture a narrower range of behaviors than the notion of indicative or symptomatic behavior.

---

[30] Both natural expressions and linguistic utterances can indeed be said to provide reliable indication of relevant psychological states, but Alston doesn't think this diminishes the difference between the two categories of expression. For, although "one way of providing someone with a reliable indication of my disgust is to tell him that I am disgusted . . . the way in which saying 'I'm disgusted' is an indication of disgust is very different from the way in which a facial expression is an indication of disgust" (1965: 20). Although in both types of cases, an inference from the expression to the state is licensed, in the case of linguistic expressions, we need to "appeal to a general practice of using the sentence in a certain way"; whereas in the case of natural expressions, we need only appeal to a "de facto correlation" between the expression and the state. As Alston goes on to explain, cases of natural expression are underwritten by regularities; cases of linguistic expression involve the operation of rules (see 1965: 21 ff.).

Earlier I took issue with Alston's suggestion that naturally expressive behavior falls exclusively under the category of behavior that
causally expresses mental conditions. I pointed out that we ordinarily
include under the umbrella of "natural expressions" not only things
that merely happen to a subject, but also things a subject intentionally
does, or at least lets happen. I now want to suggest that even when we
consider behavior that is unintentional, to regard it as a natural
expression is to see it as more than just a natural sign of the relevant
condition. Following Hauser (1996: 9), we may distinguish a natural
*sign*, which is a symptom, a behavioral manifestation or a trace that
provides information (e.g., red spots on the skin, sneezes, footprints),
on the one hand, from a *cue*, which is a natural sign that has been
selected for its capacity to convey information (e.g., bright coloration
in frogs, designed for warning away potential predators), and a *signal*,
which is a cue that can be produced in response to changes in the
environment (e.g., sexual swellings and piloerection), on the other
hand. In addition, there may be good reason to separate off a subclass
of signals, which I shall dub "communicative signals". These would be
behavioral manifestations that have the natural purpose of conveying
information to, or producing certain reactions in, some designated
audience.

Now, at one end of the spectrum of behavior that we regard as
naturally expressive, we may locate things that merely happen to an
animal, such as changes in the color of its complexion or releases of
odors, and over which it can exercise no voluntary control. It may
seem at first that there is no significant line to draw between these
and various manifestations that are merely non-voluntary side-effects
or symptoms of various conditions (such as the reddening of one's
eyes when tired.) But it could well turn out that even the non-voluntary behavioral manifestations that we count as natural expressions
still belong in the specific sub-category of communicative signals,
rather than just in the broader categories of signs or cues. (Whether
or not this is the case is, of course, not something to be determined by
pure philosophical reflection.) If so-called natural expressions are a
species of communicative signals, this would suggest a certain intuitive connection between expression and intentional action, which
could serve to bridge between $EXP_1$ and $EXP_2$. Perhaps the kinds of
behavior that we count as natural expressions are kinds that can at

least potentially be involved in intentional communicative acts of a certain sort. Many, if not most, of the behaviors we regard as natural expressions can be brought under voluntary control to some extent. And, interestingly, we would not count odors we release, over which we cannot exercise voluntary control, among natural expressions. While a change in the color of one's face or skin is not normally something one can exercise any control over, let alone induce, one can at least *let* tears roll down one's face *or not*, and in the case of behavioral manifestations such as the shaking of one's hands or the trembling of one's voice, one also can modulate the intensity of the behavior. (Dogs seem able to intensify the wagging of their tails in response to their owners' approval and suppress their barks when hushed, and babies seem able to increase or decrease their crying according as their mother moves further away or closer.) The suggestion would be that when we regard a bit of behavior as a natural expression, we presume it to be something a creature *does*, or allows to happen, which is potentially susceptible to voluntary control, or at least subject to modulation in response to input that is directed at the behavior itself, even if it cannot be produced at will.

If natural expressions fit under the general rubric of signals (in Hauser's terminology), then, *contra* Alston, they are already not merely "direct behaviouristic symptoms of the emotions or feelings to which they testify".[31] If, moreover, natural expressions are what I've called *communicative* signals, then naturally expressive behavior can be regarded as a species of communicative behavior. This would support the intuition that the notion of a natural expression has narrower application than that of a natural behavioral symptom or indicator. The organisms we encounter in our natural environment all exhibit symptoms of various conditions they are in; but not all organisms exhibit behavior that is in some way designed to communicate the presence and character of some of their conditions to some designated audience. It may be that creatures who engage in naturally expressive behavior are characteristically endowed with feedback mechanisms that allow them to have some awareness of the relevant behavior and are capable (to varying degrees) of reproducing, modulating, or suppressing the behavior. This in turn allows them to develop or acquire sets of distinctive, repeatable vocalizations, facial

---

[31] This is a suggestion Alston borrows from Stevenson (1944: 37).

expressions, bodily gestures, movements—behavioral *repertoires*—which can constitute common currency in the life of the species, or the socio-cultural group, or even the individual. Possession of such a repertoire is characteristic of creatures who engage in communicative behavior.

Note that if it is correct to suggest that common sense subsumes naturally expressive behavior under communicative behavior, this would also help to explain the intuitive distinction between natural expressions and various actions in which subjects may engage simply *as a result* of being in various mental states, and which may reliably attest to the presence and character of the states, but which do *not* express them. There are many different things a subject may do as a typical result of feeling tired, or hungry, or in pain, or anxious, or con-tented, or amused, and so on, all of which could be taken as reliable indications of the relevant state of the subject. But we think of only a small subset of these behaviors or actions as *expressing* mental condi-tions, in either the causal or the action sense. (Contrast, for example, someone taking an aspirin with her wincing or rubbing her temples.) The present suggestion is that focusing on behaviors or actions that are in some way communicative could help us to zero in more closely on the relevant subset.

This is not the place to discuss what makes for communicative behavior. A more pressing task is that of further delimiting the relev-ant subset of behaviors. What the commonsense view regards as natur-ally expressive behavior, we may agree, is not merely symptomatic of mental states; it is behavior that has as its natural purpose to commu-nicate the presence, as well as the character, of some of a creature's internal states to relevant observers. (N.B.: to say this is not to say that a creature capable of naturally expressive behavior may not engage in such behavior without *herself* having communicative purposes.) But not all behaviors that have a communicative purpose would be regarded as natural expressions. I can report to you how sad I felt yesterday, predict that if I go for a long run now I'll feel very tired later, or tell you that my daughter feels disappointed about a cancelled trip. In all these cases, I engage in behavior intended to communicate the pres-ence (past, future, or present) of various mental states; but I do not thereby express those same mental states, in any sense of expression.[32]

---

[32] My assertions about these matters may, of course, serve to express my beliefs about the presence of the states, but they will not express those states themselves.

I can also deliberately sneeze with the intention of communicating to you that I have a cold, or can intentionally place your hand on my forehead to convey to you that I have high fever. In these cases, I intentionally produce or draw attention to a natural symptom, thereby communicating that I am in a certain condition. But I cannot be said thereby to express$_1$ the condition, any more than the symptom itself can be said to express$_2$ it. One's own past and future mental states, the mental states of others, bodily conditions, diseases, and various other internal physical states are not things we take to be expressible (in either the causal or the action sense) through one's behavior.

These limits on the notion of expression (as well as additional ones that will be mentioned below) could simply be dictated by its 'logical grammar'. But it may be worth investigating whether at least some of these limits fall out of some salient feature of expression as ordinarily understood. When contrasting so-called natural expressions with linguistic expressions, Alston remarks that natural expressions *show, display, exhibit,* or *manifest* the conditions they express. This is something Alston thinks linguistic expressions do not do, which is why he thinks that two distinct notions of expression are at work here. We have seen reason to reject Alston's separation between linguistic and natural expressions. But my present concern is to see what we can make of Alston's rather intuitive suggestion that what is distinctive of natural expressions is that they actually *show* us the conditions they express, rather than merely *tell* us *that* the creatures exhibiting the expressive behavior are in the relevant conditions. For this idea seems to hold some promise.[33]

Consider, first, examples where information is naturally conveyed, but where no communicative behavior is involved. A trained mountaineer can learn about a deer's size and weight, whether it was walking or running, and so on, from its footprints. But we don't take the footprints to be showing the deer, or its foot, or its running. And a wound examined by a forensic expert is not presumed to show her the implement that inflicted the wound, or the time of the injury, though she can recover accurate information about all these things.

---

[33] My thinking about the connection between expression and showing has been helped by many discussions with Mitchell Green. But, to keep my discussion manageable, I have not paused to document every point of influence, agreement, and disagreement.

The footprint and the wound are mere traces—though highly articulated traces—of what they convey detailed information about. They are not *designed* to convey the relevant information to any natural 'consumers'. Bee dances, on the other hand, *are* designed to convey to fellow bees information about the distance and direction of a nearby source of nectar, as well as its degree of concentration. But we still wouldn't take it that a bee dance or any of its aspects serves to show the nectar either to us or to other bees. (Although in one sense the dance shows the nectar's location and direction—it tells the bees where to go to find it—it clearly doesn't exhibit or display the nectar's site.)[34] By contrast, on the present suggestion, a smile, a wince, a squeal, a growl, and so on, are regarded as also showing us the conditions they express. So a subject who intentionally produces a natural expression is doing something that constitutes more than providing evidence for the presence or character of her present mental state; she is doing something that in some way constitutes showing the state itself. And, correlatively, the consumers of a natural expression are not merely inferring the presence of the condition in the subject from her expressive behavior. Rather, they are in some way perceiving the relevant condition.

The present suggestion, then, is that our commonsense category of natural expression marks a special subclass of communicative behavioral manifestations, which are not simply designed to communicate information about the presence and character of a condition of the subject to a designated audience, but also serve to show the condition. Of course, not all showing is expressing. If I show you my house, I do not thereby express my house. If I show you a painful scar, I do not thereby express the scar, or the pain I feel. I can show you someone else's grin, but I cannot express her pleasure. What is perhaps more puzzling: I can show my courage, or integrity, as well as my expertise or wisdom, through things I do or say; yet I cannot express them. Given this, it would be helpful to understand what renders some but not other showings cases of expression. Furthermore, given the variety of kinds of things that can be shown, as well as the variety of kinds of ways of showing, we need a clearer understanding of the

---

[34] For a brief description of the structure of bee dances, see Akmajian *et al.* (1984: 12 ff.). In Hauser's terminology, bee dances are not merely signs, they are cues; for they do not only happen to convey the relevant information to us, but they are naturally designed to do so for the sake of other bees.

sense in which natural expressions show the conditions they express. I shall address the latter issue first.[35]

A mathematical or logical proof can show certain results; astronomical evidence can show the presence of a star at some location. This, however, is showing in the sense of establishing; it is showing *that* something is the case. A natural expression, on the other hand, is ordinarily taken to show us not merely *that* someone is in some particular mental state; rather, in some sense, it is taken to show us the state itself. But in what sense? A map can show us the location of a post office, or the layout of a city. The map does more than establish, or offer conclusive evidence, that the post office is in such-and-such a place, or that the city has such-and-such a layout. It shows us the post office's location by modeling some of its topographical relations to other places referenced by the map. There is some sense in which the map can be said to show us the post office, but the sense of showing involved seems still less demanding than the sense of showing I take Alston to have in mind for the case of natural expressions.

If a map shows us a place, it is not by giving us a glimpse of it. By contrast, an episode, or act, of a naturally expressive behavior (unlike an episode or act of proving *p*, or drawing a map of *x*) is a kind of display; it is itself a show. When a subject engages in expressive behavior, it might be said, she actually shows us (some of) what her feeling, attitude, or emotion looks like; she *allows us to see it.* When we confront an animal baring its teeth in anger, a child who smiles in pleasure, a man who twists his mouth in disgust, we take ourselves actually to be *seeing* the anger, the pleasure, the disgust. We also often speak of *hearing* nervousness in someone's uneven voice and *feeling* the tension in someone's body, and so on.[36] This suggests that associated with naturally expressive behavior is the kind of showing that actually *makes perceptible* the expressed states. On this suggestion, an observer of a bit of naturally expressive behavior who is suitably attuned by nature, or properly habituated or trained, will be able to perceive—see, hear, feel, etc.—the subjects' present mental condition.[37] We speak, in this vein, of children's inability to *hide* their feelings. What they do not

---

[35] In what follows, I have been helped by the analysis offered by Green (unpublished: ch. 3).

[36] The facial expressions associated with the basic emotions offer a kind of signature, which lends itself fairly readily to artistic depiction. See Green (unpublished: ch. 4).

[37] In the case of mathematical proofs we do speak of seeing the mathematical result once we have gone through the proof. But the seeing is a seeing that.

typically do is suppress behavior that would enable others to perceive their feelings. The possibility of hiding one's state may be seen as a correlative of the kind of showing that is perception-enabling.

Some support for the idea of natural expressions as perception-enabling displays of subjects' present mental states may come from the fact that, unlike cases where A merely shows us *that* B (e.g., a proof or evidence showing us that *p*), natural expressions are taken to reveal not only the presence of the state, but also its quality, degree, and object. A natural expression can display the location of a pain in the chest, as well as its severity, a mild midriff ticklishness, or a moderate agitation about a bug's flutter, or rage, as opposed to panic, at the attacker, an intense desire for a toy, great excitement at the sight of a mate, or an extreme puzzlement about a disappearing doll, and so on.[38] Indeed, it may be thought that it is by perceiving (seeing, hearing, feeling) the quality, degree, or object of someone's mental state, as those are exhibited in her expressive behavior, that we perceive the state she is in. Additional support may come from reflecting on the role that naturally expressive behavior plays in the lives of creatures capable of it. Arguably, naturally expressive behavior is effective when it meets the right responses: a parent will feed or comfort a crying child, will hand her the desired toy when she reaches for it, will try to calm her anger when she throws a tantrum, or assuage her fear when she turns away from a dog, etc. The natural purpose of naturally expressive behavior may be better served if it directly elicits appropriate reactions on the part of the observers. In empathetic creatures, appropriate reactions are perhaps likelier to ensue if the behavior enables them to *perceive* the other's condition, rather than merely enabling them to make the right inference about some hidden cause of subjects' behavior.

Much more needs to be said—and cannot be said here—about the ways in which expressive behavior can show (and make perceptible) expressed mental states. The above reflections, speculative as they are, are not intended to provide conceptual analysis of the notion of expression (or even just natural expression) in terms of showing. I do think, however, that the idea that natural expressions show the conditions they express, rather than merely communicate information

---

[38] As we shall later see, this high degree of articulation makes them candidates for replacement by linguistic expressions.

about their presence and character, is a useful one for our purposes. First, it supports the intuition that natural expressions are not simply natural signs or symptoms. Second, it can serve to capture something distinctive about natural expressions, against which we can assess the claim that there is a noteworthy similarity between avowals and natural expressions. This is important dialectically. The expressivist claim is sometimes attacked by pointing out that behavior expressive of pain, such as a wince or a cry, shows one's pain, whereas a pain avowal can only tell of it. Thus, taking seriously the claim that natural expressions show the states they express constitutes a concession to the opponent of expressivism, insofar as she is likely to press the point that natural expressions differ significantly from avowals. If, even while accepting this claim, we can still identify an important similarity between the two types of performances, the opponent's case will be significantly weakened. Third, as will continue to emerge, our intuitive notion of showing has certain features that are useful for the purpose of shouldering the explanatory burden I want to assign to the expressivist insight.

If giving a natural expression to a feeling, emotion, or propositional attitude is a matter of showing it, in the sense of making it perceptible to an observer of the expressive behavior, then it stands to reason that one cannot provide a natural expression of a past or future mental state. Perception of an object, event, or state, requires its presence (at least in the sort of cases relevant here). As we shall see later, natural expressions (understood as products) can be detached from the states they express, so that one can in principle give a natural expression to a state one is not in; one can wear a pleasurable smile on one's face, even though one is not enjoying oneself, for example. But even in such cases, we *take* the behavior, albeit erroneously, to give expression to a *present* state.

What about the mental states of others? Although I can show you someone else's smile, wince, etc. (e.g., by pointing to it), doing so does not constitute showing their pleasure or pain. Thus, although I can behave in ways that would enable you to perceive their mental states (if I enable you to see their expressive behavior), my behavior is not what does the showing. And that may explain why we cannot give natural expression to the mental states of others. What about our own non-mental states? Bodily states such as having a sunburn, or a wound, being pregnant, having a certain blood pressure, heart murmur, or ulcer, etc., can be shown, and made perceptible, in various ways (you can see the sunburn on my shoulder if I uncover it, and you can hear my heart murmur using a stethoscope). However, such conditions can only be evidenced, indicated, or signaled, but not shown *through our behavior.* Finally, what about our psychological dispositions and character traits (such as wisdom, patience, courage)? Surely, one can show courage by speaking up, show patience by sitting quietly, and so on. But intuitively, one doesn't thereby express one's courage or patience. If we are to characterize natural expressions in terms of showing, it would be helpful to understand what separates natural expressions from non-expressive showings.

The following answer (again suggested to me by Ram Neta) seems to me promising. What is distinctive about naturally expressive behavior is not only that it shows the conditions or states it expresses, but that it is behavior that is *sufficient* to show the relevant conditions or states. It is true that in the case of mental states of others, my own non-mental conditions (internal or not), and my own 'non-occurrent', or standing, psychological dispositions and character traits (as well as, incidentally, my own past and future mental states), I can often behave in ways that serve to show the relevant states, conditions, dispositions, or traits. My gesturing at my child's beaming face may allow you to see her pleasure, my exposing the sunburn on my shoulder may enable you to see it, and my speaking up in front of a big audience may show my courage. But in none of these cases does my exhibiting or engaging in the relevant behaviors suffice by itself to show the relevant items to you. If this is so, then the fact that only so-called occurrent mental states can be expressed could be explained by the fact that only in the case of the former can one engage in behavior *sufficient* to show the subject's being in the relevant state. Let me elaborate.

Consider first the case of my gesturing at my child's beaming smile. It's true that, but for my gesture, you might not have been able to see her pleasure. But that is because you wouldn't have seen the behavior that would suffice to show the child's pleasure—viz., the *child's* behavior. So *my* behavior is not what is doing the crucial showing work; and it certainly wouldn't suffice for showing my *child's* mental state. Next consider present non-mental states, say the sunburn on my shoulder or a fracture in my forearm. I can do things that will enable my audience to perceive the relevant state: I can expose my shoulder, and I can show you an X-ray image of my forearm on a screen. But here again, although the relevant state is mine, and I am the one engaging in behavior that is conducive to your perceiving my state, the behavior isn't what does the showing. As regards your ability to perceive my state, my behavior is otiose. Moreover, the behavior could not by itself suffice to show the relevant bodily state.

The case of psychological dispositions and character traits may seem more puzzling. Mitchell Green considers the case of Rosa Parks, who showed her courage by sitting at the front of the bus, and an example of someone's showing integrity by refraining from open-ing a letter with damning information about a colleague.[39] One can show restraint by remaining quiet, show maturity by following sound advice, and so on. An immediate thing to notice is that an observer of the relevant behavior would be in no position to know what trait or disposition is exhibited by the subject, absent knowledge of the relevant background. But to this one may respond that, with very few exceptions,[40] absent some background knowledge, we wouldn't know what mental state a subject is expressing$_1$. As we have already noted in passing, expressive repertoires contain culturally/socially variable elements and potentially idiosyncratic character. So what's the difference?

I think the answer is that background conditions or context can play two different roles. Take the example of someone behaving in a way that supposedly shows their courage. Here, the contextual cir-cumstances determine what *constitutes* or counts as a courageous act; they don't merely determine whether observers will be able to *know* whether a subject is displaying courage. The very same behavior—moving to the front of the bus—would not *be* an act of courage, and thus would not serve to display the *subject's* courage, given relatively small changes in the circumstances (e.g., if Rosa Parks had been invited to sit at the front of the bus by the driver). This is not to make the post-modernist-sounding claim that the psychological trait of courage is socially constructed, or constituted by convention. You

---

[39]   The latter example is due to Mitchell Green, in conversation.

[40]   I have in mind 'signature' facial and vocal expressions and gestures, which enjoy universality, and whose recognition may be innate. (See again Green (unpublished: ch. 4).)

may suppose if you like that being courageous is an entirely non-conventional matter, a 'brain-based' natural property of individuals. Nevertheless, what will make for a *bona fide* exercise (and thus a display) of this dispositional property on a given occasion will depend on background conditions. Whether Rosa Parks is being courageous or not on a given occasion is dependent on the circumstances of the candidate act. By contrast, although circumstances will no doubt causally determine whether someone will be tired, hungry, upset, thinking of $x$, scared of $y$, feeling mad at $z$, they do not determine whether at a given moment someone *is* in one of these states.

So, to know whether or not someone's behavior shows the mental state she is in, and what mental state her behavior shows, an observer may need background information. Thus, contextual background does come into the *perception* of expressive behavior. But it does not determine what constitutes being in the state that is supposed to be shown by it. On the other hand, whether someone is *being* courageous, or wise, or stupid, or careless, on a given occasion *is* determined in part by background conditions and circumstances, so the behavior that shows these dispositions or traits cannot suffice to show their presence. On the present suggestion, this is why we cannot express psychological dispositions and character traits, though we can show them through our behavior. Whereas in the case of so-called occurrent mental states, the behavior that is said to express a given state is sufficient to show it, in the case of psychological dispositions and character traits the behavior we engage in is not sufficient by itself to show them.

Some remarks are in order. First, I suggested earlier that expressive behavior shows mental states not merely in the sense of showing observers that behaving subjects are in the relevant mental states, but also in the sense of enabling observers to perceive the states. We still need to understand how this idea is connected with the idea that expressive behavior is distinguished by its being sufficient to show mental states. We also need to understand better precisely how expressive behavior fulfills its perception-enabling role. I shall have more to say about these matters in the next chapter. Second, my explanation of natural expression in terms of behavior sufficient to show the expressed state was in aid of explaining why only occurrent mental states are expressible. I do not think this explanation commits me to the behaviorist claim that naturally expressive behavior is *constitutive* of mentality. As I shall explain in the final chapter, my expressivist account in no way entails that one cannot be in a mental state unless one exhibits some expressive behavior. Nor does the account entail that merely engaging in certain expressive behaviors may be sufficient for being in a mental state. To say that naturally expressive behavior is sufficient to show your being in M is just to say that *if/when* you are in M, engaging in the relevant behavior suffices to show it, so that a suitably attuned and placed observer could perceive your M by perceiving your behavior. It is also to say that if one does not engage in any expressive behavior, then others may be unable to perceive one's mental states, though they may still be able to come to know of one's mental states in other ways. This is a far cry from the behaviorist commitment to a metaphysical dependence between mentality and behavior. (For further discussion, see Chapter 10 below.)

On the picture that emerges from our exploration of the phenomenon of natural expression, we ought to think of first-person/third-person asymmetries in a way that is rather different from traditional ways. While expressive behavior can be seen as, in a sense, equally open to view to both observer and subject, for the subject the behavior serves to give voice to, air, etc. her present mental state, whereas for the observer it is a manifestation of someone else's state. The subject is *in* the state and is expressing it through her behavior; the observer *perceives* the state. There is no assumption that only one who is in a mental state can see it with an 'inner eye', whereas others who observe her behavior can at most conjecture about it. Quite the contrary. An observer may perceive a subject's state of mind even when the subject herself is too 'wrapped up in it', or too distracted, to recognize the state she's in. Facial expressions, gestures, and bodily demeanor may betray subjects' anxiety, discomfort, excitement, even when, as we put it, 'they don't realize it'. At any rate, if we follow common sense, we should regard naturally expressive behavior as enabling us to see subjects' anger, fear, embarrassment, etc. *Pace* the traditional introspectionist view (and its contemporary heirs), we don't merely perceive the behavior and infer to the presence and character of subjects' internal states as the best explanation of the behavior we perceive; rather, we perceive their present states of mind (or, as I prefer: we perceive their being in the relevant state of mind).

In this sense, expressive behavior is *transparent-to-the-subject's-mental-condition*.[41]

This transparency has two dimensions. First, naturally expressive behavior is transparent-to-a-subject's-condition in that it can show us *what kind* of condition the subject may be in, as well as the state's degree, quality, and intentional object. The child's rolling laughter as she gazes at a clown shows us her being highly amused by the clown. The features that enable expressive behavior to have the first dimension of transparency facilitate persuasive acting. Thus, confronted with a talented actor onstage who produces a rolling laughter, we would take her to be (successfully) expressing intense amusement, though not necessarily *her* amusement. Secondly, naturally expressive behavior is transparent in that it shows us the *subject's being* in the relevant state. To regard a bit of behavior by someone S as a genuine case of natural expression, rather than successful simulation, is to regard the behavior as not merely expressive of M, but also as showing us S's presently being in M. Confronted with the child throwing herself at her father, we typically take it that she expresses not only a desperate desire for the parent to stay, but also *her* being in a state of desperately wanting the parent to stay.

A child's behavior may fail to show us what she wants, feels, etc. Children very quickly learn to tone down or suppress expressive behavior. As noted earlier, even a dog can suppress barks of excitement at his owner's command. Thus, to say that expressive behavior is transparent in the above sense is not to say that we are always guaranteed to perceive others' states of mind. Moreover, a child—even a small child—can purposely put on expressive behavior. Very young children are able to display certain forms of expressive behavior just for dramatic effect. A child can throw herself at the parent in pretense, in order to mislead, or deceive. Still, in such a case (as in the case of acting onstage) what the child would be doing is pretending to be in *that kind* of 'desiring condition'. It is just that in such a case the child will not have expressed *her* condition.[42] As observers of the child's behavior, we may fail to recognize this. Thus, to say that expressive behavior is transparent-to-the-subject's-condition is not to say that it cannot be misperceived. It is true that, if we *take* a bit of behavior to

---

[41] This notion is introduced and briefly discussed in Bar-On and Long (2001: sect. 4).

[42] For a helpful articulation of this point, see Rosenberg (1977: 156 f.).

be a genuine case of natural expression, rather than, say, dissimulation, of, say, anger, we suppose that the subject is indeed showing us her anger. We thus take ourselves to be privy to the subject's being angry right now, which is of course to presume that the subject *is* angry. After all, we take it that we are seeing her anger! But this is not to say that we couldn't be wrong. For our eyes could deceive us.

This point is easy to miss, because of the fact that "express", like "show", as well as verbs of perception and some epistemic verbs, is a success verb.[43] If we say that a subject has expressed her anger, or joy, we imply that the subject is indeed in the state cited. S cannot be correctly said to be expressing her M if that M is not there to be expressed, just as S cannot correctly be said to be showing O unless O is there to be shown, and S cannot be said to be seeing/hearing/feeling O unless O is there to be seen/heard/felt. But from this it doesn't follow that observers cannot make mistakes about expressive behavior. Consider: on a particular occasion, we could fail to be seeing a tree, even if we take ourselves to be seeing one. But the fact that we could be subject to visual mistakes and illusions does not undermine our ability to use our eyes to see objects in the world. That we may be merely under the impression that we are seeing a tree does not mean that we do not sometimes simply see trees, as opposed to indirectly inferring their presence from visual appearances. Similarly, the fact that we can misperceive behavior—take a piece of dissimulation to be the 'real thing'—does not mean that behavior cannot be transparent in the above sense. Expressive behavior can fail to show us a subject's condition; and we can regard someone's behavior as genuinely expressive of her mental state when it is not. But this does not mean that we must think of the behavior as merely an evidential basis from which to infer to someone else's mental state through fallible inference or hypothesis.

Cases of dissimulation illustrate one way in which the two dimensions of transparency-to-the-subject's-condition can pull apart: a subject intentionally and successfully expressing a certain kind of condition without actually being in the relevant condition at the given time. But the two dimensions can pull apart in the opposite way. A subject may try to express a condition she is in, but use a form of expression that is naturally associated with a different kind of condition. A subject may

---

[43] I believe that Jacobsen (1996) is mistakenly led by this feature of "express" to hold that avowals, if taken to be expressions of mental states, are strongly infallible.

intend to show her joy, but produce a strained grimace instead of a happy smile. This may be due to a scar on her face, or some other idiosyncrasy. If we know the subject, we may recognize her as expressing her joy, though with a facial expression that typically expresses (say) disgust, for *in her expressive repertoire* the grimace may serve as the right expressive vehicle for expressing joy. As we move away from basic, universal, natural expressions, what is shown by bodily expressions and gestures may be culture-dependent. More or less similar facial expressions may serve to express different kinds of conditions, depending on one's cultural environment. And when it comes to adult human beings, bodily expressions and gestures may be highly idiosyncratic, and what they show may be exceedingly context-dependent. Accurate perception of the conditions shown may require sufficient exposure to and repeated interactions with the relevant individual. But this is not to say that in the realm of expression anything goes. There are limits on expression, reminiscent of the limits pointed out by Wittgenstein in connection with the use of language: you can't say "hot" and mean *cold*. An individual may fail to express her present state even when she is in the relevant state and tries to show it through her behavior.[44]

I would like to conclude the present discussion of natural expressions with several observations. (The significance of some of these observations may emerge only later, as we move on to discuss linguistic expressions in general, and avowals in particular.) First, the illustrations of the two types of ways in which expressive behavior can fail to express the subject's present condition in no way relied on the supposition that the subject herself has made a *mistake* about her own condition. In the case of an actor onstage, we may suppose that the actor is under no illusion regarding his state of mind. He is expressing M, though not his M (assuming he's not in M). But in that case our subject is not even trying to express his M. Rather, he's utilizing his skill at duplicating the features of expressive behavior that enable it to express M, so as to *simulate* someone expressing his M. Next consider dissimulation. Here we are also supposing that the subject has not in

---

[44] A proper study of this fascinating subject may find use for an analogue for expressive behavior of the linguistic distinction between a dialect (a set of types of linguistic expressions with certain meanings that is relatively uniform across a certain group of speakers) and an idiolect (a similar set restricted to a single speaker). But even when it comes to expressive idiolects, I suspect that there are normative limits. You are not guaranteed expressive success just in virtue of sincerely giving vent to a present state in just any way whatever.

fact expressed her condition, though, unlike in the actor case, we have been deceived into thinking she has. Here *we*, the audience, have mistaken what is in fact a piece of dissimulation for a sincere, spontaneous act of expression. But again there is no assumption that the subject has mistaken her own state. On the contrary; if we take her to be deliberately and successfully deceiving us, for example, we are assuming that she doesn't herself think she is in the relevant state. Yet even in the case of a subject who has failed to use an appropriate form of expression, so the mental state that her behavior expresses is not in fact the state she is in, there is still no need (or room) for the supposition that the subject has gone wrong because she failed correctly to identify her own condition. Our ability to perceive the subject's condition through the expressive behavior is compromised, but not because of the subject's epistemic failure.

Second, the above characterization of natural expressions brings out an important respect in which natural expressions resemble linguistic expressions. I remarked earlier that naturally expressive acts do not express subjects' states in Sellars's semantic sense, since there is no conventional relation between a natural expression and the condition it expresses, and the natural expression is not *about* the condition—it does not refer to it or represent it. However, it should now be evident that natural expressions (*qua* products, not acts) do enjoy a kind of expressive autonomy that allows them to exhibit types of mental states, somewhat in the way that a picture depicts a type of scene. So an act of natural expression may display a state of a certain kind even when it fails to express the *subject's* state, in Sellars's causal or action sense. It will be important to bear this in mind when, in the next chapter, we return to avowals and their similarity to natural expressions.

Third, as we prepare to move from so-called natural expressions to linguistic expressions, we should recognize that behaviors we include in the category of natural expressions are often acquired, and culturally or socially variable. This is true not only of certain noises, such as tutting or snorting, and verbal emissions such as "Ouch!", "Yuk!", "Yippee!", "Ugh!", or "Blah", but also of various facial expressions and bodily gestures.[45] Many facial expressions, bodily gestures and

---

[45] It is in keeping with common usage to refer to such emissions, gestures, etc. as "natural expressions". The *OED*, e.g., describes tutting as "a natural utterance; . . . an ejaculation (often reduplicated) expressing impatience or dissatisfaction . . . ". Alston himself acknowledges the existence of acquired, culturally based natural expressions (1965: 24). But he doesn't recognize that it casts a doubt on the sharp distinction he wants to draw between natural and linguistic expressions.

vocal emissions are acquired before we master language, and the use of expressive words quickly becomes for us "second nature". They are routinely incorporated into spontaneous, unreflective conduct and are smoothly integrated into the human behavioral repertoires that we are born with. But their inclusion in the class of natural expressions makes for a significant heterogeneity: natural expressions are not all universally shared, nor do they all have their origin in biological nature. Much of what we include under the rubric of natural expressions involves learned behavior and socialization. And it remains to be seen what to make of the idea that the way such behavior expresses subjects' mental states resembles the way babies' cries and gurgles or a dogs' tail-waggings and growlings do.

Relatedly, the suggestion explored in this section was that what is distinctive of naturally expressive behavior is that it is behavior that suffices to show, in the sense of making perceptible, the conditions it expresses. I pointed out that this constitutes a concession to the opponent of expressivism, since it is often thought that avowals could not be thought to express subjects' conditions *in that sense*. But given the heterogeneity of the class of natural expressions just noted, the opponent may be caught in a dilemma. She could insist that acquired behaviors such as tutting, twisting one's nose, snorting, slapping one's thigh, yelling "Ouch!" or "Ugh!", and so on do qualify as showing (= making perceptible) one's mental state. In that case, she would be hard pressed to explain why more articulate linguistic expressions, avowals included, could not similarly qualify. Alternatively, the opponent could concede that these acquired behaviors do not qualify as showing the relevant mental states. But then, since such behaviors are often counted among the paradigms of naturally expressive behavior, it would seem that the conclusion to draw is either that not all so-called natural expressions express in the sense of showing (= making perceptible) the conditions, or that showing (= making perceptible) is not the distinctive mark of all natural expressions after all. Either way, we are not forced to draw the sharp distinction between natural and linguistic expressions with which we began, or to reject the idea that avowals are expressive acts.[46]

---

[46] A last remark on Alston: Alston agrees that both natural expressions and linguistic utterances can be said to provide reliable indications of relevant psychological states, but thinks they do so in very different ways (see n. 30). The facial expression shows my disgust, whereas the linguistic utterance tells of it. And Alston thinks that, where linguistic utterances are concerned, we need to "appeal to a general practice of using the sentence in a certain way"; whereas in the case of natural expressions, we need only appeal to a

Finally, and perhaps most importantly, we should notice that we now have on our hands a very strong positive reason for endorsing an expressivist account of avowals. An expressivist account can explain the following remarkable fact: that it is only self-ascriptions of *certain aspects* of our own present mental life that exhibit a distinctive security; roughly, these are self-ascriptions of the presence, character, and content of *occurrent* mental *states* issued in the 'avowing mode'.[47] On just about anyone's view, our self-ascriptions of present character traits, psychological dispositions, various 'hidden' ('subconscious', or 'subpersonal') psychological processes or events, and non-occurrent mental states, are *not* especially secure. On the Epistemic Approach, the most we can do to explain this remarkable fact is to stipulate that we just do not have privileged epistemic access to, or uniquely secure epistemic methods for the recovery of, these aspects of our present mental life. By contrast, the expressivist can appeal to the fact that only occurrent mental states are such that we can engage in behavior that suffices to show their presence, character, and content; only such states are expressible through behavior. Since the expressivist explains the security of avowals by appeal to their expressive character, the fact that only certain mental self-ascriptions enjoy distinctive security falls neatly into place.

"de facto correlation" between the expression and the state. To repeat, cases of natural expression, Alston thinks, are underwritten by regularities; cases of linguistic expression involve the operation of rules (see 1965: 21 ff.). Once the heterogeneity of what we count as natural expression is recognized, however, I think that Alston's way of drawing his sharp distinction is undermined.

[47] Transparency views of the sort discussed in Ch. 4 assign special status or 'authority' to first-person self-ascriptions of non-occurrent beliefs, desires, etc. offered in response to queries ("Do you believe *p*?", "Do you like *x*?"), but only insofar as they are construed as pronouncements on what one is *to* think, believe, want. See my discussion on pp. 134 ff.

# 8

# *Avowals: Expression, Content, and Truth*

In the previous chapter, I argued that avowals form a special category of acts: expressive acts, in which subjects directly give voice to their present mental conditions using explicit, semantically articulate, expressive vehicles that ascribe those conditions to themselves. I examined the notion of a natural expression, and gave reasons for questioning the received view that there must be a sharp distinction between linguistic and natural expressions. Though natural expressions are clearly different from linguistic expressions as products, there are significant similarities between *acts* of giving expression to one's present mental state which cut across the natural/linguistic divide. It is these similarities that our commonsense notion of expression may latch onto.

I begin this chapter with a story about how linguistic expressions in general, and mental "I"-ascriptions in particular, could acquire an expressive role similar to the role played by natural expressions, despite the important differences between these respective types of expressive vehicles. The story I shall offer is a kind of 'rational reconstruction' of how it could come to pass that avowals might play an expressive role that is similar to the role played by other expressions. The story is not intended to carry the full burden of explaining the security of avowals, or even of establishing that acts of avowing qualify as expressive acts. As I see it, the explanatory order is as follows. I have been arguing that we can best explain the distinctive security of avowals if we regard them as expressive acts that resemble other acts in which subjects give vent to their present mental states. I have tried to defend the plausibility of the expressivist claim independently by addressing potential challenges to it, and by developing an account of expression that respects intuitions regarding the phenomenon of natural expression and that can bring out the relevant respects in which avowals resemble natural expressions. The rational reconstruction I offer below is intended to add to the plausibility of the claim that there is continuity between avowals and natural expressions by explaining how mental self-ascriptions could emerge in the order of acquisition. In addition, it suggests that an expressivist account may have a better story to tell than rival accounts about the acquisition of mentalistic vocabulary.

The story I tell invokes the idea that avowals emerge, in the first instance, as *replacements* for natural expressions of sensations, emotions, and intentional states. This requires that there *be* natural expressions of those states for avowals to replace. But, clearly, numerous mental conditions do not have natural expressions that could serve as candidates for replacement. So in the second section, I explain how the replacement story can be developed so as to address this issue. I then identify more precisely the way in which avowals, *qua* linguistic self-ascriptions, can be said to express subjects' mental conditions, and try to determine whether, in addition, avowals also express subjects' self-judgments. Now, it is important for my account that although avowals, as acts, express the mental conditions they ascribe, as products they are *truth-assessable*, self-ascriptive sayings (*contra* the Simple Expressivist view). In the remainder of the chapter, I explain why avowals are governed by a special presumption of truth (*contra* the materialist introspectionist), and also how avowals *can* sometimes be false (*contra* the Cartesian).

## The Beginnings of Mental Talk: From Natural Expressions to Avowals

Recall that the core claim that is crucial for the Neo-Expressivist account is that avowals express the subject's self-ascribed condition in the same sense as do linguistic expressions that are not self-ascriptions. Strictly speaking, the core claim does not require establishing that avowals express mental states in the same sense as do natural expressions. Nevertheless, I saw fit to devote a lengthy discussion to natural expressions. This is because I think that a better understanding of the diverse and complex character of natural expressions can help to diminish the resistance to the Neo-Expressivist proposal regarding avowals. Furthermore, I think that the Neo-Expressivist account can gain support, albeit somewhat indirectly, if we consider the resources it has for explaining how mentalistic language may be acquired, and how avowals can come to play the expressive role that the account assigns to them. So in this section I start to tell a story about the beginnings of mentalistic talk, which portrays such talk as continuous with naturally expressive behavior. I should reiterate, however, that the plausibility of the story is not intended as a direct argument for the Neo-Expressivist account. I take the direct argument to consist primarily in showing that my account does a better job of explaining avowals' security than other accounts on offer by meeting the various desiderata mentioned early on (in Chapter 1).

The story I will be telling is intended as a kind of rational reconstruction, rather than a quasi-empirical theory.[1] My story will not involve denying that mentalistic terms refer to mental conditions. At the same time, it will not rely on assimilating the acquisition of mentalistic terms and their use in avowals to that of either observation or theoretical terms. (This will serve to contrast it with alternative stories that might be offered by epistemic accounts of avowals, which I will briefly sketch below.) On the expressivist story, the beginning of mental talk lies with spontaneous, non-linguistic natural behavior which is expressive of certain conditions of subjects—their pains, joys, fears, desires, angers, etc. Non-linguistic naturally expressive behavior is seen as providing the initial 'materials' for (though *not* the subject matter of) mentalistic discourse. The key idea is to regard certain talk *about* mental states as directly linked, at its beginning, with naturally expressive behavior that comes *from* the states themselves.

---

[1] I use "rational reconstruction" in a sense expounded in my (1996). The story below is offered in the general spirit of philosophical accounts of language such as are to be found in, e.g., Quine (1960), (1974); Fodor (1975); Grice (1989: Essay 18); Sellars (1963: Essay 5); Evans (1982); Putnam (1975); and Dummett (1978: *passim*) and (1993: *passim*).

With all due respect to empirical linguistics, I believe there is room for philosophical accounts of the task of acquiring language that can be offered in relative independence of empirical investigations. This is not to say that empirical studies bear no relevance to philosophical theorizing in this area. On the other hand, it seems to me wrong to suppose that such studies are themselves sufficiently philosophically innocent to have uncontroversial implications for the philosophical conceptions. The best strategy is, perhaps, to work from both ends: develop systematic philosophical arguments and considerations while at the same time conducting empirical investigations, in the hope of reaching a stable philosophical view that at least is not embarrassed by the findings of empirical studies of language.

I hinted in the previous chapter that naturally expressive behavior has its home with creatures capable of empathy. An onlooker witnessing the expressive behavior of a conspecific will be moved to action appropriate to the mental state she perceives through the behavior. But we humans do more. Confronted with a child's cry after a fall, a parent will not only hurry to comfort the child, but will emit "Ouch!" Hearing a gurgle of gustatory pleasure as the child chews on some food, we don't just give more food; we make a verbal offering: "Yummm! Tastes good!" Feeling a child's startle at the thunder, we might say, "Wow! That was loud!" As we see a child looking at a dog, we say, "Such a nice doggy!" When noticing a child's attention drawn to a ball, we may confirm, "See that big ball?" To a child rubbing her injured leg, we might say, "That hurts, doesn't it?." A child's distinctive whine will meet with "You must be hungry" or "What's the matter, you're not feeling well?"; her reaching for a ball may meet with "Do you want the ball?"; a fearful expression on her face with "You're scared of the clown, aren't you?". And so on. The verbal reactions are a mixed bag of interjections, expletives, and questions, as well as articulate descriptions peppered with adjectives, intensifiers, and mentalistic terms. On my expressivist story, the verbal responses serve, often enough, to hand the language-learner *new forms of expressive behavior*—forms which can come to supplement, and later on supplant, the non-linguistic expressive behavior witnessed by the speaker. In particular, the mentalistic terms are not to be seen as offering the child a linguistic label for the hypothesized inner cause of her state which the parent takes to be salient only to the child. Rather, the seasoned speaker is naming the condition she perceives in the naturally expressive behavior. And she hands down the mental term as a new addition to the learner's bag of expressive tricks.

Back to Jenny, the young child who is eagerly reaching for the teddy. "Jenny", we might say, "You *want* the teddy, don't you? Can you say 'I want Teddy'?" On the present story, we are here offering Jenny a different, more socially tamed, way of giving voice to her desire for the teddy. At first, Jenny might verbally embellish her reaching behavior by uttering "Teddy!" as she stretches out her hand. Soon she will learn to use more explicit ascriptions, such as "Jenny wants Teddy!" and then self-ascribe, "I want the teddy". Having acquired the verbal tools, Jenny is now able to express her desire using words in addition to manifesting it by gesture. Her ability to say "I want the teddy" can be thought of as an extension of her expressive ability to reach for the teddy; for she has learned to say such things when in the sort of condition that is naturally expressed by reaching. In no time, she will be able to produce the self-ascription with no reaching at all. The linguistic self-ascription will have *replaced* the natural expression as a means of venting, or giving voice to, her desire for the teddy, constituting what we earlier referred to as an avowal proper.[2]

The new expressive tool "I want the teddy" contains linguistic terms that represent things—an individual subject, her (state of) wanting, and its intentional object. These terms have currency in the language used by the teacher. They are governed by various linguistic conventions. It is a requirement on the learner's being able genuinely to ascribe to herself a desire for teddy using the self-ascription "I want the teddy" that she master the use of all the relevant terms. The expressivist story by itself does not tell us what such mastery amounts to. But it makes it plausible to deny that a prerequisite of Jenny's issuing a genuine self-ascription is that she form a recognitional judgment about the presence and character of the relevant condition. If we accept that the self-ascription is adopted as a new means of expressing a present condition—a means that replaces the old natural expression—then the *act* performed by Jenny when avowing "I want the teddy" may be seen as importantly similar to the act she would have earlier performed when intentionally reaching for the teddy, though its product is a different kind of product: it's a linguistic self-ascription which has specific semantic content. Using the terminology borrowed from Sellars again (see above, p. 216), the learner's condition—a present desire for the teddy—culminates in behavior that expresses it in the causal sense (at least)—reaching for the teddy bear. The teacher hands her a linguistic expression which semantically represents the relevant condition: viz., "want" as standing for states of wanting, thereby allowing her in the future to express *her* condition in the action sense, intentionally 'venting' it or giving it voice using language, rather than just reaching. Note that, once an expressive vehicle of one language is available, it can be traded for expressive vehicles of other languages. You can learn to replace "Wow!" with

---

[2] Keep in mind, though, that not all avowals begin as replacements for natural expressions. See next section.

"O la la!", "Oh, no!" with "Oy vey!", and even incorporate the foreign words into your expressive repertoire, if they are deemed more apt.[3]

It may be useful to contrast the above expressivist story of the beginnings of mentalistic discourse[4] with alternative stories that would try to assimilate mentalistic vocabulary and its acquisition to seemingly less problematic discourses. For purposes of the present discussion, let us suppose that mentalistic terms pick out internal physical conditions of subjects—say, states or processes in their brains. The question that interests us now is why, despite the uniformity of reference across different uses of mentalistic terms, their application in avowals issues in ascriptions that are distinctively secure. This is yet another ('genetic') version of our earlier question: How, in the order of acquisition of mentalistic vocabulary, does Epistemic Asymmetry emerge, despite Semantic Continuity?[5]

Consider, first, a likely introspectionist story. On this story, there is no difference in reference between first-person and third-person uses of a given mentalistic term. Mentalistic talk begins when a language-learner identifies within herself an event or state that is *observationally salient* to her alone and which is only inferred or hypothesized by others.[6] We can gloss this by saying that mentalistic terms function like observational terms in their first-person applications, whereas they function like theoretical terms in their third-person applications. This kind of duality is not without precedent. A term such as "electron" may become like an observation term for a seasoned scientist, though for a lay-person it functions as a theoretical term. Now, a scientist, for whom (we may suppose) the term "electron" has become like an observation term can teach its use as a theoretical term to a novice— say, by giving him an implicit definition, involving various theoretical truths about electrons. But when it comes to mentalistic terms, the connection with the relevant objective item, the mental state itself, is supposed to be set up observationally for the learner alone. By

---

[3] My story so far has centered on avowals in speech, since it is a story about the acquisition of mental vocabulary. I shall later explain how the expressivist idea applies to avowals in thought.

[4] Which story we could perhaps refer to as 'the myth of Jenny' (a suggestion due to Grant Dowell).

[5] What follows is not much more than a casual outline of the more obvious competitors to the expressivist story I sketched above. I do not mean to suggest that this is the best that can be done. But I hope that what I say may challenge the proponents of alternative stories to do better.

[6] As Hacker puts it, introspectionists see sensation talk as "beginning with the sensation, which the sufferer observes in *foro interno*, identifies and then represents in a description which communicates to others what is directly accessible only to him" (1993: 88).

hypothesis, the teacher is *not* in a position to observe the relevant item, but instead must conjecture about its presence.[7] It is not easy to see how to achieve the semantic convergence needed for language acquisition and linguistic communication in the face of the specific, and rather extreme, form of epistemic divergence that is built into the account in question.

To avoid this difficulty, it might be suggested that sensation terms (and all mentalistic terms) are in fact more like theoretical terms whose meanings are implicitly defined by sets of core truths provided by the relevant theory. Thus, according to the view known as "analytic functionalism" (see, e.g., Lewis (1972) and Armstrong (1980) ), a term such as "pain" is implicitly defined through a set of common-sense platitudes which comprise the folk theory of pain; e.g., "pain is typically caused by such environmental inputs as pin pricks; pain typically causes such behavioral outputs as cries and winces", and so on. If so, it could be maintained that a child learns the use of a term such as "pain" not by direct acquaintance with or perception of instances of pain within herself, but rather by mastering the relevant implicit definition. In contrast to the "observation view" suggested above, then, the child first learns mentalistic terms as theoretical terms. Later, perhaps, as the child masters what Sellars calls "a reportive use" of first-person mentalistic ascriptions, the term begins to function in his discourse more like an observational term (see Sellars (1963) ).

A growing number of philosophers and psychologists have presented what I consider to be a strong case against the idea that children acquire mentalistic concepts in a way that resembles the way they master the concepts of scientific theories.[8] Their arguments, I believe, tell against the plausibility of a functionalist acquisition story of the sort suggested above. In any event, the story does not comport very well with the special status assigned to avowals in ordinary discourse. In fact, it does not seem that it could fare any better on that score than the earlier story told on behalf of the materialist introspectionist. On that story, my own self-ascriptions are based on introspection, which is

---

[7] I am not supposing that language is taught, rather than learned or acquired, by children. I am here using "teacher" as a correlate of "learner" to denote anyone from whom the learner acquires the relevant piece of language.

[8] I have in mind philosophical and empirical arguments against the so-called 'theory'-theory of mind. For some discussion of the 'theory'-theory and for relevant references, see Davies and Stone (1995). In (2004*b*), I argue against what I dub the 'theory'-theory of linguistic understanding.

direct inspection of the ascribed states, whereas my observer's ascriptions are based on inferences from my behavior to the underlying
internal states. So there is a clear contrast, albeit a contingent one,
between the ways in which self-ascribers and their observers apply
mentalistic terms, which can be invoked when trying to explain the
epistemic asymmetries between avowals and truth-equivalent ascriptions by others. By contrast, on the above functionalist story, the application of mental terms is at bottom theoretical for everyone, though it
may become more direct, or "reportive", in first-person uses. But then
it seems that however the story elaborates what allows first-person uses
of mentalistic terms to become less theoretical, it could not improve
on the introspectionist account of Epistemic Asymmetry. If, as I argued
in Chapter 4, that account is inadequate to the task of capturing the
special security of avowals, we would have reason to reject the account
that uses the functionalist idea, as well.

The foregoing does not establish the impossibility of a plausible
introspectionist or functionalist acquisition story. But it does pose a
certain challenge to epistemic views: to construct an independently
plausible account of the beginnings of mental talk which makes good
sense of the special status assigned to avowals in mentalistic discourse.
I will not here investigate how epistemic views, can meet the challenge, but will instead try to show how the expressivist account is
well equipped to do so.

## Beyond Beginnings: Linguistic Expressions

Consider my present mental state of thinking that epistemic accounts
of avowals' security face serious difficulties. Or my wishing I could
finish up my lecture for next week. What non-linguistic behavior
could serve to express these states of mine? As Crispin Wright points
out, even when it comes to sensations, "the range of cases where there
are indeed natural, non-linguistic forms of expression ... is very
restricted" (1998: 37). Wright cites the sensation of coolness in one
foot and the smell of vanilla as examples. We might add to that having
a mental image of a bright pink ice cube. And so on. Wright himself
suggests that an expressivist account could perhaps address the worry,
though he himself does not say how. Now, on the story told in the

previous section, instead of thinking of mentalistic terms as applied on different bases in the first- and third-person uses, we are to think of first-person uses of mentalistic terms as playing an expressive role, which they can acquire through replacing natural expressions of subjects' sensations, emotions, and intentional states. But it is clearly correct to point out that numerous mental conditions do not have natural expressions that could serve as candidates for replacement. So we may wonder how avowals of such states can acquire their expressive role. In this section, I develop the replacement story further so as to answer this question.

Let us consider first the case of avowals of propositional attitudes—occurrent beliefs, hopes, wishes, and so on, whose content is articulated by a "that"-clause (or its equivalents). There are philosophers who would deny that propositional attitudes have natural expressions. Such states are partially individuated through their content, so that, for example, it makes no sense to attribute to someone a belief unless we attribute to her a belief that $p$, where $p$ serves to specify a particular content. However, it is not clear what could constitute a natural expression of the content part of the belief—an expression that would be articulate and specific enough to warrant the claim that the subject believes that $p$ rather than that $q$ (e.g., that there is food in the bowl rather than that something edible is here).[9] Now, if there were non-verbal expressions of belief (however underdetermined they are with respect to the contents of the ascribed beliefs), then verbal expressions of beliefs (e.g., assertoric utterances such as "It's raining", "There's a truck", etc.) could be seen as articulated (and refined) verbal replacements of those natural expressions. And avowals proper of belief, which involve self-ascriptions of beliefs, could in turn be seen as replacements of those. Along the lines suggested earlier, they could be seen as articulate linguistic vehicles of expression handed down by the seasoned speaker to the language-learner, upon recognizing the relevant natural expression.

But it is important to see that the expressivist account of avowals proper does not turn on there being natural expressions of beliefs. Suppose there are no natural, non-linguistic expressions of occurrent

---

[9] One might see the dispute over whether animals and pre-linguistic children have beliefs as precisely a dispute over whether there can be natural (non-verbal) expressions of beliefs. For a well-known defense of a skeptical view on animal thought, see Davidson (1975).

beliefs. Still, we can appeal to the first-order *linguistic* expressions of beliefs as candidates for replacement by self-ascriptions. The expressivist account in no way denies that there are ordinary assertoric or descriptive utterances; it only denies that self-ascriptions of mental states are always offered as assertoric or descriptive reports of one's mental states. Thus, faced with a 'ground-level' expression of belief—be it verbal *or* (if one allows) non-verbal—we can see the seasoned speaker as offering mentalistic ascriptions of propositional attitudes as partial replacements for such expressions. The child says "There's a cat" (looking at a rabbit), and the parent says, "You think that's a cat? It does look like one, but it's actually a rabbit." Next the child will learn to offer qualified expressions of thoughts by saying "I think that's a cat", and finally to express an occurrent thought by self-ascribing, "I think Mom is going to give me a surprise!" Similarly for other propositional attitudes. Confronted with a ground-level verbal expression of a wish, "Maybe grandma will buy me that toy for my birthday!", the parent may offer, "You'd like grandma to buy you that toy", so the child will next be able to express her wish using the self-ascription: "I'd like grandma to buy me that doll." Avowals of propositional attitudes understood along these lines illustrate the fact that there is no need to seek a natural expression for each kind of avowal to replace. Avowals of desires, hopes, (occurrent) beliefs, and so on, can be seen as replacing *non-self-ascriptive*, linguistic expressions of those states. These latter expressions typically articulate the intentional content of the state: "Teddy!" uttered as one reaches for the toy; "Don't leave, Dad!" said while clinging to the parent; "There's a bunny", exclaimed while looking at an animal. The articulation serves to pin down the intentional content of the state; the particular way in which the content is articulated serves to show the state to be named in the avowal—i.e. a desire, a desperate wish, a belief, etc.

The foregoing may help us with the case of sensations that have no natural expressions. Consider Wright's example of smelling vanilla scent. The expressivist story does not require that our pre-linguistic child be in possession of non-verbal, natural means of expressing her experience of smelling, specifically, vanilla. As in the case of offering mentalistic terms to replace non-self-ascriptive expressions of propositional attitudes, here too it suffices if our child is in a position to offer a verbal characterization of the experience without naming her experience. We can imagine the child sniffing and saying, "Hmm, vanilla!" Taking that to be a verbal expression of the child's olfactory experience, we may respond by saying, "Ah! You're smelling vanilla. That's right, Daddy is baking cookies." The child's subsequent articulate self-ascription, "Dad! I can smell vanilla!", can then be seen as expressing what had earlier received a non-self-ascriptive (linguistic) expression. Thus, although in telling the replacement story, I initially appealed to the familiar paradigm examples of verbal replacements of natural expressions, it is not crucial for the story that there be, in every case, natural expressions that serve as candidates for replacement by avowals. All that is required is that there be some ground-level, non-self-ascriptive expressions, whether natural or not, for avowals to replace (or supplement).

There is a great variety of non-self-ascriptive linguistic devices that can be seen as taking over the expressive role of non-verbal natural expressions (i.e., facial expressions, bodily gestures, vocal emissions). Our standard vocabulary includes inarticulate expletives ("Oh!", "Ow!", "Ooh!", "Yea!"), interjections ("Yuk!", "Yum!", "Blah"), cuss words ("Damn!"), and intensifiers ("This is *so* big!", "She's *very* tall"). In addition to descriptive adjectives (such as "blue", "round", "1-foot long", "sunny"), we also have expressive ones ("huge", "enormous", "tiny", "gross", "lovely", "puny", "pathetic"). Closer to the case at hand, we have mental-state adjectives such as "painful", "boring", "tiring", "disgusting", and a variety of adverbial modifiers, such as "She's *amazingly* smart", "He's *surprisingly* quiet", "*Hopefully*, I'll get there on time", which we standardly use to expressive effect. My suggestion is that self-ascriptions such as "I'm amazed at how smart she is", "I'm surprised at how tall she is", "I hope I'll get there on time", when issued 'in the avowing mode', can be seen on a continuum with those in being linguistic devices that are used to express, specifically, the state, emotion, attitude that they self-ascribe.

Now, however, we have to face the following objection. Granted that avowals need not replace natural expressions, but can replace non-self-ascriptive *linguistic* expressions, we may wonder how linguistic expressions, in general, can be said to express in the first place. I have spoken of natural expressions as being transparent-to-the-subject's-condition in two ways. A natural expression can show us both what kind of state the subject is in and the subject's being in that state—a child's wide-open eyes can show excitement, as well as *her* present excitement. I have tentatively accepted that we can regard the relevant showing as 'perception-enabling': a natural expression allows us to see someone's pain, hear her anger, feel her fear. But once again, it may be argued, linguistic acts paradigmatically *tell* us things. Considered on its own, a linguistic act cannot *show* us anything. In particular, if someone avows feeling tired, this can perhaps show us *that* she is tired. But it does not show us her fatigue. Thus, if avowals (and linguistic acts more generally) are regarded as acts in which a subject expresses a present condition, this must be in an entirely different sense from the sense in which acts of natural expression express mental conditions, since, to repeat, a linguistic act (as such) in no way shows a subject's mental state; it only tells of it. So even if non-self-ascriptive linguistic expressions can be seen as *coming in place of* natural expressions in the order of acquisition, we have no assurance yet that they (and, similarly, avowals) can *inherit* the expressive role of natural expressions.

This objection deserves our attention, since I think that versions of it are at the heart of resistance to an expressivist treatment of avowals. Let me first note that the objection does not strike specifically at the idea that *avowals* can be expressive of subjects' mental states. If we adopt the view that expressing is a matter of engaging in behavior sufficient to show, in the sense of enabling perception, we have to face the worry that *no linguistic expressions as such, whether self-ascriptive or not*, can be sufficient to show a subject's mental state in that sense. Can we see someone's pain in (or through) her utterance of "Ouch"? Can we hear someone's anger or frustration through her utterance of "Darn"? Can we perceive her annoyance through her utterance of "This is so annoying"? You might say that we *can* see the pain, hear the anger, and so on, as we witness the utterance, by the tone of voice, the facial expressions, or the bodily demeanor. Very well, then. The utterance, as an event in the world, may have perception-enabling features; but these are features of the linguistic *act* as performed in context. They do not attend the linguistic *product*—the expletive *word*, the *phrase*, or the *sentence*, considered on its own. By the same token, though, we might say that a self-ascription can also show us someone's pain, boredom, or anger, since we may perceive them in the way the self-ascription is produced. (After all, the word

"Darn", too, can be produced non-expressively; it may be used in a dictation.)[10]

It may be objected that in the case of natural expressions, the showing is achieved through the products and not only through the acts. Facial expressions, bodily gestures, or demeanor, as well as various sound patterns, seem capable of displaying certain feelings or emotions 'all on their own'. Think of a big smile, a 'long' face, a cowering demeanor, a sharp wail, or a rolling laughter, for example. As artists well know, the expressive power of such products can be preserved even when they are detached from individual acts of expression. Thus, a painter can portray sadness or boredom without herself feeling sad or bored, and without any pretense or intention to deceive, by reproducing 'the face of' sadness or boredom. Words, on the other hand, may seem incapable of such independent showing. So, for example, you might think that the sentence "This is boring", considered on its own, can only convey the information—tell us that—some designated item is boring. Similarly, the sentence "I feel bored", considered on its own, could only tell us that the speaker feels bored, but not show us her boredom. What, then, of the idea that avowals—and even non-self-ascriptive linguistic expressions—are similar to natural expressions in being capable of expressing subjects' mental states?

One obvious response is to concede that the *products* of linguistic acts indeed do not themselves show the mental states they express, and to point out that what matters to an expressivist is only that subjects should be able to show mental states through *acts* whose products are linguistic. Given the enormous variety of the things that we think can be shown, and given the enormous variety of ways we regard as available for showing things, I see no reason to deny that. We speak of people showing us their exercise routine, their charming smile, their resolve, contempt, integrity, loyalty, generosity, concern, conviction, cruelty, and so on. We speak of showing respect by tipping one's hat, showing confidence by casting a vote, showing resentment

---

[10] What about avowals in thought? Clearly, as observers, we cannot perceive the state allegedly expressed by a thought avowal by perceiving the subject's performance of the act of avowing, since we cannot perceive the avowing performance. But I would argue that as we reflect on the performance, and take it to be a thought *avowal*, as opposed to a theoretical self-report, e.g., we ascribe to it features such that *if* we could perceive them, we would be able to see the subject's state, just as we would if the subject were to exhibit overt behavior. (After all, we cannot perceive a subject saying *to herself* "Darn!" as she trips; yet surely we can make sense of such a mental act along expressivist lines.)

by turning away, showing one's intention to buy an item in an auction by giving a slight nod of the head, showing courage by speaking up in a meeting, showing commitment by signing a document, showing approval by raising a hand. We even speak of showing disrespect by *failing* to show up, showing neglect by *not* taking some action, showing restraint by *refraining* from saying something, and showing disregard for someone's feelings by *avoiding* their overture.[11] The heterogeneity of the above list attests to a remarkable flexibility in the commonsense notion of showing, which makes it unreasonable to insist that linguistic acts simply *could* not show subjects' mental states.

Could the showing in question be of the perception-enabling kind? It is a bit hard to say, absent a closer investigation of what is involved in perception in general and perception of mental states in particular. The notion of perception, it may be pointed out, also enjoys remarkable flexibility. Take seeing, for example. I can see the maple tree in my yard by seeing a characteristic component of it—say, one of its branches. The branch could be severed and separated from the tree, so it is possible for me to see the branch without seeing the tree. But that doesn't change the fact that *if* the tree is there, still attached to the branch, I can see the tree by seeing the branch. In other words, *if* I were to see the tree—which requires that the tree be there so as to be seen—it would be by seeing the branch that I would see it. As suggested by Green, we could perhaps think of natural expressions as exhibiting characteristic components of the states they express, so we can sometimes see the relevant state by seeing a characteristic component of it.[12]

In general, a characteristic component need not be an essential component. The tree could survive losing the branch by means of which I saw it. A characteristic component need not be universal or typical. The branch could be of a shape that is atypical among maple trees. Indeed, the branch could be an artificial graft, or painted; so a characteristic component need not be natural. Thus we can see things by seeing non-essential, idiosyncratic, and acquired components of

---

[11] Not all the examples given here are examples of expression. As pointed out in the previous chapter, not everything that can be shown can be expressed. See above, pp. 271 f.

[12] We need to be careful here. The smile (a product) is not a characteristic component of 'a pleasure'. In the sense relevant here, pleasure is not an object, like a tree. And perceiving a characteristic component of it is not perceiving a *part* (a 'chunk') of it. Rather, the act of smiling is a characteristic component of the state of *feeling* pleasure. And what we see when we see someone smiling is her *being* in a state of feeling pleasure.

them. Similarly, perhaps we could think of acts involving acquired, 'non-natural' expressions—gestures, facial expressions, vocalizations, etc.—including ones that have their roots in the cultural/social environment or in individual idiosyncrasies, and *also* including *linguistic* expressions, as characteristic components of (being in) the states they express. This could apply to rolling one's eyes, turning up one's nose, covering one's ears, tutting, and squinting, as well as sighing, cussing, and uttering "That's great!", "Well done!", "What the heck!", and so on, but also to an individual's special facial expression or tone of voice or turn of phrase.[13] In this way, a bit of behavior that has become 'second nature' could be thought to allow us to perceive someone's feeling pleasure just as much as a picture-perfect smile, by becoming a characteristic—which is not to say essential—component of the relevant state. (Later on I shall argue that this way of looking at things helps Neo-Expressivism avoid the charge of being committed to behaviorist irrealism.)

Although I think the explication of expressing in terms of showing that enables perception of characteristic components is promising, I don't think the success of the Neo-Expressivist account depends on it. The account can survive even if it turns out, upon further investigation, that this explication is either flawed or does not extend to non-natural expressions. We could let showing in the sense of enabling perception of characteristic components fall where it may, so long as we can lean on the fairly robust intuition that, avowals aside, we regularly express our thoughts, feelings, emotions, and attitudes using language. You say, looking at the sky, "It's going to rain." You have spoken of rain, and predicted its imminent occurrence. The sentence you have uttered expresses$_3$ (in Sellars's semantic sense) the proposition that it is going to rain. But in the act of uttering it, you have expressed$_1$ (in Sellars's action sense) *your present thought or judgment* that it's going to rain. Or, as you observe your little ballerina, you say, "Look at her. Isn't she dancing beautifully?" You are telling your hearer to look at your child, and posing the question whether she's dancing beautifully. But you're expressing$_1$ your joy and pride at the

---

[13] As pointed out in the previous chapter, very few of the human feelings, emotions, and attitudes, have innate, universal 'signatures' that can show them to us in the way a picture may depict a tree. Many non-linguistic gestures etc. which we would count among natural expressions have their roots in cultural, social, or even individual history and habits, if not conventional rules. Their association with the relevant mental states is not set up by nature.

child's performance. Or you say, "What you just did is a disgrace", which expresses$_3$ the proposition that what your hearer just did is a disgrace. But you're expressing$_1$ your outrage at what she did. Given the right context and background, it would be natural to take these utterances as expressing the said thoughts or attitudes, even if they were unaccompanied by any (other) expressive behavior, i.e. a distinctive facial expression, gesture, tone of voice, or demeanor. There is even at least *a* sense of "natural"—namely, where it contrasts with "contrived"—in which we might say that, when making the above utterances, you *are* naturally expressing your present thoughts, feelings, and attitudes. You're using words, not (or not just) to make a prediction about the weather, to ask a question, or to describe someone's action (respectively). You are putting a present thought or feeling of yours into words, rather than into a facial expression, a gesture, your tone of voice, or bodily demeanor. You are *speaking* from a present condition, instead of giving it some non-verbal expression.

We can often enough tell *that* someone is speaking from a present condition—'putting into their words' a present feeling, emotion, or thought, rather than, or in addition to, doing anything else that can be done with those words (describing, reporting, stating, informing, asking, commanding, etc.)—by witnessing their behavior. *What* condition someone is speaking from (venting, airing, sharing) is something we can often enough tell based on the semantic content of their utterance (when it has one) as well as a host of contextual clues. Utterances that involve one and the same sentence, semantically individuated, may express$_1$ different types of conditions of the utterers, and utterances involving different (semantically individuated) sentences may express$_1$ the same type of condition. For an obvious example of the latter, consider the following three sentences, all of which can be used, in context, to express one's annoyance: (1) "She just got up and left!"; (2) "It's annoying that she just got up and left"; (3) "Annoyingly, she just got up and left." The Neo-Expressivist claim is that avowals are on a continuum with such utterances. They are acts in which a subject speaks from a present thought, feeling, emotion, sensation, or attitude, thereby giving it articulate, self-ascriptive expression. Thus, one could also express one's annoyance by saying, (4) "I am so annoyed that she just got up and left". It is worth noting that in (4), as in (2) and (3), an aspect of the semantic content directly guides us to the condition the subject is trying to express$_1$. *And this may obviate any need to perceive the expressed condition in the product or in the accompanying behavior.* On the other hand, taking a token of (1) to express one's annoyance would seem to depend on perception of an accompanying tone of voice, facial expression, etc. (We shall return to this point in the next section.)

Now, regarding avowals as expressive acts, on a par with acts of non-ascriptive linguistic expression (and perhaps also with acts of natural expression), may seem most compelling in the case of what I've called "avowals proper". Characteristic of avowals proper is the fact that they are immediate, spontaneously volunteered reactions that can be seen as simply supplanting non-verbal reactions. It seems highly plausible to regard such reactions as expressions of a mental state, unaccompanied by any intention to inform others that one is in that state, unmediated by a judgment that one is in that state, and ungrounded in any epistemic reasons for thinking one is in that state (with that content) rather than some other state (with some other content). In the case where Jenny says "I want the teddy!", instead of eagerly reaching for the teddy, it may indeed seem that there is not the requisite 'epistemic distance' between Jenny and her condition for the notions of error in judgment, or justification, reasons, and epistemic basis to get a foothold. We can plausibly take Jenny to be speaking directly from her condition, rather than offering a descriptive report of it.

But not all avowals are like that. There are also what may be described as *non-evidential reportive avowals*.[14] Having mastered the use of "I want the teddy" as a linguistically articulate expressive device, Jenny may put that device to partially reportive use. For instance, she may offer that kind of self-ascription in answer to such questions as "Why are you looking in that drawer?" or "What do you want most right now?". In such cases, the self-ascriptive utterance may seem to shade readily into ordinary reports. If it is still regarded as more secure than such reports, we may wonder why. I suggest that, if we regard non-evidential reportive avowals as more secure than other reports, theoretical self-reports included, this is still because, or *to the extent that*, we regard them as directly expressive of the self-ascribed state.

[14] Gasking (1962: 168 f.) briefly draws attention to the possibility that avowals share some characteristics with reports.

Thus, I think it is still plausible to attribute the difference in security to the fact that there is an expressive element even in reportive avowals. In the typical case, when we invite someone to tell us how things are with them—by asking, for example, "How are you feeling?" or "What are you thinking about right now?"—what we are doing is inviting them to give voice to their present feelings, thoughts, etc. We take them to be in a special position to do more than offer a well-founded opinion, or craft a reliable report about their state of mind. The avowing subject can do what no one else can: she can speak from the very states of minds she ascribes to herself. Indeed, I would suggest that there is a direct correlation between the degree of security we would be prepared to assign to a present-tense mental self-ascription and the extent to which we take the subject to be speaking her mind. So suppose we ask Jenny, "What would you really like to do right now?" and, upon reflection, she replies, "I'd like to cuddle with my teddy". Given the context of the request, it is not unreasonable to see her as informing us about how things are with her mentally. But I submit that, insofar as we take Jenny to be avowing, we take it that she is also expressing a state she is in, and not merely presenting her findings about a state inside her. Furthermore, we would take her response to have a unique security only insofar as we take it that way.

Reflection can play (at least) two distinct roles in this context. There is the kind of reflection involved in self-interpretation, whereby the subject puts together various facts she knows about herself in order to reach a conclusion about what she now wants, feels, etc.[15] Such reflection need not rely on observation of one's own behavior, or on theoretical hypothesizing and inference. Still, it involves a certain kind of self-analysis and 'reading' that is conducted at one (or more) remove from the state one is in. But there is a kind of reflection whose point is, rather, to put the subject in the right position to give vent to her state, or speak directly from it. At any given moment, there is a lot that is going on in our minds. If a question arises about one particular aspect of what is going on at a given moment, we may have to pause to be able to offer an answer. But this isn't necessarily because we must survey our mental scene with an inner eye, or theorize about the causes

---

[15] Borrowing from Tanney (1996), Wright cites and briefly discusses a passage from Jane Austen which illustrates this kind of case (1998: 15).

of our behavior; the purpose of reflection may just be to eliminate what can be described as background noise and let the right condition come to the surface, as it were.[16]

Non-evidential reportive avowals are different from purely theoretical self-reports. A mentalistic "I"-ascription based solely on the analysis of a therapist, say, or on an application to one's own case of general scientific findings is not an avowal at all; it is *only* a self-report. The self-reporter's explicit reliance on epistemic support would clearly signal that she is not speaking from her condition. Her position vis-à-vis the condition is no different from that of an observer, as evidenced by the fact that her self-ascription is fully arrived at through epistemic routes potentially available to anyone (though she may be in a position to gather more evidence than others). We often take issue with people's self-reports. Theoretical self-knowledge is not something we presume people to have.

Actual cases of avowals are rarely as neatly divided as the above separation between avowals proper and reportive avowals may suggest. Thus consider again one of our earlier examples. You bump into a friend and you say, "I'm so happy to see you". This could be a case that neatly fits the paradigm of avowals proper, by being simply and purely a spontaneous joyful reaction upon seeing your friend. You offer the self-ascription "I'm so happy to see you" instead of saying "It's so good to see you!" or giving a joyful hug. However, the utterance could also be accompanied by a deliberate communicative intention to inform your friend about your joy. If so, it may not seem to be a purely expressive reaction.

The Neo-Expressivist account can accommodate this without accepting that in avowing "I'm so happy to see you" you must be offering a descriptive report of your present state as you find it when 'looking inside'. The presence of the communicative intention to inform of the condition does not by itself turn the self-ascription into a descriptive report. After all, the communicative intention could also accompany a non-verbal expression, such as an enthusiastic hug, yet the hug is not even a candidate for being a report, since it does not

---

[16] Hypnosis, as a therapeutic technique, may be thought of along these lines, as a systematic method for putting subjects in a position to give vent to *past* conditions, bypassing the epistemic distance introduced by selective memory and self-interpretation. The therapeutic notion of 'getting in touch with one's feelings' can perhaps be seen as trying to capture the expressive element I am talking about.

semantically express anything, let alone a self-judgment. In this latter case, it seems right to say that you are letting your friend know you're happy to see her *by* hugging her; but for all that, we would still take you to be expressing your joy through the hug. I am claiming that the same could be true of the self-ascriptive exclamation. Even if it is accompanied by the communicative intention, it can still be seen as expressing your joy at seeing your friend. You are letting your friend know that you are happy to see her by putting your feeling into your words, rather than into a bodily gesture. (In this particular type of case, we could perhaps describe the issuing of the self-ascription, somewhat artificially, as a two-stage process. You see your friend and think, "I'm so happy to see you". The thought avowal is an avowal proper; it is a silent expression of your joy. But then, as a second stage, there is the verbal performance in which you utter: "I'm so happy to see you!", thereby articulating in speech the thought avowal so as to let your friend know that you are happy to see her. Describing the case in this way makes it clear that the presence of the accompanying communicative intention need not turn the avowal into an act of expressing one's higher-order judgment.)[17]

## Avowals as Expressive of Judgments

Even an avowal proper, *qua* a genuine self-ascription, involves the intentional use of an indicative sentence (or its analogue in thought) which semantically represents a certain proposition: viz., that the avower is in a mental state M. But the intentional use by a subject of an indicative sentence meaning that *p*, when sincere and competent, is standardly associated with the expression of the subject's *belief* that *p*. Putting it in terms of Sellars's distinction, a subject who avows "I am in M" will be intentionally using a sentence that expresses$_3$ the proposition that she herself is in M, thereby expressing$_1$ her higher-order belief that she is in M, rather than expressing$_1$ her condition M. This may give rise to the following objection: the potential of an

---

[17] A closer look at this case may suggest that avowals proper, which are purely expressive, have a degree of primacy over mixed avowals, which have descriptive or reportive elements. This contrasts with the view defended by Fleming, who considers an avowal to "be doing much the same sort of thing as . . . 'I have brown hair'" (1955: 614). Fleming considers the self-descriptive, informative use to be logically primary (1955: 615). (I return to the case of mixed avowals in the final chapter.)

avowal to express$_1$ the self-ascribed condition is preempted by the avowal's expressing$_1$ the subject's belief, or judgment. In this section, I address this objection.

In earlier stages of my thinking about avowals along expressivist lines, I thought it very important to insist that avowals serve to express the avowed condition, *as opposed to* the subject's judgment that she is in that condition.[18] This was in keeping with a key aspect of expressivist views in general. Such views are initially concerned to contrast expressions of feelings and attitudes with assertions, or descriptive reports, and it is assumed that this means denying that they can express judgments. But, as we saw in the case of ethical expressivism, the expressivist view is put forth not only as a positive claim about the expressive force or function of ethical utterances, but also as a "non-cognitivist" negative claim to the effect that there are no ethical properties for ethical statements to refer to. It is the negative claim that serves to draw a contrast between ethical discourse and 'cognitive' discourses. Given the negative claim, it seems incumbent upon the ethical expressivist to insist that her view precludes the idea that ethical utterances can express judgments about ethical matters (in addition to expressing various pro- or con-attitudes of the utterer).

As an antidote to introspectionist views, which portray avowals as mediated by secure perception-like judgments about one's present state, I think it is a good strategy to present avowals as expressive of self-ascribed conditions, rather than highly secure second-order judgments about first-order states. However, I think it is a mistake of the Simple Expressivist account to couple the claim that avowals are distinguished by their expressive character with the claim that avowals involve no genuine ascription, or that the mental terms involved in them do not refer. So I reject the analogue of the ethical expressivist's negative claim. The question that still remains for my account is whether the positive expressivist claim that I *do* adopt—that an avowal expresses$_1$ the subject's first-order condition—nonetheless leaves room for the idea that it may *also* express$_1$ the subject's higher-order judgment that she is in that condition; or, conversely, that if we accept that an avowal, *qua* a sincere utterance of an indicative, expresses$_1$ a self-judgment, it cannot also express$_1$ the subject's first-order condition.

---

[18]  This is evident especially in formulations of the Neo-Expressivist view offered in Bar-On (2000) and Bar-On and Long (2001).

For simplicity, I will focus below on the case where I issue a true avowal, such as "I'm hoping that it doesn't rain tonight". The self-ascription has the semantic content that DB is hoping it doesn't rain tonight. So we might say that the avowal expresses$_3$ that judgment (expresses it in the semantic sense, that is). But, on the Neo-Expressivist account, in issuing the avowal, I express$_1$ my hope that it doesn't rain tonight. So the question is whether, in addition, I may also be expressing$_1$ my judgment that I'm hoping it doesn't rain.

Let us set aside for now the question whether the avowal expresses$_2$ (in the causal sense) my judgment. If this is a question that concerns the causal history of the avowal—whether the issuing of the self-ascription, in speech or in thought, is at least in part caused by a higher-order judgment I make (to the effect that I'm hoping it doesn't rain tonight)—then it may best be left to a more directly psychological investigation. I take the more purely philosophical question to be whether, as is often tacitly assumed, my expressing my hope in the action sense *precludes* my also expressing$_1$ my judgment that I'm hoping . . . Let me first point out that what is required for the Neo-Expressivist account is the idea that, when avowing, subjects do express$_1$ the avowed states, and, most crucially, that the special security of avowals is to be explained by reference to that fact, *rather than* by appeal to the epistemic security of the subject's judgment (if any) regarding her state. Nothing in the account as explained so far seems to require denying that, when avowing, a subject expresses$_1$ her judgment that she is in the avowed state, *as well as* the self-ascribed condition. So unless there are independent reasons to think that one cannot express$_1$ two distinct states with one bit of intentional behavior, we should perhaps remain neutral on the matter.

It seems true to the phenomenology of avowals—particularly of avowals proper—to compare them to natural expressions in point of expression$_1$, and to play down the role of the subject's higher-order judgment to the point of even denying its presence. The subject who issues an avowal proper does not pause to consider whether she is in the state she avows; she may not even attend to it. Like the subject who grimaces in pain, or smiles with joy, she engages in a bit of unre-flective (though not unintentional or pointless) behavior. She simply 'comes out' with the self-ascription, just as she might 'come out' with a bit of non-verbal behavior. This similarity is worth seizing upon when trying to articulate a clear alternative to epistemic views of avowals' special security. But it still seems true that my alternative account of this security does not *require* supposing that the subject does not in addition make or express$_1$ any higher-order judgment about the state she expresses$_1$. And I see no general reason to maintain that one cannot express$_1$ more than one state with a bit of behavior. Intuitively, one can express$_1$ both one's fear and one's loathing with a single contortion of one's face. By the same token, one could in principle express$_1$ both one's hope and one's judgment that one's hoping in one verbal (or mental) act. In the case of expressing one's pro- or con-attitude when using ethical terms, the expressivist has a special reason to deny that we may express an ethical judgment at the same time as we express our pro-attitude. But the Neo-Expressivist account does not inherit (an analogue of) this special reason.[19]

In characterizing the special security of avowals, I suggested that their epistemic immediacy can be captured through their distinctive immunity to ascriptive errors. This immunity consists in the fact that, when avowing "I am in M", I have *no more reason* for thinking that I am in some state or other than whatever reason I have for thinking I am in M. I also pointed out that an avowal such as "I'm so glad to see you" *no more* needs to rest on, or be epistemically grounded in, some recognitional judgment I make regarding the presence, character, or content of my present state than the hug I give to my friend. Neither claim entails that as I issue the avowal, I do not express$_1$ the self-judgment that is semantically expressed by the self-ascription. Let us dub the idea that, when I avow, unlike when I engage in naturally expressive behavior, I express$_1$ not only the avowed condition but also my judgment that I am in that condition "the Dual Expression thesis". Should this thesis be embraced or rejected?

I can think of at least three reasons favoring the Dual Expression thesis. First, we have modeled our understanding of the special immunity to error of avowals on the (more limited) immunity to error of proprioceptive reports and their likes. Since the point of presenting such reports as immune to error was originally to explain their unusual epistemic status, while preserving the idea that they

---

[19] If when I avow I do express$_1$ a self-judgment, what kind of judgment might this be? Is it justified in any way? Do I have reasons for it, even if it is not grounded in any evidence, inference, observation, or recognition? These questions will be taken up in Ch. 9.

represent self-judgments, we may be advised to continue to think of avowals as representing self-judgments as well (albeit epistemically different from theoretical mental self-judgments, as well as bodily ones). Secondly, and relatedly, adopting the Dual Expression thesis might make it easier to render plausible the idea that avowals (can) represent genuine self-knowledge. For, we might think that, unless I do express₁ my judgment or belief that I am in M when I avow M, I could not be said to *know* that I am in M. (This issue will be discussed at some length in the next chapter.) Thirdly, at least among philosophers of language, it is commonplace to think of the sincere utterance of an indicative sentence $p$ as expressing the utterer's judgment or belief that $p$. This general supposition would, of course, have to be finessed in cases where it is thought that there can be no judgment or belief involved (as Ethical Expressivism maintains in the case of ethical utterances). However, since the Neo-Expressivist account does not traffic in "mental non-cognitivism", it may seem advisable for it not to depart from that general supposition, and so to adhere to the Dual Expression thesis.

A further reason to adhere to this thesis has occurred to me, but upon reflection I think it should be rejected. (I have included it here, because it may help illuminate an important point about the Neo-Expressivist account.) You might think that, if we focus on the case of thought avowals, the Dual Expression thesis would seem inevitable. After all, if I am thinking, as opposed to saying, "I'd love some ice cream right now", then I am articulating in thought that I'd love some ice cream right now. Doesn't that mean, *ipso facto*, that I am making the judgment that I'd like some ice cream? Our discussion of self-verifying thoughts in the previous chapter should be instructive here. That discussion suggested that there is room for a distinction between merely thinking $p$, on the one hand, and judging, or believing, that $p$ is the case. Absent an argument to the contrary, we should not suppose that any case of tokening a thought with content $p$ must amount to a case of (occurrently) affirming/judging/believing that $p$. For, as we have seen before, it seems that one may entertain a thought with content $p$ without affirming (subscribing to or endorsing) $p$. If so, this supports my effort to develop the Neo-Expressivist account in a way that cuts across speech and thought. To the extent that thinking a self-ascriptive thought does not constitute expressing one's judgment that one is in the self-ascribed state, self-ascriptions in thought can be seen to share with those issued in speech a key feature needed to make sense of the idea of avowals in thought. Both in speech and in thought, a subject may engage in an expressive act whose product is a self-ascription, but where what the subject expresses$_1$ is the self-ascribed state, rather than her judgment affirming that she is in that state.

For the record, there are also apparent reasons that tell against the Dual Expression thesis. One apparent reason comes from the gloss offered earlier on the distinction between EXP$_1$ and EXP$_2$ (see Chapter 7, pp. 249 f.). On that gloss, recall, to express M in the action sense is to have M as one's reason for the relevant behavior. Thus, if an avowal of M is to express$_1$ one's judgment that she's in M, that self-judgment must itself be one's reason for the avowal. By itself, this is not a problem; it just means that accepting the Dual Expression thesis requires accepting that, in general, one may have (and perhaps offer) more than one reason for one's action. There is nothing unusual about this idea. If asked, "Why did you suddenly duck?", one might say, "Because that ball was coming at me", but also "Because I saw the ball coming at me" (or "Because I thought the ball was coming at me"). Both a perceived state of affairs and one's perception of or judgment about it may be cited as reasons for one's action. In the particular case of avowals, however, it might be noted that one would *not* typically offer one's self-judgment as a reason for avowing. If asked "Why are you saying this?" upon avowing "I'm so mad at you", it would be odd to respond, "Because I think I'm mad at you". Such a response would naturally be read as your taking back the avowal. Whereas responding, "Because I'm mad at you", would be perfectly sensible. This may suggest an oddity in regarding a subject's self-judgment as her reason for avowing. So, as long as we adhere to the construal of EXP$_1$ in terms of reasons for action, we may hesitate to apply the Dual Expression thesis to avowals, unless we can explain away the oddity (perhaps by appeal to some Gricean pragmatic explanation). A second apparent reason for rejecting the Dual Expression thesis in the case of avowals is that there may seem to be a conflict between the idea that an avowal expresses$_1$ one's self-judgment and the Neo-Expressivist construal of avowals as epistemically immediate, and ungrounded in epistemically secure self-judgments. However, we should bear in mind that claiming that an avowal expresses₁ a subject's self-judgment is portraying the self-judgment as the subject's *reason for action*; it does not commit us to taking the avowal itself (as product) as having *epistemic* reasons, or seeing the expressed self-judgment as itself being made on any epistemic basis. Since neither of these apparent reasons for rejecting the Dual Expression thesis seems compelling, and since it does not seem to detract from the Neo-Expressivist account of avowals' special security to accept that they express₁ self-judgments, in what follows I shall leave it open that avowals may express₁ subjects' higher-order self-judgments as well as their first-order (and self-ascribed) mental condition.

## The Asymmetric Presumption of Truth and Transparency-to-the-Subject's-Condition

It is worth pausing to see, in a schematic way, how we are faring with respect to my overall goal of offering a non-epistemic account of avowals' security, as represented by Epistemic Asymmetry, without compromising Semantic Continuity. What I have called Epistemic Asymmetry has 'subject-oriented' aspects and 'audience-oriented' aspects.[20] On the subject side, there is the fact that, when avowing, doubt as to whether one is indeed in the self-ascribed state, or whether the state has the intentional content one assigns to it, seems entirely out of place. We may refer to this as the *relative indubitability* of avowals. In addition, avowals seem 'groundless' and to be issued with a distinctive effortlessness. We may refer to this as the *epistemic directness or immediacy* of avowals. Correlatively, on the audience side, there is the fact that we do not expect an avower to have reasons or grounds for her avowal. We also do not stand ready to correct or challenge an avowal. We may refer to this as the *relative incorrigibility* of avowals.

I have argued that we can explain these aspects of Epistemic Asymmetry by appeal to avowals' distinctive immunity to error of misascription. And this ascriptive immunity to error, in turn, I have explained by appeal to the expressive character of avowals. But there

---

[20] In the case of avowals made in thought, audience-directed aspects may be construed as pertaining to how *we*, who envisage the subject's mental act of avowing, regard it.

is another component to the ascriptive security of avowals that bears
both on their relative corrigibility and on what the Cartesian view
identifies as their infallibility. When people avow being in pain, or
thinking about their aunt, or feeling apprehensive about an upcoming test, and so on, it is not only that we would refrain from subject-
ing what they say (or think) to epistemic criticism or correction.
We would also strongly presume their avowals to represent *truths*
concerning their present conditions. Indeed, this strong presumption
of truth seems to lie behind the idea that avowals, in contrast with
natural expressions, represent a privileged kind of self-*knowledge* that
subjects possess. It is linked with what is often referred to as "first-
person authority" (or, as I prefer, first-person privilege), and serves to
distinguish avowals from other empirical pronouncements, including
ordinary perceptual reports. I now want to turn to an explanation of
this asymmetric presumption of truth that governs avowals.

A precondition of presuming avowals to be true is taking them to
be truth-*apt* (or truth-assessable). Thus, the first issue to address is
avowals' *truth-aptness*. I have emphasized throughout that, on the
Neo-Expressivist account, the expressive character of avowals is not a
fact about their semantic content, but rather has to do with the use of
a self-ascription, or the kind of act performed, in the given situation.
Suppose I utter "I am really thirsty", as I desperately reach for a glass
of water. I am using a sentence that has the grammar and meaning of
a self-ascription. It is true under the same conditions as your com-
ment, "You are really thirsty", when you're observing me gulp down
a whole cup of ice water. For all that, in uttering the sentence I may
not be *reporting* my thirst but rather *expressing* it. A familiar comparison may help. I utter, "I promise to take you to dinner tonight." I am
using a sentence that is true if and only if DB promises to take
[so-and-so] to dinner [on a certain evening]. But in uttering the
sentence, I am not reporting this promise, I am making it. Or I say,
"I intend to finish reading your article tonight." My utterance is true
if and only if at a given time DB has the intention of finishing reading
the book tonight. But my utterance may very well constitute a declaration of my good intention, rather than a report of the presence of
that intention. In these cases, the form of words used in self-ascriptions
allows them to be truth-assessable—to have truth-evaluable content—
without automatically making them into descriptive reports.

The suspicion that any expressivist account of avowals must fall foul of their truth-aptness may be due to a false comparison to ethical expressivism (discussed in Chapter 7, pp. 233–40). As I have pointed out, the ethical expressivist couples the claim that ethical utterances express pro- or con-attitudes with the denial that there *are* such properties as goodness, justness, and the rest for us to make truth-apt judgments about. The analogue of this in the case of the expressivist account of avowals would be the claim that avowals express mental states coupled with denying that there are such things as being in pain, etc. for us to make truth-apt judgments about. But I have emphasized that the negative claim is by no means part of the Neo-Expressivist account. Of course there are mental states; otherwise we couldn't express them! In virtue of its semantic content, the *product* of an avowal—a self-ascription—refers to these states and ascribes them to subjects; it says, *truly or falsely*, that someone is in a particular mental state. But, for all that, the *act* of producing the self-ascription may be an expressive act in which the avower gives vent to the self-ascribed condition. Thus, my Neo-Expressivist account adopts the Simple Expressivist main insight that avowals resemble natural expressions in terms of the acts they perform, without maintaining that they are like natural expressions in failing of truth-aptness.

When I exclaim, as I desperately reach for a glass of water, "I feel so thirsty", I am using a meaningful sentence of English that is capable of being true or false. In point of grammar and meaning avowals, my sentence is an ascription to an individual of a present state, which can be exchanged with other sentences that can be used simply to report my state ("She/DB is so thirsty" or "I was so thirsty then"). This is how Semantic Continuity is preserved. But truth-apt sentences can be put to all sorts of uses, and not every such use is an assertion or a report.[21] To reiterate, when Mary angrily says to John, "I intend to leave you", what she says is true just in case she intends to leave him, and yet she may not be reporting her intention, but rather declaring it. She may *also* be reporting her intention. But her performance would not be properly understood unless it is recognized that she is declaring her intention. Analogously, in ordinary contexts an utterance of "I feel

---

[21] The idea is familiar. Peter Strawson has suggested that truth-aptness is a matter of meaning, whereas assertive or reportive function is a matter of use. Strawson's example is "The present King of France is bald", used in a context where there is no king of France. See his (1950).

so thirsty" is to be understood as an act of expressing, not reporting, my thirsty condition. In the case of avowals, as in the familiar cases of so-called other moods, grammar and meaning may not line up with force or with use. And this can serve to explain Epistemic Asymmetry.

Now to say that avowals (as products) are truth-apt is to accept that they can be true *or* false. The question I want to answer next is why the self-ascriptions that are the products of avowals are taken to enjoy an asymmetric presumption of truth. My strategy in addressing this question will be to think of avowals from the perspective of the actual or potential audience—the consumers of their products, who stand to learn something from them (actually or potentially) about the avowing subject's condition. But here, too, I will advert to the expressive character of avowals. I will be relying on the following idea, introduced in the previous chapter (see pp. 278ff.). There I argued that, when witnessing expressive behavior, we take it that the subject is in the condition that we perceive in the product of her act: we presume, as I have put it, that the behavior is *transparent-to-the-subject's-condition*. To anticipate, I will be arguing that this presumption of transparency is what becomes, in the case of semantically articulate, self-ascriptive expressions, the asymmetric presumption of truth.[22]

I have been claiming that, to understand the status of avowals, we should think of them as bits of behavior, doings, overt or covert, which belong in the category of expressive acts. Beginning with avowals proper, I have urged that semantically articulate self-ascriptions, like natural expressions, can be seen as 'pressed from' the subject, and that their production can be seen as equally epistemically direct or immediate. Understanding their status does not require appeal to the subject's attempt (conscious or not) to recognize or ascertain the presence or character of the condition she self-ascribes. (The condition need not be seen as the subject's epistemic target, as I've put it.) In this, avowals proper are different from descriptive or assertoric reports, and similar to acts of natural expression. Like natural expressions, avowals proper are seen as directly presenting to us the subject's condition, rather than the subject's well-founded *judgment that* she is in that condition. This similarity is reflected in observers' typical responses to

---

[22] In this, I am following the discussion in Bar-On and Long (2001: sect. 4). But some of what I have to say about the presumption of truth will depart from that discussion.

avowals proper. To someone who exclaims, "I think she's about to fall", we do not say, "No, you don't", but something like, "No, she's not—she's too far from the edge". We negate the propositional content of the avowed belief, and perhaps try to correct a mistake, rather than deny the self-ascription of belief. To the child who says "I'm scared of the bear", we say, "But he's so gentle", at once rejecting the implicit judgment that the bear is scary and trying to assuage the child's fear, rather than denying the self-ascription of fear. And to the person who says "I've got a terrible headache", we hand an aspirin, trying to alleviate the painful condition, rather than deny the pain self-ascription.

What is striking about these kinds of cases is that, as observers, we respond to the ascribed condition itself, not to the self-ascription that can be recovered from the avowal's grammatical form. We take it for granted that the subject is in the condition indicated by the mental term, and go on to address the condition itself in whatever way we deem appropriate. We concur with an expressed belief or try to correct it; we attempt to fulfill an expressed desire for a teddy bear by handing it to the child or try to eliminate the desire by showing the teddy bear to be undesirable; we do our best to alleviate the pain or . . ., and so on. Just as a subject who merely gives vent to her condition is not thereby offering a report of it, so an observer who takes her to be venting will typically not be concerned to offer a correction or corroboration of the self-ascription based on her own judgment. What typically corresponds to the subject's non-reportive spontaneous verbal expression is the observer's 'non-judgmental' spontaneous response to the condition he recovers from the expression.

When we take an act whose product is a self-ascription to be an avowal proper, we regard the self-ascription as taking us directly to the subject's mental condition. In this way, we treat avowals proper as sharing in the transparency-to-the-subject's-condition of naturally expressive acts. I distinguished two dimensions of this transparency: expressive behavior is transparent inasmuch as we can see in it the *kind* of condition we take the subject to be in (e.g., a teddy desire, a wish that dad will stay), and also inasmuch as we can take it that the subject's behavior shows us *her* being in the condition (e.g., *Jenny's* wanting the teddy bear, or wishing daddy to stay). So far, my comparison of avowals proper to acts of natural expressions has focused on the second dimension. For I have tried to make the case that avowals proper are acts in which a subject speaks from a present condition. But my characterization of natural expressions and the replacement story I have offered suggest a way of pushing the comparison a bit further.

Consider again Jenny's avowal, "I really want the teddy!". I have conceded that the product of Jenny's act—i.e., a self-ascriptive sentence-token—does not display Jenny's desire the way her eager reaching for the teddy bear does, or even the way her accompanying tone of voice might. We could even concede that the sentence itself cannot show us the kind of condition in question (in the perception-enabling sense); rather, it only tells of the desire, by expressing the proposition that someone has that desire. The product is a linguistic item that, in virtue of its grammatical form and semantic content, ascribes the relevant state to Jenny. But this means that, when it comes to verbal expressions that replace natural expressions, our ability as observers to tell what kind of condition the relevant behavior (i.e., the verbal utterance) expresses is actually enhanced immensely. Self-ascriptive verbal expressions *wear the conditions they are supposed to express on their linguistic sleeve*, as it were. A linguistic utterance (and its analogue in thought) directly reveals the *kind* of condition it is intended to express through its semantic content. It contains a component that semantically represents the relevant kind of condition. So all that is required for our recognizing the kind of condition the subject's performance purports to express is linguistic uptake. I suggest that we can take this to be the analogue of the first dimension of transparency-to-the-subject's-condition in the case of semantically articulate verbal expressions.

Saying that verbal expressions wear the conditions they purport to express on their linguistic sleeve is another way of saying that the expressive vehicles used in avowals reveal the intended condition through what they express in Sellars's *semantic* sense. An "I"-ascription such as "I hope we get some rain today" will semantically express the relevant judgment by *explicitly naming a kind of condition* (a hope) *and articulating its content* (that it rain today), as well as *ascribing it to a certain individual*. The present point is that linguistic understanding of what the "I"-ascription says—i.e., what it expresses in the semantic sense—suffices for knowing what kind of condition the subject would be in if she were expressing *her* condition in Sellars's action sense. Unlike in the case of natural expressions, we do not need to recover that information through our perception of the expressive behavior. It is made available to us through the linguistic vehicle used in the act of avowing.

Thus, suppose it is insisted that avowals as products are different from natural expressions in that they do not display or exhibit the kind of conditions they express. The above suggestion is that the perception-enabling features of naturally expressive behavior that show us the kind of condition being expressed are taken over by the *semantic* features of avowals. What plays the role of showing the kind, quality, and object of the expressed state in the case of avowing is the subject's calling out the condition's name, as it were, and articulating its intentional content when it has one, in the course of an act of giving vent to her condition. And what plays the role of the observer perceiving the kind of condition being expressed is her understanding of the semantic content of the avowal.[23] In this way, although, semantically speaking, the expressive vehicles used in avowals—i.e., articulate mentalistic "I"-ascriptions—are importantly different from natural expressions such as grimaces, smiles, frightened gestures, etc., avowals can still be seen as possessing both dimensions of the transparency-to-the-subject's-condition characteristic of natural expressions. We can see avowals as lying at one end of a continuum of expressions. The continuum begins with universal natural expressions, followed by acquired facial expressions and gestures, inarticulate verbal emissions, expletives, and interjections. Next come semantically articulate linguistic expressions that do not semantically represent the expressed condition (such as "This food is great" or "This was a terrible result"). Then we have a variety of linguistic expressions that do make mention (at least indirectly) of the relevant condition, such as "You're so *annoying*"; "*Surprisingly*, she got there early". And these are followed, finally, by avowals such as "*I* feel *bored* to death". (See above, p. 261.)

We are now in a position to offer an expressivist rendering of the presumption of truth governing avowals. To regard a linguistic act as an avowal is to take it as an expression rather than a mere report of the

---

[23] Here again it is important not to construe competent language use and linguistic understanding in *epistemic* terms. For the subject to be making a genuine self-ascription, she must *mean that* she is in M by her avowal. And her hearer, or, alternatively, the person taking her to be avowing in thought, must *understand* her that way. But I would argue that neither accomplishment requires making reference to the subject's epistemically secure judgment that she is in M.

ascribed condition. It is to take the avowing subject to be speaking directly from her condition, where the self-ascription tells us *what* condition is to be ascribed to her. All that we as audience need to know to identify the condition being expressed is linguistic uptake. Note, however, that insofar as we take the subject to be expressing *her* condition (in the causal and action senses), we take it that she *is* in the relevant condition—the condition that is semantically referred to by the self-ascription, which is *the very condition that would render the self-ascription true*. Thus, the judgment that is semantically expressed by her avowal is what we take to be *true*, as long as we take Jenny to be expressing her condition. What is unique about avowals, in contrast even to linguistic expressions that mention the expressed condition in some way, is that they are *self*-ascriptive: they proclaim the very condition they supposedly express. When someone says "This is boring", we may recognize her act as an act of expressing her boredom. But what she says will be true just in case what she refers to *is* indeed boring. And there is no special presumption that, if anyone says that $x$ is boring, $x$ is indeed boring. On the other hand, if someone says "I feel so bored", recognizing her act as an act of expressing *her* boredom will *ipso facto* imply presuming her avowal to be true.[24]

On epistemic accounts, an avowal expresses the subject's own higher-order judgment about her present mental condition. And the asymmetric presumption of truth reflects our trust in the avowing subject's ability to judge *correctly*—and on a more secure epistemic basis than anyone else—what mental condition she is presently in. By contrast, on the Neo-Expressivist account advocated here, the asymmetric presumption of truth has to do with our taking avowals to be expressing the subject's (first-order) self-ascribed mental condition itself. What I suggest is that the asymmetric presumption of truth reflects our taking the subject's act as an expressive performance, where such performances are presumed to be transparent-to-the-subject's-condition. My proposal, then, is that *the asymmetric presumption of truth is what becomes of the presumption of transparency when the expressive performance has a truth-assessable self-ascriptive product.* If we

---

[24] Jacobsen (1996) makes a similar connection between expression and truth. However, he does not utilize the distinction between expressing M and expressing *your* M, and (perhaps consequently) takes the connection to be too strong. On his account, the truth of avowals is guaranteed, once they are understood as expressive of the mental states they ascribe. (See also Finkelstein (2001).)

take the author of an "I"-ascription at her word, if we do not question or correct what she says, and strongly presume it to be true, this is because, and to the extent that, we take her to have genuinely expressed her mental condition, as 'transparently' as she would if she were to produce a natural expression. An avowal is asymmetrically presumed to tell us the truth about the subject's condition insofar as it is taken to be the product of an expressive act of avowing—an act whose point is to give vent to the subject's present condition—and thus is seen as taking us directly to the state it ascribes.

Note that transparency-to-the-subject's-condition is a notion applicable to phenomenal as well as intentional avowals, and it is conceived from the point of view of an audience which either witnesses the avowal made in speech or considers it made by the subject in thought. It thus differs from Evans's and Moran's transparency-to-the-world discussed earlier (see Chapter 4). The latter is a notion reserved for intentional avowals—avowals that explicitly specify some worldly matter or object outside the subject. And, as you will recall, it is presented in terms of the way in which the subject would answer questions regarding what she presently thinks, believes, hopes, etc. (As a reminder, Evans, Moran, Gallois, and others point out that, if asked, "Do you believe the Democrats will win?", you will not typically answer by looking inside; you will instead consider the proposition "The Democrats will win" directly and answer on that basis.) On the Neo-Expressivist account, the transparency-to-the-world of intentional avowals will fall out as a consequence of the expressive character of *all* avowals, and will have as a correlative their transparency-to-the-subject's-intentional-state. If asked whether you believe *p*, you will directly consider whether *p* is *to be believed*. We can think of this as a way of putting yourself in a position to give direct voice to your (first-order) belief, which is what the Neo-Expressivist account says you do when avowing. You consider whether things are as the proposition says, and then simply pronounce on it, though you are using a self-ascriptive expressive vehicle. And your audience, having recognized you as avowing a belief, will confirm or take issue with the first-order belief she takes you to have expressed, rather than with the self-judgment semantically expressed by your self-ascription.

Avowals of intentional states are also special in having a commissive aspect. (See Chapter 4, pp. 135ff.) But this, too, can be seen as a consequence of their expressive character. On the present account, if one's self-ascription of a belief is an avowal, it serves to give expression to one of one's (first-order) beliefs. But this is to say that in avowing a belief one simply expresses what one takes to be true. When one ascribes a belief to another, one is not thereby committed to the truth of the other's belief. This is so even when one ascribes the belief empathetically (that is, by projecting to the other a transparent judgment about what there is to believe), because even then one's judgment about what is to be believed is only a conditional judgment: it is conditional upon assuming the other's point of view, which one need not do. Thus, the first-person/third-person contrast in commitments pointed out by proponents of the commissive view of avowals falls out of the contrast between reports and avowals that I have drawn in terms of expression.

We can now characterize more precisely the asymmetric presumption of truth that separates avowals from all other reports, however epistemically secure:

Understanding a mental "I"-ascription to be an avowal is taking it that the avower is expressing$_1$ *her* present condition, which means taking it that the avower is in the condition she self-ascribes. But that just means taking her self-ascription to be true. By contrast, understanding a mental "I"-ascription (purely) as a report does not require taking it to be true. A sincere report of the form "I am in M" may be understood as expressing$_1$ only the reporter's *judgment that* she is in M. But we can consistently understand it that way without supposing that she really is in M, and thus without taking the judgment to be true.[25]

Summing up: we can see the ascriptive immunity to error of avowals and the asymmetric presumption of truth that governs them as both due to the expressive character of avowals. On the present account, both are taken to be a consequence *not* of a highly secure epistemic route or basis available to avowing subjects, but rather of the fact that avowals constitute, and are understood as, acts in which a subject directly speaks from a present mental condition, rather than offering a descriptive report of it. Though, when avowing, a subject

---

[25] Thanks to Ram Neta for urging me to offer a more succinct articulation here.

produces a truth-assessable self-ascription of a mental state, the mental state is no more an epistemic target for her than it would be if she were to produce a natural expression. Her self-ascription is immune to errors of misascription (as well as misidentification) and is thus protected from ordinary epistemic assessments. At the same time, the self-ascription is asymmetrically presumed to be true. And this is because, taking the self-ascription to be an avowal means taking it to be a product of an expressive act, and I've suggested that such acts, in general, are presumed to be transparent-to-the-subject's-condition. In the case of avowals, this presumption amounts to the presumption of truth. For to presume that the avowal takes us directly to the subject's condition is to presume that she *is* in the relevant condition, which is just to presume that her self-ascription is true. This is not so in the case of acts whose products are natural expressions or non-self-ascriptive verbal expressions, since such products do not *say that* the avower is the expressed state. Moreover, the presumption of truth thus understood separates avowals from reports. This is because to take it that a self-ascription was indeed produced in an act of avowing is to take the avower at her word—to presume that what she has said (or thought) is *true*; not so if we take the self-ascription to be produced purely as a self-report.

## Expressive Failures

Avowals, I have maintained, are semantically continuous with other ascriptions, specifically, with other, more alienated "I"-ascriptions of occurrent mental states. For the products of avowals are truth-apt self-ascriptions. They can be true or false. I have also explained why, due to the expressive character of avowing, avowals are governed by an asymmetric presumption of truth. This presumption, however, does not amount to a guarantee of truth. In this section, I want to consider a variety of cases where avowals do seem to go wrong and offer the Neo-Expressivist take on such cases. This would serve several purposes.

First, I want to support the intuition that the distinctive security of avowals does not amount to absolute infallibility or incorrigibility. I take it as an advantage of the Neo-Expressivist view over *both* Cartesianism and Simple Expressivism that it makes room for the falsity of any given avowal. Some opponents of these views are still wedded to the idea that at least phenomenal avowals (avowals of present sensations, for example) cannot be false. This requires drawing a sharp distinction between phenomenal and intentional avowals in terms of their security, a distinction which seems to me ungrounded in the ordinary treatment of avowals. By contrast, my characterization of avowals' security in terms of ascriptive immunity to error and an asymmetric presumption of truth allows that the same kind of security is enjoyed by intentional and phenomenal avowals alike, and makes room for the falsity of both types of avowals. Indeed, as you will recall, the only potential candidates for guaranteed truth that I have considered are self-verifying avowals of presently entertained thoughts, which are clearly intentional avowals (i.e., avowals that articulate the intentional content of the self-ascribed state). (See above, Chapter 6.)

Secondly, admitting the possibility of false avowals may seem in tension with the idea that avowals are immune to both errors of misidentification and errors of misascription. It may seem that with these immunities in place, there is no room left for *any* kind of error. So how could avowals be false? My answer will be that the epistemic directness or immediacy captured by the notion of immunity to error, which I have explained by appeal to the expressive character of avowals, protects avowals only from the possibility of a certain kind of error: *brute (local) epistemic error* on the self-ascriber's part in ascribing to herself a present mental condition and in assigning it intentional content (when it has one). What we do not seem to have in the case of avowals, whether phenomenal or intentional, is the analogue of the notion that the self-ascriber has *simply got it wrong*. There is a way of going wrong that we do not associate with avowals, as opposed to other ascriptions. But a subject who has not *gone* wrong can still *be* wrong, in the sense that her avowal can be false, for she can issue a false self-ascription through what I shall refer to as *expressive failure*.

So, thirdly, I want to offer an understanding of false avowals, of both the phenomenal and of the intentional variety, as cases of expressive failures. This will be important, because it is sometimes thought that at least intentional avowals are subject to a variety of distinctive errors; most notable here are the prevalent cases of wishful thinking and self-deception. Such cases can seem puzzling for my account for two reasons. They seem to undermine the security of at least a large class of intentional avowals. And they seem to lend themselves readily to an epistemic interpretation, according to which the wishful thinker or the self-deceiver genuinely *mis-takes* one of her present mental states for another. On the analysis I shall offer, however, the phenomena of wishful thinking and self-deception do not yield true analogues of straightforwardly false, corrigible perceptual reports, on the one hand, or false self-reports of limb position, location, or orientation, on the other hand. Neither the wishful thinker nor the self-deceiver must be regarded as a victim of brute local epistemic error comparable to the error of someone who thinks that there is a red car outside when there is not, or that her legs are crossed when they are not. So, although these phenomena can illustrate the possibility of false intentional avowals, and thus show that the presumption of truth governing intentional avowals may be overridden, they do not show that avowals do not enjoy a distinctive security as understood by the Neo-Expressivist account.

On my Neo-Expressivist view, though an avowing subject may not have her condition as an epistemic target—though she may simply be giving it verbal expression—it is still possible for her to say something false. An example will help here. I sit in the dentist's chair. Having a long history of dental work, I dread what is to come. The dentist puts a sharp-looking instrument in my mouth, and I wince, or grunt. If I could speak, I might say (something which I may in fact *think* to myself), "Ow, that tooth!" or, more explicitly, "My tooth hurts so much!" I would be speaking from a present condition, in the sense of giving it vent, rather than issuing an introspective report about it. But for all that, I may not be suffering a toothache; so my explicit self-ascription would be false. Or, consider another example. A freshman being initiated in to a fraternity and primed to think he will be harmed may, upon having a piece of ice pressed to his neck, scream, "Stop it! My neck hurts!" The freshman's utterance seems just like an avowal proper—a spontaneous, sincere verbal expression of pain; yet for all that, we may be convinced that the guy is not really in pain.[26]

Something goes wrong in such cases, but I want to resist the conclusion that the subject in such cases must have *mis*-taken one

---

[26] This is an example discussed in Bar-On and Long (2001). The diagnosis offered there, however, is different from the one I offer here.

state for another through some kind of epistemic failure—a misperception, mis-impression, or recognitional failure. On the introspectionist model, we should suppose that our subject was deceived in some way by inner appearances. She somehow mistook her fear for pain, perhaps because her fear appeared just like pain to her, as she was looking inside.[27] In any event, what went wrong is that she was led to form a *false recognitional judgment* that she was in pain, which has led to the judgment she expressed in her avowal. The Neo-Expressivist account denies that the avowal must be the upshot of some recognitional judgment concerning inner goings-on. It maintains that a self-ascription may be produced expressively: not to report on how things are with you based on internal appearances or scanning, but rather to express your present state. So the question is how we are to represent cases like the above ones in which a subject *cannot* actually be expressing her state, since she simply is not in the relevant state.

The above cases are cases of failed expression. What has gone wrong in such cases, I suggest, is that, assuming the subject is not in pain, her expressive act has failed in a certain way: though she has successfully expressed *pain*, she has not succeeded in expressing *her* pain. She could not have expressed her pain, since there was no pain for her *to* express. The subject has used an expressive tool that is referentially associated with one condition (a toothache, or a hurt neck, respectively) to give vent to a different condition. We have already seen instances of this separation in the case of non-linguistic, natural expressions. A child may pretend to feel hurt to gain sympathy or attention, and an actor onstage can effectively fake natural expressions of pain—grimaces, grunts, etc.—to convey a character's being in pain. The possibility of separation attests to the fact that expression$_1$ is aligned with expression$_3$ rather than with expression$_2$ in not being a purely causal notion. Expressing$_1$, like representing, and like showing, requires a certain fit. A facial expression, a tone of voice, a vocal emission, a bodily gesture, do not express$_1$ whatever state has caused them. Also, a piece of behavior can express a state without being caused by it—it can express M, without expressing someone's present M. Thus there can be various mismatches between expressive behavior and the states it expresses.

---

[27] The inner scanner version of introspectionism (see Ch. 4, pp. 96 f.) will presumably have an analogous story to tell, though perhaps not in strictly perceptual terms.

Dissimulation, of course, can occur in speech as well as in non-verbal behavior. The actor onstage declares, "I feel so happy!", though she's actually rather sad. And the liar uses a semantic expression of the belief that *p* (uttering "It's going to rain later", or "I think it's going to rain later") as though it expressed *her* belief that *p*. We are also familiar with simple cases of mis-speaking, due to slips of the tongue: saying "Jim is here!" to express one's belief that John has arrived. These are all examples of expressive mismatches, in which what is expressed is not the condition the subject is in. In such cases, however, we would take it that there is no corresponding avowal in thought on the subject's part. For example, the actor—unless she is an exceptional method actor—is presumably only saying, but not thinking, "I feel so happy!" What is distinctive about the case of false avowals (if I am right that there are indeed such) is that they are mismatched expressions in which the subject is issuing a false self-ascription in the course of giving vent to a present condition, whether in speech or in thought. What renders her act one of a false avowal is that the expressive means she uses—a self-ascription of a particular kind of state—is not associated (through meaning or context) with the condition she is in. Nonetheless, I want to say, she may still be avowing.

I think it's important to acknowledge that avowals can be false, since we do sometimes find occasion to reject an avowal, as the above examples show. But it is also important to make room for false avowals, if we are to preserve the distinction between self-verifying self-ascriptions (e.g., "I am thinking about being deceived by an evil demon" as an avowal of an entertained thought passing through my mind) and other avowals. Put in the above terms, the difference between the self-verifying and the non-self-verifying cases is as follows. Barring slips of the tongue (or their equivalents in thought, if there are such), an avowal of an entertained thought that *p* is an expression of *one's* thought that *p*, because one cannot make such an avowal without *ipso facto* entertaining the ascribed thought, thereby making the avowal true. (And there may be other self-fulfilling acts, where self-ascribing a mental state actually makes it true, at least causally speaking, that one is in the state.) However, even barring slips of the tongue, the same is not true for ordinary avowals of beliefs or hopes or desires that *p*. I can avow a desire to go to the movies without thereby making it true that I have that desire; similarly for phenomenal avowals.

In general, it seems possible to make expressive use of a tool that is semantically associated with a mental condition without being in the relevant condition, and thus without expressing *one's* condition, even when one does not intend to deceive or engage in dissimulation or act playing. For this reason, I reject expressivist views that maintain that a subject's avowing a mental condition *conceptually guarantees* her being in the condition (so the avowal must be true), as long as the subject is linguistically or conceptually competent and sincere.[28] Such views fail to take account of the distinction between expressing M and expressing one's M, and also between avowals as products and avowals as acts. Of course, if it is *true* that the subject is *expressing her condition* (in the action and causal sense) then she must *be* in the relevant condition. (This simply follows from the fact that "expressing one's M" implies success, like "knowing that *p*", "seeing O", and so on.) But this still leaves room for a variety of cases in which one's expressive act succeeds in expressing M but fails to express one's actual, present M.

However, the possibility of false avowals raises a question for the Neo-Expressivist account. In explaining the presumption of truth governing avowals, I have in effect appealed to the fact that expressing is a success verb. I have said that to take a self-ascription to be an avowal of M is to take it as expressing the subject's being in M, and thus to take the self-ascription "I am in M" (where "I" refers to the subject) to be true. But this may seem to rule out the possibility of false avowals. A subject may issue a false self-ascription, but if she does, she can no longer be seen as expressing *her* M. In that case, though, how can her act be seen as an avowal? On the other hand, intuitively, from the point of view of the subject and what she does, there may be nothing to distinguish her saying "My tooth hurts" when it does indeed hurt from her saying it when it doesn't. She is not trying to deceive, or pretend, and neither is she offering a report of her present condition, made on some basis. She is not only just *saying* "My tooth hurts"; she is also (we may suppose) *thinking* "My tooth hurts". And as she produces the self-ascription, she would be as disinclined to subject it to doubt as she would any true avowal. From the audience's point of view, though there is ultimately reason to retract the presumption that

---

[28] For expressivist views that endorse a guarantee of truth, see, e.g., Jacobsen (1996); Falvey (2000); and Finkelstein (2001).

the self-ascription is true, given the context, as well as the audience's perception of the subject's behavior, there may seem to be as little room to ask her for reasons for the self-ascription, or to question how she knows her tooth hurts, as there would be if her self-ascription were true. In other words, intuitively speaking, the false self-ascription seems to share key aspects of the security of avowals as I have characterized it (minus, of course, the presumption that it's true, since we are supposing from the outset that it is not). But, since it cannot be said to express the subject's present pain, given that it's false, how are we to adhere to the idea that it still constitutes an avowal?

The Neo-Expressivist account seems to face a dilemma here. If we give up the idea that false self-ascriptions can constitute avowals, we lose some of the advantages mentioned earlier. Moreover, we would then have to accept that some non-avowals share key aspects of the security of avowals as I have characterized it, which may seem to cast doubt on the claim that the Neo-Expressivist account captures what is distinctive about avowals. On the other hand, if we want to adhere to the possibility of false avowals, it seems as though we have to give up that part of the explanation of Epistemic Asymmetry which appeals to the connection between expression and truth. Either way, important aspects of the account would seem to be compromised.

I think that the key to avoiding this apparent dilemma is, again, to pay careful attention to the act/product distinction. Acts of avowal are intentional acts. There is a certain systematic ambiguity in the characterization of such acts. When we describe someone as turning the lights on, or drawing a tree, or raising his arm, we are characterizing what they are doing partly in terms of the intention with which they are acting, or the purpose of their behavior—what they are *aiming* to do—and partly in terms of the *result* of their effort—what they have accomplished. When all is well, purpose and result line up. But they don't always. If I ask you what you're doing, you may sincerely answer: "I'm turning the lights on", yet I can see that the lights are still off. There is a mismatch between what you present yourself as doing and what you've actually succeeded in doing. A natural way to describe the situation is by retreating to the language of trying: "You're *trying* to turn the lights on, but they're not going on"; "You may be *trying* to draw a tree, but look at what came out!" What is notable about these descriptions is that they serve to signal the occurrence of unsuccessful actions, while allowing us to acknowledge a commonality between the successful and the unsuccessful cases, a commonality that has significance from both the agent's perspective and the audience's perspective. If you ask me to draw a tree and I begin to comply, then, unless I have reason to doubt my prospects of succeeding, I would be inclined to describe myself as drawing a tree, as opposed to merely *trying* to draw a tree. But so would you, at least prior to seeing the rotten fruits of my efforts.[29]

We can deploy this idea when trying to make room for the possibility of false avowals without compromising the Neo-Expressivist explanation of the presumption of truth. Suppose I utter, "My tooth hurts!" If I am an actor onstage, my audience may assume I am not giving voice to my own pain; my self-ascription is a simulated or pretend avowal, not a genuine one. Now suppose I am producing the self-ascription not onstage, but in the course of trying to deceive you. Again, my act is one of a pretend avowal, though this time you may not appreciate it—you may take it to be a genuine avowal, in which case you'd be presuming, erroneously, that you're presented with *my* present pain. But now let's suppose, as in our earlier example, that my utterance is produced while in the dentist's chair, when I am in fact not in pain, so that my self-ascription is false. From my point of view, we may suppose that there is no difference between that case and the case in which I produce the self-ascription and it is in fact true. (As I said before, we may suppose that I produce the self-ascription in thought, without uttering the words.) The utterance is produced as spontaneously and unreflectively, and I myself would be able to offer no reason for producing my utterance other than that my tooth hurt. Furthermore, if you were to witness my performance, not knowing anything about my dental history, you would take my utterance at face value, and regard it as expressing my present pain. And even when you begin to suspect that perhaps I am not actually in pain, you would not scrutinize my self-ascription for reasons or recognitional errors, any more than you would a painful sigh that I might have produced instead. In other words, you would still treat my utterance as though it were an avowal, except that you would retract the presumption that it is true, given what you now know about me.

---

[29] However, to identify the commonality in terms of trying is not thereby to accept that each act must separate into two independent parts: the trying part and the succeeding part.

Can you still regard my utterance as an expressive act? Think first of a non-linguistic analogue of the above case. For expressive mismatches are not the sole province of linguistic expressions. Instead of saying "My tooth hurts", I might have just winced or moaned, even though I was not in pain. Now, in discussing natural expressions in the last chapter, I suggested that to give natural expression to a mental state M is to engage in behavior sufficient to show it. Of course, if one is not in M, no behavior will suffice to show M, since M is not there to be shown; "show" is clearly a success verb, a feature that "express" can be seen to inherit from it. Still, we can recognize someone as having engaged in behavior that would suffice to show her M, *had* she been in M. Thus, when I moan, you could see me as sincerely engaging in behavior that would suffice to show my pain, but for the fact that I am not in pain. Though I will have failed to express my pain through my behavior, you can still see me as engaging in an expressive act. This, I think, can point us toward a way of preserving the idea that false avowals share in the expressive character of true avowals without compromising the earlier expressivist explanation of the presumption of truth governing them. If you have good reason to suppose I am *not* in pain, my sincere utterance "My tooth hurts" notwithstanding, then of course you will not regard my utterance as expressing *my* present pain; you will already have retracted the presumption of truth. But you can still see me as speaking my mind, *as opposed to* engaging in some other kind of act. You may still recognize me as speaking directly from a present condition, rather than issuing a self-report on some basis, or, alternatively, acting or trying to deceive. Though my act may have been unsuccessful, so it would be misleading to describe me as having expressed my pain, we can still cleave to the idea that my (false) self-ascription was produced in the course of avowing, as opposed to some other kind of act. Just as true present-tense mental self-ascriptions can be produced through all sorts of acts, so can false ones. Armed with distinctions I have provided throughout, I think we can capture the differences without appealing to the subject's false impressions or mistakes about her present state, and without giving up key aspects of the Neo-Expressivist explanation of avowals' security.

Earlier, I mentioned Wright's claim that phenomenal avowals, such as avowals of pain, thirst, etc., are "strongly authoritative": "If somebody understands such a claim, and is disposed sincerely to make it about themselves, that is a *guarantee of the truth* of what they say" (1998: 13, my emphasis). Wright, however, contrasts phenomenal avowals with "attitudinal avowals" (what I am calling "intentional avowals") on this score, for he claims that the latter are only "weakly authoritative". As evidence for the higher degree of vulnerability of intentional avowals he cites the fact that "there is space for relevant forms of self-deception or confusion", so that "sincerity-cum-understanding is no longer a guarantee of truth of even basic self-ascriptions of intentional states" (1998: 17). I think the kinds of case described above (at the dentist, at the fraternity initiation) give the lie to the claim that sincere, competent self-ascriptions of states such as pain are guaranteed to be true. In defense of the Neo-Expressivist construal of phenomenal avowals, I have denied that the possibility of false phenomenal avowals requires us to see the avowing subject who says something false as someone who has *gone* wrong, epistemically speaking. Now, I think the same line of defense is equally open in the case of false intentional avowals, the label "self-deception" notwithstanding. Thus, I want to take exception to Wright's explicit claim that there is a decisive difference between intentional avowals and phenomenal avowals in terms of the possibility of falsehood, and also to the implicit claim that the difference in some way poses a threat to a uniform expressivist account of avowals.

Consider, first, an instance of so-called wishful thinking: a father whose only son is lost in battle volunteers, "I am confident my son is still alive", in the face of all evidence that the son is dead. This kind of case, although it may involve something describable as confusion on the subject's part, does not lend support to Wright's claim; nor should it be regarded as posing any threat to the Neo-Expressivist account. For what we have here is not a case of a *false* avowal at all, but rather an avowal of a belief that is (most likely) false, and that was arrived at in a deviant way. Instead of being responsive to the evidence, the belief is driven, at least in part, by the subject's wishes. The expressivist account can easily accommodate this type of case. On my construal, recall, avowals can take over the role of *non-self-ascriptive expressions*. In the case of intentional avowals, the relevant non-self-ascriptive expressions would be ground-level expressions of, e.g., a belief, a thought, a want, a hope. These will often be verbal expressions: e.g., sincerely uttering (or thinking), "There's a red Buick!", "My poor aunt is on her way to Atlanta now", "Let me have that shirt", "Maybe the rain will stop by noon, so we can go out", respectively. In the present case of wishful thinking, the relevant non–self-ascriptive expression might be the utterance (or thought), "My son is definitely still alive". What we should bear in mind is that if the father is indeed a victim of wishful thinking, the non–self-ascriptive expression of his belief would be as much a product of the wish as his self-ascriptive "*I am confident* that my son is still alive". What is (deviantly) driven by a wish is the father's first-order state of believing his son is alive. If there is confusion of the father's part, it is to do with the process that leads to the formation of that (first-order) belief in him. The expressivist account is only saying that an avowal of the belief can be as much an expression of that first-order state itself as a non–self-ascriptive utterance that expresses it. It does not preclude the possibility of malformation of beliefs.

We are now ready to confront cases of so-called self-deception. Self-deception is different from wishful thinking, I take it, in that, in the cases relevant to us here—cases of avowing a present belief, desire, hope, etc.—the subject's confusion does lead to her making a false avowal. So, for instance, I say, "I find this painting very interesting", where (let us suppose) I do not really think anything like that. But I am not being insincere, or trying to deceive someone else. Rather, I am a victim of *self*-deception, as we put it, brought on by, say, some kind of social or personal pressure to think well of the painting. Here it may seem that we are forced into an epistemic explanation of the avowal's falsity: there are pressures on me to find the painting interesting, and that makes me judge wrongly that I find the painting interesting. If so, then the avowal should be seen as simply expressing a higher-order judgment that I have *erroneously formed* regarding my first-order state, and not my first-order state itself. I have made a mistake about my state, taking it to be one of finding the painting interesting, and the avowal reflects that mistake.

However, I think an alternative account of this case is possible, one that is perfectly in line with the expressivist understanding of avowals (i.e., with the idea that in avowing an intentional state, one is giving vent to a first-order intentional state, without having one's mental condition as an epistemic target on which one passes judgment). Indeed, this case can be accommodated on the expressivist account along the same lines offered in explaining how false phenomenal avowals are possible. To see this, notice again that in the case as described I would equally be prepared to offer a non-self-ascriptive expression; I would be equally inclined to say, "This painting is very interesting". Assuming I do not actually find the painting interesting, the non-self-ascriptive expression could not actually express *my* state of finding the painting interesting, though it does *semantically* express the thought that the painting is interesting. So my utterance would be just as much of an expressive failure. And it could equally be thought to be a product of self-deception.[30]

As an act, saying (or thinking), "I find his painting is very interesting", may be an expressive performance, without being successful. The act can fail. Since the expressive vehicle used may semantically express a state the subject is not in, as a matter of fact, expressive success is not guaranteed. A subject may be led to express herself by issuing self-ascription that fails to express a state she is in. A psychological explanation for such expressive failure may be readily available. At least in some cases of mismatched expression, it is plausible to suppose that it is in some way advantageous or helpful or comfortable for the subject to say and think certain things. What I don't think is plausible is to insist that the explanation *must* always be an epistemic one, invoking the basis on which the subject passes (or would pass) judgments about her present beliefs, desires, etc. In particular, it does not seem reasonable to take any *non*-self-ascriptive expression of the thought that the painting is interesting to be the upshot of my *judgment that* I find the painting interesting, any more than it is plausible to see the winces or cry of "Ouch!" by the person in the dentist's chair as the upshot of her intervening judgment that she is in pain. To treat all non-self-ascriptive expressions of mental states as underwritten by self-judgments would amount to denying that there can be direct expressions of mental states. Furthermore, it would have an unfortunate consequence for *epistemic* accounts of avowals; for such accounts portray avowals as *contrasting* with non-self-ascriptive utterances in virtue of being upshots of subjects' (especially secure)

---

[30] Could there be self-deception in thought? The idea would be that thinking, "This painting is very interesting", can fail to express one's finding the painting interesting; it could fail to be the upshot of that state, and be instead the upshot of the aforementioned pressures. If we think that this is problematic, we may be pushed to analyze putative self-deception in the way we analyzed wishful thinking, where we take the self-deceiver to have the avowed beliefs, desires, etc. but where we regard them as malformed.

judgments about their own present states. The (alleged) contrast would be lost if it turns out that non-self-ascriptive utterances, too, are such upshots.

I do not wish to deny that there is a genuine phenomenon of being confused or making an error *about* one's own mental states, even about one's own present state of mind. Sometimes we do undertake to survey our mental states and report our findings (to others or to ourselves). We can, in such cases, use a variety of methods, from clinical to deliberative or self-interpretive. And we can no doubt go wrong and consequently produce false mentalistic "I"-ascriptions. What I am denying is that every case in which one says (or thinks) something false about one's present state of mind must be treated as representing *epistemic* failure, due to misperception or other failures of recognitional self-judgment. I maintain that one can produce a false "I"-ascription of an intentional state in a genuine act of speaking one's mind. By way of supporting my position I have pointed out that one can even produce natural expressions—and, more generally, non-self-ascriptive expressions—which fail to express one's mental condition. And I suggested that cases of false avowals—whether phenomenal or intentional—could be understood on the model of such expressive mismatches. If this is so, then the possibility of false avowals, intentional or phenomenal, should not lead us to favor epistemic accounts over the Neo-Expressivist account advocated here.

Both the Cartesian view and the Simple Expressivist view deny the possibility of sincerely made, competent, yet false avowals. But, as we have seen, the possibility of such avowals can be readily appreciated once we see how expressive mismatches can arise, and do arise even in the case of natural expressions. Still, the Neo-Expressivist account can accommodate the intuition that there is a certain kind of mistake to which avowing subjects are not vulnerable: a *brute error* about the condition they are in. In this, avowals contrast with perceptual reports, including those based on proprioception or kinesthetic sense. A competent individual can be fooled into thinking that there is a cup in front of her, even when all her faculties are in perfect order. The world can simply play tricks on her, by presenting her with a perfect counterfeit. More fancifully, a subject's brain could also, unbeknownst to her, be so hooked up to someone else's legs that she would be caused to issue false "I"-reports on the position of her limbs, for example. But, it may be insisted that if a sincere, competent subject avows, "My tooth hurts!" when it doesn't, or "I really like this painting" when she doesn't, then there will always be some psychological explanation for the mismatch between her actual condition and the self-ascription she has produced.

It should be appreciated, however, that on the Neo-Expressivist account, if brute error is not possible, this is not because we are somehow guaranteed recognitional success, and are assured of never mistaking one mental state for another. Rather, it is because, in a sense I have explained earlier, the distinctively secure self-ascriptions we issue about our present mental states—our avowals—do not rest on 'judgments of appearances'. Though when I avow, my self-ascription can be false, its being false will not be due to my erroneously thinking that it is M I am in, though rightly thinking I am in some mental state or other. As I have construed it, my epistemic position when I avow is one in which I have no reason for thinking I am in some mental state, though perhaps not M, other than whatever reason I have for thinking I am in M.

Before concluding my discussion of expressive failure, I want to digress briefly in order to discuss a kind of *success* that may seem problematic for the Neo-Expressivist account. So far, I have considered only examples of avowals that affirm the presence of a mental state, ones involving self-ascriptions of the form "I am in M". But we often issue *negative* self-ascriptions. Suppose, looking at the sky, you volunteer, "I don't believe it's going to rain today". Or suppose, as you see me doing something, you say, "I don't think that is such a good idea". Or suppose, in response to my question, you say, "No, I'm not hungry". The worry here is that, on their face, these self-ascriptions seem to be issued just like avowals, not on the basis of observation, evidence, or inference, and they seem to share in the security of avowals. As in the case of false avowals, the subject is not in the mental state named by the self-ascription. But, unlike cases of false avowals, these negative self-ascriptions are true; they truly proclaim the absence of the relevant mental state. The question is how the Neo-Expressivist can explain the security of such self-ascriptions, and in particular the presumption that they are true, given that there is no relevant M for the subject to be speaking from (so, again, the subject cannot be said to have expressed *her* M). Like the question about false avowals, this too is a question that pertains to the scope of the Neo-Expressivist account. Just as we asked whether there can be genuine avowals that are false, so we can ask whether there can be genuine avowals that are 'negative' (i.e., avowals that proclaim the absence of a mental state). And in both cases, we want to understand why certain self-ascriptions are treated just like avowals when they may not be.

I do not think there are as good reasons to preserve the possibility of avowals of 'absent mental states' as there are reasons to preserve the possibility of false avowals. But first let me point out that many grammatically negative self-ascriptions are not self-ascriptions of absence but rather ascriptions of 'complementary' mental states. I would propose the following as the most natural readings of negative self-ascriptions offered in the 'avowing mode':

"I don't want to go" → "I'd like to stay/not to go";
"I don't like this" → "I dislike this";
"I don't think this will work" → "I think this won't work";
"I don't think so" → "I think not";
"I'm not feeling hungry" → "I'm feeling satiated";
"I don't believe $p$" → "I believe not-$p$".

I conjecture that spontaneously volunteered self-ascriptions that fit the characterization of avowals proper, even if containing a grammatical negation, will always likewise have readings on which they self-ascribe a present state rather than the absence of one. I think this is often true even of negative self-ascriptions offered in response to queries ("Are you feeling tired/nervous?"—"No, I am not". "Do you mind?"–"No, I don't").

Sometimes, a negative self-ascription is offered not by way of avowing the presence of a corresponding 'positive' state, but rather by way of avowing an 'indeterminate' state. For example, you may avow "I'm not sure about this" to express a present state of feeling uncertain or undecided about whatever "this" refers to. (Using some anecdotal evidence, it is not unreasonable to surmise that languages will differ in the extent to which they have simple lexical elements containing no negation to name various occurrent states.)[31]

---

[31] For example, in Hebrew it is more natural to answer "Are you hungry?" by offering the equivalent of "No, I am [satiated/full]" than it is to offer the equivalent of the negative "No, I am *not* hungry".

To get a genuine negative avowal, we would need to be forced to a reading on which the subject is denying that she is in M *simpliciter*. So, for example, the subject is asked, "Do you believe *p*?", and her answer "No, I don't believe *p*" has to be understood neither as an affirmation of not-*p*, nor as expressing hesitation or uncertainty regarding *p*, nor yet as expressing the belief that either *p* or not-*p* is the case. Or, the subject is asked, "Do you want/hope for *q*?" And her negative answer is to be understood simply as meaning that she has no desire or hope one way or the other (not, mind you, as expressing indifference). I suspect that actual cases fitting this bill will not be easy to find. But if we find them, I see no compelling intuitive reasons to regard them as avowals. If we imagine a case like this, we need not, of course, suppose that the subject bases her negative answer on some evidence or inference. The answer may seem as 'groundless' as in a genuine case of avowing, though clearly the subject will not be speaking from any present mental state, there being no such relevant mental state for her to speak from. If we wonder how the subject can confidently pronounce on the absence of the relevant state, we may, if we like, invoke introspection here. Asked whether she believes that *p*, or desires/hopes for *q*, the subject instantly surveys her present state of mind, and finds no belief that *p* or desire/hope for *q*. Neo-Expressivism doesn't require denying that we do sometimes employ genuine introspection as a mode of access to our present state of mind.

However, in such a case the resulting (negative) self-ascription—understood as simply affirming the absence of the named mental state—is best understood as a self-report of the subject's negative finding about her present state of mind. Such a self-report would *not* seem to share in the special security of avowals. It would seem open to doubt, questioning, requests for reasons/explanation, etc., much like proprioceptive self-reports, for example, and unlike the cases earlier described as false (but genuine) avowals. We may even presume such a self-report to be true. But, unlike in the case of genuine (and true) avowals, the presumption would obviously not be tied to our understanding of it as expressive of the subject's state. We *can* have a proper understanding of its character as an act while taking it to be false. I thus conclude that, while the Neo-Expressivist account should accommodate the possibility of false avowals, there is no reason for it to recognize the existence of genuinely negative avowals.

## Ascriptive Immunity, the Presumption of Truth, and First-Person Privilege

So far, my task has been to explain Epistemic Asymmetry while preserving Semantic Continuity. I believe that my construal of the distinctive security of avowals in terms of ascriptive immunity to error and an asymmetric presumption of truth allows us to understand why avowals are assigned the special status that has passed for indubitability, incorrigibility, and infallibility. But it does not do so by excluding avowals from the category of (true or) false utterances, as does the Simple Expressivist Account. Nor does it do so by taking the security of avowals to be due to the epistemic security of the self-judgments they represent, as epistemic accounts would have it. Rather, the Neo-Expressivist account of avowals defended here identifies a *non-epistemic* basis for the asymmetries between avowals and all other ascriptions, most notably, theoretically based mentalistic "I"-reports.

Note that there is no need for the Neo-Expressivist account to deny that subjects do enjoy various epistemic advantages over their observers. To be sure, when we undertake to report what goes on in our minds, great familiarity with the subject is on our side. We generally have more information about our mental lives than others possess about us, so we do not *need* to generate hypotheses, consult evidence, or draw inferences as much as others do. We often do not even need to look inside. Moreover, there is no reason to deny that we do possess an introspective faculty that allows us to look inside in cases where others are restricted to observing our behavior. Perhaps we *are* endowed with a Cartesian inner eye, or with a built-in brain-scanner! The present account only denies the explanatory benefits of appealing to whatever epistemic advantages we may have over our observers in explaining the relatively non-negotiable status of avowals.

In pointing out the limitations of epistemic views, I claimed that they are not able to answer adequately the following question: Why should it matter to the security of claims about some contingent matter of fact that they concern the *very person* issuing the statement, and that they refer to *occurrent mental states*? (see p. 122 above). It is with this question in mind that I set out to develop my non-epistemic Neo-Expressivist account of avowals' security. I believe we have now assembled the materials for answering this question more adequately. Avowals indeed tell of contingent matters of fact. An avowal says that an individual, *a*, is in some mental condition, M. And what it says, like any semantically equivalent pronouncement, *can* be either true or false. However, avowals are issued by the very person who is said to *be* in the relevant condition, at the very time she is said to be in it, in the course of *speaking her mind*. Speaking my mind is something I am in a unique position to do. Only I can express, or give voice to, *my own* present states of mind; and it is only states of my *mind* that I can express (in the relevant, non-semantic sense); for it is only in the case of such states that I can engage in behavior sufficient to show them.

So we are now in a position to identify a special first-person privilege of avowing subjects, a privilege that applies only to one's *occurrent mental* states which are *contemporaneous* with one's "I"-ascription. On the Neo-Expressivist account, first-person privilege is not a matter of privileged epistemic access to mental conditions. It is not a matter of epistemic credentials, authority, or expertise possessed by the self-ascriber or assessed by her audience. On the other hand, the account does not entail that first-person privilege is similar to the authority granted, e.g., to the performer of a naming ceremony or to the author of a promise—that is, the authority involved in bringing some state of affairs into existence. For the condition expressed by an avowal is not here portrayed as being of the self-ascriber's own making. First-person privilege, as construed here, is like 'performative' or legal authority in being granted, or assigned, to the self-ascriber when we consider her "I"-ascription in a certain way—as the product of an expressive performance. But it is like epistemic authority in relating the subject to an independently existing condition.[32]

This way of portraying first-person privilege has several advantages. First, we can see why avowals are not only more secure than third-person mental reports, but are also more secure than non-mental "I"-ascriptions, including those that are immune to error through misidentification. For avowals can also be said to enjoy ascriptive immunity to error. We can also see why avowals are more secure than certain mental present-tense "I"-ascriptions, notably

---

[32] The metaphysical issue regarding the ontological status of mental conditions and the degree to which they are independent of expressive behavior will be revisited in the final chapter.

alienated or theoretical "I"-ascriptions, which are arrived at on the basis of evidence, inference, etc. Given that such ascriptions are evidence- or theory-based, they will also not enjoy ascriptive immunity to error. It should be remarked, however, that first-person privilege is not something a subject forfeits as soon as she makes a reportive use of a present-tense mental "I"-ascription. I suggested that the expressive element characteristic of avowing extends beyond avowals proper. One may offer an "I"-ascription such as "I prefer to go to restaurant", upon reflection, in response to a query. Such reportive avowals will enjoy special security to the extent that we see their authors as (also) directly expressing a present condition. First-person privilege is forfeited only when a subject ceases to avow altogether, when she no longer speaks her mind, but talks about her mental conditions only as she might talk about the mental conditions of someone else.

Second, on the Neo-Expressivist account, first-person privilege is a privilege had by subjects in virtue of their capacity to express their present mental states in self-ascriptions of those states. As pointed out earlier, this means that the account can explain the remarkable fact that our special first-person privilege extends only to some aspects of our present mental lives. On my account, this fact is to be explained by the coinciding of what is avowable with what is expressible. The account correctly predicts that first-person privilege can be exercised only in issuing self-ascriptions that ascribe an expressible mental state to the subject.

It should be noted that construing the security of avowals in expressivist terms leaves room for considerable flexibility regarding the status of the various "I"-ascriptions that subjects are capable of producing. On the present account, the degree of special security assigned to an "I"-ascription (and the corresponding privilege assigned to its producer) correlates with the extent to which it can be taken to be a direct expression of the self-ascriber's condition. We regard an "I"-ascription as sharing in the distinctive security of avowals insofar as, and to the extent that, we regard it as expressive of the self-ascribed condition. At the most secure end of the spectrum we find avowals proper: spontaneous or reactive, unreflective self-ascriptive utterances or thoughts. By the same token, to the extent that we do not take an "I"-ascription to be a direct expression of the subject's condition, we may regard it as less secure. At the least secure end of the spectrum we find theoretical, or alienated, "I"-ascriptions, such as those based purely on what a therapist or a scientific study has taught one.

Finally, while the Neo-Expressivist account associates first-person privilege with subjects' expressive capacity, it does not require treating all exercises of this capacity as on a par. First-person privilege as construed here accrues to subjects who *speak* their mind; it does not extend to those who grimace and grunt. Though we will not take issue with the products of such acts of natural expression, we do not regard them as *true* self-pronouncements. Unlike the Simple Expressivist account, the Neo-Expressivist account does not purchase first-person privilege at the cost of portraying avowing subjects, unreasonably, as simply protected by grammar from making false self-ascriptions when they avow. By distinguishing the products of avowals from products of acts of natural expression, the account can preserve logico-semantic continuities between avowals and other ascriptions. At the same time, by portraying avowals as expressive acts with *self-ascriptive* products, the account can offer an explanation of the special presumption of truth that separates avowals from other linguistic expressive acts that have truth-assessable products. Most importantly, perhaps, as we shall see in the next chapter, the Neo-Expressivist account leaves it open that the exercise of first-person privilege can issue in genuine avowable self-knowledge.

## 9
# Speaking My Mind: Expression, Truth, and Self-Knowledge

In Chapter 1, I mentioned several desiderata that should be met by an adequate account of avowals' security (see p. 20). I believe I have shown so far how the Neo-Expressivist account does a better job than its competitors in explaining the distinctive, unparalleled security of avowals and the first-person privilege enjoyed by avowing subjects (thereby meeting desiderata D1–D4). The explanation provided by my account preserves the logico-semantic continuity of avowals with other ascriptions (desideratum D5), without requiring us to endorse the absolute infallibility or incorrigibility of avowals (desideratum D6), and while avoiding commitment to Cartesian dualist ontology (desideratum D7). In this chapter, I turn to the final desideratum on an adequate account of the special security of avowals:[1]

D8. It should allow for the possibility that avowals represent privileged self-knowledge.

On the Neo-Expressivist view offered in the previous chapters, the basic position from which a subject ascribes present mental states to herself is not, as the Epistemic Approach would have it, a perspective or a point of view *on* those states. Rather, it is the position of someone *in* various mental states, engaging in behavior that serves directly to express those states. Some of the behavior becomes supplemented, and sometimes supplanted, by verbal expressions ranging from inarticulate exclamations, such as "Ouch!", to articulate "I"-ascriptions, such

---

[1] Portions of this chapter are based on a joint paper with Douglas Long (2003). However, at several points in the chapter I offer my present take on self-knowledge, which may not be entirely shared by Long.

as "I have a terrible migraine!" Though the articulate "I"-ascription, in virtue of its form and meaning, *can* be used by the self-ascriber in a 'third-person mode', for purposes of issuing a theoretical report on some condition of hers, it is most typically offered and treated as a first-person expression of the condition itself. Thus, the special first-person privilege enjoyed by avowing subjects turns out not to be due to the fact that they are in a better position to obtain *knowledge of* their own present minds. Rather, it is due to the fact that avowing subjects are uniquely capable of ascribing various current mental conditions to themselves in the course of speaking from those conditions. But this gives rise to the question: *Do* we have a special form of self-knowledge which avowals represent? In this chapter, I will try to show how the Neo-Expressivist account can meet desideratum D8, by sketching several substantive accounts of self-knowledge that are consistent with it.[2] Filling out the sketch will be left for future work.

## Secure Avowals and Self-Knowledge

The Neo-Expressivist account of avowals' security was designed to answer the question

(i)  What accounts for the *unparalleled security of avowals*? Specifically, why is it that avowals, understood as true or false ascriptions of contingent states to an individual, are so rarely questioned or corrected, are generally so resistant to ordinary epistemic assessments, and are so strongly presumed to be true?

In developing an expressivist answer to this question, I made considerable efforts to show that seeing avowals as performances that serve to express subjects' first-order mental conditions does not preclude regarding them as genuine true or false sayings which ascribe the expressed conditions to particular individuals. These efforts were made with an eye to removing a major source of resistance to traditional expressivist accounts of avowals: namely, that expressivist accounts must fall foul of Semantic Continuity. I have also offered an

---

[2] For a summary of how the Neo-Expressivist account meets all the desiderata, see the opening section of Ch. 10.

answer to the question of why avowals are so strongly presumed to be true, as well as protected from various epistemic errors. However, since the answer did not invoke an especially secure way that avowing subjects have of obtaining knowledge about themselves, the explanation I offered falls short of providing a positive answer to question (ii):

(ii) Do avowals serve to articulate *privileged self-knowledge*? If so, what qualifies avowals as articles of knowledge at all, and what is the source of the privileged status of this knowledge?[3]

The following challenge may, then, be presented to my view. On the Neo-Expressivist view, though avowals are semantically continuous with other ascriptions, they still belong in a class of performances that cannot be regarded as *epistemically* continuous with other classes of ascriptions. Even if avowals are truth-assessable pronouncements (and even when true), *qua* direct expressions of subjects' first-order mental states, they cannot be taken to articulate things we genuinely know about ourselves, and, *ipso facto*, they do not represent a privileged kind of knowledge that we have. I shall refer to this as the *deflationist challenge*, since we can see it as claiming that my view, like other expressivist views of the security of avowals, must pay the price of embracing a *deflationary* view about self-knowledge, to wit:

To the extent that avowals are seen as expressive performances protected from doubt and epistemic correction because made on no epistemic basis, they cannot represent *any* kind of knowledge, let alone an especially secure form of knowledge.

There may be various reasons (social? pragmatic?) why we dignify ordinary mental self-ascriptions with the title "self-*knowledge*". But, on the deflationary view, they do not really deserve this title. Consider for example my rejection, in Chapter 5, of the recognitional conception of self-knowledge, which was in aid of showing that our ordinary self-ascriptions of content (and of mental states) are secure against skeptical alternatives. It might be thought that recognition (broadly understood) is our best model for non-theoretical knowledgeable telling, at least as far as knowledge of empirical matters of

---

[3] See Ch. 1, where I distinguished between (i) and (ii), as well as a further question (iii) ("Avowals aside, what allows us to possess privileged self-knowledge?"), which will be discussed later on.

fact is concerned. The deflationist challenge enjoins us to say what, in the absence of recognition, could possibly allow my self-ascriptions of content to constitute a kind of knowledge about my present states at all, let alone a highly secure and privileged kind of knowledge. If avowals do not rest on any legitimate method of obtaining substantive knowledge concerning the relevant facts, how can they represent genuine self-knowledge? Yet the Neo-Expressivist story as told so far does not tell us why we should think of avowals as representing not only truths about subjects' mental lives, but also things of which they have real knowledge.

Knowledge of oneself can be gained in a variety of ways. People often learn things about themselves by observing how they behave in various situations: everyday or contrived situations, even ones set up by psychological experimenters. One can also gain self-knowledge by talking to other people and seeing oneself reflected in their comments and attitudes. For example, you may not realize how conceited you are until someone points it out to you, or until you see their reactions to your conduct. You will then gain self-knowledge or self-understanding that you lacked before. Some forms of therapy may work by teaching one how to internalize various methods of learning about oneself. Knowledge obtained in these ways, it seems, could be equally (and sometimes even more easily) obtained by others, since others can observe, or gain various kinds of access to, what another person says and does.

However, avowals have traditionally been thought to articulate a different kind of self-knowledge—I've referred to it as "basic self-knowledge"—which is especially secure and uniquely limited to the first-person perspective. For present purposes, I want to recall two contrasting views of basic self-knowledge: the Cartesian introspective view and the Simple Expressivist view. On the Cartesian view, we do have substantive basic self-knowledge, which is privileged because underwritten by a special kind of epistemic access. By contrast, on the Simple Expressivist view, what we take to represent our special basic self-knowledge—our everyday avowals—are simply glorified replacements of natural expressions. Whereas when you say of me, "She has a toothache", you are making a genuine ascription of a state to a particular individual, when I utter, "I have a toothache", I do something that is epistemically on a par with grimacing or holding my cheek. The avowal no more represents a piece of knowledge I have about myself than does the grimace.

As I see them, the Cartesian and the Simple Expressivist views both rely on the following presupposition:

If I can be said to have privileged knowledge that I am in a certain state of mind, then this knowledge must have some *distinct epistemic basis*; there must be a special epistemic method or route (a special 'way of knowing') that I use to obtain this knowledge.

The Cartesian takes it as non-negotiable that we do have privileged (basic) self-knowledge. Impressed by the secure character of this knowledge, he searches for a special, infallible method that we have for obtaining it. The proponent of the Simple Expressivist view, on the other hand, seizes on the fact that avowals are as resistant as natural expressions to epistemic assessment (e.g., to questions of *how* we know, to requests for reasons or justification, to doubt, etc.), and ends up denying that avowals can be candidates for knowledge any more than natural expressions. As we shall see, the Distinct Epistemic Basis presupposition (as I shall refer to it) is inherited by contemporary successors of the Cartesian and the Simple Expressivist accounts.[4]

In my attempt to answer question (i), I have denied that explaining avowals' special security requires invoking an especially secure way of knowing, or an especially secure epistemic basis on which avowals are made. Indeed, the Simple Expressivist account mentioned earlier provides a prime example of an explanation that clearly avoids doing so; it thus provides a non-epistemic answer to (i). But answering question (ii), which is about whether avowals represent privileged self-knowledge, directly calls for an epistemic answer, in that it demands an explicitly epistemological investigation as to what (if anything) qualifies avowals as representing genuine knowledge, and what (if anything) renders this knowledge privileged. We can see the Cartesian as beginning with question (ii), which is concerned directly with the status of self-knowledge. Having identified a special epistemic

---

[4] I think, though I cannot elaborate on it here, that this presupposition is behind the recognitional conception discussed at some length in Ch. 5. Given the presupposition, there is strong pressure on anyone impressed by the security of avowals to seek some distinctive epistemic method available to subjects for obtaining reliable (even if not infallible) information about their present mental states. Inner recognition, which works through a perception-like mechanism, or else through some other form of detection or tracking, is supposed to fit this bill.

route—in terms of the privileged introspective access—which we each possess to our present states of mind, the Cartesian can go on to represent avowals as articulating self-judgments grounded in the exercise of this special way of knowing, thereby offering an epistemic answer to (i). The proponent of the Simple Expressivist account, by contrast, can be seen as aiming, in the first place, to explain the special security of avowals as a class of performances. She sets out to answer question (i) first, and offers a non-epistemic answer to it. However, since she shares with the Cartesian the Distinct Epistemic Basis presupposition, but thinks that avowals' security is underwritten by grammar, rather than by any special epistemic basis, she is moved to give a negative answer to question (ii). She thus ends up with a deflationary view of self-knowledge, denying that avowals articulate a privileged kind of self-knowledge.

In the next section, I shall consider a more sophisticated grammatical account of avowals that is also deflationary regarding self-knowledge. For the record, I think that the Neo-Expressivist account I have presented *can* be coupled with a deflationary view of self-knowledge. However, I will be arguing that, although the Neo-Expressivist account of avowals' security, like grammatical accounts, offers a non-epistemic answer to question (i), it does not preclude non-deflationary views of self-knowledge, since it leaves room for a positive, substantive answer to (ii). Nothing in the Neo-Expressivist account, I shall argue, entails that we do not possess avowable knowledge—even privileged knowledge—of our present states of mind. If this seems paradoxical, it is due to the unquestioned acceptance of the Distinct Epistemic Basis presupposition mentioned earlier (which is the claim that where there is special knowledge, there must be an especially secure epistemic method of obtaining it, so that in the absence of such a method there could be no privileged knowledge for avowals to articulate). Once this presupposition is rejected, it becomes possible to combine a non-epistemic account of avowals' security, such as the Neo-Expressivist account, with a non-deflationary view of self-knowledge. Since I take it that such a view ought to explain what makes avowals especially apt to represent judgments that are both true and epistemically warranted, I shall later sketch several such accounts, which I take to be consistent with the Neo-Expressivist account of avowals' security.

## Self-Knowledge: A Deflationary View

On what I have called the Epistemic Approach, recall, a subject's avowals represent the subject's higher-order judgments about her independently existing, first-order mental states. These judgments enjoy a high degree of *epistemic* security, since they are arrived at through the exercise of a highly secure epistemic method, or are made on a highly secure epistemic basis.[5] An avowal represents, as Crispin Wright puts it, a genuine "cognitive achievement, based on cognitive privilege" that subjects enjoy; and this privilege can, in turn, explain "first-person authority" (1998: 42). On an alternative proposal, which Wright attributes to Wittgenstein, there is no legitimate explanatory project connected with so-called first-person authority. There are indeed first- third-person asymmetries; but these "belong primitively to the 'grammar' of the language-game of ordinary psychology". The fact that psychological discourse exhibits these features should simply be regarded as part of what makes it *psychological* discourse (1998: 41 f.). On the alternative account, then, the special status enjoyed by avowals is not due to the special nature of the states they ascribe (viz., mental, as opposed to non-mental), or the special epistemic relation between subjects and their own mental states. Rather, it is "a *constitutive principle*" of mentalistic discourse, which "enters primitively into the conditions of identification" of the subject's mental states.

Later, Wright expounds the proposal in terms of the *truth-conditions* of mentalistic ascriptions. The truth-conditions of such ascriptions are governed by a special constraint, which Wright formulates as follows: "unless you can show how to make better sense of her by overriding or going beyond it, [a subject's] active self-conception, as manifest in what she is willing to avow, must be deferred to" (1998: 41). Mastery of the semantics of mentalistic ascriptions, on the present proposal, requires recognizing that, unless there are good reasons to the contrary, one must accept what a subject is willing to avow, and only make ascriptions to her in accordance with what she herself is willing

---

[5] The method may be an absolutely infallible form of inner perception, as on the Cartesian view, or just a highly reliable kind of tracking (perceptual or not) as on materialist introspectionist views. Indeed, it could bypass introspection altogether, as proposed on Evans's Transparency view (see Ch. 4).

to avow. Wright dubs this the "Default View", since it presents "a subject's opinions about herself" as "default authoritative and default limitative" (1998: 41).[6]

The Default View takes the practice of psychological ascription to provide a kind of bedrock in accounting for asymmetries between avowals and other ascriptions. On this view, the presumed truth of avowals and the fact that they are not subject to ordinary epistemic assessment are to be regarded as simply a product of the facts about the concepts involved. The default status of avowals is part of what fixes our concepts of mental states; it is not a product of non-conceptual facts about subjects' mental life or their relationships to their mental states. Mentalistic ascriptions are all ultimately answerable to the subject's own avowals *because this is how mental concepts work*. This is the sense in which the Default View presents the epistemic asymmetries between avowals and other ascriptions as a consequence of logical grammar, rather than substantive epistemological differences. At the same time, the Default View, unlike the Simple Expressivist view, can accommodate the semantic continuities between mental ascriptions to oneself and to others. For there is nothing in the Default View as described so far to stand in the way of taking the surface grammar similarities between these two types of ascriptions at face value. For example, nothing seems to stand in the way of taking my self-ascription "I am in pain" as sharing truth-conditions with your ascription "She is in pain".

The Default View offers a clear contrast between mentalistic ascriptions and other ascriptions. But, on its face, it seems at risk of severing certain continuities between ascriptions of mental states and ascriptions of other kinds of states to subjects. For the view presents our practices of mentalistic ascription as ultimately "not accountable to any reality" (1998: 39) in a way that, presumably, our ascriptions of, e.g., height, weight, distance, etc. to subjects would (or at any rate should) not be. But this may just highlight the way in which the Default View chooses to capture the unique status of mentalistic self-ascriptions. And it remains to be seen whether any view that succeeds

---

[6] Wright presents the Default View in his (1989), (1991), and (1998). Note that it is not obvious how the above constraint captures the *truth*-conditions of avowals, as opposed to describing our practice of *accepting* them as true. (Thanks to Dylan Sabo here.) It would take some work, and quite possibly a contentious view of meaning, to link the fact that the linguistic practices surrounding avowals are governed by the constraint with the conditions under which avowals are true.

in adequately capturing the perceived asymmetries between mental and physical self-ascriptions could avoid severing this kind of continuity between mental and other ascriptions in a similar way.[7]

However, it is not clear how well the Default View is equipped to capture the crucial epistemic asymmetries between first- and third-person ascriptions. Wright suggests that this is achieved through building the (default) correctness of first-person ascriptions into the truth-conditions of mentalistic ascriptions by definition, or "primitively" (as he puts it). But note that this means that mentalistic discourse *as a whole* is constrained by a default assumption that accords special authority to present-tense mental "I"-ascriptions. The constraint is presented as a global constraint that is built into mentalistic discourse in virtue of some constitutive features of mentalistic concepts. But such a conceptual constraint, while it may reflect a crucial contrast between mental and non-mental concepts, does not seem by itself capable of telling us in what ways mental present-tense "I"-ascriptions differ from *other mental ascriptions*—specifically, ascriptions of mental states to others, or to oneself at other times, and most notably, evidential present-tense "I"-ascriptions. After all, all such ascriptions use mental concepts; so they would be equally governed by the constraint (though the consequences of the constraint may be different for different ascriptions). We still need to hear what makes applications of mental concepts in one's *own* case in the *present tense* and in a *non-evidential* way special. An account that builds first-person authority into the truth-conditions of *all* mental ascriptions seems too glib to capture that contrast, which arises *within* mentalistic discourse, and, intuitively, seems sensitive not only to the semantic content of avowals but also to the special way in which they are issued.

In offering the Default View as an alternative with the Cartesian view, Wright is partially motivated by an analogy with other areas of discourse where it seems misguided to conceive of successful judgments as tracking a completely independent reality—e.g., color judgments, and, on some views, ethical judgments. In these areas, Wright thinks that it may be explanatory to suppose that there is *judgment-dependence*: what is true about an object's color, for example, may not be entirely independent of the color judgments of a well-placed

---

[7] See Ch. 10 below.

perceiver. Similarly, he suggests, what is true of a subject's mental state may not be independent of a subject's own judgments at the time she is in the mental state.[8] This is what the default assumption is designed to capture. However, in these other cases we do not find the variability in the security of the judgments reflected in the first-person/third-person asymmetries. In the case of mental ascriptions, it makes a difference *who* ascribes M to S (as well as when and in what way). What calls for explanation in the case of avowals is (partly) the contrast between a subset of the mental "I"-ascriptions (avowals) and other mental ascriptions. To cite the dependence of mentalistic facts on the *subject's own* judgments is just to reiterate the contrast, not to provide an account of it. This becomes especially clear when we consider that among the asymmetries we have noted is one that arises *within* the class of mental "I"-ascriptions. We have seen that avowals enjoy more security than alienated, or theoretical, mental "I"-ascriptions. But the notion of judgment-dependence offered by Wright in expounding the Default View does not seem apt to explain or even capture this asymmetry.

A proponent of the Default View may object that the above complaint misses the point. The whole idea behind the view is to deny that there is any substance to the idea of first-person authority, anything 'behind' the special status assigned to avowals, beyond the conventions of mentalistic discourse. If so, the above complaint simply serves to expose how radical—and ultimately unsatisfactory—the Default View really is. To adopt the Default View is to deny that "the features of avowals . . . which seem to betray something remarkable about self-knowledge" reflect any deeper facts about the subject matter of avowals, or subjects' relationship to it (Wright 1998: 39). The view is that there is nothing *to* explain concerning the special security of avowals. We can note the security as marking a constitutive feature of mentalistic discourse; but it is futile to try to offer a substantive explanation of it. If so, then the answer offered by the Default View to question (i), regarding the special security of avowals, like the answer offered by the Simple Expressivist account, is a purely grammatical answer (and a less satisfying one at that, since it makes nothing of the correct, expressivist insight of that account). And, like the

---

[8] I return to the comparison in Ch. 10.

Simple Expressivist account, the Default View adopts a negative answer to question (ii) and a thoroughgoing deflationary view of self-knowledge. To accept the Default View is to deny that avowals are apt to represent a special kind of knowledge deserving the epithet "privileged self-knowledge" that can be articulated by avowals. Thus, as Wright himself remarks in criticism of the view, adopting the Default View may be nothing more than "merely an unphilosophical turning of the back" on issues surrounding avowals and self-knowledge (1998: 41).[9]

## No Cognitive Achievement

Deflationary views of self-knowledge are sometimes introduced as putting forth the claim that mental self-ascriptions that are ordinarily considered authoritative do not involve any *cognitive achievement*, and are thus not candidates for privileged self-knowledge. Both the Simple Expressivist account we considered earlier (see Chapter 6) and the Default View discussed above would seem to qualify. What does it mean to say that there is no cognitive achievement involved in self-knowledge?

Elizabeth Fricker (1998: 173) offers the following as one reading of the 'no cognitive achievement' claim:

NCA1 It is not the case that veridical self-knowledge is an 'achievement' in that it is the upshot of something which the person can do, or try to do, an effort of some kind which she may make, in order to achieve it.

Under things a person can do, Fricker lists the making of an inference, or an observation, or a judgment, based on attending to one's experience. As an example of beliefs that do not involve cognitive achievement in this sense, she cites beliefs that one simply finds oneself with. (An *idiot savant*'s beliefs about mathematical products or the dates of events may qualify as prime examples.)

---

[9] For further discussion of the Default View, see Boghossian (1989); McDowell (1998); Bilgrami (1998); and Moran (2001). Fricker (1998) distinguishes Wright's proposed Default View from a view she calls "the Pure Artefact of Grammar Theory", which she argues can be ruled out of court. It is not clear to me that the "impure" view, when spelled out to answer various pertinent questions, will not in the end collapse into the pure view. (Fricker may not disagree.) I return to the Default View briefly later on, in Ch. 10 (pp. 410 ff.).

SPEAKING MY MIND: EXPRESSION, TRUTH 351

As a blanket claim intended to apply to *all* true present-tense mentalistic self-ascriptions, NCA1 is implausibly strong. Surely, at least sometimes we make substantive claims about ourselves using self-ascriptions. We do sometimes obtain psychological self-knowledge, even concerning present mental states, just as we obtain such knowledge about others; and what better way to articulate it than by present-tense mentalistic self-ascriptions? This point can also be pressed by noting that NCA1 is presumably designed to capture a significant contrast between mental self- and other-knowledge. But to do so, NCA1 would have to be coupled with the claim that things we say (or think) about others' mental states *can* represent cognitive achievements on our part, and *can* amount to genuine knowledge. But if so, then, given the interchangeability of third-person present-tense ascriptions of mental states with first-person ones, we may ask: *Why* is it that a subject cannot put herself in an epistemic position analogous to that of others (as well as herself at other times) with respect to her present condition? Or, to put the problem in more ontological terms, if there is an objective state of affairs which constitutes my being in the relevant mental state at a given moment, why is it that I, in contrast to others, and even to myself at other times, am peculiarly barred from obtaining knowledge about it at the time it occurs, by making an appropriate cognitive effort that would yield a knowledgeable description or report of it?

The Neo-Expressivist account is not committed to NCA1 understood as applicable to all present-tense mentalistic self-ascriptions, since it recognizes the existence of genuine mentalistic self-reports (viz., reports of one's present state of mind arrived at on the basis of, e.g., therapy, general scientific findings, or deliberate self-interpretation). Such reports are not only interchangeable with third-person reports about oneself, they are also answerable to evidence, revisable, and sensitive to theoretical considerations. Like their third-person counterparts, self-reports can straightforwardly represent cognitive achievements and are clear candidates for genuine knowledge. But perhaps NCA1 should be understood as a more restricted and less radical claim that concerns what I have earlier called *basic* self-knowledge, the kind of knowledge allegedly represented by avowals. The claim would be that there really is no such thing as genuine basic self-*knowledge*, since avowals do not represent any cognitive achievement. But even this claim may seem too strong. Consider what I have described as reportive avowals. Suppose someone asks me, concerning my recently injured arm, "How does your arm feel now?" or "What would you prefer, coffee or tea?" I may need to refocus my attention to be able to respond. My answers to these questions: "I can still feel a mild ache", or "I'd like some tea please", would not represent spontaneously volunteered avowals proper. Still, on my Neo-Expressivist account, I could be seen as avowing, and my answers could be regarded as immune to ascriptive error and governed by an asymmetric presumption of truth, to the extent that they can be seen as directly 'giving vent' to my present condition. However, non-evidential, reportive avowals do involve "an effort of some kind" made by the subject "in order to achieve" them. So at least in that sense they can be seen as representing cognitive achievement, *contra* NCA1.

What about avowals proper? I run into you on the street, and I exclaim, "I'm so happy to see you!" or, coming back from a run, I say, "I'm *so* thirsty!" as I reach for a glass of water, or, as we are both sitting quietly, I suddenly volunteer, "I'm thinking about what happened to Jenny last night". The mark of such avowals is that they seem to 'bring to the surface' one's present mental states, with an immediacy and epistemic directness equal to those of naturally expressive acts. But, as emphasized in previous chapters, this similarity to natural expression does not imply semantic similarity between the products of avowals proper and natural expressions. The product of an avowal proper is an articulate, acquired, verbal expression. The mature avower, who initially acquired the verbal expression "I want ice cream" as a simple replacement for the gesture of reaching for the ice cream, has to have mastered the grammatical, logical, and epistemological machinery required for competent application of the component concepts. Moreover, the avower of a belief, for example, has to satisfy the necessary conditions for *having* the belief she avows, and, *qua* believer, she is subject to rational criticism. These are all cognitive achievements necessary for fully competent self-ascription.

Still, it is true that, on the Neo-Expressivist view, at least avowals proper do not involve the subject's own direct attempt to gain or convey information about her present mental state. The mental state she ascribes to herself, I have said, is not an epistemic target for her. The products of such acts can convey information about the subject's state of mind. But *qua* expressions of the subject's first-order present mental states, they do not represent any effort on the subject's part to get things right. Moreover, the cognitive achievements we just spoke of belong on the side of general prerequisites (for example, mastery of the concepts involved in the self-ascription is necessary for making a competent self-ascription in the first place). They are not the result of the subject's attempt to recognize, identify, or ascertain the presence and character of the *specific* condition she ascribes to herself.

However, if avowing involves no cognitive achievement in that sense, this does not entail that avowals do not represent any *epistemic* achievement. That one has made no cognitive effort to obtain information about oneself does not entail that one's self-ascription must be epistemically ungrounded, no better than a lucky shot in the dark. Thus, accepting this reading of NCA1 does not by itself commit one to a startling, deflationary view of self-knowledge. (What, if anything, may qualify avowals as representing epistemic achievements is something that will occupy us in the next section.)

Now, Fricker (1998: 173) offers another reading of the 'no-cognitive-achievement' claim:

NCA2 It is not the case that a person's first-level mental states and her judgements self-ascribing them are ontologically distinct states, and that the second reliably track the first.

I have already mentioned the temptation to associate all expressivist views of mental self-ascriptions with an implication that there simply are no independently existing mental states of subjects to ground the cognitive success *or* failure of mental self-ascriptions. I have mentioned that ethical expressivism typically couples the claim that ethical utterances express subjects' pro- and con-attitudes with ethical 'non-cognitivism'—the claim that there are no genuinely cognitive ethical judgments which concern independently existing ethical states of affairs.[10] The expressivist claim in this case is offered as an *alternative* to a seemingly tempting cognitivist construal of ethical discourse, which supposedly incurs unwanted ontological commitments. By contrast, the Neo-Expressivist view deploys the idea of expression, in the first instance, in order to deny that avowals represent subjects'

---

[10] For a recent example of construing expressivism about mental self-ascriptions in this way, see Jacobsen (1996).

special way of *knowing about* their own mental conditions. There is no reason to saddle the view with the ontological denial, or with the intention of uprooting all cognitivist understanding of mentalistic discourse. If avowals turn out not to represent genuine knowledge on the Neo-Expressivist view, this will only be because it turns out that regarding avowals as acts expressive of self-ascribed conditions leaves no room for the right epistemic relation between avowing subjects and the conditions they avow, not because the view casts doubt on the ontological status of the mental conditions themselves.[11]

Nothing in the Neo-Expressivist account requires it to endorse NCA2. NCA2 maintains an ontological dependence between a subject's first-level mental states and her higher-order *judgments about* those states. But it is no part of the Neo-Expressivist view to maintain such dependence. On this view, one can *be* in a certain mental condition without *judging* that one is. The case of natural expressions illustrates this possibility; for ordinarily we don't suppose that a subject who gives natural expression to her present condition thereby expresses her present judgment that she is in the condition (or even necessarily makes one). Though I have left it open that avowals, unlike natural expressions, *may* express the subjects' self-judgments in addition to expressing their self-ascribed conditions, I can still consistently maintain that being in a mental state does not *require* that the subject make the judgment that she is in it.[12] I can also consistently maintain that someone may judge that she is in a mental state without actually being in that state. For one thing, one can surely reach a false conclusion, based on misleading evidence, regarding one's present mental states. But even if we take it that all avowals express self-judgments, in addition to expressing the self-ascribed states, I have allowed that one can issue a false avowal, and so make a false self-judgment, due to expressive, rather than epistemic, failure. Judging that one is in pain, or believes that it's raining, or wants ice cream does not make it so. So the

---

[11] As suggested earlier (see Ch. 7, p. 239), there is something odd if not self-defeating, about the analogue of the non-cognitivist claim in the case of mental self-ascriptions. Are we to accept that there really are no independent mental states (sensations, emotions, attitudes) that we can genuinely ascribe to people, and yet mental ascriptions serve to express our attitudes?

[12] From this it does not follow that the relevant mental state cannot be a conscious one. This would only follow on the (in my opinion, controversial) assumption that a state's being conscious is a matter of one's having a higher-order judgment about the mental state. For a defense of this assumption, see, e.g., Rosenthal (1986). The assumption entails that a creature incapable of higher-order judgments about her present states will not have conscious states, which seems highly unintuitive to me. (I return to the issue of judgment-independence in the next chapter.)

view of avowals I have defended here is consistent with the notion that "a person's first-level mental states and her judgements self-ascribing them are ontologically distinct states", contrary to NCA2.

It may be thought that while the Neo-Expressivist view can consistently allow the ontological independence of mental states from self-judgments, it must be committed to some ontological dependence between mentality and expressive behavior. Indeed, expressivist proposals are often understood as reflecting a certain kind of behaviorist irrealism about mental states. Whether or not this association is warranted is something I leave for the next chapter. For now, I want to register that, as I understand it, the 'no cognitive achievement' claim concerns the epistemology of self-ascriptions, whereas the 'no independent existence' claim concerns the ontology of mental states. While the Neo-Expressivist view *may* be committed to the epistemological 'no cognitive achievement' claim NCA1, it rejects the ontological claim NCA2. The view has been developed with an eye to allowing the independent reality of mental states. Furthermore, it is intended to be compatible with the possibility of robust knowledge of such states, even by the subject who is in those states.

## Knowing What Mental State You Are In

As expressions of subjects' mental states, avowals are not performances appropriately subjected to epistemic assessment, yet they can serve as an especially articulate source of reliable information about subjects' present conditions. If a subject *is* in the state she ascribes to herself in an avowal, so that her avowal is true, we can take it that an observer who has understood the avowal will have gained knowledge of the subject's present condition. This tells us something about the epistemic situation on the *consumer* side of things. But it does not by itself afford an answer to question (ii) above, which concerns *self*-knowledge. Could avowing subjects themselves be credited with genuine knowledge about their present states of mind? If so, what makes such knowledge privileged? One can acknowledge that we have a distinctive ability to produce secure mental self-ascriptions, without thereby accepting that the exercise of this ability is apt to yield any kind of knowledge. For one can maintain that possessing genuine knowledge requires more than the production of true self-ascriptions that enjoy expressive security. This is just another way of raising the deflationist challenge presented earlier in the chapter (see p. 342).

In Chapter 5, I argued that we can see our way clear to a rebuttal of a certain kind of skepticism about ordinary self-knowledge, if we reject the recognitional conception of self-knowledge and replace it with an alternative non-recognitional conception. Toward offering such an alternative, I recalled Evans's and Shoemaker's analysis of judgments that are immune to error through misidentification. As a brief reminder, on their analysis, judgments such as "I am sitting down", or "My legs are crossed", when made in the normal way, are *immune to error through misidentification*. Though the relevant "I"-ascription can be false, there is no room for an error on my part of misidentifying the subject of my ascription, of wrongly taking someone else to be me. You might ask: What about counterfeits? Couldn't it be that, for all I know, it is my identical twin who is sitting down? Well, that possibility would seem entirely irrelevant to an assessment of the judgment I've made, given that I do not tell that it is me who is sitting down by telling myself apart from other candidates. I can falsely judge that I am sitting down. But, since in the normal case, my "I"-ascription does not rest on my recognition of myself as the individual who is sitting down, there seems to be no room for a reasonable doubt on my part as to whether it is indeed me, rather than someone else (whom I misidentify as me), who is sitting down. Nor is there room for asking me why I think, or how I know, that I am the one sitting down. For, in the normal case, I would have no reason for thinking that someone (though perhaps not me) is sitting down that is independent of whatever reason I have for thinking that *I* am sitting down.

Neither Shoemaker nor Evans is inclined to deny that, when issuing a self-ascription that is immune to error in this way, I do have knowledge of the relevant fact (viz., that *I* am sitting down). Although my self-ascription does not rest on a recognitional judgment to the effect that it is I, as opposed to someone else, who am sitting down, the self-ascription can still represent something I know *about myself*. How can that be? Evans notes that we possess two general capacities for gaining information about some of *our own* states and properties. First, we possess "a general capacity to perceive our own bodies" (which includes "our proprioceptive sense, our sense of balance, of heat and cold, and pressure"), and second we also have a capacity for determining our own "position, orientation, and relation to other objects in the world . . . upon the basis of our perceptions of the world" (1982: 220, 222). It is the exercise of these capacities that gives rise to judgments that are immune to errors through misidentification. For, when a subject gains information that he himself is F (for the relevant range of Fs) in one of these ways,

[T]here just does not appear to be a gap between the subject's having information (or appearing to have information), in the appropriate way, that the property of being F is instantiated, and his having information (or appearing to have information) that *he* is F; for him to have, or to appear to have, the information that the property is instantiated just is for it to appear to him that *he* is F. (1982: 221)

For this reason, when an "I"-statement is arrived at in the appropriate way, it will make no sense to wonder: "Someone may be F, but is it I who am F?" ("Someone's legs are crossed, but is it my legs that are crossed?"; "Someone is moving, but is it I?"). Evans denies that the possibility of error of such "I"-ascriptions, even an error regarding *who* is F, is sufficient to show that, in 'non-deviant' cases, my claim to know that I am F would have to be supported by my (correct) recognitional identification of myself as the individual who is F (1982: 221). True, if, unbeknownst to me, my brain is hooked up to your nervous system, so that I get proprioceptive information about your legs, rather than mine, I may judge "My legs are crossed" when it's actually *your* legs that are crossed. But I think that, on Evans's view, though my "I"-ascription in such a case would be false regarding the subject, I would still not be victim of an error of *misidentification*. And the possibility of such falsehood should not lead us to regard my "I"-ascription as epistemically grounded in an identification judgment. For even in the case imagined, I would still have no reason for thinking that *someone's* legs are crossed that is independent of my reason for thinking (albeit falsely) that *my* legs are crossed. My "I"-ascription in such a case will be false (and thus will not constitute knowledge); but it will still enjoy a certain measure of epistemic security.

If we accept the above analysis, then we have an interesting and powerful model of epistemically secure self-ascriptions that will be useful in understanding the *epistemic* status of avowals. This model is marked by the following features of certain self-ascriptions:

(i) Though not absolutely infallible, they are *immune to a certain kind or error and doubt* (concerning the identity of the subject of ascription).

(ii) When true, they can potentially represent *knowledge* that something is the case (viz., that *I* am F).

(iii) The relevant knowledge is *non-recognitional*, in the sense that it is not grounded in recognition of that which is the case (viz., a recognitional judgment identifying the person who is F as me). If I know that *I* am F, this is not because I have grounds for thinking someone, whom I correctly take to be me, is F, over and above whatever grounds I have for thinking that I am F.

In Chapter 3 (pp. 61 f.), Russell's 'knowing which' requirement was mentioned: a prerequisite for a thought's being about a particular individual is that the thinker *know which* individual her thought is about. If an "I"-ascription that is immune to error through misidentification is to be about a particular individual in the world, if it is to specify a particular individual who is said to be F, the self-ascriber must know which individual it is who is said to be F. Thus, if my "I"-ascription "I am spinning around" is to represent a genuine thought about me, I must know who, among all the individuals in the world, is *me*. I take Evans to be denying that I can only know which individual in the world is me, and thus know, in a particular case, that it is I who am F, if I have made a recognitional identification of myself as the one who is F. But then, how is it that I can obtain the relevant information? Evans's suggestion, I think, is that I obtain it in a more 'practical' manner, by putting to use certain distinctive capacities for gaining information about the relevant state of affairs (viz., my spinning around), which capacities I normally have only with respect to certain of my own states. However, we should note that what Evans does not do is offer a positive epistemic account that explains what renders self-ascriptions that represent information obtained in this way *knowledgeable* as regards its being me who is spinning around.

Now I have proposed that we apply Evans's analysis to the ascriptive component of avowals. Suppose I avow, "I am nervous about this dog," or "I am hoping that you'll join us tonight". In opposition to the No Ascription view of avowals, I maintain that the avowal genuinely ascribes to me a state M with content $c$. But, in addition, I now want to suggest that my self-ascription represents *knowledge* I have that I am in state M, rather than M′, with content $c$, rather than $c$.[13] Applying Evans's suggestion, we might deny that I can only have knowledge that I am in state M with content $c$ if I have separable recognitional grounds for thinking that it is $M$, rather than M′, that I am in, or that it is $c$, rather than $c'$, that is the content of my state. I have argued that, in the normal case of avowing, I do not have any grounds for thinking that I am in some state or other, or that the state has some content or other, independent of whatever grounds I have for thinking that *I* am in state M with content $c$. (The analogous claim in the case of judgments that are immune to error through misidentification (only) was that I do not have any reason for thinking that it is I who am F that is independent of whatever reason I have for thinking that *I* am F.) But then the question is: How can I obtain the information that I am in state M (with content $c$)?

Here, too, we might resort to a more practical manner I have for obtaining the information that, e.g., it is a state of hope I am in, and that it has the content *that dinner will be served soon.* When issuing an intentional self-ascription in the avowing mode, as opposed to reporting my findings about my present mental conditions on some evidential basis, I put to use a distinctive capacity that I have only with respect to certain of my own states. It is the capacity to *express* my mental states by speaking from them *in an explicit, self-ascriptive way.* I can speak from (give voice to) a present mental state of mine using all kinds of linguistic means: I can say, "It's so great to see you!", "Hmmm, so tasty!", or just "Yum!". But when I avow being in state M (with content $c$), I issue a self-ascription which expresses$_3$ (in the semantic sense) the proposition that I am in the very state I express$_1$ (with the very content that I spell out in the course of doing so). We saw in the previous chapter that this expressive capacity is one I have only with respect to my *own present mental states,* since only in the case of states of mind that I am in at the time of avowing can I engage in *behavior that suffices to show* someone's being in those states. I can show

---

[13]  If we apply Russell's 'knowing which' requirement to the ascriptive component of my self-ascription, then for me to be making a genuine self-ascription, I need to know what states are M states, and, if my self-ascription specifies an intentional object or proposition content ("intentional content", for short), what intentional content I am assigning to it. What recognitional capacities must be involved in such 'knowing which' is a matter for debate.

my non-mental states in various ways: I can expose the sunburn on my shoulder, I can point to the decay in my tooth, I can display a reading on an instrument that shows my blood pressure, and so on. But what I cannot do is exhibit behavior that suffices to show these conditions. As for the mental states of others, while I can draw attention to them (as well as to my own past or future mental states), I cannot exhibit behavior that suffices to show them. And though my behavior can serve to show various psychological traits and dispositions of mine, it is not sufficient by itself to show them.

It is important to highlight the following difference between self-ascriptions that are merely immune to error through misidentification and self-ascriptions that are, in addition, immune to errors of misascription. A self-ascription that is immune to error through misidentification can still represent a judgment made on some epistemic basis regarding one's present (bodily) state. It's just that the self-ascription does not rest on a recognitional judgment concerning the identity of the *bearer* of the state (viz., oneself). By contrast, on my proposal, avowals of one's present mental state, which are also immune to errors of misascription, do not rest on one's recognitional judgment about *either* the identity of the state's bearer (oneself) *or* the presence and content of the particular state in oneself. This is what renders them immune to errors of misascription, as well as to errors of misidentification. Thus, if we want to maintain that avowals do express subjects' self-judgments, in addition to expressing their first-order (and self-ascribed) mental states of wishing, hoping, being scared, hungry, etc., the self-judgments should not be understood as epistemically grounded in any kind of mental self-recognition. And, of course, if the Neo-Expressivist account is accepted, avowals' security must not be understood as due to whatever epistemic security is enjoyed by the self-judgments. Bear in mind, however, that if we take avowals to represent self-judgments that are not epistemically based on recognition, but are afforded by the exercise of distinctive expressive capacities, we still have to explain what confers on them a positive epistemic status, which could qualify them as instances of genuine (and privileged) knowledge. If we are to address the deflationist challenge adequately, we will need to provide a positive epistemic account that explains what renders avowals knowledgeable as regards what states we are in (and as regards what, if any, content they have).

## Expression, Self-Knowledge, and the JTB Model

Let us take stock. The deflationist challenge introduced earlier enjoins us to explain how, given the Neo-Expressivist account of avowals' security, it can be maintained that avowals represent articles of genuine, and privileged, self-knowledge. The deflationist challenge can be seen as partially motivated by the Distinct Epistemic Basis presupposition— the thought that possessing privileged knowledge that I am in a certain state of mind requires having some special epistemic method or route that I use to obtain this knowledge. By way of undermining this presupposition, I invoked Evans's treatment of bodily self-judgments that are immune to errors of misidentification, since on his view such self-judgments supposedly represent knowledge we have about ourselves—viz., that it is *I* who *am* F—which do not rest on a distinctive epistemic basis. In the case of such self-judgments, the relevant information is obtained not through recognitional identification, which can provide a separate *reason* or grounds for the relevant judgment, but rather by putting to use certain distinctive practical abilities. I suggested that, similarly, in the case of avowals, which are in addition immune to errors of misascription, the relevant information (concerning what mental state one is in, and what its content is) is also obtained through the exercise of distinctive practical abilities. Even if a subject who avows being in state M with content *c* has not made a recognitional identification of M as the state she is in, or of *c* as the content it has, she may possess the relevant information through the exercise of her expressive capacity.

However, it is fairly clear that the deflationist challenge has not yet been fully met. Even in the case of Evans's immune bodily self-judgments, one may wonder what justifies Evans in taking such judgments to represent *knowledge* that it is *I* who *am* F, even granting that I have a distinctive non-recognitional way of obtaining information about certain bodily features I myself possess. While having a distinct epistemic basis may not be necessary for possessing knowledge, surely merely having information is not sufficient for it. (As remarked earlier, Evans doesn't really offer a positive epistemic account of what makes it legitimate to take immune bodily self-judgments to be knowledgeable as regards the identity of their subject.) When it comes to avowals, one may worry that, if avowals are understood as on the Neo-Expressivist account, then they are not even in the running as candidates for any kind of knowledge, since, *qua* expressions of first-order mental states, they do not represent self-*judgments* in the first place. And even if they do represent self-judgments, given the expressive character of avowals, avowing subjects would not stand in the right epistemic relations to the facts they pronounce on to qualify as possessing genuine (let alone privileged) knowledge of those facts. But then the deflationist challenge still stands.

The present worry can be perspicuously couched in terms of the familiar conception of knowledge (known as the JTB model) according to which knowing that *p* requires (at least) having a *justified and true belief* that *p*. On this view, having self-knowledge in the relevant sense would presumably require having true beliefs about one's present mental states for which one possesses a distinctive kind of epistemic justification. The proponent of the Neo-Expressivist view thus faces two challenges: first, to explain whether and how, on that account, avowals are apt to represent *beliefs* or judgments that avowing subjects have about themselves; and second, to explain in what one's *special epistemic justification* for those beliefs could consist. (So the second task is itself twofold: to explain not only what makes it the case that avowing subjects have *any* epistemic justification for the beliefs represented by avowals, but also what makes this justification special.) If the proponent of the Neo-Expressivist account cannot meet these challenges, then, as long as she adheres to the JTB model, she would be forced to endorse a deflationary view of self-knowledge. She would have to acknowledge that, although avowals may be especially secure pronouncements that, unlike natural expressions, are truth-assessable, and, moreover, have to be presumed true (if they are regarded as expressions of self-ascribed states). Still, just like natural expressions, avowals cannot amount to any kind of knowledge.

The JTB analysis of knowledge has come under much attack with respect to the sufficiency and necessity of both the "belief" and the "justification" conditions.[14] Nonetheless it is useful to refer to that analysis

---

[14] See, e.g., Gettier (1963) for the famous challenge to the sufficiency of the conditions. Zeno Vendler (1972: 138–49) has argued that having knowledge actually contrasts with believing. This is because to know that *p* is to be in robust "epistemic contact" with the fact that *p*, or with the state of affairs that *p* represents; whereas to believe that *p* is to be in a certain relation, perhaps psychological or cognitive, to the proposition that *p*. And Timothy Williamson, while not endorsing Vendler's account of the contrast,

as a benchmark in explaining how the Neo-Expressivist account of avowals' special security is compatible with a non-deflationary view of self-knowledge. The JTB analysis attempts to capture two requirements on knowledge that seem intuitively correct. First, it does seem that the subject who is said genuinely to know something must somehow be cognitively related to that which she is said to know. And, second, if a subject is said to know something, it seems that she cannot merely *happen* to believe what is in fact true; her having the belief cannot be a mere accident. If we take the JTB requirements in this intuitive spirit, then it is reasonable to investigate whether Neo-Expressivism makes room for genuine self-knowledge by examining the extent to which avowals could satisfy the conditions laid down by the traditional JTB conception.

Let us consider the "belief" condition first. The Neo-Expressivist account maintains that, if avowals are distinctively secure, this is because they give voice to subjects' first-order conditions, and not because they articulate their higher-order judgments regarding those conditions, which they have formed in an epistemically secure way. This seems at first glance to tell against the idea that avowing involves a subject's having a *belief that* she is in a particular mental state. Since the JTB model requires one to have a belief in order to be said to know, then avowals would seem to fail one of the JTB conditions on knowledge. However, even if we accept that belief *is* a necessary component of knowledge, and even if we understand belief as a cognitive relation to propositions, true or false, it seems appropriate to distinguish two different senses in which one may believe that *p*. In what we may call the *opining* sense, one believes that *p* if one has entertained the thought that *p* and has formed the active judgment that *p* on some basis, where one has (and could offer) specific evidence or reasons for that judgment. The Neo-Expressivist may wish to deny that avowals represent beliefs in this 'opining' sense. An avowing subject is not of the opinion, e.g., that he is in pain, or that he would like some tea. And we have noted that one aspect of Epistemic Asymmetry is that it seems inappropriate to expect the subject to be able to offer any kind of evidence for her avowal, or to be able to support individual aspects

argues that knowing (like seeing and remembering) is, whereas believing is not, a success verb designating a relation that one can have only to truths (1995: 551). If knowing *p* contrasts with believing *p* in these ways, then it may be mistaken to analyze knowing *p* in terms of believing *p*.

of her self-ascription with any epistemic reasons (other than whatever reason she has for thinking, simply, that she is in M). But there is a second, more liberal, sense of belief, in which a subject believes that *p*, provided (roughly) that she would accept *p* upon considering it. This *holding-true* sense, as we may refer to it, is the one we apply when we say that people have beliefs concerning matters they have not yet even considered. For example, I may not presently have any active opinion, formed on some specific basis, regarding matters such as the color of rain in Spain, or the sum of some numbers, or that a building within my field of vision is taller than a tree standing next to it. Yet, if suitably prompted, I would affirm the relevant claims.[15]

Earlier, I presented the belief requirement on knowledge as intended to capture the intuitive idea that a subject who is said to know that *p* must have some appropriate cognitive contact with *p*. It also seems to me reasonable to understand the requirement as independent of the justification requirement. In other words, it should not be built into the belief requirement that someone can meet it only if she has gone at least some way toward meeting the justification requirement—for example, if she has made some epistemic effort to acquire the belief that *p*, or has formed the judgment that *p* on some basis (however inadequate). It seems to me that judgments one simply finds oneself with should not be ruled out of court as potential candidates for knowledge by the belief requirement alone. Thus, I see no reason why a subject who believes that *p* in the sense of holding *p* to be true cannot satisfy the belief condition on knowledge, even if, as the case may be, she is not in a position to offer reasons for, or support with evidence, that which she holds true. It will of course require an additional step to show that such a subject can meet the justification condition on knowledge. But as far as I can see, that step is a separate one.

---

[15] Brie Gertler (in correspondence) has complained that the 'holding true' sense is too liberal, since in that sense I could be said to believe that I'm thinking while asleep, since *if* I were to consider whether I am thinking, I would accept that I was. This suggests that belief in the holding-true sense may be too liberal to capture beliefs we have about occurrent matters. But see below, where I explain that in the case of avowals, a more restricted notion than the purely dispositional holding-true is applicable.

There is in the literature an even more minimal notion than that of holding-true reserved for so-called tacit beliefs. One may tacitly believe *p* even if one would not accept *p* upon consideration. For example, linguists often claim that speakers have tacit beliefs regarding rules of their language, though they lack the theoretical understanding that would allow them to affirm statements of those rules. There is much debate on the cogency and appropriate analysis of the notion of tacit belief. (For relevant articles, see George (1989).) On one recent analysis, due to Crimmins (1992), to have a tacit belief is just to act *as if* one had a belief in a more demanding sense.

Now, I think it's fairly clear that the Neo-Expressivist account makes room for the idea that avowals represent beliefs that subjects have about themselves in the holding-true sense. Recall that, on the Neo-Expressivist view, avowing involves using an expressive vehicle that has the semantic content of a self-ascription. The product of an avowal says something about the self-ascriber. Suppose I now avow, "I am feeling really thirsty". Let us assume (with the Neo-Expressivist) that the avowal need not represent a belief I have acquired or a judgment I have formed regarding my present state on this or that basis. Even so, the avowal's product semantically expresses that self-judgment. It represents a proposition concerning a present state of mine, which, we may assume, I understand perfectly well. This proposition can reasonably be regarded as something that I hold to be true, where, to repeat, holding true requires only that I would accept $p$ if I were to consider it. If so, then even if in avowing "I am feeling thirsty" I am not opining that I am feeling thirsty, I may still be said to believe it, at least in one sense of belief. But we can say something stronger. In the case of avowals, unlike in the case of purely dispositional beliefs, a subject actively and intentionally engages in an act of producing a mental self-ascription (in speech or in thought). It isn't merely that *if* you asked me, upon my having avowed feeling thirsty, whether I believe I am feeling thirsty, I would say that I am. On the Neo-Expressivist account, when avowing feeling thirsty, I am actually self-ascribing to myself feeling thirsty; I am *saying* or *thinking that* I am feeling thirsty. If merely holding true that I'm feeling thirsty is sufficient for having the requisite cognitive contact with the relevant state of affairs, then actively issuing a self-ascription that semantically represents the state of affairs surely should be too. But then the Neo-Expressivist can allow that avowals represent beliefs that subjects have about themselves not only in the sense of holding true (as expounded above) but in a more robust, 'self-ascriptive' sense. Subjects can be credited with the relevant beliefs to the extent that they can be seen as intentionally issuing self-ascriptions that represent those beliefs when avowing. If so, then we can maintain that avowing involves a subject's expressing her first-order mental condition without denying that avowals represent beliefs we have in the sense required for knowledge.

Now, in the previous chapter (pp. 307 f.), I suggested that the Neo-Expressivist may endorse the thesis that avowals do express$_1$ (express in the action sense) a subject's own self-judgment *in addition to* expressing₁ the self-ascribed condition itself. I pointed out that the account needs to insist only that avowals' *distinctive security* derives from the fact that they serve to express₁ subjects' self-ascribed conditions, *rather than* from whatever epistemic security accrues to any self-judgments avowing subjects may express₁. I pointed out that a Neo-Expressivist who endorses this Dual Expression thesis (as I referred to it) would still want to deny that the mental self-judgments that are expressed₁ are formed on this or that basis, in which case it may still be inappropriate to regard them as beliefs in the opining sense, given our characterization above. But we now have a way of accommodating the Dual Expression claim, using the more liberal 'self-ascriptive' notion of belief. A subject may be said to express₁ *her* self-belief simply in virtue of actively making the relevant self-ascription. *All there is* to having a self-belief in the case at hand, it might be held, is the (intentional) issuing of a self-ascription. Armed with our self-ascriptive notion of belief, we can also make sense of the idea that, when reporting in the normal way that I am standing up, I can be credited with the belief that it is *I* who *am* standing up, even though I haven't formed an opinion about the matter. Not only do I hold it true that *I* (and not anyone else) am the one standing up, but when making the report, I am also actively ascribing the property of standing up to myself. Similarly, I can be credited with the belief that, e.g., it is hunger I feel when I avow feeling hungry, even if I have not formed any opinion as to the type of state I am in, so long as I am ascribing hunger to myself.

I think, then, that the belief requirement on self-knowledge can be satisfied by avowing subjects consistently with the Neo-Expressivist account of their security. But now we need to consider whether the beliefs that avowing subjects can be said to have regarding their present states of mind can meet the justification condition on self-knowledge. As noted earlier, the condition aims to capture a general contrast between knowing and merely having a true belief. This contrast would presumably apply even to belief understood as either holding true or self-ascribing; for it may be reasonably insisted that genuine knowledge requires more than accidentally holding true what is in fact true or even making a genuine and true self-ascription. Epistemic views, which take avowals to express beliefs that we form on a secure epistemic basis, in a way already build in the idea that we possess a straightforward epistemic justification for our avowals. By contrast, it may seem that, by the standards of JTB, the Neo-Expressivist account could at most credit us with beliefs about our present mental states that we simply find ourselves with, or with self-judgments that we simply find ourselves unable to deny, or are moved to accept, upon consideration.

Is there an appropriate notion of justification that is applicable to the case of avowals? Suppose it is held that a knowledge claim can be justified only if the person making the claim has reached a judgment through some epistemic effort or act, such as drawing an inference or judging on the basis of evidence, or perhaps at least observing, or even just attending to, the relevant phenomenon. If a person reaches a judgment on such an epistemic basis, then she is justified, because she has reasons or grounds for her judgment. The Neo-Expressivist view does seem to exclude such justifications, at least in its portrayal of avowals as direct expressions of one's self-ascribed present mental states. But it seems unreasonable to expect that every knowledge claim should be backed up by justification in this sense. There are other cases of knowledgeable though not explicitly justified beliefs, such as ordinary memory claims, inference rules used in logical reasoning, and other apriori judgments. In addition, the knowledge we gain via perception is not plausibly described as involving beliefs (opinions) that require justification. In seeing that the vase is broken, I can be said to have discovered, realized, or ascertained, and thus to come to know, that it is. But it might be argued that seeing the broken vase is just a way of grasping that fact, rather than forming or arriving at the belief that it is broken on the basis of some reasons. Avowing being in pain may be another case in point, where there isn't even a need for me to ascertain or discover that I am in pain.

In fact, it might be argued that even in the case of perception, I do not always do something to ascertain or discover what I can properly be said to know. Suppose I'm staring out of the window on a bright sunny day, and a robin lands on a branch right in front of my eyes. It seems to me that I can be said to see the robin, and, assuming I am aware of it, I can be said to have a perceptual belief, or to be making a perceptual judgment that there is a robin in front of me. Moreover, my belief would not seem to be true merely accidentally. It would be unreasonable to deny that I have perceptual *knowledge* in this case, even though I have not, strictly speaking, made any *observation* that could justify my perceptual belief.[16] (I shall not here attempt to characterize in positive terms what qualifies this as a case of knowledge.) If so, then some perceptual knowledge can be had without meeting the justification condition understood as above.[17]

Earlier, I mentioned a presupposition shared by both deflationary and epistemic accounts of self-knowledge, which I dubbed the Distinct Epistemic Basis presupposition. In its general form, the presupposition says that possessing any distinct kind of knowledge requires making judgments or forming beliefs *on some distinct epistemic basis*. We can now see this presupposition as simply expressing commitment to a certain understanding of the JTB belief and justification conditions. I have argued that the Neo-Expressivist account is compatible with the belief condition on a suitably relaxed reading. My rejection of the Distinct Epistemic Basis presupposition can be seen as a rejection of an overly narrow reading of the justification condition. But now we must see whether there is a more appropriate reading of the justification condition that would still allow one to separate avowals from merely accidental self-judgments, consistently with the Neo-Expressivist account of their distinctive security.

Let us accept that knowledge properly so-called requires, in addition to truth, some kind of *epistemic warrant*, even if it does not require justification understood narrowly. Accepting this is consistent with rejecting the narrow reading of the justification condition. For justification in the narrow sense of relying on a distinct epistemic basis may

---

[16] Making an observation, I take it, requires minimally that one intentionally turn one's eyes in the right direction, look, or focus one's gaze. In the case at hand, it seems that I need do none of these things to be able simply to see the robin. (And see next note.)

[17] To deny that perceptual reports require justification in the traditional sense (including the need to discover or ascertain) is not to erase the epistemic asymmetries between them and avowals. On my view, perceptual reports such as "The vase is broken" or "There's a broken vase on the table" are not immune to error through misascription *or* misidentification. Perceptual *self*-reports ("I see a broken vase") *are* immune to error through misidentification, but are not immune to error through misascription. Using the intuitive test for immunity to error, if I report "I see a broken vase" in the ordinary way, although it makes little sense for me to wonder whether it is I who am seeing the broken vase, it makes perfect sense for me to wonder whether it's a vase I'm seeing or rather a planter, or . . . and also whether the vase I'm seeing is broken or rather oddly shaped, or . . . In more theoretical terms, when I judge that I see a broken vase, I do have reason for thinking it's a *vase* I'm seeing (or that the vase I'm seeing is *broken*) that is separate from the reason I have for thinking that I'm seeing a broken vase. And I can retain my judgment that I'm seeing *something* even as I give up the judgment that it's a broken vase that I'm seeing.

be only one kind of epistemic warrant. There may be others. In other words, the slack between knowing and holding true what is in fact true (or, in our case, making a true self-ascription) may be picked up by something other than justification in the narrow sense. If so, then we can reject the Distinct Epistemic Basis presupposition without doing an injustice to the spirit of the JTB model. Below I sketch three alternative views that would allow us to regard avowals as articulating self-knowledge, even though they do not represent justified beliefs in that narrow sense. I then propose a possible synthesis of the three views, which draws directly on key ingredients in the Neo-Expressivist account of avowals' security.

## The Low Road to Self-Knowledge

According to the epistemological view known as Reliabilism, beliefs a subject has can constitute knowledge even when they are not justified by reasons the subject has (and can offer) for thinking the beliefs to be true. Rather, they can amount to knowledge "due to their being reliably produced by truth-conducive mechanisms or processes, such as memory and perception", where "[r]oughly speaking, a belief-producing mechanism is reliable, or truth-conducive, only if it tends to produce more true beliefs than false beliefs in the relevant situations" (Moser 1986: 5). On other versions of the Reliabilist view, what renders beliefs knowledgeable is the fact that belief states carry reliable information about the world, or reliably track the truth in some counterfactual way.[18] These Reliabilist views do not deny that a subject's true beliefs must meet a further condition to count as knowledge, but they do reject the "internalist" conception of this condition. On the Reliabilist view, the knowing subject need not herself know or be aware of the conditions that allow her beliefs to constitute knowledge.

The Reliabilist model has seemed especially suited to accommodate the justificatory pedigree of perceptual beliefs, where it is not plausible that the subject makes any inference, or uses any evidence,[19] in reaching the belief. The Reliabilist insists that we can possess genuine

---

[18] For these alternative, "informational" and "tracking" versions of Reliabilism, see Dretske (1970) and Nozick (1981), respectively.  [19] Or even makes an observation—see above, pp. 367f.

knowledge of such propositions as "There's a moose in front of me" or "This dress is red", even if the relevant beliefs are in some sense epistemically unmediated, provided only that there is some sort of appropriate reliable connection between our beliefs and the facts. The reliability of the connection suffices to render the beliefs epistemically warranted.

This feature of the Reliabilist view suggests a possible marriage between the Neo-Expressivist explanation of the special security of avowals and Reliabilism concerning self-knowledge. On this combination, avowals do not represent beliefs that are arrived at by a subject on the basis of inference or any other form of justification that is available to the subject from an 'internal' point of view. Nor is the special security of avowals to be understood as a consequence of their expressing a subject's own reliably formed beliefs about her present states. To explain the security of avowals in that way would be to adopt the Epistemic Approach, which we have rejected. Rather, the Reliabilism envisaged now endorses the Neo-Expressivist idea that avowals' distinctive security is due to the fact that they express the first-order mental conditions they self-ascribe. Still, avowals do represent beliefs that subjects have, if only in the more modest, holding-true or self-ascriptive senses. The products of acts of avowing are truth-assessable self-ascriptions, which do not just *happen* to correlate well with the mental states they ascribe. They are apt to be true, because the mechanisms underlying expressive behavior are truth-conducive. (The Reliabilist might appeal to the reliability of natural expressions as indicators of subjects' mental conditions, and tell a story about how articulate self-ascriptions could inherit that reliability. Or she could argue that expressive behavior carries reliable information about underlying mental states. And so on.) Avowals are apt to represent self-knowledge courtesy of the reliable connection between what avowals say and truths of the matter.

To clarify: I am here envisaging a Reliabilist answer to question (ii): What gives avowals the status of knowledge? I have rejected the Reliabilist answer to question (i) (viz., What makes avowals especially secure?) along with other epistemic answers.[20] Adopting the Neo-Expressivist account of avowals' security means denying that avowals'

----

[20] See Ch. 4.

security comes from whatever epistemic security is enjoyed by the self-judgments they represent (if any). But it is consistent with explaining what renders avowing subject's self-ascriptions epistemically warranted by appeal to the reliability of the mechanism(s) underlying self-ascriptive expressive behavior, for example. When issuing a self-ascription in the avowing mode, a subject does not merely affirm what is in fact true. Avowals do not merely happen to be true; they are reliably connected with the mental conditions they ascribe. Note that the Reliabilist need not require that the avowing subject *know* that her self-ascriptions are produced by a reliable mechanism, or reliably track her mental states, and so on, in order to be warranted in taking them to be true. Consistently with her overall epistemic externalism, the 'Expressivist-Reliabilist' could insist that the subject need only know what her mental states are, since there is no need for her to *know that she knows* what they are. Therefore, she is required only to produce self-ascriptions that are in fact reliably connected with her mental states; she does not have to establish that she does.

This stark Reliabilist picture may not be very appealing as a basis for an account of self-knowledge. As in other cases, here too the knowing subject is portrayed as a kind of input–output device, like a computer that flashes appropriate self-ascriptive messages about its internal processes on a display screen. No matter how reliable the subject's self-ascriptive output, it is not at all clear why we should call it knowledge.[21] In the case at hand the starkness of the Reliabilist proposal may be more disturbing than in other cases. To see why, consider, by contrast, a possible Reliabilist answer to the question of how *observers* know of an avowing subject's mental states. The answer might appeal to the reliability of the processes through which observers form their beliefs about others' mental states upon witnessing their expressive behavior. Presumably, the reliability of the processes would be underwritten by the reliability of avowals as indicators of the mental states. The above Expressivist-Reliabilist story, however, does not propose that avowing subjects have self-knowledge by virtue of forming beliefs about their mental states through reliable processes. The Expressivist-Reliabilist I am imagining is, of course,

---

[21] For the computer analogy, see Putnam (1960). Long (1994) offers reasons for denying that an inanimate device, however complex, is a proper subject to which to ascribe mental states, let alone genuine knowledge of its own states.

not supposing that avowals serve as a reliable source of information *for the subjects themselves*. Rather, the Expressivist-Reliabilist story purports to tell us what allows avowals to represent self-knowledge, given an expressivist understanding of the character of avowals. Now, one may complain (as I have) against the Epistemic Approach that it introduces excessive epistemological machinery that puts the avowing subject at one remove from her present mental life, as though she were witnessing her mental states and reporting on them, rather than undergoing them and giving them direct voice. But the Expressivist-Reliabilist account may seem to stray too far in the opposite direction. If avowers' possession of the relevant self-beliefs amounts to nothing more than their intentionally issuing self-ascriptions in the course of expressing their first-order mental states, then there's a clear sense in which their beliefs are not *responsive to* any evidence. On the Expressivist-Reliabilist proposal, an avowing subject possesses knowledge provided only that she erupts appropriately—i.e., issues a true self-ascription that is reliably connected with the state expressed.

It may be possible for the Expressivist-Reliabilist view to go beyond the idea that having avowable self-knowledge is simply a matter of producing largely correct, semantically articulate reliable signs of one's present states. It is doubtful, however, that the view could ground a distinctive form of knowledge deserving of the epithet "*privileged self-knowledge*". On the Reliabilist picture, self-knowledge appears optional. Whether, and to what extent, the avowals of any given subject represent self-knowledge is completely contingent upon whether and to what extent the subject's expressive behavior is reliable. Not only is it a biological accident that, in addition to having mental states, we have avowable knowledge of those states, but it is quite possible for an individual subject to lack such knowledge entirely. Yet our ordinary ascriptions to individuals of avowable self-knowledge do not seem to ride on ascertaining their individual reliability in producing true mental self-ascriptions. Unless linguistic competence or sincerity is in question, we are prepared to credit individuals with avowable knowledge of their basic beliefs, attitudes, feelings, and sensations. If the reliability of subjects' self-ascriptions is relevant to avowable self-knowledge, it does not seem to be what makes or breaks it. Furthermore, it seems that the Reliabilist could not accommodate the idea that basic self-knowledge is different in kind from other types of reliably obtained knowledge, such as perceptual knowledge. Whatever privileged status is assigned to basic self-knowledge, the Reliabilist would have to regard it as reflecting nothing more than a (contingently) higher degree of reliability of expressive mechanisms. It is hard to believe that the commonsense belief in privileged self-knowledge is informed by an assessment (even tacit) of that reliability.

Even though one could adopt a Reliabilist epistemology of self-knowledge while accepting our (non-Reliabilist) Neo-Expressivist account of avowals' special security, doing so risks distorting the true picture of self-knowledge. A Reliabilist answer to question (ii), regarding the nature of self-knowledge, may seem to compromise *privileged* self-knowledge, for much the same reason that the Reliabilist answer to question (i) would end up compromising Epistemic Asymmetry.[22] Just as the Reliabilist answer to question (i) can accommodate some of Epistemic Asymmetry, but cannot do justice to its full scope, so the Reliabilist answer to question (ii) would not do justice to the privileged status of self-knowledge, even if it could accommodate the existence of avowable self-knowledge. Still, it is important to recognize that the Expressivist-Reliabilist view represents one avenue potentially open to a proponent of the Neo-Expressivist account who does not wish to deny that avowals can represent self-knowledge.[23]

## The High Road to Self-Knowledge

The Expressivist-Reliabilist account builds up self-knowledge from below, adhering to the causal facts about avowals—specifically, the fact that their production is sustained by reliable mechanisms. It relies on a minimalist analysis of self-knowledge that is designed to be equally applicable to other kinds of knowledge. It thus assures us that there is nothing extraordinary about avowable self-knowledge. In this sense, it paves a "low road" to self-knowledge. At the other end of the

---

[22] See above, Ch. 4, pp. 90 ff.

[23] Dylan Sabo has wondered whether the Reliabilist can accommodate the distinction between an avowal being a causal expression of an underlying state and a *subject* expressing her state (in the action sense). If she cannot, then it may turn out that a Reliabilist account of self-knowledge cannot be built upon the basis of my Neo-Expressivist account of avowals' security. I have tacitly assumed, for purposes of articulating the Reliabilist proposal, that the Reliabilist can avail herself of a suitably pared down notion of agency (however unsatisfactory such a notion may be), and, correlatively, of a distinction between expressing in the causal and action senses.

spectrum of non-introspectionist views of self-knowledge lies a "high road" approach, according to which avowals represent genuine knowledge that, additionally, enjoys a highly unique status. Whereas on the low-road approach, possessing avowable self-knowledge is entirely optional, on the high-road approach it can be argued on apriori grounds that avowable self-knowledge is obligatory.[24]

As suggested above, one can be epistemically warranted in one's claim or belief even if one is not justified in the narrow sense—even if one has not engaged in any epistemic effort to form an opinion about the relevant matter, and even if one cannot provide any reasons for what one says or thinks. In "Our Entitlement to Self-Knowledge", Tyler Burge says:

> I take the notion of epistemic warrant to be broader than the ordinary notion of justification. An individual's epistemic warrant may . . . also be an entitlement that consists in a status of operating in an appropriate way in accord with norms of reason, even when these norms cannot be articulated by the individual who has this status. We have an entitlement to certain beliefs or to certain logical inferences even though we lack reasons or justifications for them. (1996: 3)[25]

A familiar and useful analogy comes from the legal domain: one can be legally entitled to something without engaging in any specific action or effort designed to secure one's legal hold. One can be legally entitled to do something, for example, provided only that in doing it one acts in accordance with applicable legal norms, regardless of whether one is aware of those norms. Similarly, it might be argued that a person avowing her mental states is epistemically entitled to her pronouncements, because her avowal is made "in accord with norms of reasons". Epistemic entitlement in this case consists in being epistemically reason*able* in one's avowals, which does not entail being prepared to offer reasons.

---

[24] The proposal articulated in this section draws mainly on ideas presented in Tyler Burge's influential work on self-knowledge. See especially Burge (1988), (1996), and (1998a). Moran (2001) contains some related ideas. Shoemaker (1996) (see especially 'First-Person Access') and Bilgrami (1998) offer different apriori reasons for the necessity of self-knowledge, which could be incorporated into a high-road proposal. For helpful exposition and critique of Shoemaker's arguments, see Siewert (2003). I should perhaps emphasize that my concern here is to articulate a non-deflationary view of self-knowledge that is compatible with the Neo-Expressivist account of avowals' security, rather than to provide an accurate exegesis of these authors' writings.      [25] See also Sellars (1988: 301 f.).

   We now need to consider what would give one a special entitlement to one's avowed self-ascriptions. Consider self-ascriptions of thoughts and occurrent beliefs. There is an important difference between ascribing such states to oneself in an alienated or theoretical way and ascribing them to oneself from the first-person perspective. It is one thing to ascribe to myself the belief that I am leery of my neighbor's friendliness purely as a result of taking my therapist's expert word for it. It is another thing to ascribe that same belief to myself with the expressive directness of an avowal. To avow a belief is at least to endorse the belief and to adopt an intellectual stand on its content. It is thereby to incur an intellectual commitment to the avowed belief that is equal only to the commitment one incurs when giving the belief a non-self-ascriptive expression. If I avow (in speech or in thought), "I believe the Democrats will win", and I am apprised of facts that point against victory for the Democrats, it becomes rationally incumbent upon me to alter or find other support for my first-order belief. No such pressure arises in connection with ascriptions of beliefs to others, or alienated self-ascriptions. (I can easily ascribe to someone else a belief I think is false. And I can do so even in my own case, provided I adopt a theoretical or third-person stance.)

   Avowing in general puts one in a special relationship to what is avowed. Avowing does not allow disowning the avowed state in the way one can disown states ascribed to another, or even states ascribed to oneself in a detached, theoretical (or observational) manner. Although high-road proponents focus their treatment upon avowals of doxastic propositional attitudes, the basic idea is perhaps also applicable to avowals of non-doxastic states—occurrent wants, preferences, emotions, feelings, and perhaps even sensations. Just as an avowal of a belief or thought involves taking a direct intellectual stand on the subject matter of the thought, so an avowal of an occurrent desire, emotion, or feeling involves genuinely claiming one's state. Thus, for me to avow "I prefer to have tea rather than coffee right now" is not merely to voice a neutral judgment that I have a preference for tea over coffee right now. If I *avow* such a preference, I place myself under some commitment to opt for tea over coffee, circumstances permitting. It is for this reason that analogues of Moore's paradoxical sentences can be formulated for attitudes and states other than belief—e.g.: "I am so bored by this and it's not boring" or "This is very enjoyable, and I am not enjoying this", and so on.[26]

It can also be argued that engaging in rational deliberation or critical reasoning requires being able to ascribe to oneself knowledgeably not only beliefs, thoughts, judgments, etc., but also emotions, feelings, and sensations from the first-person perspective, or in the avowing mode. Charles Siewert has recently explained the point regarding the necessity for rational deliberation of having avowable first-person knowledge of one's beliefs and other states as follows:

> Any humanly rational agent must be able to try to determine what is the case, based on a consideration of reasons: you must be able to justify (some of) your beliefs . . . in many cases, we are disposed to justify our beliefs by citing facts about how we came by those beliefs—the sources of those beliefs. And to justify your beliefs by explaining why you have the beliefs you do, you have to represent yourself as a believer. Moreover [the facts ordinarily thought relevant] . . . include answers to questions such as: do you believe that *p* because it *looks* (or otherwise *appears*) to you as if *p*? . . . It seems that your ability to cite reasons in support of everyday beliefs, in a way that manifests basic human rationality, depends on your being able to take such facts— . . . —into account. (2003: 135)

A parallel point can be made regarding practical deliberation. To be a practical deliberator, it is obviously not enough that one *have* first-order desires, intentions, feelings, etc. One must in addition be able to self-ascribe those states as part of one's deliberative processes. To be a practical deliberator, one has to be able to justify (some of) one's choices and actions. In many cases, we do so by citing facts about the states (emotions, feelings, sensations, as well as beliefs, thoughts, and other propositional attitudes) that have moved us to choose or act in certain ways. But this means that our ability for practical deliberation depends on our ability to self-ascribe mental states.[27]

Two questions arise. First, granted that our normal practices of rational and practical deliberation require mental self-ascriptions,

---

[26] As pointed out earlier (p. 219), Moore-type conflicts can be generated in utterances that have only partial propositional form (e.g.: "[Yawn] this is really interesting").

[27] Burge and Shoemaker (as well as Siewert) tend to focus explicitly only on rational attitudes. Indeed, Burge explicitly says: "I regard knowledge of one's sensations as requiring separate treatment from knowledge of one's thoughts and attitudes" (1996: n. 13). However, against the background of the Neo-Expressivist account of avowals, extending the high-road approach to basic self-knowledge to cover non-rational attitudes and sensations, and calling on considerations about practical deliberation, seems natural (as well as in the spirit of Shoemaker's and Burge's discussion).

why must the self-ascriptions be *knowledgeable*? Indeed, why must they even be (at least largely) *correct* (let alone especially warranted)? Siewert answers this question by citing the general *de facto* success of these practices. The correctness of our self-ascriptions is required to explain how we are able "to justify (cite reasons in support of) [our] beliefs [and choices/actions] as well as we (the humanly rational) do" (Siewert 2003: 136). Second, we may wonder whether the relevant self-knowledge could not be obtained in an evidential, third-person way, as it is in the case of ascriptions to others. In other words, what reason do we have for supposing that the mental self-ascriptions we offer by way of giving our reasons for belief or action must be issued in the first-person way (i.e., why they must be *avowals*)? Siewert points out in response that when "justifying decisions or claims in ways that appeal to information about one's desires, beliefs and sense experience, one often, even usually, won't actually have *done* anything that could explain how one came by this information" (Siewert 2003: 135). He also thinks that third-person self-ascriptions have to bottom out in (what I have here described as) non-evidential avowals, on pain of regress (2003: 135 f.). And he summarizes:

Maybe one can know or be justified in believing that *p*, without being able to justify the assertion that *p*. Still, an ability to justify claims and choices is a fundamental aspect of human rationality. And if the practice of justifying, as we engage in it, requires the ability to cite accurately what beliefs, desires and experiences we have, and if there is often no available third-person source for these citations, one must be able to represent one's own attitudes and experiences to oneself accurately by a distinctively first-person means. (2003: 136)

It is worth pondering a bit further the reason why avowable self-knowledge might be thought essential to our capacities as rational and practical deliberators. It seems that when we offer theoretical reasons for our beliefs or practical reasons for our actions, we normally do something markedly different from offering a purely psychological explanation of our coming to believe or do something. The reasons we cite are usually presented as having direct rational and motivational force for us: they are offered as reasons *to* think or do as one has or does. Asked "Why do you believe that the Democrats will win?", I may say: "Because I think they've put on a strong campaign." I self-ascribe a thought in giving a reason for my belief, but I do not merely speculate on the causal history of my present belief that the Democrats will win; I give a reason *to* believe this, which I presently endorse. Similarly, when I say "I want to make sure you're safe", in response to my child's question "Why are you following me into the building?", I am giving a reason *for* following her, which has the force of a hypothetical imperative that I am presently subscribing to (something like: if one wants to ensure one's child is safe, then one should not let her walk to her destination on her own). In other words, the self-ascriptions we cite as our reasons are offered as avowals, expressive of the very wants, beliefs, thoughts, wishes, etc. that we self-ascribe, rather than as mere third-person reports on our present mental states.[28]

If it were true that being a rational and practical deliberator required being in a position to self-ascribe mental states in the avowing mode, then the special entitlement that grounds privileged self-knowledge could be seen as follows. As an avowing subject, I would be entitled to the self-judgments that my avowals semantically express insofar as these self-judgments are necessary elements in my rational and practical deliberation. This entitlement would derive not from contingent facts about the reliability of my pronouncements as indications of my present states (cf. the low-road approach), but rather from the assumed fact that I am by and large a *successful* rational and practical deliberator, plus the (alleged) apriori derived fact that the truth of the self-judgments semantically expressed by my avowals is necessary for successful rational and practical deliberation. The derivation could take the following, transcendental form:[29]

If successful rational and practical deliberations are possible, deliberators' own avowals of present beliefs, thoughts, preferences, hopes, feelings, etc. must enjoy a special epistemic status. These avowals enjoy a special epistemic status only if the deliberator possesses a special entitlement to the judgments expressed by those self-ascriptions. Since we, normal

---

[28]  This is the kind of observation that motivates some accounts of self-knowledge to focus on the transparency-to-the world of avowals and on their commissive character considered in Ch. 4.

For some discussion of the contrast between theoretical knowledge of one's attitudes and the kind of knowledge reflected in avowals, see Burge (1996: 21 ff.). See also Moran (1997). Moran suggests, for example, that the job of a therapist who tries to persuade a patient that she hates her brother would not be regarded as complete until the patient actually came to avow the emotion, as opposed to merely self-ascribing it as a result of believing that the therapist's analysis is correct.

[29]  Inspired by Burge's discussion in (1996).

human beings, do successfully engage in rational and practical deliberation, we must possess a special entitlement to the judgments semantically expressed by our avowals.

There is much that is attractive about the high-road approach. It clearly speaks to the intuition that, at least in some sense, avowable self-knowledge is not optional, and that avowals hold a special place among the things we can be said to know. Authors who may be considered representatives of the high-road approach point out connections between avowals and rational deliberation, action, free agency, and so on, that seem both interesting and important to understanding the role played by avowable self-knowledge in our epistemic lives. All this represents an improvement on the stark low-road approach described earlier. However, one may shy away from some of the stronger claims these authors make in the course of fleshing out these connections. As regards the above transcendental argument, it may be thought that the argument gets things backwards. For it may be argued that if avowals are apt to serve as crucial steps in rational and practical deliberations, this is *because* they represent things we are in a special position to know, rather than the other way around. Thus, suppose it is granted that we must possess avowable self-knowledge in order to be successful practical and rational deliberators. And suppose, further, that we take it as given that we are indeed such deliberators. At most, this commits us to the claim that we do possess avowable self-knowledge, so that (on the present suppositions) the deflationary view of self-knowledge must be rejected. We may still seek an explanation of what renders avowals knowledgeable. The acknowledged necessity of avowable self-knowledge seems insufficient for this purpose.

Some proponents of the high-road approach connect their apriori reasons for thinking that we must possess self-knowledge with the idea that there is a "constitutive" relation between being in mental states and making true avowals (so if S sincerely avows being in a mental state M, then S must be in M, and vice versa, at least when certain general conditions are assumed to hold). Thus, Shoemaker (1996) argues that certain deep connections between rationality and self-knowledge preclude the possibility of "self-blindness" (i.e., of a rational human being who has first-order mental states but lacks all knowledge of those states). In the course of defending the necessity of avowable self-knowledge, he maintains that there is a certain logical guarantee of the truth of avowals. And Bilgrami (1998) tries to establish that the following condition holds "under the condition of responsible agency": If S believes/intends/desires/ . . . that $p$, then S believes that S believes/intends/desires . . . that $p$, and vice versa.[30] But it may be thought that, even if the possibility of an individual who is "chronically unreliable" in her avowals is somehow ruled out on more than purely empirical grounds, this does not yet tell us what renders particular (true) avowals knowledgeable.

There is perhaps a more telling difficulty with the high-road approach. As a general approach to knowledge, I think it derives its strongest support from considering apriori knowledge, which is not easily accommodated by either standard internalist or Reliabilist accounts of justification. We can plausibly be credited with knowledge of basic logical principles, such as the law of non-contradiction. I may be said to hold this principle true, even if I do not entertain an occurrent opinion affirming it. Furthermore, my entitlement to hold it true seems not to be a matter of brute reliability; nor does it seem to require me to engage in any epistemic effort. I may be entitled to hold it true in a sense hospitable to the high-road approach: it is the principle that (we may suppose) is required by the exercise of my capacity for critical reasoning. But principles such as the law of non-contradiction are general formal principles. The contribution they make to particular instances of reasoning does not depend on the particular circumstances in which one is credited with knowledge of them. It's not as though I am warranted in believing the principle, because I am warranted in affirming its particular instances (e.g., that NOT (it's raining and it's not raining) ); if anything, it's the other way around. So there is no *prima facie* pressure to search for a specific epistemic achievement on my part whenever I am credited with knowledge of the principle (or even its particular application). By contrast, if avowals represent knowledge, the knowledge is of contingent, transient matters of fact. When avowing "I am hungry/scared of the dog/etc", my alleged knowledge is of a particular fact, which may

---

[30] It is not clear whether Burge would subscribe to such a constitutive thesis, since (at least in the works cited here) he does not explicitly articulate any such thesis. But to the extent that he thinks that self-*knowledge* is required for rational deliberation and critical reasoning, it seems that he would be committed to our avowals having to be at least largely true (as well as to our possessing special epistemic entitlement to them).

have failed to obtain altogether, may not have obtained a minute ago, and may cease to obtain in a moment. (In this respect, my avowable knowledge does appear to be a 'tracking' kind of knowledge, just like perceptual knowledge, which is one main reason why I think the perceptual model of self-knowledge continues to exercise its force on us.) Furthermore, what I am said to know when I avow are things others cannot know as I do, whereas the special place reserved for knowledge of logical principles, courtesy of its essential role in reasoning, is indifferent to the special position occupied by any individual user of those principles.

## A Middle Road to Self-Knowledge

It is interesting to note a certain commonality between the low-road and high-road approaches. Both ground the epistemic warrant of avowing subjects in what (in some sense) lies outside the subject's epistemic perspective in the relevant situation. On the low-road approach, true avowals can amount to knowledge because of the *de facto* truth-conduciveness of self-ascriptive expressive mechanisms. On the high-road approach, true avowals count as knowledge courtesy of necessary connections between our capacity to avow and other central capacities we possess. (Thus, on the particular high-road proposal considered above, avowals constitute necessary steps in rational and practical deliberation.) But it might be thought that if I am said to have special knowledge of some of my states that no one else can have, it is partly because of a special relation that I have to the actual subject matter of my knowledge, or due to my being in a special position to have that knowledge, in the relevant circumstances. Consonant with the Neo-Expressivist account, both the low-road and the high-road approaches accept that this relationship need not involve my forming a self-judgment on some distinctive epistemic basis, or possessing reasons for my avowals, or otherwise being aware of what warrants me in making them. So we might wonder in what way my having knowledge of my present states of mind can still count as some kind of epistemic achievement on my part. One might argue that, even if my being warranted in issuing a self-ascription does not require me to have made any epistemic effort, if I am to be credited with knowledge of a present state of mind I am in, then my possession of this self-knowledge must be due to something I myself have done, and am in some way responsible for, in the particular situation. If so, it may be felt that the low-road approach and the high-road approach are both guilty, each in its own way, of taking self-knowledge out of the hands of avowing subjects.[31]

In this section, I would like to articulate a 'middle-road' approach that avoids the main difficulties raised for the other approaches. This approach grounds the epistemic warrant enjoyed by avowing subjects in the special epistemic position they are in when issuing *particular* avowals. In doing so, it draws on specific resources offered by the Neo-Expressivist account of avowals' security. On that account, recall, the special security of avowals derives from the fact that they are expressive of subjects' first-order mental states. When presenting the Neo-Expressivist account, I appealed several times to the distinction between three senses of expressing: the action($_1$), the causal($_2$), and the semantic($_3$) senses. My main concern there was to separate the first two senses from the semantic sense, so as to point out that an avowal can express$_3$ a judgment that the avower is in some state while at the same time expressing$_1$, and possibly expressing$_2$, the state itself and without necessarily expressing$_1$ or expressing$_2$ the avower's own higher-order judgment that she is in the state.

Now, the low-road, Reliabilist approach focuses on the fact that avowals often enough express$_2$ the subject's mental state. It maintains that the causal reliability of avowals plus the fact that they express$_3$ truth-assessable claims about the subject that are held true by the subject should suffice to give them the status of self-knowledge. By contrast, the middle-road approach calls upon the fact that an avowal *expresses$_1$* the subject's mental state. Whereas we can say of a subject's pronouncements that they are more or less reliable indicators of a condition she is in, properly speaking, it is only the subject herself whom we can describe as warranted in making the pronouncements, and thus credit with self-knowledge. As a first step toward putting self-knowledge back in the hands of avowing subjects, the middle-road proponent

---

[31] As against the low-road approach, the point could be seen just as an application of a familiar objection raised by critics of epistemological externalism, in general, and Reliabilism, in particular. But I should mention that in the present context it is not motivated by wholesale opposition to epistemological externalism (much less by wholesale endorsement of epistemological internalism).

highlights the fact that avowing, properly understood, *is something the subject does*; it is an action—overt or covert, in speech or in mind—that is performed by an agent. Beginning with the idea that avowing is a certain kind of expressive act which a subject performs, the middle-road proponent tries to identify something in the character of this type of action that may yield a special epistemic warrant for avowing subjects.

From the subject's perspective, avowing involves intentional use of a semantically articulate self-ascription, in thought or in speech, so as to give voice to a condition she is in. Avowing is not merely something that happens to a subject, like the appearance of a rash, or a sneeze. In the typical case, it is something she intentionally does: an act of *speaking* her mind. To accomplish the expressive act involved in avowing, one must be a master of self-ascriptive expressive means, and must use them intentionally so as to produce a self-ascription. But, as pointed out earlier, the semantic achievement of self-ascription need not be underwritten epistemically. The self-ascriptions produced in the course of speaking one's mind are *epistemically simple*, in a sense I have explained: a subject has no more epistemic reason to affirm that it is she who is in M, or that it is M that she is in (or that it is *c* that is its content) than whatever reason she has for thinking, simply, that she is in M. This is what renders her self-ascription immune to errors of misidentification and misascription.

Although the notion of immunity to epistemic error was introduced by way of proposing a *non-epistemic* account of avowals' security, it can also be used to support the idea that subjects enjoy a special kind of *epistemic entitlement* when avowing. To see the idea, let's consider again the phenomenon of immunity to error through misidentification. If I say or think "I am sitting down" in the ordinary way, I am not in a position to wonder whether it is I myself, or perhaps someone else, who am sitting down. This is because my bodily self-ascription is in no way based on an identification of the subject of the ascription. But now consider the question: Do I *know* who it is who is sitting down? Assuming it is true that I am sitting down, am I epistemically warranted in accepting that truth? The natural answer would seem to be "Yes", even though I have not engaged in any epistemic effort aimed specifically at ascertaining the identity of the person who is sitting down. Of course, I may be wrong—say, if unbeknownst to me, my brain is hooked up to someone else's body, and he is the person sitting down. In that case, I could not be said to know that it is I who am sitting down—simply because it would not be true. But from this it does not follow that even when it is true that I am sitting down, I cannot be warranted in my belief to that effect.

Still, we want to understand the nature of the epistemic warrant I have for thinking it is I who am sitting down, in light of the fact that I have no (positive) reasons for thinking that, other than whatever reasons I have for thinking that I am sitting down, and have done nothing to ascertain it. Given my epistemic situation with respect to its being me who is sitting down, it seems entirely inappropriate to hold me epistemically responsible to alternatives that would defeat my claim to knowledge. My epistemic situation in this case is rather different from the situation of someone who sets out to determine, for example, whether one of the people he can see sitting down in a photograph is himself. Such a person can plausibly be held responsible to the possibility that the person he identified as himself in the photo might actually be his cousin. But the person who judges "I'm now sitting down" in the normal way, though he *is* recognizing proprioceptively that he's sitting down (rather than standing up), and though he could even be wrong about its being him who is sitting down (if, say, he's hooked up to someone else's limbs), is not in any way *taking* some other individual to be himself. So there is no room to appeal to the possibility of his *mis*-taking someone else for himself as a way of undermining his claim to know that *he* is sitting down. Since the identity of the subject of his judgment is not something he is in any way trying to determine, it makes little sense to see him as potentially *going wrong* in the matter of that identity. Yet, if he has the belief that *he* is sitting down, this belief is not one he merely *happens* to have, nor is it accidentally true. As Evans points out, proprioception is a (nonrecognitional) capacity that normally delivers information about oneself. What the proponent of the middle road proposes is that a subject in the epistemic situation just described is *entitled by default* to the relevant belief.

In general, entitlement by default, as understood here, can be seen as the epistemic cash value of immunity to error. So one can be said to be entitled by default to whatever judgment, or aspect of a judgment, that is immune to error. For an example that does not involve self-ascription, consider the following. If I judge, "It's raining", my judgment will be immune to error of 'mislocation', as well as to temporal error. I have no reason for thinking it's raining *here*, or *now*, over and above whatever reason I have for thinking that it's raining. And it would make little sense, as I make this judgment, to wonder: it is raining, but is it *here* (or *now*) that it's raining? In the normal case, I do not base my judgment that it's raining on a judgment to the effect that here is the place where (or now is the time when) it's raining. On the present suggestion, I can still have knowledge that here is the (a) place where it's raining, or now is the (a) time when it's raining. I have done nothing to establish this as the location or time of rain. However, in the normal case, I am nevertheless entitled by default to these judgments.

Since avowals are not only immune to error through misidentification, but also immune to error through misascription, a subject avowing being in M will have entitlement by default (on the present proposal) not only as regards her belief that it's she who is in M, but also as regards her belief that it's M that she is in (and that $c$ is its content). If she issues the self-ascription in the course of simply speaking her mind, alternatives to its being state M that she is in do not mark ways she might have gone wrong in her ascription, epistemically speaking, and thus we would not hold her epistemically responsible to such alternatives.[32]

To say that when avowing, subjects are warranted by default, is not to say that avowals (as products) have to be true. We saw that one can produce false self-ascriptions in the course of speaking one's mind; it is possible to avow having a sensation or feeling or belief that $p$ when one is not in fact in the relevant mental state.[33] Thus, the middle-road proposal is not that avowals are true by default. So it should not be confused with the Default View (see above, pp. 347 f.), which builds the truth of avowals into the truth-conditions of mentalistic ascriptions through a default assumption. Rather, the proposal that avowing

[32] One way to understand the middle-road proposal is as a species of a 'relevant alternatives' view (see, e.g., Dretske (1971) and Goldman (1976) ): certain defeating alternatives are simply not relevant to the assessment of whether an avowing subject knows she is in M. What renders the alternatives irrelevant is whatever renders the self-ascription immune to errors of misascription (as well as misidentification). I defer discussion of this version of the present proposal and its limitations for another occasion.

[33] On the Neo-Expressivist view, this would be due to expressive failures, which are to be explained psychologically rather than epistemically. (See Ch. 8, pp. 320 ff.)

subjects enjoy default entitlement to the self-ascriptions they produce reflects the recognition that such subjects are in a special epistemic position as regards the relevant truth, one that is different from the position subjects are in when setting out to discover or ascertain the truth about their present mental states. When avowing a mental state, in contrast to reporting on it, one's present mental state is not for oneself an epistemic target. One need not be able to back up the self-ascription one issues by the usual sorts of reasons in order to be epistemically warranted; nor is one to be held responsible to 'defeating alternatives'. Avowals' truth is not guaranteed logically; but this does not mean that to have knowledge of what they say, subjects must actively engage in some epistemic act or effort to ensure they 'get it right'. A subject whose mental self-pronouncement is taken to be an avowal will be credited with epistemic entitlement by default, so long as we take her to be a normal subject with normal expressive capacities. If her avowal is thought to be true, as it normally will be, then she will be credited with knowledge of her present state of mind. Thus, default entitlement can be seen as built into our ordinary practices of attributing basic self-knowledge, analogously to the way in which the presumption of truth is supposed by the Default View to be built into our practices of assessing the truth of avowals. The advantage of the 'default entitlement' view is that it is consistent with a robust realism about mentality. What depends on avowing subjects' special position, on this view, is not the *truth* of what they say or think; rather, it's whether they can count as *knowing* the relevant truth.

For yet another (though in some ways related) type of case where the idea of default entitlement could get a purchase, consider the knowledge one has of what one is doing in the course of doing it. You ask me, "What are you doing?" I say, "I am beating an egg," "I am drawing a house," "I am planting a bulb." As I give these answers, it is plausible to credit me with believing the relevant claims, for I intentionally self-ascribe the relevant action with affirmation (we may suppose). But in this type of case, too, it would seem odd to suggest that I am of the relevant *opinions*; and it would also seem out of place to ask me *how* I know what I am doing, or expect me to have reasons for the beliefs, or be able to justify them. Yet we normally credit people with knowledge of what it is they are doing, in the course of doing it. Note that such knowledge is by no means infallible. There may not be eggs in the bowl; what comes out on the paper may be a tower, not a house; what I am putting in the ground may be a pebble, not a bulb. (And, of course, I may be wrong in even more radical ways.) So in each case, you may not credit me with knowledge of what I am doing, but that would be because of the *falsity* of my claim, *not* because I am not warranted in making it. Falsity always trumps a knowledge claim, since one cannot know what is false (hence the "truth"-condition on knowledge). But what is at issue is whether one can know that *p*, when *p* is true, even if one has not ascertained the truth of *p*, or has done nothing epistemic to rule out the possibility of *p*'s being false. And the case of knowledge of what one is doing may illustrate nicely that one can. If I say or think that I am raking the yard when I am in fact raking the yard, I do not merely happen to hold true what is true. Though I may not be able to produce reasons for my self-ascription beyond citing again what I am doing, it seems reasonable to suppose that I am warranted in issuing it. But my warrant does not rest on any epistemic effort I have made to verify what I am doing. As the agent of my action, I am in a special position to pronounce on what I am doing, without having to engage in such an effort. I have, if you will, an 'executive' entitlement, which is a kind of default entitlement.[34]

In a similar vein, we may speak of 'expressive' entitlement as another kind of entitlement by default. Expressing my first-order mental states is what I, as the *subject* of those states, am uniquely placed to do. Whereas others (as well as I) can ascribe mental states to me using various epistemic routes, no one but I can ascribe the relevant states to me in the avowing mode. Others can know of my state of mind only by forming a belief about it, and the belief will be warranted only if it rests on some appropriate epistemic basis. But in my own case, I can (also) simply give voice to my state using a semantically articulate self-ascription. And when I do so, I am immune to the kinds of epistemic errors that could otherwise defeat my claim to knowledge of what

[34] Note that I am not claiming that self-ascriptions of action share all aspects of the security of avowals. They are immune to error through misidentification, but, much like proprioceptive reports, they are open to doubt by the self-ascriber. As I say or think "I am raking the leaves", I can perfectly sensibly wonder: "I'm doing something, but is it raking the leaves?" Note, too, that like proprioceptive reports, and unlike avowals, pronouncements on one's actions are straightforwardly open to challenge and correction by others. Presumably, such pronouncements in part rest on proprioceptive, as well as perceptual judgments, so they inherit the latter judgments' vulnerability to ascriptive error. Most importantly, perhaps, self-ascriptions of action are not governed by the asymmetric presumption of truth that governs avowal, since they are not *expressions of* that which they ascribe. My raking the leaves is not something I can express, any more than I can express my seeing a tree.

state I am in. Given the way I issue my self-ascription, it would be entirely inappropriate to hold me epistemically responsible to such possible errors; this is what the notion of default entitlement is intended to reflect. Only *I* am in this kind of position; only *I* can have avowable knowledge of my states of mind, since only *I* can issue true ascriptions of present mental states to myself and be entitled by default in accepting them.

The middle-road view goes beyond the mere contingent reliability of the products of avowals as indicators of mental states, but it remains shy of claims about the apriori necessity of avowable self-knowledge. It connects the possibility of possessing privileged self-knowledge with the special character of acts of speaking one's mind. However, at least as presented so far, the middle-road proposal seems to leave out some of the connections emphasized by the other approaches: between avowals and truth, on the one hand, and between avowals and central human capacities, such as the capacities for rational reasoning and action, on the other hand. The first connection seems crucial to the epistemic credentials of avowable self-knowledge (so described); the second seems important for capturing fully its privileged status. So although the middle-road proposal is, so far, the closest in spirit to the Neo-Expressivist account of avowals' security, it may still seem at least incomplete as an answer to our question (ii), viz.: What qualifies avowals as articles of *knowledge* at all, and what is the source of the *privileged status* of this knowledge?

## Avowable Self-Knowledge: A Synthesis

My main aim in this chapter was to argue that a defender of the Neo-Expressivist account of avowals is not consigned to a deflationary view of avowable self-knowledge. I have sketched three alternative non-deflationary views of avowable self-knowledge that such a defender could pursue, without attempting a conclusive adjudication among them. It may be that such adjudication is not possible or advisable; for it may be that the correct view of privileged self-knowledge ought to draw on ideas of all three types of view.

Developing an appropriate synthesis would require a more careful epistemological investigation than I can pursue here. In particular, it would require a much more extended study of the similarities and differences between avowable self-knowledge and other cases that do not appear to fit the straitjacket of the traditional JTB analysis of knowledge, such as perceptual knowledge and knowledge of one's present actions, as well as knowledge through memory, knowledge by testimony, and apriori knowledge. This is something that must be left for future work. However, I would like to conclude by indicating briefly one way in which such a "synthetic" account might proceed.

As emphasized throughout, on the Neo-Expressivist account, avowals' security is not due to subjects' possession of a special way of knowing, but is rather connected with being a subject who *has* mental states and who is a competent user of self-ascriptive vehicles for the expression of those mental states. A subject who avows being happy to see her friend, like a subject who spontaneously hugs her friend, gives her joy expression in the action sense. But the avowal, unlike the hug, is a semantically articulate self-ascription; it tells of a condition the self-ascriber is in by semantically representing the subject's condition. At the same time, the self-ascriptions produced in avowing typically come directly from the subject's present condition. So, as emphasized by the low-road approach, true mental self-ascriptions produced in avowing do not merely *happen* to be true. There is a highly regular (though not exceptionless) correlation between avowing a mental state and being in the avowed mental state; thus, there is a highly reliable correlation between engaging in acts of avowing and producing true mental self-ascriptions. Moreover, in contrast to other epistemically unmediated pronouncements, such as proprioceptive reports, or self-ascriptions of one's present actions, avowals provide not only a reliable, but also a crucial, source of truth. Others' epistemic access to a subject's mental state normally depends on the subject's avowals. I do not usually need you to tell me whether you are sitting or not, or where your arms are; and at least in basic cases I can judge for myself what it is you are doing by just looking. But, unless you speak your mind, even some of your most basic mental states may elude me.[35]

On the other hand, the avowing subject herself does not need to rely on her own avowals in order to have knowledge of her present

---

[35] Even if there were telepaths, their reliability (and their claim to *be* genuine telepaths) would be measured against the avowals of the subjects whose minds they are said to be able to read.

states of mind. In avowing, she knows the state of mind she is in. As the subject is avowing (in speech or in thought), she accepts as true, at the time of avowing, something that is very likely to *be* true; and when it is, it does not merely happen to be true. Furthermore, as emphasized by the middle-road view, when speaking her mind, the subject is acting in epistemic innocence, and is thus not held responsible to alternatives that would defeat the truth of her avowal. Given the expressive nature of her act, the subject's avowal is not only likely to be true; she also enjoys entitlement by default.

But perhaps we can say something stronger. Recall the Neo-Expressivist account of what renders avowals expressive acts. An avowal is an act in which a subject expresses in the action sense (expresses$_1$) a present mental state M, where expressing$_1$ M requires having M as the 'rational cause' of the act. When I avow "I am thirsty", my feeling thirsty is my *reason for the act* of issuing the self-ascription. Quite often, as in the case of avowals proper, as well as avowals in thought, being in the relevant state may be my *only* reason for that act.[36] Now it might be suggested that the avowed state itself, M, is also what provides the *epistemic reason* for my self-ascription, or what warrants me in avowing M. The state is not a justifier in the traditional sense, since it represents no epistemic effort on the subject's part. But the subject is still epistemically warranted—warranted simply through *being* in the state—and the avowal can still be said to represent an epistemic achievement on the subject's part. For the self-ascription semantically expressed by an avowal is not something that merely pops into the subject's head; it is *epistemically grounded* in the avowed state.

On the present proposal, what is epistemically unique about avowals is that the very same thing—one's being in M—provides both a rational reason for the avowal understood as an (expressive) act and an epistemic reason for the avowal understood as representative of the subject's self-judgment. An avowal as product (i.e., the self-ascription, or the judgment it expresses$_3$) requires no other warranting reason than whatever gives reason for the avowal as act (on the given occasion), thereby rendering it an act of expressing$_1$ the subject's M. It will thus turn out that whatever grounds avowals as expressive acts is also what allows them to represent a genuine *and* unique kind of knowledge.

[36] I'm setting aside for a moment the possibility (presented by the Dual Expression thesis) that my judgment that I'm thirsty is also my reason for the avowal.

Although one can obtain genuine knowledge of others' states of mind, and can be justified in various ways in having beliefs about one's own states of mind, *only when avowing can one's epistemic warrant be the same as the rational cause of one's behavior.*

The idea that a subject's state can provide her with epistemic warrant for certain beliefs is not new.[37] Nor is the idea that avowable self-knowledge, specifically, is epistemically grounded in the avowed states themselves without precedent. For example, Christopher Peacocke has proposed that our basic self-ascriptions of conscious sensations and occurrent thoughts have those very states as their epistemic reasons:

Conscious thoughts and occurrent attitudes, like other conscious mental events, can give the thinker reasons for action and judgment. They do so also in the special case in which they give the thinker a reason for self-ascribing an attitude to the content which occurs to the thinker, provided our thinker is conceptually equipped to make the self-ascription. (1999: 214)[38]

There is a standard problem for views that take the epistemic grounding of a belief to consist (at least in part) in the 'truth-maker' of the belief. The problem has to do with the warrant of *false* beliefs. The traditional notion of epistemic justification invokes 'good-making' epistemic features of beliefs that can supposedly accrue to even false beliefs. Thus, on some traditional views, my belief that there is a cup in front of me may be equally justified regardless of whether there is a cup in front of me or not (though, of course, if there is no cup in front of me, the belief will not amount to knowledge). If the presence of the cup is what is said to ground my belief, then, if my belief is false, it will lack epistemic grounding. In the specific case of self-knowledge, if what warrants me in my self-ascription of M is my state of being in M itself, then if my self-ascription is false, I will not just fail to know that I am in M due to my failure to meet the truth requirement on knowledge; I will also lack epistemic warrant. So in point of epistemic warrant, there will be nothing in common between true and false avowals.

The view known as "disjunctivism" embraces this consequence.[39] But disjunctivism in general is not without difficulties. In the case of

---

[37] See, e.g., McDowell (1995).

[38] For a discussion of Peacocke's view and an extension of it to basic self-knowledge of non-phenomenal states such as beliefs, see Zimmermann (unpublished *a*).    [39] Again, see McDowell (1995).

perceptual knowledge, disjunctivists maintain that one does not have the same epistemic grounds for believing that *p* (where *p* is the content of some perception of the external world) when one actually perceives that *p* as when one merely hallucinates that *p* or is fooled by a facsimile. The alleged difficulty with this view comes from the persistent intuition that whatever makes a perceptual belief into knowledge (the 'J' component) should remain invariant between veridical and the non-veridical cases. As Michael Tye puts it:

[W]hile there is certainly *a* difference between one's state of mind in seeing a table, say, and one's state of mind in hallucinating a table— . . . —intuitively, there is also something important in common. Intuitively, the reason why one may *think* that one is seeing a flat, square surface not only when one is seeing such a surface but also when one is hallucinating is that one can have a visual experience of the same phenomenal type in both cases.

This seems to me unquestionably the common-sense view of the matter, and it is also the view taken by scientists studying the psychology of vision. In scientific work, it is taken for granted that the same conscious visual state can occur whether or not the cells on the retina are activated by light reflected from a seen object or by artificial stimulation. (2003: 33 f.)

Note that the intuition invoked by Tye in the perceptual case is that there is a common *psychological* element shared by episodes of believing veridically and non-veridically. We may, if we like, describe this element as a certain visual experience, or the way things appear to one. But in order to raise a difficulty for the disjunctivist view, what has to be shown is that there is a common *epistemic* element. What one needs to establish, by way of posing a difficulty for the disjunctivist view, is that the common ('phenomenal') element that is psychologically invariant between the veridical and non-veridical cases is *relevant to the epistemic justification* of the relevant (true or false) perceptual belief. Nothing in what Tye says establishes that.

An opponent of disjunctivism in the perceptual case could try to argue from the presence of an element of psychological invariance to the presence of a separable 'judgment of appearance' which can serve as the requisite element of epistemic invariance between the veridical and the non-veridical perceptual judgments. When I make a judgment such as "There's a red cardinal on the tree", I do, even in the normal case, stand ready to retreat to a judgment of appearances: "Well, it *looks* to me as though there's a red cardinal on the tree." As pointed out before, a similar retreat in the case of mental self-ascriptions would represent taking back the avowing status of the utterance or thought. As emphasized by the middle-road view, the self-judgments represented by avowals enjoy a certain epistemic simplicity even relative to perceptual reports. When I avow being in M, my epistemic position is *not* one of somehow moving from a judgment that someone, who appears to me to be me, is in some mental state, which appears to me to be M, to the self-ascription that I am in M. I have no reason for thinking that someone is in M, or that I am in some mental state—other than whatever reason I have for thinking, simply, that I am in M. In particular, I have no reason for the self-ascription that is based on my recognition of M (or of myself). To accept this characterization of the epistemic position of an avowing subject is to give no purchase to the idea that a self-ascription I produce when avowing is ultimately grounded in the way things appear to me. But this means that to accept the Neo-Expressivist account of avowals is just to reject the intuition that, in the case of avowals, just as in the case of perceptual reports, there is an internal judgment of appearances, which may remain invariant between true and false avowals *and* is relevant to their epistemic warrant.[40]

If this is so, then even if the standard objection facing disjunctivism could be made to work in the perceptual case, it would have no force in the case of self-knowledge. On the proposal we have been considering, when a subject issues a true self-ascription of M in the avowing mode, she is expressing₁ her M, which is to say that M is her reason for the act of issuing the self-ascription. Moreover, she can be said to know that she is in M, because she will be epistemically warranted in issuing it. What gives the subject epistemic warrant in that case is the very same thing that gives her reason for the act of issuing the self-ascription: namely, her being in M.

What about the case in which a subject avows being in M though she is not? On the present proposal, in such a case the avowal could not represent something she knows, not only because the avowal would be false, but also because it would fail to be epistemically grounded (there being no M to ground it). However, here, unlike in

---

[40] We may remain neutral on the *psychological* question whether, when I avow, there is some psychological state I am in that does remain invariant regardless of whether I am in the avowed state or not. What is crucial is to deny that any such psychologically invariant element will be relevant to my epistemic warrant in making the self-ascription or the epistemic grounding of the self-ascription.

the case of a subject issuing a false perceptual report, there should be no temptation to invoke some 'subjectively identical state'—a self-impression, or a judgment concerning internal appearances—that could plausibly serve as an alternative candidate for the subject's epistemic reason for her avowal. Even if we suppose that there is a way in which the subject's present mental state appears to her, to the extent that we take the subject to be speaking her mind, we deny the relevance of such a self-impression to the epistemic assessment of the avowal, regardless of whether the subject avows truly or falsely.[41]

Someone may still object to the disjunctivist view of basic self-knowledge on the grounds that there must still be *something* of epistemic relevance shared by a false avowal and the corresponding true one, even if it is denied that that something is a (true) judgment of appearances on which they both rest. And I think the Neo-Expressivist account affords a satisfying way of accommodating this residual intuition. To see this, we need to call on our earlier discussion of false avowals, and the support given to the idea that true and false avowals, understood as acts, may have something in common, even though, if someone falsely avows being in M, it cannot be said that she has expressed *her* M.[42] Thus, suppose I avow "I'm feeling thirsty" as I look at a tall glass full of some enticing drink, while in fact I am not really thirsty. My utterance does not have my thirst as its brute cause; rather, it is caused by the sight of the enticing drink. So I have not expressed$_2$ (in the causal sense) my thirst, since expressing$_2$ is clearly a success verb. What about expressing$_1$? On the assumption that I am not actually feeling thirsty, though I may have succeeded in expressing$_1$ the presence of thirst, by virtue of intentionally issuing a self-ascription that expresses$_3$ thirst, I will have failed to express$_1$ *my* feeling of thirst (since there is at present no such state as *my* feeling thirsty). In this sense, my feeling thirsty cannot be the rational cause of my uttering "I'm feeling thirsty", any more than it can be its brute cause.

Now, a disjunctivist view of reasons for *action* would have it that my false avowal cannot share its rational grounding with a corresponding true avowal. Nevertheless, there seems to be room for a rational characterization of my behavior that refers to my (non-existent) thirst. If

---

[41] In (unpublished *b*), Aaron Zimmermann offers a different argument to the conclusion that "introspective disjunctivism" is more plausible than disjunctivism in the case of perceptual beliefs.

[42] See Ch. 8, pp. 396 f.

asked, "Why did you say that?", I would naturally answer: "Because I'm feeling thirsty." I may have had no more intention to deceive, mimic, or achieve some effect on my audience than I would have if I were simply to reach eagerly for the drink. And there may be no more reason to insist that my utterance was intended to inform any-one, or even just register, my (erroneous) judgment that I am thirsty than in the case of my non-verbal (though intentional) act of reach-ing. Since, by hypothesis, I am not feeling thirsty, it would of course be misleading for *you* to cite my feeling of thirst as the reason I had for my utterance. But a proper understanding of my behavior and the ways in which it succeeds or fails as intentional, purposive behavior would still cite, or make mention of, the (non-existent) feeling of thirst. As with other cases of unsuccessful acts, we could still describe the person who avows M falsely as having *tried* (but failed) to give voice to her M. In the above example, I can still be said to have tried to express$_1$ my thirst, and we can still recognize that *if* my behavior has a (rational) cause, or reason, it is none other than my thirst. Since there is no such thing as my present feeling of thirst, we cannot cor-rectly cite my thirst as the reason for my behavior. But we can still give sense to the intuition that there is a common element shared by acts of avowing truly and acts of avowing falsely: both are acts of speaking one's mind whose characterization as *reasonable* acts may require mentioning the (possibly absent) self-ascribed state of mind.

Along similar lines, I want to suggest that we can accommodate the residual intuition that false avowals share something of epistemic relev-ance with true ones, even though (as the disjunctivist about self-knowledge maintains) they cannot be epistemically grounded in the avowed state. Note that false avowals, understood as products (i.e., false self-ascriptions) will still be indubitable to the avowing subject. Moreover, although when we somehow recognize an avowal as false, we retract the presumption of truth, other aspects of Epistemic Asymmetry characteristic of our treatment of avowals remain in place. A false avowal may still be regarded as immune to errors of misascription, as well as misidentification. On the Neo-Expressivist account, to take someone's utterance to be an avowal is to regard it as an act in which she is speaking her mind, and thus to see it as pro-tected from certain kinds of epistemic challenges or criticisms. This is so even if the product of the act is thought to be false. This means that, even if we take an avowal to be false, and thus take the subject to *be* wrong, we may still not take her to have *gone* wrong, *epistemically* speaking, through mistaking one state for another, for example. And we will still expect that *if* the avower has any *epistemic reason* for her self-ascription, it will be *none other than* being in M. Thus, although a false avowal of M will not be epistemically grounded in M, we can still identify a kind of epistemic virtue (albeit a negative one) that it may share with a true avowal of M. In terms of the middle-road view, false and true avowals may equally enjoy entitlement by default.[43]

A synthetic account along the above lines would afford an answer to the question of what allows avowals to represent genuine knowledge, which is not only consistent with the Neo-Expressivist account of avowals, but makes essential use of some of its key ideas. It remains for us to articulate how such an account would capture the *privileged* character of basic self-knowledge. Earlier I introduced the notion of *first-person privilege*. First-person privilege is something each of us enjoys specifically with respect to the mental states that we ourselves are in at a given moment. It is not shared by others, and it is only exercised when one is speaking one's mind, as opposed to merely issuing a third-person report on it. There *is* something special about such an exercise, something that the high-road approach tries to capture. According to high-road views, our conception of human beings as rational and practical agents and deliberators cannot be divorced from the idea that they possess basic self-knowledge. On the present proposal, the connection is captured by noting that, when I speak my mind, *I proclaim the very states*—the thoughts, hopes, wants, pains, etc.—*that move me in thinking and in acting, at the same time as I ascribe those states to myself.* My avowals can be seen as offering up the very states that *provide reasons* for what I think and do, as well as having those states as their own epistemic reasons. In this, avowable self-knowledge is different from other kinds of knowledge, including perceptual knowledge, non-observational knowledge of one's bodily states, and immediate knowledge of what one is doing. Avowing subjects are *knowing selves* who exercise a special first-person privilege; thus their (true) avowals represent what is rightly described as privileged self-knowledge.

---

[43] See above, pp. 384 ff.

# 10

# Speaking My Mind: Grammar, Epistemology, and (Some) Ontology

Avowals of present thoughts, feelings, sensations, etc. enjoy a high degree of security; they exhibit striking epistemic asymmetries with other ascriptions, including, in particular, relatively secure "I"-ascriptions of non-mental states, and non-avowing "I"-ascriptions. The special security of avowals may seem puzzling and demands philosophical explanation. My aim in this book has been to provide such an explanation. In Chapter 1, I spelled out eight desiderata for an adequate account of avowals' security. I would like to begin this concluding chapter by summarizing the ways in which the Neo-Expressivist account of avowals' security succeeds in meeting these desiderata, tying a few loose ends along the way.

I claim as one advantage for my account of avowals' security the fact that it does not commit us to a Cartesian dualist ontology (which allows it to meet one of the above-mentioned desiderata). However, the question arises whether my account, like grammatical accounts that I reject, requires compromising the 'metaphysical robustness' of mental states in some way. In particular, an opponent of my account may raise the worry that Neo-Expressivism, with its portrayal of avowals as a species of expressive behavior, requires tacit commitment to a form of behaviorist irrealism about mental states. And so, in the remaining sections of the chapter, I will address an issue that has remained so far in the background: the metaphysical status of mental states and the relationship between mental states and expressive behavior. My discussion will inevitably be sketchy and somewhat speculative. I intend it to point the way for future investigation.

## Neo-Expressivism Meets the Desiderata

From the outset, I have sought an account of avowals' special status that fully respects Epistemic Asymmetry. I argued that epistemic views that try to assimilate the status of avowals to that of ascriptions that are merely especially well-founded, or highly reliable, fail to do so. Now, one who is committed to capturing Epistemic Asymmetry in its full scope seems to face a certain dilemma. She can explain Epistemic Asymmetry by making a Cartesian appeal to the infallible knowability of (present) mental states. But such an appeal, even if it were to succeed in explaining the asymmetries, carries with it an undesirable commitment to Cartesian Egos. Alternatively, she can chalk the asymmetries up to grammar, maintaining that avowals are excluded by their logical grammar from the category of things that represent truths or knowledge (as does the Simple Expressivist), or else claiming that the asymmetries are simply built into the truth-conditions of mentalistic ascriptions definitionally (as does the Default View). The trouble with purely grammatical accounts, how-ever, is that they do not leave room for genuine, privileged self-knowledge that can be reflected in "I"-ascriptions. In addition, they compromise the metaphysical reality of mental states, in ways I shall indicate later. In other words, familiar accounts of the security of avowals either fail to respect Epistemic Asymmetry in its full scope or have undesirable implications for the metaphysics of mind (or both).

I claim that my Neo-Expressivist account does better. First, it allows us to respect Epistemic Asymmetry in its full scope, thereby meeting desiderata D1–D4 on an adequate account of avowals' secur-ity (mentioned in the Introduction). Consider first:

**D1.** The account should explain what renders avowals protected from ordinary epistemic assessments (including requests for reasons, chal-lenges to their truth, simple correction, etc.).

On the Neo-Expressivist account, our ordinary present-tense self-ascriptions of mental states (whether made in speech or in thought) are protected from ordinary epistemic assessment because, or to the extent that, they are direct expressions of the self-ascribed states. A subject who issues an avowal, much like a subject who gives natural expression to her sensations, thoughts, or feelings, acts in epistemic innocence: she is speaking directly from a mental condition, rather than issuing a report that is based on her judgment about it. Avowals, I have proposed, are not only immune to errors of misidentification, but are also immune to ascriptive errors—errors of misjudging the state one is in (or its content). Epistemically speaking, there is no more mediation between the "I"-ascriptions we issue when avowing and the conditions we self-ascribe than there is between non-self-ascriptive expressions and the conditions they express. This is why it seems as inappropriate to correct, challenge, or request reasons for an avowal of a sensation, or a thought, as it would in the case of a natural (or non-self-ascriptive) expression of such states.

The Neo-Expressivist account also meets the second desideratum:

**D2.** [The account] should explain why avowals' security is unparalleled: why there are asymmetries in security between avowals and all other empirical ascriptions, including (truth-conditionally equivalent) third-person ascriptions and non-mental first-person ascriptions. In particular, it should explain why avowals are so strongly presumed to be *true*.

On the account I have offered, avowals are unique in being expressive acts in which subjects express, the *very conditions* that the acts' products ascribe to the subjects, in virtue of the products' semantic content. The uniqueness of avowals is reflected in the fact that they combine *saying that* the subject of the ascription is in the relevant state while at the same time serving to express that very state. In this way, my account, unlike any of its rivals, captures nicely the line that separates avowals from all other ascriptions. Mental self-ascriptions to others or to oneself at other times do not serve to express the ascribed state; and neither do non-mental self-ascriptions or self-ascriptions of character traits and psychological dispositions. A subject *can* give a natural expression, or use a non-ascriptive verbal vehicle to give expression to a present mental state M; but such expressive acts do not have self-ascriptions of M as their products. Natural expressions have no semantic content; they do not ascribe anything to anyone. And non-ascriptive verbal expressions, though they ascribe all sorts of things, do not ascribe the very mental state they express.

Of particular interest in this connection are what we can refer to as "perceptual self-reports"; e.g., "I am seeing a tree", "I am hearing footsteps", "I'm tasting chocolate", "I'm feeling/touching a cotton ball", "I'm smelling cinnamon". Interestingly, such self-reports meet Evans's and Moran's Transparency Condition (discussed above, Chapter 4). If asked whether I'm seeing a tree, I will do nothing more than look to the world, to see whether there's a tree in front of me. But my visual self-report "I'm seeing a tree" does not share in the security of avowals. It is straightforwardly corrigible, dubitable, subject to requests for reasons, and so on. On the Neo-Expressivist account this falls neatly into place. Insofar as we understand a perceptual self-report 'factively', i.e., as ascribing to the subject a visual, aural, olfactory, etc. state that relates her to a present item or state in affairs which obtains in the world (as opposed to ascribing to her a visual, aural, etc. sensation), we will not regard it as simply expressing the self-ascribed state. Someone's state of actually seeing a tree, hearing a tune, tasting chocolate, touching silk, or smelling a rose is not expressible, it seems. And the Neo-Expressivist account can explain why: as regards such states, one cannot engage in behavior that will suffice to show one's being in the relevant state, just as one cannot engage in behavior that will suffice to show one's character traits or psychological dispositions. We *could* (and maybe do sometimes) understand an utterance of "I'm seeing a tree" as serving to express$_1$ my tree-ish visual sensation. But, semantically speaking, the self-ascription produced through such an utterance does not ascribe to me that sensation, but rather ascribes to me actually seeing a tree. Since the truth of this self-ascription requires that there be a tree that I am seeing, understanding the utterance in this way does not require us to regard it as true. Using the terminology of Chapter 8, perceptual self-reports, unlike avowals, are not transparent-to-the-subject's-condition, even though, like many avowals, they are transparent-to-the-world. Thus, we can see why perceptual self-reports are *not* governed by the asymmetric presumption of truth governing avowals.

Intuitively speaking, no one else can express a mental state I am presently in, and I cannot express any mental states other than my own. I can express dismay without expressing *my* dismay; but I cannot through my behavior, verbal or not, express($_1$) *your* dismay rather than mine. On the account of expression I have developed, this is also to be explained by appeal to the fact that I cannot engage in behavior that suffices to show that someone other than myself is in a present mental state. Suppose I were hooked up to your brain and nervous system, so that when someone stepped on your foot, I would be yelling "Ouch!". Depending on the details of the case, it might be natural to suppose one of two things: either that I *was* in pain, and when uttering "Ouch" I was expressing *my* pain, or that I wasn't actually in pain, and my utterance "Ouch" was an instance of failed expression, explicable by appeal to the unusual causal set-up. It seems to me that in no case would we be inclined to take it that I was expressing *your* pain. I think that this is because we take it that my own behavior is only apt to be sufficient to show *my* mental states. My reports, by contrast, are clearly not similarly restricted. Taking avowing to be a species of expressive behavior, then, enables the Neo-Expressivist account to meet the third desideratum:

**D3**. [The account] should explain the non-negotiable character of the security—the fact that it is 'non-transferable' and 'inalienable'.

I regard it as a distinctive advantage of the Neo-Expressivist account over certain other non-introspectionist accounts that it also meets the next desideratum:

**D4**. It should apply to *both* intentional and non-intentional avowals alike, and allow us to separate avowals from other ascriptions in terms of their security.

Familiar accounts that oppose introspectionism have failed to meet this desideratum. For example, the Simple Expressivist account is usually introduced by pointing out close similarities between avowals of, specifically, sensations such as pain or emotions such as joy or fear, on the one hand, and natural expressions of such states, on the other hand. That account is not elaborated in a way that readily extends to all avowals, in particular to avowals of intentional states that do not appear to have natural expressions. On the other hand, non-introspectionist views that seize on the feature of transparency-to-the-world usually focus on intentional avowals, and it is far from clear how they can extend to avowals that do not involve any specification of intentional content. Now, the Neo-Expressivist account was introduced through the limit case of self-verifying avowals of presently entertained thoughts, which clearly fall under the rubric of intentional avowals. However, I went to great length to explain how avowals *in general* can be understood as expressive acts in which subjects express$_1$ a self-ascribed mental state and have shown how the expressivist insight applies to both intentional and phenomenal avowals. Moreover, I have explained why, among the various kinds of mental self-ascriptions, *only* avowals can be understood as such acts. Thus, my Neo-Expressivist account has identified something distinctive of *all and only* avowals.

Meeting D1–D4 amounts to accounting for Epistemic Asymmetry in its full scope, which, I have argued, epistemic views (other than the Cartesian view) fail to do. But another important point in favor of my account, as against, most notably, the Simple Expressivist account, is the fact that it doesn't purchase the explanation of Epistemic Asymmetry at the cost of Semantic Continuity. It also meets the next desideratum:

**D5**. [The account] should accommodate the continuities in semantic and logical structure between avowals and other ascriptions. In particular, it should present avowals as truth-assessable.

Using the distinction between acts and their products, I was able to endorse the expressivist idea that there are certain similarities between avowals and natural expressions, in point of the acts performed, while insisting that avowals, like acts of assertion, reporting, and so on, have as their products semantically articulate ascriptions, which say of some individual that he or she is in some state. The expressive character of avowals that is highlighted in the explanation of Epistemic Asymmetry pertains, broadly speaking, to the pragmatics (or action-theoretic features) of avowing, not to its semantics. Just as an utterance such as "This is a great show!" may serve to express one's pleasure rather than, or in addition to, one's assessment of some show's merits, so an utterance of "I'm annoyed at you" may serve to express one's annoyance rather than (or in addition to) one's judgment that one is annoyed. In each case, whether the subject is expressing the first-order feeling or attitude rather than (or in addition to) the judgment semantically expressed by her utterance is a matter of the way the utterance is issued, not a matter of what it says. This is not to deny, however, that *which* state or *what* judgment is expressed may well be systematically related to the semantic content of the utterance. In virtue of its semantic content, an avowal (understood as a certain product—a self-ascription made in a given context) will have definite truth-conditions; it will be true just in case the producer of the avowal is in the state the avowal ascribes to her. On the Neo-Expressivist account, to regard an utterance (in speech or in thought) as an avowal of M, as opposed to a report of M, is to regard it as expressive of the avower's present M. Since the avowal says that the avower is in M, and it is true just in case the avower is in M, to regard an utterance as an avowal is to take it to be *true* (hence the Neo-Expressivist explanation of the asymmetric presumption of truth governing avowals).

At the same time, my account can accommodate the possibility of false, and correctable, avowals, thereby meeting the following desideratum:

**D6.** The account should avoid portraying avowals as absolutely infallible or incorrigible.

We can make sense of the possibility of false avowals by bringing them under the rubric of *expressive failures*, as cases in which a subject is misspeaking her mind. A subject can wince, or smile, or say "Ouch!" when not in the condition naturally associated with the relevant behavior, even without any dissimulation. Similarly, a subject can sincerely self-ascribe a feeling, emotion, or thought, in the avowing mode, though she is not in the self-ascribed condition. Her act is one of directly speaking from a present state of mind, rather than issuing a self-report based on a false self-judgment; but the product of her act is a false self-ascription. We, her observers, may be in a position to recognize her avowal as a failed expression, if we have independent reason to suspect that what she says is false. We thus may be in a position to correct the avowal. So, in contrast to the Cartesian view, as well as certain grammatical views (including certain expressivist views), on my account, avowals are not portrayed as absolutely infallible or incorrigible.

Admitting that avowals can be false does not undermine the Neo-Expressivist explanation of the asymmetric presumption of truth governing them; it just shows that the presumption can be overridden. Note, too, that allowing that any given avowal (even an avowal of a present pain sensation) can be false does not commit us to the possibility of wholesale, or global, failure of avowals, or even to the possibility of a single subject all of whose avowals are false (viz., what Wright describes as a "chronically unreliable" avower). I think that whether the Neo-Expressivist account is committed to such possibilities will depend on the character of the link it forges between expression and mentality. I shall return to this issue in the next section.

In developing the Neo-Expressivist account, I was also mindful of the following desideratum:

**D7**. [The account] should avoid appealing to Cartesian dualist ontology.

I do not think that the full appreciation of avowals' distinctive security forces on us—or even encourages—Cartesian dualism. I argued in the early chapters (2 and 3) that the peculiar security of uses of "I" 'as sub-ject' in no way requires invoking infallibly recognized Egos, even if "I" genuinely refers to a certain individual. In a similar vein, I argued in later chapters that the special ascriptive security of avowals does not require appealing to infallibly knowable states of immaterial minds, even as we take avowals to involve genuine ascription of mental states to oneself. The key to understanding the (genuine) asymmetries between avowals and other ascriptions, while adhering to the logico-semantic continuities between them, is to recognize that avowals play a role similar to that of non-self-ascriptive expressions, in that their *primary* contextual function is to express first-order conditions rather than higher-order judgments about those conditions. There is no need to identify a special epistemic route, or method, or basis, which under-writes subjects' privileged epistemic access to their present mental states, and which explains the special security of avowals. Equally, there is no need to appeal, as does the Cartesian account, to the special *nature* of the states of which avowals speak. It remains to be seen what *non-Cartesian* ontology of mental states befits the Neo-Expressivist account, and whether it can accomplish its explanatory task without compromising the metaphysical reality of mental states.

By meeting the above desiderata, I have provided what I take to be a fully adequate '*non-epistemic*' answer to the first question I set out to answer, namely:

(i)  What accounts for the *unparalleled security of avowals*? Why is it that avowals, understood as true or false ascriptions of contingent states to an individual, are so rarely questioned or corrected, are generally so resistant to ordinary epistemic assessments, and are so strongly presumed to be true?

However, I have taken as an additional, final desideratum on an adequate account of avowals' special security:

**D8**. It should allow for the possibility that avowals represent privileged self-knowledge.

Having developed a non-epistemic, expressivist answer to (i), I set out, in Chapter 9, to show that the Neo-Expressivist account does not preclude a substantive, non-deflationary answer to a question that is often of central interest to philosophers studying avowals, namely:

(ii)  Do avowals serve to articulate *privileged self-knowledge*? If so, what qualifies avowals as articles of knowledge at all, and what is the source of the privileged status of this knowledge?

I sketched three kinds of views that portray avowals as representing items of privileged (even if not infallible) self-knowledge, consistently with the Neo-Expressivist account of avowals' security. I concluded with what I take to be a promising synthesis of these views, which makes direct use of key ingredients of the Neo-Expressivist account of avowals' security. On the synthetic view I sketched, avowals do not simply represent reliably produced true pronouncements that observers will presume to be true to the extent that they take them to be expressions of subjects' present mental states. In addition, avowing subjects enjoy a special epistemic warrant, since their pronouncements, when true, are epistemically grounded in the very states they ascribe to themselves, which states also serve as the reasons for their acts of avowing. This special warrant accrues to subjects only when issuing present-tense self-ascriptions of occurrent mental states, and only when they do so in the avowing mode—that is, only when they exercise their first-person privilege. Avowals (when true) can thus be seen as representing items of genuine and privileged self-knowledge.

I did not offer a direct answer to another question about self-knowledge identified in the first chapter, namely:

(iii)  Avowals aside, what allows us to possess privileged self-knowledge? That is, how is it that subjects like us are able to have privileged, non-evidential knowledge of their present states of mind, regardless of whether they avow being in the relevant states or not?

Questions (i) and (ii) begin with the fact that we often pronounce on our mental states through avowals (in speech or in thought), and that when we do, our pronouncements enjoy a special security and appear to represent privileged knowledge we have of ourselves. By contrast, question (iii) presupposes that there is a certain datum of self-knowledge, which we may describe as the existence of 'unarticulated self-knowledge': whether or not we bother to pronounce on a present mental state in speech or thought, if we are in a mental state, we *know* it, and know it in a privileged way. Given that we do have privileged self-knowledge, whether or not it is articulated by avowals, (iii) seeks to find out what allows us to have such knowledge.

Throughout my discussion, I have avoided commitment to the Cartesian idea that our mental states are transparent to us, in the sense that a subject who is in a mental state is somehow guaranteed to know that she is. I think there are several reasons not to endorse this very strong thesis of 'self-intimation' (as it is sometimes referred to). For one thing, at least our post-Freudian common sense has grown quite accustomed to the notion of a subconscious emotion, feeling, or propositional attitude, which we harbor at a given moment, and which affects our behavior and other aspects of our mental lives, but which is, for one reason or another, deeply hidden from us. There are also various findings of contemporary cognitive science suggesting that our behavior and actions may be guided by mental states (including perceptual states) and reasoning processes of whose presence and character we are entirely ignorant.[1] I take it as an advantage of my view that it does not require us to deny such possibilities of self-ignorance. But even setting aside such possibilities, a proponent of the thesis of self-intimation has to tell us what to make of subjects who possess mental states, but, due to conceptual limitations, are incapable of passing any judgment on—and thus (presumably) of *knowing* of—their mental states. Views of self-knowledge that tie the explanation of its privileged character to self-intimation either have to deny that 'unknowing selves', such as brutes or otherwise conceptually challenged creatures, can have mental states (something Descartes himself was willing to do), or have to add the stipulation that the thesis of self-intimation applies only in the case of creatures capable of self-judgment. Neither option seems desirable to me.[2]

---

[1] See, e.g., Nisbett and Wilson (1977), and Nisbett and Ross (1980).

[2] My student Charles Olbert has pointed out the following consequence of the thesis of self-intimation. If the thesis says: "If a properly endowed subject S is in M, then S will think/occurrently believe that she is in M," then it faces a regress. For, *thinking* that one is in M is itself an occurrent mental state. So, by the thesis

The idea that only a creature capable of warranted judgments concerning its present mental states should be capable of *being* in mental states is sufficiently implausible on its face, and its corollary—that animals and very young children could not have mental states—is sufficiently widely rejected, that I feel justified in setting it aside here. Authors who endorse the thesis of self-intimation more often opt for the second option, of restricting the thesis to rational creatures like us, who are capable of self-reflection.[3] They claim that *in a creature who is capable of mental self-judgment or self-ascription*, it is not in general possible, conceptually speaking, that the creature should *be* in a mental state M, without knowing that she is. Now, it seems intuitively clear that only a creature conceptually capable of thinking of her own mental states should be able to possess any kind of self-knowledge. But it is far from obvious how having the relevant conceptual wherewithal brings in its train any kind of conceptual guarantee that when one is in a mental state one will *know* that one is in it.[4] Why should having the conceptual capacity for mental self-judgment guarantee (a) that one will always *exercise* the capacity for mental self-judgment when in a mental state by tokening the relevant judgment or thought, and (b) that the ensuing self-judgment will be *correct* (as well as warranted)?

Now, behind (iii) may lie the naïve thought that a creature, whether human or brute, who is feeling pain or pleasure, hunger, fatigue, anger, fear, etc., regardless of whether she says, or thinks to herself, that she is in the relevant state, knows it, and knows it the way no one else does. This is just part of what it is to be in a state of this kind. This naïve thought gives rise to the objection that, *contra* the Neo-Expressivist view, possession of privileged self-knowledge must be independent of any (overt or covert) self-ascriptive expressive behavior.[5] *Privileged* basic self-knowledge, the objector would say, is something a subject has whenever she is in a conscious mental state, and such knowledge is only incidentally articulated by avowals.

---

of self-intimation, one will think that she thinks she's in M; and so on, *ad infinitum*. The proponent of self-intimation may, however, be willing to accept this consequence.

[3] Cf. Shoemaker 'First-Person Access' (in his (1996) ). Shoemaker defends a (non-Cartesian) version of the self-intimation thesis by developing an argument that 'self-blindness' is impossible. Peacocke (1996) offers a different version of self-intimation. Both authors restrict the claim to subjects who are conceptually capable of thinking about their own mental states.

[4] It may be true that a creature like us *will (almost) always*, as a matter of brute causal fact, believe she is in M whenever she is. But the defenders of self-intimation in question are after more than mere causal guarantee.          [5] This way of thinking of (iii) has been suggested to me by Keith Simmons.

But note that on this line of thought, "S has privileged (first-person) knowledge that she is in M" is simply taken to be entailed "S is in a conscious state M". And note, too, that it will turn out that any creature who has conscious mental states will *ipso facto* possess privileged basic self-knowledge. Although I think it is true that only so-called conscious states are avowable, I have taken the question about privileged self-knowledge to be a substantive epistemological question that is not automatically answered positively by appealing to the conscious character of avowable mental states. That is to say, I have sought a substantive account of self-knowledge on which it could turn out that (when avowing) we can be said to have especially warranted true self-beliefs. If it is accepted that simply being in conscious mental states is sufficient for having privileged self-knowledge properly so-called, then there is no need for such an account; we should instead be seeking an account of what renders some states conscious, something I have definitely not undertaken in this book.

It may be suggested, in response, that simply *being* in a conscious mental state is not sufficient by itself for possessing the relevant self-knowledge; one also has to *attend to* or *reflect on* one's present mental state (which is something only some creatures with mental states are capable of). The thesis of self-intimation may seem more plausible when it is taken to require actual attention to one's present mental state. Thus restricted, the thesis will say that, as a matter of conceptual necessity, *if* someone attends to her present state of mind, then, if she thinks she is in a mental state M, she will be correct (as well as warranted).

However, if this is what the thesis of self-intimation amounts to, the Neo-Expressivist can clearly take it on board, as long as it is understood as allowing for the possibility that a subject may be wrong about her present mental state. After all, thinking that one is in M is just self-ascribing M in thought. Such self-ascriptions can, on the Neo-Expressivist account, qualify as avowals, provided they are not made on the basis of any behavioral evidence, inference, etc., and serve to express M itself. As suggested in Chapter 8, self-ascriptions issued upon attending to one's present state of mind are naturally regarded in this way. Attending need not be construed as an epistemic method of obtaining information or discovery; it can be seen instead as a psychological device for putting oneself in a position to *speak directly from* one's condition. In the special case of avowing in thought, there is, of course, no speaking. Still, there is an issuing of a self-ascription—some mental tokening that qualifies as thinking *that* one is in M. Now, on my account, thought-avowals, like avowals in speech, can be seen to enjoy distinctive security: we would not expect any reasons or justification for such avowals, beyond the subject's simply being in the self-ascribed state. And, to take someone to be avowing M in thought is to take her to be expressing (to herself) her M, which means presuming that her avowal is true. Moreover, assuming the avowal is indeed true, we would take the subject who avows to have privileged knowledge that she is in the state she thinks she is in.

An opponent of the Neo-Expressivist account may still be worried that the account commits us, implausibly, to the idea that a subject could *only obtain* privileged basic self-knowledge by actually engaging in self-ascriptive expressive behavior. So, in the absence of expressive behavior, the subject would have no immediate, first-person way of knowing her own states of mind.[6] This seems to me to involve a misunderstanding of the account. The Neo-Expressivist is not saying that we *reach* or *achieve* self-knowledge *by producing avowals* (in speech or in thought). Expressing one's present state is not an act one engages in so as to obtain self-knowledge. This is not to deny that speaking one's mind is something one can get better at, and in that sense, that one can perhaps become more self-knowledgeable. There are presumably things one can do to become better able directly *and correctly* to speak from one's present states of mind. Certain forms of therapy (including hypnosis) could perhaps be construed as, in part, aiming to minimize expressive failures—to help get one 'in touch with' oneself, as we say. I have no objection to this way of cashing out the idea that subjects may have methods of obtaining self-knowledge.[7] But this is a far cry from

---

[6] For a published version of this worry, see Wright's brief discussion of the hypothetical case of a secret agent who, under torture, still gives no expression to his pain (1998: 37). But I have heard this worry voiced on various occasions when presenting the Neo-Expressivist account.

[7] One can strive to become, in general, better able to speak one's mind, so that one's self-pronouncements will bear the marks of privileged self-knowledge more often. But, on particular occasions, too much cognitive effort invested in trying to 'get things right' concerning one's present states of mind can actually get in the way of such achievement. Arguably, people sometimes feel the need to engage in self-analysis or self-interpretation precisely when they feel unable simply to give voice to a present thought, feeling, or emotion. What they avow in such circumstances is typically uncertainty, or hesitation ("Let's see, what *do* I think? How *do* I feel about what she just did? Hmmm, I'm not quite sure. Maybe it's that ... or ... "). And, unless our effort culminates in what is properly regarded as an expression of our present (possibly just acquired) state, our audience (actual or potential) will not hesitate to challenge our claims. It is not uncommon for the products of self-analysis or self-interpretation to be treated as disputable speculations, not to be taken at face value.

the traditional idea of privileged access. Thus, it seems to me to go against the grain of the Neo-Expressivist account to insist that avowable self-knowledge is a result of a distinctive method we employ or route we take, and to seek a systematic answer to the question how, avowals aside, subjects can arrive at basic, privileged self-knowledge.

## Speaking My Mind: Expression and Reality

When someone avows "I feel awful!", is there a state of affairs, a distinct 'bit of the world' that makes her "I"-ascription true? I intend the view of avowals that I have developed in this book to be fully compatible with a positive answer to this question. My expressivist view of avowals has been put forth with a fairly robust commonsense realism in mind, at least as regards basic mental states, such as feeling hungry, cold, tired, achy, having a pain in one's stomach, wanting ice cream, preferring to have some tea, thinking about $x$, feeling angry at $y$, and so on. Though such states are states of subjects, they are not of subjects' own making. At the same time, however, in developing the Neo-Expressivist view of avowals, I have not committed myself to any particular view of what *being* in a mental state of these kinds consists in. Apart from avoiding commitment to Cartesian dualism, I have tried to remain relatively neutral on the question of the nature of mental states. However, it may seem that the Neo-Expressivist account cannot avoid compromising the metaphysical reality of mental states. While developing a positive metaphysical account of the nature of mental states clearly goes beyond the scope of this work, I would like to take some steps towards addressing this worry.[8]

One familiar way in which a metaphysical view in a given domain is thought to compromise metaphysical reality is by maintaining that the facts in the relevant domain are ultimately dependent upon our judgments about those facts. Thus, recall the Default View presented in the previous chapter. On that view, avowals do have truth-conditions; they can be true or false. However, when a self-ascriber succeeds in

---

[8] Some of the ideas presented in this and the next section were first introduced in a talk that Doug Long and I gave at UNC Chapel Hill in November 1997. Discussions with Long have helped shape my thinking about the metaphysical issues surrounding avowals, though he may take exception to the ontological conservatism I advocate in what follows.

making a true avowal, this success is not a matter of making a correct judgment that tracks bits or aspects of an independent mental reality. For it is part of the truth-conditions of mentalistic ascriptions that self-ascribers' judgments are assigned default correctness. Strictly speaking, mental reality is not what makes mentalistic ascriptions true, since it is in good part the making of mentalistic ascriptions by self-ascribers which itself renders mentalistic ascriptions true.

As mentioned in Chapter 9 (pp. 348f.), Wright thinks that it's possible to "exculpate [the Default View] from the charge of dogmatism" by appealing to a comparison between mental discourse and other areas of discourse where it may be misguided to conceive of successful judgments as tracking a completely independent reality. For example, it may be suggested that whether or not some object is red is at least in part dependent on the color judgments of well-placed perceivers. Similarly, on some views, whether or not an action is right or wrong, a state of affairs good or bad, may not be a matter of features of the world that are entirely independent of the judgments of moral agents. In these areas, truth is *judgment- (or response-) dependent.*[9] In the case at hand—the mental realm—the claim would be that whether the avowal "I feel awful" is true or not, and whether or not the self-ascriber does feel awful, is not entirely independent of what she thinks about her state. Since this dependence on the subject's own verdict constrains any ascription of a mental state to her, if someone said of me, "She feels awful", the truth of her ascription would presumably also not be independent of what *I* take to be the case about my state. If so, it should be no surprise that there is such a fit between what a subject says (or thinks) about her condition and the truth of the matter, and ultimately no point in seeking a substantive explanation of the asymmetries between avowals and other ascriptions—hence the Default View.

I do not think this attempt to rescue the Default View from the charge of dogmatism succeeds, though expounding my reasons will take us too far afield. Very briefly, the idea of judgment-dependence involves specifying conditions on what it is that qualifies someone as well placed—what equips her with "a suitable cognitive endowment"—to make the judgments on which the truths in the given domain

---

[9] For discussion of this idea, see, e.g., Wright (1994).

allegedly depend. In general, there is a question whether the relevant conditions can be specified in a non-circular way—whether, for example, we can characterize the well-placed observer of color in a way that does not appeal in any way to her ability to make correct (...) color judgments. But in the present case there is an additional problem. For, the idea of judgment-dependence here is not the idea that what is true in the mental realm depends on the judgment of *any* well placed judge concerning any arbitrarily chosen mental fact. It is built into the case that subjects can be well placed *only with respect to their own present mental states*, so that being well placed will systematically depend on whether the relevant mental state is the subject's or some-one else's. But then we may still be under explanatory pressure: *why* is it that subjects are to be systematically presumed *better* placed than their observers to pass truth-determining judgments on certain facts in the mental realm?

An obvious answer is that *being* in a mental state is partially consti-tuted by thinking that one is in the mental state, so that facts in the mental realm are determined in part by what self-ascribers take them to be. In the previous section, I canvassed some difficulties with this answer, and will not reiterate them here. In any event, endorsing this answer seems to require settling for a certain irrealism about mental states, which many would find problematic. On a more robust realist view, it would be held that, at least in the case of basic mental states (for example, those we share with non-human animals and pre-cognitive children), whether someone is in a given mental state does not depend on whether she takes herself to be in the mental state. And, in devel-oping the Neo-Expressivist view, I wanted to allow this much real-ism about mental states. On the metaphysical view I have had in mind, the mental conditions expressed by avowals are not, in general, dependent on subjects' own best judgments. Being in a mental state is one thing; passing a judgment that one is in the mental state is another. Nothing in the Neo-Expressivist account is supposed to depend on the idea that avowable mental states are states whose very existence requires that the subject make a judgment that she is (or takes herself to be) in the state.

It is worth reiterating in the present context that the Neo-Expressivist view also allows that someone may judge that she is in a mental state without actually being in that mental state. Passing judgment on a contingent matter of fact is a risky business, here as elsewhere. However reliable one is, one may get it wrong. There are all sorts of ways of coming to make a judgment that one feels depressed, or hopes for something, or wants something, or even is in pain, and they can lead us astray. With the possible exception of self-verifying thoughts (discussed at length in Chapter 6), there is no apriori reason to deny that one can reach a judgment that one is in a mental state even when one is in fact not in that state. There may well be particular mental phenomena that do fit Wright's characterization of the judgment dependence of mental ascriptions, where one's judgment that one is in the mental state actually makes it the case that one is, or at least partially constitutes one's being in the state.[10] But I do not believe this to be the general case. In general, judging that one is in some mental condition does not make it so. Furthermore, I have maintained that there can be false avowals. This means that there can be, on my view, self-ascriptions issued in the avowing mode (in speech *or* in thought) when the subject is not in the avowed state. If those self-ascriptions are taken to represent ('unreflective') self-judgments,[11] then cases of false avowals will provide a pertinent illustration of the possibility of a subject's judging she is in a mental state without in fact being in the state. Unlike grammatical views, expressivist views included, my Neo-Expressivism does not associate with avowals a logical or conceptual guarantee of truth. It also does not recognize an interesting sense in which mental states in general are of subjects' own making.

It may be thought that my acceptance of a 'no-cognitive-achievement' claim in connection with avowals (see Chapter 9, pp. 352f.) commits me to a compromised view regarding the independent existence of mental states. But I do not think this is so. The (limited) 'no-cognitive-achievement' claim I endorse is the claim that avowals do not reflect a cognitive effort, some epistemic doing, whose target is one's present mental state. Avowing as such is not a matter of trying to 'get it right' regarding how things are with one at present mentally. But this does not mean there are no independent facts of the matter constituting how things are with the subject mentally. That there

---

[10]  See Taylor (1985); Moran (1988); and Tanney (1996).

[11]  So that avowals are taken to express self-judgments, in addition to expressing the mental state they self-ascribe, in keeping with the Dual Expression thesis (see pp. 304ff.).

is no epistemic targeting of the condition on the avowing subject's part does not mean there are no conditions that are potential targets. The 'no-cognitive achievement' claim I have accepted concerns the epistemology of self-ascriptions. It is distinct from the 'no-independent-existence' claim, which does concern the ontology of mental states.

However, there may be another reason for thinking that my account of avowals' security and self-knowledge commits me to some form of irrealism about mental states. Even if the Neo-Expressivist allows that mental states exist independently of self-ascribers' judgments, it may seem to tie the existence of mental states to expressive behavior. In Wittgenstein, for instance, the expressivist thesis is closely aligned with the 'non-designative' thesis: the claim that mental terms do not designate inner items the way physical terms designate physical items or the way color terms designate colors of things.[12] Partly in light of this thesis, it is often thought (mistakenly, I believe) that Wittgenstein champions a certain kind of behaviorist irrealism about mental states. This attribution is typically fostered by reading the combination of the non-designative thesis and the expressivist thesis in a certain way. If, as the non-designative thesis seems to maintain, terms like "pain", "anger", "hope", "intention", etc. do not stand for anything 'inside' subjects, then such terms do not designate anything at all (this is sometimes thought to be the upshot of the famous beetle-in-the-box passage in Wittgenstein's *Investigations* (1953: §293)). But then self-ascriptions which employ such mentalistic terms can at most amount to glorified moans and groans, stylized bits of behavior; so all there could be to mentality then would be subjects' surface behavior. This would be the upshot of the expressivist thesis. And reports on subjects that contain mentalistic terms could then at most be seen to offer descriptions of such behavior (or perhaps of dispositions to it). Thus, behaviorist irrealism.

Can the Neo-Expressivist account that I have offered be protected from this threat of behaviorist irrealism? Or does it commit us to the view that being in pain, for example, or thinking of Vienna, cannot amount to anything more than displaying (or being disposed to display) certain kinds of characteristic expressive behavior, overt or covert? The worry is that, in its effort to avoid Cartesian dualism, the

---

[12] On the relationship between Wittgenstein's expressivist thesis and the non-designative thesis, see Peacocke (1982), and Foot's reply (1982).

account will end up compromising the metaphysical reality of mental states, by tying mental states too closely to expressive behavior.

More than three decades ago, Richard Rorty (1970a) set an agenda for properly realist, or non-eliminativist, views of mentality. Rorty argued that, to engage Descartes's arguments for dualism, such views must provide an acceptable demarcation of the mental from the physical, one that does justice to what I have called Epistemic Asymmetry. Like Descartes, Rorty thinks that this requires giving the demarcation in terms of incorrigibility: the mark of the mental is the fact that subjects' ascriptions of such states to themselves are incorrigible. And, like Descartes, Rorty understands incorrigibility in epistemic terms; if subjects' self-ascriptions of mental states are to be incorrigible, this is because subjects are in an unassailable position to know of those states. However, if, as Rorty himself suspected, there could be no states answering to this description, then the existence of distinctively mental states will be impugned—hence the possibility of eliminativism, a position which Rorty himself later embraced (see his (1970b) ). If Rorty is right, then we may be caught between the Scylla of eliminating distinctively mental states and the Charybdis of endorsing non-materialist Cartesian ontology. Either we recognize the existence of specially knowable mental states over and above physical states (and Egos over and above human bodies), or we must give up on the idea of mental states as a distinct category of states with respect to which subjects enjoy a special privilege.

Traditional behaviorism does appear to provide for a non-dualist mental/physical demarcation. But it does not escape Rorty's dilemma, for two reasons. First, the behaviorist demarcation does not make room for the idea of a special status for basic self-knowledge, or of what I have called first-person privilege.[13] Secondly, since traditional behaviorism rejects the idea of mental processes, states, and events—specifically, of occurrent mental *episodes*—in favor of behavioral dispositions, it clearly falls under Rorty's rubric of eliminativism. Unlike traditional behaviorism, the Neo-Expressivist view offers a mental-physical demarcation that not only avoids Cartesian dualism but also does justice to the commonsense notion of first-person privilege and to the special status of basic self-knowledge. Or so I have argued. It remains to be seen whether, unlike traditional behaviorism, the account can stay clear of objectionable irrealism about mentality.

---

[13] See Ryle (1949: ch. 6).

It might seem that there is an easy way to preserve robust realism about mental states while still accommodating the insights of the Neo-Expressivist account, thereby steering between the horns of Rorty's dilemma. Suppose, in adherence to a certain form of materialism, we took mental conditions to be independently existing states or events inside subjects' bodies, but accepted that our mentalistic self-ascriptions do not always serve to report these internal happenings. Sometimes they only serve to express them; and then a special kind of first-person privilege can indeed be associated with them, just as the Neo-Expressivist account would have it.[14] The point of making this 'materialist expressivist' proposal should be clear: it is to provide for a complete detachment of mental conditions from expressive behavior, so as to avoid the threat of behaviorist irrealism, while taking advantage of the expressivist account of avowals. The materialist expressivist view as I envisage it would maintain that being in a mental condition is fully constituted by the presence of a relevant internal (brain) state. The presence of that state inside a subject is what provides the worldly condition that makes an avowal true; and that presence is completely detachable from the presence of any expressive behavior on the subject's part whatsoever.

To capture the role played by expressive behavior in understanding mentality, our expressivist materialist may elaborate the proposal along functionalist lines, as follows.[15] Ontologically speaking, mental states just are internal neurophysiological states of individuals, and mental terms refer to these states. However, our typical *epistemic access* to these states (at least in the case of others) is mediated by our perception of their typical causes and behavioral effects, which include expressive behavior. Expressive behavior can then perhaps be thought of as relevant to the *meaning* of mental terms, or to our standard ways of *fixing the reference* of such terms. We pick out someone's state of fatigue, say, not directly as a certain internal state of their brain or nervous system, but rather as the *underlying, hidden cause* of characteristic observable fatigue behavior (where the state itself also has typical observable causes). Given this understanding, a mental state can be thought of as completely detachable from expressive behavior, since internal causes of typical behavior need not actually cause the behavior

---

[14] This proposal is due to Keith Simmons.    [15] See, e.g., Lewis (1972) and Armstrong (1980).

on any given occasion, and might have never caused it. Still, the expressivist materialist may take on board the idea that, when avowing, say, a desire for ice cream, a subject gives articulate truth-assessable expression to the desire itself, and that this explains the special security of her avowal. This can be accepted, as long as we do not suppose that there is any necessary connection between mentality and expressive behavior.

Although I myself would welcome a reading of the Neo-Expressivist account which renders it consistent with materialist ontology, I think that the foregoing crude attempt to graft an expressivist account onto a materialist understanding of mentality will not do as it stands. This is because the reading requires setting aside key features of the Neo-Expressivist account of avowals' security and privileged self-knowledge. On the proposal sketched above, we are to understand the real mental action as taking place inside subjects' bodies, with goings-on that constitute the underlying mental reality. Crucially, the proposal portrays our commonsense notion of a mental state as that of a state hidden from plain view, whose presence and character are hypothesized by observers on the strength of characteristic behavioral effects that they can observe. The proposal does not tell us what to make of the idea that certain behaviors are *expressive of* mental conditions. Specifically, it does not tell us what to make of the idea, so central to the Neo-Expressivist account, that bits of expressive behavior are not mere signs or symptoms, which serve as reliable indications of their causes. But how, then, are we to capture the insight that expressing a mental state is showing it, and that in the case of our own mental states, unlike the mental states of others or our own physical states (internal or not), we can engage in behavior *sufficient to show* our being in those states?

In expounding my view of expression, I tried to argue that our commonsense notion of expression separates expressive behavior from behavior that merely indicates, evidences, or signals the presence of an underlying condition; expressive behavior is not merely symptomatic of the conditions it expresses. The products of expressive behavior, even when not produced intentionally, are not related to the expressed conditions purely causally. Expressive behavior in general, I have suggested, is transparent-to-the-subject's-condition in that we can see (hear, etc.) the subject's condition in the expressive behavior, as opposed to merely using it to infer or hypothesize about its presence in the subject.[16] On the materialist expressivist view described above, we are to think of expressing, say, pain as just a matter of displaying behaviors that are the typical effects of the internal condition that constitutes being in pain. But then it seems that we could not look to the notion of expression to give us an account of the special security of avowals and of distinctive first-person privilege. For we do not regard behavioral effects as enjoying the kind of transparency-to-the-subject's-condition assigned to expressive behavior (on my construal). If we indeed thought of behavioral expressions as mere effects of internal conditions, it would remain puzzling why we should treat avowals (understood as expressions) as providing more than contingently secure clues for causal inferences on the part of observers. In other words, we would be hard pressed to explain Epistemic Asymmetry in its full scope by appeal to the notion of expression.

Our overall task seems clear conceptually. We want to preserve the Neo-Expressivist account of first-person privilege while avoiding behaviorist irrealism about mental conditions. What makes this difficult to achieve is the fact that the account appears to require tying mental conditions conceptually to expressive behavior, whereas the rejection of behaviorist irrealism appears to require their conceptual detachment. The materialist can preserve the metaphysical robustness of mental states. However, unless she can somehow allow for the requisite link between expressive behavior and the conditions expressed, it seems that she must give up the expressivist account of the special status of avowals and of first-person privilege. If the materialist expressivist proposal cannot be made to work, then we seem caught in a new dilemma (not unrelated to Rorty's): give up materialism or give up the most promising account of Epistemic Asymmetry.

Before addressing this apparent new dilemma, I'd like to examine more closely the worry that the Neo-Expressivist account does not provide for an appropriate detachment of mental conditions from behavior. We have already seen that there is nothing in the account that stands in the way of detaching the presence, on an occasion, of a mental condition from a subject's displaying the relevant expressive behavior. I have allowed that a subject may be in a mental condition that she does not express through her overt behavior. Silent expressions—e.g.,

---

[16] See Ch. 7, pp. 279 ff.

thinking to oneself, "Ow! That hurts!"—form an integral part of the view as I presented it. Moreover, I see no reason to deny the possibility that a subject can, on a particular occasion, be in a mental condition to which she gives no expression, overt or covert. Going in the other direction, I have made room for a variety of cases of dissimulation. For example, a subject may display behavior expressive of pain (onstage, in pretense, to deceive, etc.) which, on the given occasion, does not express her pain. Indeed, I have allowed for a seemingly more extreme form of detaching expressive behavior from the reality of a subject's mental condition. In some cases, a subject may avow a condition without really being in the condition she ascribes to herself. This was illustrated by the case of the patient in the dentist's chair, the freshman initiated in to a fraternity, the wishful thinker, and the self-deceived person who avows a desire she doesn't have. These were all intended to be cases of genuinely expressive behavior: not only is the subject's self-ascriptive utterance not mediated by the subject's own judgment about the condition she is in, but there is also no intention to dissimulate, no deliberate attempt to 'put on' the behavior. The subject's behavior is a spontaneous expressive performance; she speaks from a condition, yet what she says fails to express her condition, because by hypothesis the subject is not really in the relevant condition.

The cases I have allowed all trade on the possibility of pulling apart the mental condition which the subject appears to us to be in from the mental condition she is really in. They do so in different ways. We can distinguish at least three types of cases:

A. Cases of silent or absent expression, when the subject is in a certain expressible condition without the subject's expressing it overtly or at all, and thus without appearing to anyone to be in the condition she is in.[17]
B. Cases involving dissimulation, in which the subject engages in behavior expressive of, say, pain without expressing *her* pain, and the behavior is deliberately put on. In such cases the subject may appear to others to be in a certain state without being in the state.

---

[17] Note that, I am not relying on the idea that in any of these cases expressive behavior pulls apart from the subject's condition because it appears *to her* that she is in a condition she is not really in. I have insisted throughout that spontaneous expressions (natural or acquired) should not be understood as upshots of the subject's own judgment on, assessment, or even awareness of her own condition. To see, e.g., the freshman's exclamation as an expression, rather than a report or a description, is to deny that it aims to represent even how things appear to her.

C.  Cases of 'misplaced' expression, such as the dental patient case, the fraternity ice case, wishful thinking, and self-deception. In these cases the subject may also appear to be in a condition she is not really in. But the behavior is not deliberately 'put on'.

Cases of type A trade on the possibility of a subject concealing or suppressing or failing altogether to exhibit any expressive behavior. Cases of type B trade on the fact that, once in a subject's (overt or covert) behavioral repertoire, a piece of expressive behavior can put it to use for illicit purposes or for play. And cases of type C trade on the fact that expressive behavior can be 'pressed from' subjects inappropriately, so as to express a condition they are not really in. All three types of case constitute expressive failure of one sort or another. Such failures can clearly interfere with our ability to perceive a subject's mental conditions. But, as far as I can see, they do not tell against the Neo-Expressivist attempt to explain Epistemic Asymmetry by appeal to a connection between expressive behavior and mentality: specifically, the idea that expressibility through behavior is the mark of avowable mental conditions.

Note that in making room for the various kinds of detachment between expressive behavior and mental conditions, I have followed the ordinary, everyday conception of mental conditions. Common sense already allows for the above types of case; and we already seem to have in place ordinary grounds for claiming that in the cases described, mental reality and behavioral appearances pull apart. In developing my account, I simply tried not to go against what common sense prescribes in this regard; it is for this reason that I have made room for the possibility of unavowed mental states and of false avowals. This is not to say that I take common sense to be sacrosanct. It is just to highlight the following fact: drawing the appearance/reality distinction that is dictated by realism about mental states does not immediately require use of metaphysical resources that are available only to those who pin mental reality on goings-on that are hidden inside subjects—states of their immaterial soul *or* events in their material brains. Consider, for instance, the fraternity example. It does not seem as though acknowledging that the freshman is not in pain even though he screams "It hurts!" requires any more metaphysical resources than acknowledging the possibility of dissimulation. In particular, it does not by itself require us to appeal to the subject's internal affairs in order to ground the claim that the freshman really is not in pain, his expressive behavior notwithstanding. (I shall return to this point shortly.)

It may be thought, however, that the Neo-Expressivist account still incurs a commitment to some form of behaviorist irrealism through its use of the notion of expressive behavior as behavior that *suffices to show* subjects' mental states. (This idea, recall, was used in explaining why only our *own, occurrent* mental states are expressible.)[18] In response, I want to reiterate that the claim that expressive behavior is sufficient to show the conditions it expresses is not the same as (and does not entail) the claim that expressive behavior is *constitutive* of the conditions it expresses. First, nothing in the idea of behavior sufficient to show a given mental state is intended to imply that engaging in expressive behavior is *necessary* for being in a given mental state. The Neo-Expressivist use of the notion of expression does not preclude the possibility of someone's being in a mental state M without engaging in any expressive behavior (indeed, without engaging in *any* behavior). If a person doesn't engage in any expressive behavior, others may be unable to *perceive* her being in M, although, of course, they may still be able to come to know of her mental states in other ways. All that my account of expression commits us to is the claim that *if* one is in M and *does* engage in expressive behavior, the behavior will show one's being in the state, and thus enable a suitably attuned observer to perceive it. Second, to say that expressive behavior is sufficient to show the state it expresses is not to say that engaging in the behavior *suffices for being* in the relevant state. We have seen that one can exhibit behavior sufficient to show one's being in M even if one isn't in M. To say that expressive behavior is sufficient to show your being in M is just to say that *if/when* you *are* in M, engaging in the relevant behavior suffices to show it, and also that a suitably attuned and suitably placed observer could perceive your M by perceiving your behavior. Thus, on the view I have developed, in contrast to traditional behaviorism, engaging in expressive behavior is neither necessary nor sufficient for being in mental states.

Traditional behaviorism can be seen as closely tying mentality to behavior through two commitments: first, a commitment to a logical analysis of mental state ascriptions in terms of behavioral disposition

---

[18] Thanks to Dylan Sabo for inviting the following clarification.

ascriptions, and second, a commitment to denying the existence of genuine mental episodes over and above characteristic behavioral dispositions. I would argue that it is the conjunctions of these two commitments that saddles the traditional behaviorist with an implausibly irrealist position in the philosophy of mind. However, I believe that the Neo-Expressivist account avoids both commitments. For it lays no claim to the possibility of translation of mental ascriptions into behavioral ascriptions, and it affirms the existence of mental episodes. The only commitment regarding a connection between mentality and behavior that the account incurs is through the claim that mental states, unlike non-mental bodily states and psychological dispositions and traits, *can* be and often *are* shown (and made perceptible) through subjects' behavior.

Now, it may be true that, if the expressive behavior you're witnessing can suffice to let you see my being in M, the behavior must in *some* sense be part of my being in M. But this does not mean that for any given M there will be characteristic expressive behavior that is *essential* to being in M. (Analogy: I can see the tree in my yard by seeing one of its familiar branches, which is clearly part of the tree. Still, the branch is not an essential part of the tree.) A given mental state could be shown through behaviors that may vary across cultures, individuals, and even occasions. Moreover, the fact that one's being in M *can* be shown through one's behavior does not entail that being in M *must* be accompanied by *some* expressive behavior (characteristic or not). For, to repeat, an individual may be in M without engaging in any behavior that shows it.[19]

On my construal of the commonsense view, we think of mental states as expressible states of individuals that are often, though not always, made perceptible through expressive behavior. Common sense allows subjects often to be engaging in behavior that suffices to show suitably attuned and suitably placed observers the very states it expresses. This means that mental states are not ordinarily thought of as essentially hidden or private conditions inside subjects, which are in

---

[19] *Could* there be creatures who, like us, have a range of mental states, but who never engage in any expressive behavior whatsoever, overt or covert? I think that, if we are to remain faithful to the commonsense conception of mental states, we should probably refrain from any firm commitment on this matter. The most we can derive from that conception, I think, is a sense of how very exotic the envisaged possibility would be, and how utterly different from us the imagined 'inexpressive creatures' would be, if they could exist.

principle perceptible only by them. Nor are they accidentally hidden physical conditions that are contingently perceptible by their subjects only. Thus, on my reading, the commonsense conception of mental states is neither Cartesian nor materialist introspectionist. But neither is it behaviorist. For there is nothing in the conception as I have portrayed it that entails that *being* in a mental state is constituted by exhibiting, or even being disposed to exhibit, characteristic behavioral manifestations.

The Neo-Expressivist view does allow that mental states *can* be and often *are* shown (and made perceptible) through subjects' behavior. And this represents a subversion of traditional ways of thinking about first-person/third-person asymmetries. I have rejected the received assumption that, as a matter of necessity, or even just as a matter of contingent fact, only a subject who is in a mental state can perceive it with 'inner sense', whereas others who observe her behavior can at most infer to its presence and character from her behavior. Quite the contrary, I have argued that, as common sense would have it, expressive behavior is transparent-to-the-subject's-mental-condition: it enables us to see (hear, feel, etc.) the subject's anger, fear, embarrassment, etc. We don't merely perceive the behavior and infer to the subjects internal state as the best explanation of the behavior we perceive; rather, we perceive the subject as being in the relevant state of mind. At the same time, the various possible detachments and mismatches between expressive behavior and mental states clearly suggest that, as common sense would have it, being in a mental state is not constituted by engaging in expressive behavior. If we think of the presence of the behavior as what *enables* us to perceive someone's being in a mental state, this suggests that there is something more, or something else, to her being in the state than engaging in the perception-enabling behavior. (Analogy: if we see the tree by seeing one of its branches, seeing the tree is not the same thing as seeing the branch.) So, in a way, it is misconceived to try to saddle the expressivist with the idea that engaging in certain characteristic expressive behaviors is constitutive of being in particular mental states.[20]

To summarize: the Neo-Expressivist explanation of first-person/third-person (as well as mental/physical) asymmetries invokes certain aspects of the commonsense conception of mental states. On the commonsense conception, I have suggested, mental states are not taken to be internal states in their subjects' bodies, identifiable as mental states

---

[20]  See relevant discussion in Ch. 7, pp. 277 ff.

in a manner that is entirely independent of our ordinary ways of recognizing mental conditions such as pain, hunger, desires, etc. These ways crucially involve various forms of expressive behavior. Expressive behavior is, importantly, not understood as merely symptomatic of the 'real' and hidden mental conditions; rather, it is behavior in which, we take it, the conditions themselves can be perceived by observers. On the commonsense conception, as I understand it, these ordinary recognitional means do not merely claw at the effects through which we infer the presence of independently existing items hidden from the untrained observer's view. At the same time, the commonsense conception does not pin the reality of particular mental states—their presence or character—on the presence or character of particular forms of expressive behavior. Thus, the commonsense conception, as I see it, is neither Cartesian nor materialist *nor* behaviorist.

The question remains, however: What is the commonsense notion of a mental condition, if it is neither the notion of some internal state (material or not), nor the notion of a disposition to certain kinds of behavior? How are we to understand, for example, the claim that our fraternity freshman is not really in pain, though he winces and grimaces, and avows being in pain? Here is a tentative proposal. It is inspired by the rational reconstruction of the beginnings of mental talk, which I offered earlier, in Chapter 7. On the expressivist story I offered there, mental terms are handed down to learners as components of new forms of expressive behavior. If so, we can regard them as keyed to the conditions that users of the terms perceive in subjects' expressive behavior. What we take subjects to express, however, are *conditions the subjects are in, not states that are in the subjects.* As expressing is something we take subjects to be doing, mental conditions are taken to be conditions *of* subjects, or conditions they are in, rather than states *inside* them.[21] It is these conditions that are perceived by the seasoned users of mental terms in the learning situation. And it is these conditions to which their use of the relevant terms is keyed. The ordinary concept of a mental state, then, we might say, is the concept of a subject's condition that is expressible in various characteristic ways, rather than the concept of a state inside the subject that has such-and-such typical (causes and) effects, or the concept of a brute disposition to display certain kinds of behavior.

---

[21] For relevant discussion, see Blackburn (1993: ch. 13).

Metaphysically speaking, what does the distinction between conditions of subjects, states they are in, on the one hand, and states in subjects' bodies, on the other, amount to? I don't at present have a satisfying answer to this question. But I want to conclude my discussion by suggesting that there is no reason as yet to suppose that the appeal to the contrast between states of subjects and states in them automatically puts us at risk of compromising materialist ontology. What we need to give up is not the materialist *ontology*, but the materialist *ideology* (to borrow a distinction from Quine). We can, provisionally at least, accept the materialist's parsimonious ontology of bodies, physical states and features, causal relations among them, and so on. At the same time, we can recognize that our ordinary *concept* of a mental state is not the materialist concept of a state inside a body, and not even the functionalist causal role concept. Rather, it is the concept of an expressible condition of a subject. From this I don't think it follows that there must be subjects, and conditions of subjects, or special properties of them, *over and above* human bodies and their states and properties. For consider: when describing a chair as broken, or a shirt as discolored, we are saying something about a condition a certain object is in. We are not plausibly making a claim about an internal state of the relevant object, or some underlying hidden condition inside which causes it to appear or behave in certain ways. Yet shirts and chairs, I assume, are wholly physical entities, with only physical states and properties.

If it is accepted that our conception of mental states connects mentality with expressibility, and, correlatively, that our ordinary concept of a mental state is the concept of an expressible state a subject can be in, then the materialist conceptual framework, at least as currently propounded, may be ill-suited to fully capture the demarcation that Rorty sought between mental and non-mental states. The materialist framework provides us with a point of view on organisms and their states from which internal states and their causal relations to behavior and to other states are visible. But this point of view is inevitably a limited, 'impersonal' one. Arguably, it is not a point of view from which we can adequately describe and understand human agency, or even animal intentional action.[22] Insofar as the materialist conceptual

---

[22] See Hornsby (1993), for the distinction between the "personal" and the "impersonal" perspectives, which make visible different aspects of action. Also relevant is Heal (1995).

framework does not allow us to capture what is distinctive about expressive behavior, as opposed to behavioral effects of internal causes, the special status of avowals and first-person privilege as understood on the view I have developed in this book are also not apt to be visible from the materialist point of view. Confined to the conceptual resources of the materialist, we cannot articulate the expressivist answer to the question: Why should it matter to the presumed truth of claims about some contingent matter of fact that they concern the very person who happens to pronounce on the matter, and that they refer to mental states contemporaneous with the person's pronouncement? But, while the Neo-Expressivist answer to this question may require resources not dreamt of in materialist ideology, I don't see that it requires overhauling or expanding materialist ontology.

## Some Concluding Remarks

My overall goal in this work has been to explain what I have called Epistemic Asymmetry in its full scope in a way that respects Semantic Continuity. In offering the explanation, I aimed to sustain the possibility of privileged self-knowledge, without committing myself to an implausible view of the nature of mental states. Rather than seek a transcendental demonstration that avowals must be uniquely secure, or that we must possess privileged self-knowledge, I have tried to ground avowals' security and privileged self-knowledge in natural abilities we have as minded creatures. Subjects who experience pain, hunger, joy, fear, desire, and so on, are characteristically capable of showing their mental states by giving vent to them. Human subjects are in addition endowed with linguistic and conceptual abilities that enable them not only to show, but also to tell of their mental conditions by speaking from them. I can show my pain by crying out, but I can show *and* tell it by saying "I'm in pain". And, with this ability to speak from one's mental condition comes the possibility of an intriguing form of privileged self-knowledge worthy of philosophical attention both in its own right and for what it can teach us about knowledge more generally.

Early on, I concurred with Wittgenstein that we should resist the temptation, posed by the distinctive features of some of our uses of

"I", to postulate Cartesian Egos. As Wittgenstein observed, uses of "I" as subject indeed rest on no recognition of "a particular person by his bodily characteristics" (1960: 69). Yet, as he suggests, this should not lead us to suppose that they rest on recognition of someone by *non*-bodily characteristics. However, the temptation of which Wittgenstein speaks seems parasitic on a more basic Cartesian temptation connected with our first-person (or 'subjective') uses of mental terms. Given that we so often ascribe mental states to ourselves without any reliance on recognition of physical features of those states, we may be seduced into thinking that mental states have *non*-physical features that we are intimately acquainted with 'from our own case'. With the Neo-Expressivist account in place, however, I hope that we can see how to avoid both temptations at once.

A crucial ingredient of my account involved portraying avowals' security as a joint product of their immunity to error through misidentification and their ascriptive immunity. Speaking of a joint product may suggest that there is a clear separation of the secure status of avowals into two components, corresponding to the logico-semantic components of reference and predication. It makes it seem as though there is, on the one hand, the security of speaking (or thinking) about oneself and, on the other hand, the security of pro-nouncing on the condition one is in. However, it should now be clear that the securities in question cannot be ultimately pulled apart in this way. When I avow, I am telling you things about my mental states in acts of speaking from them. There is an important sense in which the immunity to error through misidentification of the subject of the avowal is parasitic on the immunity to error through mistaking the subject's condition (and its intentional content, when it has one). When I speak from a present mental condition, I have no need for recognitional identification of the subject of my self-ascription pre-cisely because I am the one expressing my condition—witness the 'subjectless' "It hurts!" If one is giving vent to one's condition, the need to use any means of identification of the bearer of the condition is obviated. As Wittgenstein puts it: "The man who cries out with pain, or says that he has pain, doesn't choose the mouth which says it" (1958: 68).

While philosophers may readily accept Wittgenstein's point regarding "the man who cries out with pain", many would balk at applying the point to the case of articulate verbal utterances that are taken to represent self-knowledge. The common philosophical stereotype of such utterances is that of thoughtful Self-centered acts accompanied by various communicative intentions, whose products represent objective information that we have obtained in distinctive ways. So it may seem puzzling initially how such utterances could be related to the subject's condition of pain, say, in a way similar to the way his crying out would be; or, if they are so related, how they could still represent genuine self-knowledge.

My aim throughout has been to persuade the reader that this puzzlement is due to a failure to separate the semantics of avowals from their epistemology and use. When avowing in speech, I may want to let someone know about my present condition, and I do produce a genuine self-ascription; but for all that, my utterance will not be an act of reporting that is epistemically underwritten by special privileged access to my inner Self. What renders my avowals especially secure and affords me privileged self-knowledge is rather this: as a subject who is in a mental state, and who is also an agent endowed with certain linguistic and conceptual capacities, I am uniquely placed to give self-ascriptive expressions to my present states of mind. I can only inform you about someone else's state of mind by conveying my belief about it. But in my own case, I can do it also by speaking my mind.

Speaking my mind is something I am in a unique position to do. Only I can express, or give voice to, my own present states of mind. And it is only states of my mind that I can express, or give voice to. Bodily conditions such as having high blood pressure, a raised arm, or a weak heart are not conditions one can speak from. I can speak my mind, but I cannot speak my body.

In the end it is perhaps with this, rather than with Cartesian incorrigibility, that our search for an epistemic mark of the mental should rest.

# Bibliography

Akmajian, Adrian, Demers, Richard, and Harnish, Robert (1984), *Linguistics: An Introduction to Language and Communication, 2nd edn.* (Cambridge, Mass.: MIT Press).

Alston, William (1965), 'Expressing', in Max Black (ed.), *Philosophy in America* (Ithaca, NY: Cornell University Press), 15–34.

Anscombe, G. E. M. (1965), 'The Intentionality of Sensation', in R. J. Butler (ed.), *Analytical Philosophy*, 2nd ser. (Oxford: Oxford University Press), 158–80.

—— (1975), 'The First Person', in Samuel Guttenplan (ed.), *Mind and Language: Wolfson College Lectures, 1974* (Oxford: Oxford University Press), 45–65.

Armstrong, David (1968), *A Materialist Theory of the Mind* (London: Routledge).

—— (1980), *The Nature of Mind* (Brisbane: University of Queensland Press).

Aune, Bruce (1965), 'On the Complexity of Avowals', in Max Black (ed.), *Philosophy in America* (Ithaca, NY: Cornell University Press), 35–57.

Austin, J. L. (1961), 'Performative Utterances', in *Philosophical Papers* (Oxford: Oxford University Press), 220–39.

Ayer, A. J. (1946), *Language, Truth and Logic* (New York: Dover).

Bar-On, Dorit (1990), 'Scepticism: The External World and Meaning', *Philosophical Studies*, 60, 207–31.

—— (1995), 'Reconstructing Meaning: Grice and the Naturalization of Semantics', *Pacific Philosophical Quarterly*, 76, 83–116.

—— (1996), 'Anti-Realism and Speaker Knowledge', *Synthese*, 106/2, 139–66.

—— (2000), 'Speaking My Mind', *Philosophical Topics*, 28/2, 1–34.

—— (2004a), 'Externalism and Self-Knowledge: Content, Use, and Expression', *Noûs*, 38/3, 430–55.

—— (2004b), 'Semantic Eliminativism and the 'Theory'-Theory of Linguistic Understanding', in *New Essays in Philosophy of Language and Mind*, suppl. vol., *Canadian Journal of Philosophy*.

—— and Long, Douglas, (2001), 'Avowals and First-Person Privilege', *Philosophy and Phenomenological Research*, 62/2, 311–35.

—— —— (2003), 'Knowing Selves: Expression, Truth, and Knowledge', in Brie Gertler (ed.), *Privileged Access: Philosophical Accounts of Self-Knowledge* (Aldershot: Ashgate Publishing Ltd.), 179–212.

Bernecker, Sven (1998), 'Self-Knowledge and Closure', in Peter Ludlow and Norah Martin (eds.), *Externalism and Self-Knowledge* (Stanford, Calif.: CSLI Publications), 333–49.

Bilgrami, Akeel (1998), 'Resentment and Self-Knowledge', in Crispin Wright, Barry Smith, and Cynthia MacDonald(eds.), *Knowing Our Own Minds* (Oxford: Oxford University Press), 207–41.

Blackburn, Simon (1984), *Spreading the Word* (Oxford: Oxford University Press).

—— (1993), *Essays on Quasi-Realism* (Oxford: Oxford University Press).

—— (1995), 'Theory, Observation, and Drama', in Martin Davies and Tony Stone (eds.), *Folk Psychology: The Theory of Mind Debate* (Oxford: Blackwell), 274–90.

Boër, Steven, and Lycan, William (1975), 'Knowing Who', *Philosophical Studies*, 28, 299–344.

Boghossian, Paul (1989), 'Content and Self-Knowledge', *Philosophical Topics*, 17, 5–26.

Brandom, Robert (1994), *Making It Explicit* (Cambridge, Mass.: Harvard University Press).

Bradley, R. D. (1964), 'Avowals of Immediate Experience', *Mind*, 73/290, 186–203.

Bratman, Michael (1989), 'Two Faces of Intention', *Philosophical Review*, 93/3, 375–405.

Brown, Jessica (1995), 'The Incompatibility of Anti-Individualism and Privileged Access', *Analysis*, 55, 149–56.

Brueckner, Anthony (1992), 'What An Anti-Individualist Knows A Priori', *Analysis*, 52, 111–18.

—— (2000), 'Externalism and the Aprioricity of Self-Knowledge', *Analysis*, 60, 132–6.

Buckley, J., and Hall, L. (1999), 'Self-Knowledge and Embodiment', *Southwest Philosophical Review*, 15/1, 185–96.

Burge, Tyler (1979), 'Individualism and the Mental', *in Midwest Studies in Philosophy*, (Minneapolis: University of Minnesota Press), 73–122.

—— (1988), 'Individualism and Self-Knowledge', *Journal of Philosophy*, 85/11, 649–63.

—— (1996), 'Our Entitlement to Self-Knowledge', *Proceedings of the Aristotelian Society*, 96, 1–26.

—— (1998a), 'Reason and the First Person', in Crispin Wright, Barry Smith, and Cynthia MacDonald (eds.), *Knowing Our Own Minds* (Oxford: Oxford University Press), 243–70.

—— (1998*b*), 'Memory and Self-Knowledge', in Peter Ludlow and Norah Martin (eds.), *Externalism and Self-Knowledge* (Stanford, Calif.: CSLI Publications), 351–70.

Cassam, Quassim (1994) (ed.), *Self-Knowledge* (Oxford: Oxford University Press).

—— (1997), *Self and World* (Oxford: Oxford University Press).

Collingwood, R. G. (1940), *An Introduction to Metaphysics* (Oxford: Oxford University Press).

Crimmins, Mark (1992), 'Tacitness and Virtual Beliefs', *Mind and Language*, 7, 240–63.

Davidson, Donald (1968–9), 'On Saying That', *Synthese*, 19, 130–46.

—— (1973), 'Radical Interpretation', *Dialectica*, 27, 313–28.

—— (1974), 'Belief and the Basis of Meaning', *Synthese*, 27, 309–23.

—— (1975), 'Thought and Talk', in Samuel Guttenplan (ed.), *Mind and Language: Wolfson College Lectures,* 1974 (Oxford: Oxford University Press), 7–23.

—— (1984), 'First Person Authority', *Dialectica*, 38/2–3, 101–11.

—— (1987), 'Knowing One's Own Mind', *Proceedings and Addresses of the American Philosophical Association*, 60, 441–58.

Davies, Martin (1998), 'Externalism, Architecturalism, and Epistemic Warrant', in Crispin Wright, Barry Smith, and Cynthia MacDonald (eds.), *Knowing Our Own Minds* (Oxford: Oxford University Press), 321–61.

—— and Stone, Tony (1995) (eds.), *Folk Psychology: The Theory of Mind Debate* (Oxford: Blackwell).

Dennett, Daniel (1981), 'Where am I?', in *Brainstorms* (Cambridge, Mass.: MIT Press/A Bradford Book).

—— (1987), *The Intentional Stance* (Cambridge, Mass.: MIT Press/A Bradford Book).

Descartes, René (1998), *Discourse on Method* and *Meditations on First Philosophy*, 4th edn. trans. Donald Cress (Indianapolis: Hackett Publishing Company, Inc.).

Devitt, Michael (1981), *Designation* (New York: Columbia University Press).

Donnellan, Keith (1966), 'Reference and Definite Descriptions', *Philosophical Review*, 75, 281–304.

—— (1970), 'Proper Names and Identifying Descriptions', *Synthese*, 21, 335–58.

—— (1979), 'Speaker Reference, Descriptions and Anaphora', in Peter French, Theodore Uehling, and Howard Wettstein (eds.), *Contemporary Perspectives in the Philosophy of Language* (Minneapolis: University of Minnesota Press), 28–44.

Dretske, Fred (1970), 'Epistemic Operators', *Journal of Philosophy*, 67, 1007–23.

—— (1971), 'Conclusive Reasons', *Australasian Journal of Philosophy*, 49, 1–22.

—— (1988), *Explaining Behavior* (Cambridge, Mass.: MIT Press/A Bradford Book).

—— (1999), 'The Mind's Awareness of Itself', *Philosophical Studies*, 95, 103–24.

—— (2003), 'Externalism and Self-Knowledge', in Susana Nuccetelli (ed.), *New Essays on Semantic Externalism and Self-Knowledge* (Cambridge, Mass.: MIT Press/A Bradford Book), 131–42.

Dummett, Michael (1978), *Truth and Other Enigmas* (London: Gerald Duckworth & Company Ltd.).

—— (1991), *The Logical Basis of Metaphysics* (Cambridge, Mass.: Harvard University Press).

—— (1993), *The Seas of Language* (Oxford: Clarendon Press).

Evans, Gareth (1981), 'Understanding Demonstratives', in Herman Parret and Jacques Bouveresse (eds.), *Meaning and Understanding* (Berlin: Walter de Gruyter), 280–303.

—— (1982), *The Varieties of Reference*, ed. John McDowell (Oxford: Oxford University Press).

Falvey, Kevin (2000), 'The Basis of First-Person Authority', *Philosophical Topics*, 28/2, 69–99.

Finkelstein, David (2001), 'Wittgenstein's "Plan for the Treatment of Psychological Concepts"', in Timothy McCarthy and Sean Stidd (eds.) *Wittgenstein in America* (Oxford: Clarendon Press), 215–236.

Fleming, Brice Noel (1955), 'On Avowals', *Philosophical Review*, 64/4, 614–25.

Fodor, Jerry (1975), *The Language of Thought* (Cambridge, Mass.: Harvard University Press).

Fogelin, Robert (1976), *Wittgenstein* (London: Routledge and Paul).

Foot, Philippa (1982), 'Peacocke on Wittgenstein and Experience', *Philosophical Quarterly*, 33/131, 187–91.

Frege, Gottlob (1960), 'On Sense and Reference' in P. T. Geach and Max Black (eds.), *Translations from the Philosophical Writings of Gottlob Frege*, 2nd edn. (Oxford: Blackwell), 56–78.

—— (1967), 'The Thought', trans. A. M. and Marcelle Quinton, *Mind*, 65/259, 289–311.

Fricker, Elizabeth (1998), 'Self-Knowledge: Special Access vs. Artefact of Grammar—A Dichotomy Rejected', in Cynthia MacDonald, Barry Smith, and Crispin Wright (eds.), *Knowing Our Own Minds* (Oxford: Oxford University Press), 155–206.

Gallois, André (1996), *The World Without, The Mind Within* (Cambridge: Cambridge University Press).

Gasking, Douglas (1962), 'Avowals', in R. J. Butler (ed.), *Analytical Philosophy* (Oxford: Basil Blackwell and Mott Ltd.), 156–86.

Geach, Peter (1965), 'Assertion', *Philosophical Review*, 84, 449–65.

Georgalis, Nicholas (1994), 'Asymmetry of Access to Intentional States', *Erkenntnis*, 40/2, 185–211.

George, Alexander (1989) (ed.), *Reflections on Chomsky* (Oxford: Blackwell).

Gettier, Edmund (1963), 'Is Justified True Belief Knowledge?', *Analysis*, 23, 121–3.

Gibbard, Alan (1990), *Wise Choices, Apt Feelings: A Theory of Normative Judgment* (Cambridge, Mass.: Harvard University Press).

Ginet, Carl (1968), 'How Words Mean Kinds of Sensations', *Philosophical Review*, 77, 3–24.

Goldman, Alvin (1976), 'Discrimination and Perceptual Knowledge', *Journal of Philosophy*, 73/20, 771–91.

—— (1986), *Epistemology and Cognition* (Cambridge, Mass.: Harvard University Press).

—— (1989), 'Interpretation Psychologized', *Mind and Language*, 4, 161–85.

—— (1992), 'In Defense of the Simulation Theory', *Mind and Language*, 7, 104–19.

—— (1993), *Philosophical Applications of Cognitive Science* (Boulder, Colo.: Westview Press).

Goodman, Nelson (1968), *Languages of Art* (Indianapolis: Bobbs-Merrill Company Inc.).

Gordon, Robert (1986), 'Folk Psychology as Simulation', *Mind and Language*, 1, 158–71.

Green, Mitchell (1999), 'Moore's Many Paradoxes', *Philosophical Papers*, 28, 97–109.

—— (unpublished), *Self-Expression*.

Greenwood, John D. (1991), 'Self-Knowledge: Looking in the Wrong Direction', *Behavior and Philosophy*, 19/2, 35–47.

Grice, H. P. (1989), *Studies in the Way of Words* (Cambridge, Mass.: Harvard University Press).

Hacker, P. M. S. (1993), *Wittgenstein: Meaning and Mind* (Oxford: Blackwell).

Hauser, Mark (1996), *The Evolution of Communication* (Cambridge, Mass.: MIT Press/A Bradford Book).

Heal, Jane (1989), *Fact and Meaning* (Oxford: Blackwell).

—— (1995), 'Replication and Functionalism', in Martin Davies and Tony Stone (eds.), *Folk Psychology: The Theory of Mind Debate* (Oxford: Blackwell), 45–59.

Heil, John (1988), 'Privileged Access', *Mind*, 97, 238–51.

—— and Mele, Alfred (1993) (eds.), *Mental Causation* (Oxford: Clarendon Press).

Higgenbotham, James (1998), 'On Knowing One's Own Language', in Crispin Wright, Barry Smith, and Cynthia MacDonald (eds.), *Knowing Our Own Minds* (Oxford: Oxford University Press), 429–41.

Hornsby, Jennifer (1993), 'Agency and Causal Explanation', in John Heil and Alfred Mele (eds.), *Mental Causation* (Oxford: Clarendon Press), 161–88.

Jacobsen, Rockney (1996), 'Wittgenstein on Self-Knowledge and Self-Expression', *Philosophical Quarterly*, 46/182, 12–30.

Kaplan, David (1975), 'How to Russell a Frege-Church', *Journal of Philosophy*, 72, 716–29.

—— (1989), 'Demonstratives', in Joseph Almog, John Perry, and Howard Wettstein (eds.), *Themes from Kaplan* (New York: Oxford University Press), 481–614.

Kenny, Anthony (1966), 'Cartesian Privacy', in George Pitcher (ed.), *Wittgenstein: The Philosophical Investigations* (Garden City, NY: Anchor Books), 352–70.

Kobes, Bernard (1995), 'Telic Higher Order Thoughts and Moore's Paradox', *Philosophical Perspectives*, 9, 291–312.

Kripke, Saul (1972), 'Naming and Necessity', in Donald Davidson and Gilbert Harman (eds.), *Semantics of Natural Languages* (Dordrecht: Reidel), 253–355.

—— (1977), 'Speaker's Reference and Semantic Reference', in Peter French, Theodore Uehling, and Howard Wettstein (eds.), *Contemporary Perspectives in the Philosophy of Language* (Minneapolis: University of Minnesota Press), 6–27.

—— (1982), *Wittgenstein on Rules and Private Languages* (Cambridge, Mass.: Harvard University Press).

Lewis, David (1972), 'Psychophysical and Theoretical Identifications', *Australasian Journal of Philosophy*, 50, 249–58.

Lichtenberg, G. C. (1971), *Schriften und Briefe,* ii (Munich: Carl Hanser Verlag).

Loar, Brian (1987), 'Subjective Intentionality', *Philosophical Topics*, 15/1, 89–124.

Long, Douglas C. (1994), 'Why Machines Cannot Think and Feel', in Dale Jamieson (ed.), *Language, Mind, and Art: Essays in Appreciation and Analysis, in Honor of Paul Ziff* (Dordrecht: Kluwer Academic Publishers), 101–9.

Ludlow, Peter (1998), 'Externalism, Self-Knowledge, and the Prevalence of Slow Switching', in Peter Ludlow and Norah Martin (eds.), *Externalism and Self-Knowledge* (Stanford, Calif.: CSLI Publications), 225–9.

—— and Martin, Norah (1998) (eds.), *Externalism and Self-Knowledge* (Stanford, Calif.: CSLI Publications).

Lycan, William (1987), *Consciousness* (Cambridge, Mass.: MIT Press/A Bradford Book).

—— (1996), *Consciousness and Experience* (Cambridge, Mass.: MIT Press/A Bradford Book).

—— (2000), *Philosophy of Language* (London: Routledge).

MacDonald, Cynthia (1998), 'Externalism and Authoritative Self-Knowledge', in Crispin Wright, Barry Smith, and Cynthia MacDonald (eds.), *Knowing Our Own Minds* (Oxford: Oxford University Press), 123–54.

McDowell, John (1977), 'On the Sense and Reference of a Proper Name', *Mind*, 86, 159–85.

—— (1984), '*De Re* Senses', *Philosophical Quarterly*, 34, 283–94.

—— (1982), 'Criteria, Defeasibility, and Knowledge', *Proceedings of the British Academy*, 68, 455–79.

—— (1990), 'Peacocke and Evans on Demonstrative Content', *Mind*, 99, 255–66.

—— (1995), 'Knowledge and the Internal', *Philosophy and Phenomenological Research*, 55, 877–93.

—— (1997), 'Reductionism and the First Person', in Jonathan Dancy (ed.), *Reading Parfit* (Oxford: Blackwell), 230–50.

—— (1998), 'Response to Crispin Wright', in Crispin Wright, Barry Smith, and Cynthia MacDonald (eds.), *Knowing Our Own Minds* (Oxford: Oxford University Press), 47–62.

McGeer, Victoria (1996), 'Is "Self-Knowledge" an Empirical Problem? Renegotiating the Space of Philosophical Explanation', *Journal of Philosophy*, 93/10, 483–515.

—— (2001), 'Psycho-Practice, Psycho-Theory and the Contrastive Case of Autism: How Practices of Mind become Second-Nature', *Journal of Consciousness Studies*, 8/5–7, 109–32.

McKinsey, Michael (1991), 'Anti-Individualism and Privileged Access', *Analysis*, 5, 9–16.

McLaughlin, Brian, and Tye, Michael (1998), 'Externalism, Twin Earth, and Self-Knowledge', in Crispin Wright, Barry Smith, and Cynthia MacDonald (eds.), *Knowing Our Own Minds* (Oxford: Oxford University Press), 285–320.

Marcus, Ruth Barcan (1960), 'Extensionality', *Mind*, 69, 55–62.

—— (1961), 'Modalities and Intensional Languages', *Synthese*, 13, 303–22.

Mills, Andrew (unpublished), 'Assertions, Indicative Utterances, and Non-Cognitivism'.

Moore, G. E. (1959), 'Wittgenstein's Lectures in 1930–33', in *Philosophical Papers* (London: George Allen and Unwin Ltd.), 252–324.

Moran, Richard (1988), 'Making Up Your Mind: Self-Interpretation and Self-Constitution', *Ratio*, NS 1/2, 135–51.

Moran, Richard (1994), 'Interpretation Theory and the First Person', *Philosophical Quarterly*, 44/175, 154–73.

—— (1997), 'Self-Knowledge: Discovery, Resolution, and Undoing', *European Journal of Philosophy*, 5/2, 141–61.

—— (1999), 'The Authority of Self-Consciousness', *Philosophical Topics*, 26/1–2, 179–200.

—— (2001), *Authority and Estrangement: An Essay on Self-Knowledge* (Princeton: Princeton University Press).

Moser, Paul K. (1986) (ed.), *Empirical Knowledge: Readings in Contemporary Epistemology* (Totowa, NJ: Roman and Littlefield).

Neale, Stephen (1990), *Descriptions* (Cambridge, Mass.: MIT Press / A Bradford Book).

Nisbett, Richard, and Ross, Lee (1980), *Human Inference: Strategies and Shortcomings of Social Judgement* (Englewood Cliffs, NJ: Prentice-Hall).

—— and Wilson, Timothy DeCamp (1977), 'Telling More Than We Can Know: Verbal Reports on Mental Processes', *Psychological Review*, 84, 231–59.

Nozick, Robert (1981), *Philosophical Explanations* (Cambridge, Mass.: Harvard University Press).

O'Brien, Lucy (1995), 'Evans on Self-Identification', *Noûs*, 29, 232–47.

Peacocke, Christopher (1982), 'Wittgenstein and Experience', *Philosophical Quarterly*, 32, 162–70.

—— (1992), *A Study of Concepts* (Cambridge, Mass.: MIT Press).

—— (1996), 'Our Entitlement to Self-Knowledge: Entitlement, Self-Knowledge, and Conceptual Redeployment', *Proceedings of the Aristotelian Society*, 96, 117–58.

—— (1999), *Being Known* (Oxford: Clarendon Press).

Pears, David (1987), *The False Prison* (Oxford: Oxford University Press).

Perry, John (1977), 'Frege on Demonstratives', *Philosophical Review*, 86/4, 474–97.

—— (1979), 'The Problem of the Essential Indexical', *Noûs*, 13/1, 3–21.

Pryor, James (1999), 'Immunity to Error through Misidentification', *Philosophical Topics*, 26/1–2, 271–304.

Putnam, Hilary (1960), 'Minds and Machines', in Sidney Hook (ed.), *Dimensions of Mind* (New York: New York University Press), 148–79.

—— (1975), 'The Meaning of "Meaning" ', in Keith Gunderson (ed.), *Minnesota Studies in the Philosophy of Science, vol. 8: Language, Mind and Knowledge* (Minneapolis: University of Minnesota Press), 131–93.

Quine, Willard Van Orman (1960), *Word and Object* (Cambridge, Mass.: Cambridge University Press).

—— (1974), *Roots of Reference* (La Salle, Ill.: Open Court).

Rorty, Richard (1970a), 'Incorrigibility as the Mark of the Mental', *Journal of Philosophy*, 12, 399–424.

—— (1970b), 'In Defense of Eliminative Materialism', *Review of Metaphysics*, 24/1, 112–21.

Rosenberg, Jay (1977), 'Speaking Lions', *Canadian Journal of Philosophy*, 7/1, 155–60.

—— (2002), *Thinking about Knowing* (Oxford: Oxford University Press).

Rosenthal, David (1986), 'Two Concepts of Consciousness', *Philosophical Studies*, 94/3, 329–59.

Rovane, Carol (1987), 'The Epistemology of First-Person Reference', *Journal of Philosophy*, 84, 147–67.

Russell, Bertrand (1905), 'On Denoting', *Mind*, 14/56, 479–93.

—— (1912), *The Problems of Philosophy* (London: Williams & Norgate).

Ryle, Gilbert (1949), *The Concept of Mind* (London: Hutchinson).

Salmon, Nathan (1986), *Frege's Puzzle* (Cambridge, Mass.: MIT Press / A Bradford Book).

Sellars, Wilfrid (1963), *Science, Perception, and Reality* (London: Routledge and Kegan Paul).

—— (1969), 'Language as Thought and as Communication', *Philosophy and Phenomenological Research*, 29, 506–27.

—— (1988), 'On Accepting First Principles', *Philosophical Perspectives*, 2, 301–14.

Shoemaker, Sydney (1968), 'Self-Reference and Self-Awareness', *Journal of Philosophy*, 65/19, 555–67.

—— (1994), 'Self-Knowledge and "Inner Sense"', *Philosophy and Phenomenological Research*, 54/2, 249–314.

—— (1996), *The First-Person Perspective and Other Essays* (Cambridge: Cambridge University Press).

Siewert, Charles (2003), 'Self-Knowledge and Rationality: Shoemaker on Self-Blindness,' in Brie Gertler (ed.), *Privileged Access: Philosophical Accounts of Self-Knowledge* (Aldershot: Ashgate Publishing Ltd.), 131–45.

Smith, Barry (1998), 'On Knowing One's Own Language', in Crispin Wright, Barry Smith, and Cynthia Macdonald (eds.), *Knowing Our Own Minds* (Oxford: Oxford University Press), 391–428.

Stevenson, C. L. (1944), *Ethics and Language* (New Haven: Yale University Press).

Strawson, P. F. (1950), 'On Referring', *Mind*, 59/235, 320–44.

—— (1959), *Individuals* (London: Routledge).

—— (1974), *Subject and Predicate in Logic and Grammar* (London: Methuen).

—— (1994), 'The First Person— and Others', in Quassim Cassam (ed.), *Self-Knowledge* (Oxford: Oxford University Press), 210–15.

Strong, William John (1992), *McCormick on Evidence*, 4th edn. (St Paul, Minn.: West Publishing Company).

Stroud, Barry (1983), 'Wittgenstein's "Treatment" of the Quest for "a language which describes my inner experiences and which only I myself can understand" ' in Paul Weingartner and Johannes Czermak (eds.), *Epistemology and the Philosophy of Science: Proceedings of the Seventh International Wittgenstein Symposium, Kirchberg*, 1982 (Vienna: Oxford University Press), 438–45.

Tanney, Julia (1996), 'A Constructivist Picture of Self-Knowledge', *Philosophy*, 71, 405–22.

Taylor, Charles (1985), 'The Concept of a Person', in *Human Agency and Language: Philosophical Papers*,; (Cambridge: Cambridge University Press), 97–114.

Tye, Michael (2003), 'Representationalism and the Transparency of Experience', in Brie Gertler (ed.), *Privileged Access: Philosophical Accounts of Self-Knowledge* (Aldershot: Ashgate Publishing Ltd.), 31–44.

Vendler, Zeno (1972), *Res Cogitans* (Ithaca, NY: Cornell University Press).

Weiskrantz, Lawrence (1986), *Blindsight: A Case Study and Implications* (Oxford: Clarendon Press).

Williamson, Timothy (1995), 'Is Knowing a State of Mind?', *Mind*, 104/415, 533–65.

Wilson, Margaret (1978), *Descartes* (London: Routledge & Kegan Paul).

Wittgenstein, Ludwig (1953), *Philosophical Investigations*, trans. G. E. M. Anscombe (Oxford: Blackwell).

—— (1958), *The Blue and Brown Books* (New York: Harper & Row).

—— (1980), *Remarks on the Philosophy of Psychology*, 2 vols. (Oxford: Blackwell).

Wright, Crispin (1989), 'Wittgenstein's Rule-Following Considerations and the Central Project of Theoretical Linguistics', in Alexander George (ed.), *Reflections on Chomsky* (Oxford: Blackwell), 233–64.

—— (1991), 'Wittgenstein's Later Philosophy of Mind: Sensation, Privacy and Intention,' in Klaus Puhl (ed.), *Meaning Skepticism* (Berlin: Walter de Gruyter), 126–47.

—— (1994), *Truth and Objectivity* (Cambridge, Mass.: Harvard University Press).

—— (1998), 'Self-Knowledge: The Wittgensteinian Legacy', in Crispin Wright, Barry Smith, and Cynthia MacDonald (eds.), *Knowing Our Own Minds* (Oxford: Oxford University Press), 13–46.

Wright, Crispin, Smith, Barry, and MacDonald, Cynthia (1998) (eds.), Knowing Our Own Minds (Oxford: Oxford University Press).

Zimmermann, Aaron (unpublished *a*), 'Basic Self-Knowledge: Answering Peacocke's Criticisms of Constitutivism'.

—— (unpublished *b*), 'Knowing What You Want: Introspective Disjunctivism and the Direct Access Account'.

# Index